Hierarchy

HIERARCHY

Persistence and Transformation in Social Formations

Edited by

Knut M. Rio

and

Olaf H. Smedal

Berghahn Books
New York • Oxford

Published in 2009 by

Berghahn Books

www.berghahnbooks.com

© 2009, 2011 Knut M. Rio and Olaf H. Smedal
First paperback edition published in 2011

Library of Congress Cataloging-in-Publication Data

Heirarchy : persistence and transformation in social formations /
edited by Knut M. Rio and Olaf H. Smedal.
  p. cm.
Includes bibliographical references and index.
ISBN 978-1-84545-493-7 (hbk)—ISBN 978-1-84545-490-6 (pbk)
  1. Hierarchies—Case studies.   2. Power (Social sciences)—
Case studies.   3. Elite (Social sciences)—Case studies.   4. Democracy.   I. Rio, Knut Mikjel.   II. Smedal, Olaf H.
HM716.H45 2008
305.5'209—dc22   2008015215

British Library Cataloguing-in-Publication Data

A catalogue record for this book is available from the British Library

Printed in the United States on acid-free paper

For Bruce Kapferer

CONTENTS

ACKNOWLEDGEMENTS

The initiative to this book was taken in the Department of Social Anthropology at the University of Bergen and it represents the effort of a core group of scholars in renewing the interest in the concept of hierarchy and exploring its potential for a future anthropology. The idea was launched by Bruce Kapferer and thereafter distributed to the authors. We wish to extend our deepest gratitude to them for having maintained their engagement with this project throughout the lengthy process from its conception to its publication. Their investment in this has come as a result of their visits to Bergen and familiarity with our department and it reflects our admiration for their anthropological work.

We also wish to thank Marion Berghahn for the encouraging enthusiasm she has shown since we first presented our book proposal, and Frederick H. Damon for giving advice on all chapters and graciously conceding to write the Afterword.

The volume is dedicated to Bruce Kapferer in the hope that he will find much in it to disagree with.

Knut M. Rio and Olaf H. Smedal
Bergen, February 2008

CHAPTER I

Hierarchy and Its Alternatives

An Introduction to Movements of Totalization and Detotalization

Knut M. Rio and Olaf H. Smedal

You know who I am,
you've stared at the sun,
well I am the one who loves
changing from nothing to one.

Leonard Cohen, from "You Know Who I Am," on
Songs from a Room, 1969

The aim of this volume is to convey in ethnographical terms what is characteristic of what we will call hierarchical societies. The contributors to the collection have taken on the task of describing unique hierarchical social formations in their respective areas, in order for anthropology to rethink not only variation in social forms, but also what it is that unites different social movements and how they can be compared. This task has been carried out without an initial coherent theoretical framework, but, unavoidably, most contributions engage with Dumont's concept of hierarchy, critically or otherwise. Regionally, we have chosen to avoid Dumont's areas of expertise, India and Europe, and all contributions deal with what we might call the rim of Dumont's regional interests and influence—the Ottoman Empire, Mongolia, Southeast Asia, Indonesia and Oceania.

In this chapter we intend to clear the way for these contributions by engaging critically with Dumont's conceptual pair of hierarchy and individualism. We do this, not in order to get entangled in the highly charged field populated by the allies and enemies of this controversial figure, but because we see reasons for again giving a place to the concepts of hierarchy, value and totalization in our understanding of ethnographic realities.

Notes to this section begin on page 56.

The various contributions demonstrate in different ways both the constitution of hierarchical social forms in terms of values and the degree of persistence in these social forms in the face of individualist concepts. Importantly, Dumont set up his concept of hierarchy in India in order to unravel an alternative to individualist society, but also because he aimed to establish a standard for laying bare the fundamental structural premises in individualism as an extreme version of a system of values (Dumont 1970). Individualism was an expanding system of values, not only denying and resisting its own character as a system, but also denying any value at all apart from the singular supremacy of the individual. Historically and regionally this could be seen as the outcome of a highly specific development in the Western world.

But whereas Dumont could maintain that he had described hierarchy in India in its pure historical form and individualism as an emergent form in Europe, we must take into account that Western concepts and regimes—such as democratization, free market, human rights and individual freedom—are now spreading, emerging in various guises across the globe at an epidemic pace. We note, too, that in social science it is becoming increasingly difficult to even think hierarchical relationships and holism in Dumont's terms—and even more so to make our audiences believe in them—to even think and write beyond personal initiative, narration and construction of identities, beyond aspects of power relations, beyond economic motives, beyond the immediately perceived agencies and lifeworlds of individuals. Therefore we must question not only our empirical material but also our analytical tools for conceiving of agency and social forms. However, as pointed out by Sahlins in his most recent book (2004) we should not rest content in critiquing radical individualism with its centering of individuals and its oblivion to social relations and structures on the macro level. We should also call into question what he calls "leviathanology"—the tendency to conceive of social or cultural structures as supra-individual mechanisms, such as Adam Smith's "Invisible Hand," Althusser's "interpellation," or Foucault's "discourse"—and its spread into anthropology as an "anthropology of subjects without agency" (Sahlins 2004: 144). Out of this leviathanology comes what is conceived of as a natural fact in social systems—power. Take Foucault's framework and its manifold uses in anthropology in recent years: "Here is power as irresistible as it is ubiquitous, power emanating from everywhere and invading everyone, saturating the everyday things, relations, and institutions of human existence, and transmitting thence into people's bodies, perceptions, knowledges, and dispositions" (Sahlins 2004: 147). The problem with all this insistence on power is that it strips away the specificity of all kinds of social structures (family, state, religion, and so on) and reduces them to their "functional-instrumental effects of discipline and control" (2004: 147). Sahlins's point is that both the radical individualism of the right and the leviathanology of the left have been emerging dialectically in the historical development of Western thinking. Both directions follow the mythmaking of popular and academic Western orientations alike, and we realize the full potency of the combination of individualism and leviathanology in the topic of hierarchy as it has been debated since Dumont.

Hierarchy, Holism, and Value

In order to benefit from the Dumontian framework—taking into account its advantages and its problems, we begin by accounting for what we see as the direction in Dumont's work and his definition of hierarchy. (For in-depth studies of Dumont's concept of hierarchy, see Madan 1982; Raheja 1988; Parry 1998; Parkin 2003; Celtel 2005; also Iteanu in this volume and Tcherkézoff in this volume). Our effort here is to try to convey an understanding of Dumont's concept of hierarchy in order to extend it toward other regions and new horizons of conceptualization—once more using empirical evidence as witness to the diversities and complexities in social forms.

Dumont himself pointed out in his Radcliffe-Brown lecture in 1980 that, "I have been trying in recent years to sell the profession the idea of hierarchy, with little success, I might add" (Dumont 1986a: 235). So what was he trying to sell? It is difficult to answer this question in a few sentences and even more difficult to do so outside an evaluative framework: Dumont's corpus is nothing if not controversial. In this chapter, we will return repeatedly not only to what we think are his especially salient observations, but also to remaining problems that have become apparent in more recent ethnograhic contributions—availing ourselves of the rich literature bearing on both—and will attempt at least to provide a brief, impassioned answer in this section.

India, Dumont claims, is fundamentally and irreducibly religious—Hindu thought permeates it thoroughly. This religious ideology is premised on the notion that everything—including human beings—can be classified according to a hierarchical scheme consisting of an opposition of purity and impurity. The gradation of humans along the purity and impurity axis produces caste. But caste can only develop into its full form as a system—the system that is unique to India—when religious *status* is separated systematically and totally from politico-economic *power*.[1] The justification for such separation is found in the classical Hindu texts, where priesthood (the Brahmans or Brahmins) and royalty (the Kshatrias) are distinguished absolutely; and where the priests—on account of their purity—are superior to the kings: They are closer to God. This is the paradigmatic hierarchical relation: While priesthood and royalty are conceptually *opposed*, the nature of this opposition is *hierarchical* in that royalty is subsumed under—or encompassed by—priesthood. It is crucial to Dumont's theoretical edifice bearing on India that this relative, value-laden distinction between status and power—the supremacy of priesthood over royalty—is operative on the primary level, that of ideology, since this is the level of the totality. On the secondary, politico-economic level, the spiritual authority of the priests gives way to the temporal authority of the kings. In having kept (religious) status and (politico-economic) power separated in this way for millennia, Indian history differs fundamentally from that of the West. According to Dumont, the failure of most observers to recognize the full impact of this difference has led to much regrettable misunderstanding. One problem is to mistake political and economic developments for systemic change. While there has been much of the former there has been none of the latter: "Everything happens as though the system tolerated change only within one of its secondary spheres" (Dumont 1980: 228). We note that his insistence on this point is precisely what has provided Dumont's followers with what we might call "a sudden liberating thought" and, conversely, most irked the majority of his critics.

The next stage of Dumont's scholarship took place closer to his home in Paris: until his death in 1998 he immersed himself in the study of European, and more generally Western ideology (or "culture"), much in the manner of a historian of ideas. It is sometimes assumed that Dumont's work on individualism and egalitarianism came about simply through a reversal of the gaze, a methodological innovation: by applying, as it were, Indian categories on the West. There is much truth in this, but as Jean-Claude Galey (2000: 327) has pointed out, already in his early work on South Indian kinship Dumont had become aware of a cognitive scheme of two countervailing forces, hierarchy and egalitarianism. Suspecting that the accommodation of these forces might be a universal concern, and that any valorization of the one would willy-nilly entail a corresponding disapproval of the other, he set about investigating the emergence of egalitarianism in Western ideology. His conclusions were that if in the Indian case hierarchy is fundamental to the notion of (the whole) society, in the Western case egalitarianism is coupled with the unassailable notion of the individual. And whereas hierarchy is integral to the preeminence of religion over the politico-economic spheres, individualism is essentially tied up with the emergent precedence of economy and power over religion. Yet, given the putative universality of the countervailing forces, one must expect the suppressed force always to exist and—even if from submerged, unacknowledged recesses of the social—provide the grounds for unpredictable, sometimes violent, social movements, prompting equally violent reactions. If individualism has no place in the Indian scheme of things, except by exception, hierarchy is also inimical to the West. Precisely because hierarchy is so revolting, so *unthought*, to Westerners—how can there be a place for it in societies that have affirmed the value of the individual in their constitutions?—Western analysts, victims to their knee-jerk reflexes, have refused to recognize it not only in its full bloom in India, but also in the eclipsed position it occupies in the West itself, where the hierarchical impulse—negated as such—can only express itself as discrimination. The best way to understand the obscured nature and appalling effects of hierarchy in the West is by applying what can readily be known about it from societies, such as India, where hierarchy is, as Dumont puts it, "clear and distinct" (1980: 262). Dumont's comparativism consists of such an approach. So much for our brief summary.

It goes without saying that Dumont's complaint about his lack of success with the concept of hierarchy was meant primarily for a British audience. He was addressing the British with certain ideas that—if unfamiliar to them—were deeply founded in the French tradition. Here we see a conflict over how anthropology should confront the fundamental issues of society and the individual, and it is with reference to Dumont's concept of totality that we want to explore in this chapter how we can conceive of social formations.

In an essay on Marcel Mauss, Dumont takes care to point out especially two important elements in the legacy of Mauss (Dumont 1986a, chapter 7). One is the role of comparative work—and as he points out "it was with Mauss that concrete knowledge began to react upon the theoretical framework" (1986a: 184), so that the science of anthropology could emerge in the encounter between (Durkheim's) philosophy and ethnographical material from around the world. The other point is the primacy in the analysis of a social whole: "the aim of research was to study not bits and pieces but a whole, a total, something with an internal consistency one can be sure of" (Dumont 1986a: 193–194). But unlike his British colleague Radcliffe-Brown, who would assume and take for granted the status of the totality of society as an organism (Radcliffe-Brown 1957), Mauss would prefer to look empirically for "the total social fact"—that is, specific social phenomena that could more realistically be said to *make manifest* social wholes. There is a difference here that should be spelled out. In a comment on the concept of "the total social fact," Alexander Gofman points out how "the ambiguity of this concept does not derive from theoretical construction, but from theoretical nonconstruction; in other words, from Mauss's refusal to theorise. . . . Doubtless, this pursuit of the 'total' resulted from Mauss's dissatisfaction with the traditional intra- and interdisciplinary divisions which partitioned reality in an artificial way" (Gofman 1998: 65). And, more importantly, the concept of totality in Mauss's usage addresses—although ambiguously—how social phenomena (acts, persons, institutions) manage to totalize—to take in, draw together, social wholes. The concept marks a process from within and not from without—such that for instance in the potlatch, the act of destruction or sacrifice, "the killing of wealth," is a totalizing act that *brings about* the social whole of fame, nurture, juridical aspects, and politics through the act itself. This is also why anthropology had to be a "science of the concrete" for Mauss, since the scale and implications of social totality were always open and undecided until accounted for. As Gofman points out, for Mauss total social facts were "specific ontological entities" (Gofman 1998: 67) that could be understood in their manifestation as "the constitutive elements, the generators and motors of the system." Of course, Mauss operated within an evolutionary social framework, and he would point out these totalizing societies as "archaic" societies. In advanced societies total social facts, such as the gift, would be transformed and reduced to fragmented institutions. Totalization as a social process would have lost its force. In Dumont's framework we see the same qualitative evolutionary evaluation, as individualism and egalitarianism are found to be a historical development of holistic or hierarchical systems (see also Kapferer 1988: 8–11). We shall come back to this later in this chapter.

In his review of Mauss's framework, Dumont seems to be struggling with the concept of totality. He questions the concept of the "whole" and suggests that Mauss was not really after discrete wholes or bounded totalities as such—but social *realities* or, as he says, "less extended complexes, where the 'whole' can be more easily kept within view" (Dumont 1986a: 194). From the point of view of lived sociality this "keeping within view" is quite different from postulating society as an organism, or taking society for granted as a bounded system. Mauss's almost mystical sense of totality then emerges as a perspective on social interaction, where society as a whole is always already present in the acts themselves. Acts are inbuilt with a totalizing perspective in these particular societies.

In his *Introduction to the Work of Mauss*, Lévi-Strauss had claimed the birth of a methodology in Mauss's work, but under his influence and rewriting of Mauss's project, the idea of the "whole" was more systematically turned into an abstract notion (Lévi-Strauss 1987). As pointed out by Dumont, Mauss's search for a "privileged phenomenon" was "to transcend the categories through which he approaches it" (Dumont 1986a: 194), that is, to benefit from the encounters with alternative social realities in order to deepen the understanding of the categories themselves. But Lévi-Strauss opposed this—dismissing it as immature—and argued that a mature science would always start out with the whole system of communication. With reference to Mauss's theory of the gift, he claimed that the Maori *hau*, for instance, as well as the religious concept of *mana*, were imagined signs in the universal tendency of man to try to "supply an unperceived totality" to ongoing life (Lévi-Strauss 1987: 58). They could not explain the gift as a universal system of reciprocity.

In his insistence on taking the system of exchange as his point of departure, and not some singular indigenous notion of a "spirit of the gift" as he claimed that Mauss had done, Lévi-Strauss also takes the "whole" of society away from "total" social facts and transfers it over to a "sign system" consisting in reciprocity as communication. Although Dumont would never protest against this development of Mauss, in his work on the Indian caste system the Maussian perspective on totality remains. Just as Mauss had departed from the idea of the Maroi *hau*, or "spirit of the gift," in his understanding of the gift as a human condition, Dumont departed from Indian "encompassement of the contrary" in his comparative understanding of hierarchy. As a scientist of the concrete, Dumont built his anthropology of India not on a predetermined idea that Indian society was an undifferentiated whole or a universe of signs, but on the emerging tendency in *practices* of totalization to be working toward a unifying principle on the ideological level. This can easily be misunderstood in *Homo Hierarchicus* (hereafter *HH*), since he begins by addressing totality *before* addressing the material. We can perceive this as a way of hypothesizing on the basis of material already digested in a Maussian fashion.[2]

With this legacy of Mauss[3] and conceptions of a "science of the concrete," Dumont brought with him a certain view of totality to his Indian material. What he was trying to sell was a newly designed concept of hierarchy that was adapted to the ethnographical setting of Indian caste society.

The Awkwardness of a Concept

This concept of hierarchy was in many ways hard to grasp, and in fact Dumont points out in his preface to the second English edition of *HH* that very few had been able to even think hierarchy the way he had proposed it. It was "at the heart of the 'unthought' (l'impensé) of modern ideology"—and both its critics and its supporters had misunderstood it (1980: xvi). The whole intention of *HH* had been to try to understand Indian caste on its own premises; to demonstrate the logic of a society that could not be explained within the framework of existing theories found in Western systems. In earlier accounts of the caste system, one had tried to explain the division of castes from reasons lying within a logic of political domination. Dumont would require that one bracket one's own preconception of sociopolitical relations and open up to another orientation of social organization. The concept ran counter to a materialist idea of hierarchy as stratification or a system of unequal distribution of resources. It ran counter to the idea that social systems—even their narrowly "political" aspects—by necessity were based on power. In the study of the Indian caste system, a focus on religious values and status overtook the Eurocentric focus on economy and power that could itself be verified genealogically through the history of Western thought (see Dumont 1977). Of course, the concept of hierarchy was associated in its etymology—hierarchia in medieval French was used for the ranked division of angels—with religious values and a specific mythological ordering of the universe. Dumont wanted to overturn the modernist preoccupation with *inequality* and return to the vision of a religiously and cosmologically founded hierarchy. Thus the concept of hierarchy for the Indian caste society revolved around the axis of purity and impurity as a privileged opposition that would govern values and practices of all kinds in Indian society. As religious values were primary in this hierarchy, purity would not only encompass impurity, but by extension religion would encompass politics as religious status would encompass political power.

The awkwardness of this concept consisted not just in its counterintuitive qualities, but also in its apparent intellectualism. It appeared as a puzzle to the mind of the most brilliant of scholars—the test being if one had managed to slip out of one's own Western belief system (governed by the economy-power analytic pair) sufficiently to be able to imagine such an all-embracing social formation as that given by the historical Indian case (governed by the value-status analytic pair). Hierarchy became a concept for dealing with holism, but not only that. It was a concept for expanding Lévi-Straussian binary structuralism toward the question of values and practice, but not only that. It was an empirical case for a kind of social organization that reproduced itself as a totality in all of its parts, but not only that either. It was challenging certain ways of conceptualizing society, by turning the focus away from actors and specific Indian localities and instead trying to adopt a view of social process implicated by the pratices of Indian people and their own ideas about sociality. In this claim of an indigenous model, the system of values would—in a constant motion of regulations, prohibitions, and purifications—accord all existing things, ideas, and spaces particular values. This "coding of the flow"—to use Deleuze and Guattari's terms in their work on "social machines" in *Anti-Oedipus* (1983: 141)—would be seen to be a self-perpetual motion in Indian society. It would work as a totalizing movement, all the time collecting new things, new statuses, and new events into the grasp of the regime of purity.

All attempts to pin this concept of hierarchy down to specific ethnographic circumstances would be mistaken—at least if they were made in the attitude of a crude empiricism that would only conceive of something as "true" if it were true to all participants in the event.[4] And, as pointed out by Iteanu (in this volume), the concept caused violent reactions, since it turned against the deeply entrenched epistemological premise of thinking hierarchy as a "chain of command" and as an expression of the universality of power relations. By turning the meaning of hierarchy away from power and command that were the intuitive contents of the concept in the Western context, Dumont also introduced a total relativism into the study of political systems. As Iteanu emphasizes further, this turn was crucial for the comparative project of anthropology, since it "helps overcome the absolute reification resulting from the dominating extension of the notions of power." (Iteanu in this volume, p. 333). That position certainly created as many problems as it solved, since anthropology as a practice was at least as much rooted empirically in regionalism as it was comparative. The gap between being relative and comparative on the one hand, and providing the detail that would satisfy regional specialists on the other, has in many ways been unbridgeable. Of course, to create the category of India as a totality immediately provokes the empiricist questions of where and when the boundaries of this totality are to be found, whether and how the general claims correspond to local realities, and whether local concepts would survive the essentialization inherent in such generalizations (see Fuchs 1992; Tyler 1973).[5]

But, again drawing on Iteanu (in this volume), we could say that, in the middle of this disciplinary, rather bumpy terrain, the concept of hierarchy really offers itself as a model for anthropological analysis, as "an asymmetrical translation between two societies," and "a displaced notion" that could not be found in the discourse of either of these societies (as hierarchy in the sense used by Dumont could be found in the vocabularies neither of the West nor of India), only in the anthropological apparatus serving crosscultural understanding. Therefore hierarchy as a hybrid concept could only be approached in a partial way: as encompassment, as holism, as a regime of value, but always inside the comparative relation to Western individualism, to egalitarianism or to a regime of power. Awkward indeed, and indeed difficult to think, but such intermediary concepts have been crucial to the building of the discipline. And against claims such as that made by Appadurai (1986: 745) that *HH* was a swan song for old ways of thinking, we believe that the maintenance of hierarchical thinking—and the insistence on methodological holism and sensibility to society as part of ontological reality—is of crucial importance to the anthropological project in its ambitions to understand world developments also in the future.

It is no secret that Dumont's work has met with intense scepticism since it was launched in the mid 1960s: we think here of the publication of *HH* in French in 1966 and the first English edition four years later.[6] While largely leaving to one side the reception of that book among Dumont's French colleagues—and of the numerous articles and books that ensued, in what follows here we want to fix on the reactions from those steeped in British and North American intellectual traditions, first and foremost from anthropologists, and to express some of our own reservations as we go along. Thus we proceed by working our way through Dumont's concepts of holism and hierarchy, taking note of some of the criticism those concepts have met with, aiming expressly for an alternative conception of sociality. Taking into account the influence of Mauss and the ideas of "total social facts" and "privileged phenomena" as ways of conceiving sociality as an open, ongoing, momentary process of totalization, we shall review how Dumont approaches the issue of totality.

The definitions Dumont gives for hierarchy are, in general, "an order resulting from the consideration of value," and specifically: "The elementary hierarchical relation (or hierarchical opposition) is that between a whole (or a set) and an element of that whole (or set)—or else that between two parts with reference to the whole" (1986a: 279). This does not help us in understanding what the "whole" is in social terms, and further if "[w]e can call holist an ideology that valorizes the social whole and neglects or subordinates the human individual" (1986a: 279), then we get confused about the proposed relation between the ideology that is holist and the social whole that then appears as a result of this ideology.

We are not alone in being distracted by these assertions. In fact a fairly common reaction to Dumont's analytical approach stems from its explicitly "global" or "universal," "holistic" or "total" nature. Of course these aspects are internally connected, which makes the divide between scholars, such as Marriott, Appadurai, or Dirks on the one hand, and Dumont (and his students, two of whom—Iteanu and Tcherkézoff—contribute to this volume) on the other, virtually impossible to bridge. The title Dumont gave one of his papers, "The individual as an impediment to sociological comparison and Indian history" (in Dumont 1970a), is in this respect programmatic.[7]

Already in the introduction to *HH*, Dumont makes very clear that the theory of Indian caste it contains is also an attack on the Western concept of the individual and on the concept of society—wherein the individual is a monad and society a collection of such monads—as "the tyranny of numbers" (1980: 4–5). The concept of society as a whole was then specifically not a question of creating such artificial discrete entities. It was in fact crucial for Dumont to demonstrate that the split between individual and society was an artefact of Western social ontologies, and that these concepts needed to be rethought ideologically. What he found in the Indian material was a mode of sociality set on other premises. In the latter it was the ordering of the world from Hindu ideology that regulated the life of human beings, gods, and every other kind of being, and laid out the parameters of sociality so that each person, each entity in the world, would represent a form of agency different from how we conceive of individual agency. All creations, all kinds of agency on all levels of society, would be seen to represent the differentiated agency of the whole. In such a society, where all happenings and actions on the part of men or gods would be understood as aspects of the larger motion of the whole of society, it would be insufficient, for instance, to study relations of power, relations of economy, or individual will without taking into consideration the aspect of the whole—as an agency of the social machine—again to invoke the parallels with Deleuze and Guattari. About the case of India and its "contrary ideology" of individualism, Dumont writes :

> In our case [that is, in India, eds.], in every concrete whole we find the formal principle at work, but we also find something else, a raw material which it orders and logically encompasses but which it does not explain, at least not immediately and for us. This is where we find the equivalent of what we call relations of force, political and economic phenomena, power, territory, property, etc. Those data which we can recover thanks to the notions we have of them in our own ideology may be called the (comparative) concomitants of the ideological system. Certain authors select them for study without noticing that the devaluation which they undergo in the present case alters them profoundly. The specialist steeped in modern ideology expects everything from these phenomena, but here they are bound by the iron shackles of a contrary ideology. . . . *It is only in relation to the totality thus reconstructed that the ideology takes on its true significance* (Dumont 1980: 38, original emphasis).

In this sense, the totality that consists of Indian men and women, in living out hierarchical oppositions in concrete life, "*makes the idea visible to us*" (1980: xvii, emphasis added). The idea of hierarchy as a social form is visible from observing practice in the historical and ethnographic setting of India.

Much of the criticism of the concept of hierarchy has been directed at its seemingly predetermined status as a whole, its postulation that in societies of a certain type there is a preexisting social totality that warrants the label "holistic." For the purpose also of understanding the various empirical contributions to this book as instances of hierarchical social formations in settings outside of India, we should here benefit from focusing more closely on what is meant by a "whole" or "totality" when it comes to social process—despite the uncomfortable feeling that such concepts trigger in modern anthropology.

Against Totality

The attacks on Dumont's holism have been manifold. One angle was that the theory of hierarchy as an encompassing totality is predetermining the analysis so that "social theory becomes an ontology" (see M. Fuchs 1992: 25–26). Dumont's descriptions of Indian caste were allegedly merely a projection of a preconceived idea of the primitive world. Hierarchy could then no longer be a question of rank, nor even about opposed categories, only a model of society being imposed on the material. What Dumont presented was really a nostalgic vision of a complete social totality—invested entirely inside the matrix of purity. In Dirks's framework there is the historically grounded disbelief that such a holistic system ever existed. Parallel to much other simultaneous writing on the "invention of tradition," Dirks postulated that caste was a modern phenomenon: namely "the product of an historical encounter between India and Western colonial rule" (2001: 5).[8] He claimed that it was under British rule that the term "caste" came to stand for the totality of Indian society, set up not as a discovery of holism already there, but as a straitjacket imported by the colonial apparatus with the intention to mystify Indian social structure as religiously determined by Hinduism. Instead Dirks portrays hierarchy as tied to the political rule of the king less than as determined by the religious role of the Brahmans:

> When Dumont and other ethnological commentators insist that the high position of the Brahman is the ideological proof of the hierarchical nature of the "caste system"—arguing that despite the great muddle in the middle, the strict hierarchy placing Brahmans on the very top and "untouchables" on the very bottom indicates the absolute priority of the categories of purity and pollution—they mistake a part for the whole. Brahmans may have been necessary, both for a great many aspects of thought and practice and for the ideological maintenance of Hindu kingship, but they neither defined nor provided the principles that organized hierarchy for the entire Indian social order throughout all time (Dirks 2001: 70–71).

This objection echoes Berreman's early reaction to *HH*: "From this book, one would think that Professor Dumont had been talking with, reading and believing Brahmins and their friends. That is not wrong, it is just inadequate to an understanding of caste in India or anywhere else" (1971b: 515, also 1971a).[9] It is also paralleled by Inden's fitting of the Orientalist critique onto

Dumont (Inden 1986), and it is repeated in the most recent assessment we have come across, where the author not only dismisses Dumont's efforts ("It was not as if Dumont was saying anything that has not been said before" [Gupta 2005: 410]), but also laments their lasting effect on the discipline:

> A single all embracing, all acquiescing, hierarchy was, of course, expressed with the expected hyperboles in Brahmannical texts such as the *Yagnavalkyas-mriti* and *Manusmriti*, but it was the nineteenth century Indologists who were the modern propagators of this point of view and gave it wider respectability. Sadly, social anthropologists, who could have corrected this notion with their field observations, also succumbed to this position (see Dumont 1988: 149) (Gupta 2005: 411).[10]

Another closely related and equally influential criticism has been against the tendency of totalization in Dumont's work: "Such totalization probably has its roots in the German romanticism of the early 19th century and comes to us in all the variations of the idea of the Geist (spirit) of an age or a people. Canonized in Hegel's holism, its most important result was the subsequent Marxian commitment to the idea of totality" (Appadurai 1988: 41). In tracing the genealogy of the concept of hierarchy, Appadurai claims not only to have traced its intellectual roots in Hegel's holism, but also its regional roots in a multitude of ethnographical regions through the writings of Bouglé, Evans-Pritchard, Hocart, Robertson Smith, and Maine:

> Dumont's conception of hierarchy leads from India in at least four major topological directions: Africa, in regard to its conception of the parts; ancient Arabia, for its conceptions of religious segmentation and solidarity; ancient Rome, for its conception of jural order in the absence of a powerful state; and the South Pacific (via Ceylon), for its conception of the power of taboo and the ritual implications of specialization (Appadurai 1988: 45).

According to Appadurai the issue of totality was in fact an emerging idea, arising within the ethnography of many different societies under the pretence of being specifically Indian. But this of course also corresponds to the explicit claim made by Dumont that Western societies are abnormal in this way, and that "among the great civilizations the world has known, the holistic type of society has been overwhelmingly predominant" (1977: 4).

Other critics take a somewhat different tack. Thus the gist of the "new wind" view—after the title of a well-known collection of essays (David 1977)—boils down to an accusation that Dumont's position denies India even the slightest positive valuation of individual agency, or indeed even of intra-Indian sociocultural variation. Dumont's reply to this charge was that whatever we might think about the valuation in India of individual agency or how we might construe the scholarly or indigenous recognition of sometimes great variation is beside the point when the historical developments of Western and Indian ideology are taken into account. The emergence of Western individualism is internal to the development of Christianity, and the relationship between the single individual soul and conscience and God is paramount in European history. Furthermore, in the next turn the State gradually superseded the role of the Church. What followed, while the position of the individual was continually being fortified, was that the category "economy" became separate and with it a host of other, truly modern categories and institutions—all under the State umbrella— but with "the economic view" rising to primacy. This could even be traced in Marx's labor theory of value, predated in turn by Locke's disquisitions on the inalienable right of all free individuals to the fruits of their labor (see Dumont 1970b).[11] In combination, of course, what emerges is economic individualism—a great advance on how the serfs of previous times were subordinated under sovereign monarchs—and political systems, the purpose of which was to protect property relations. Another way to formulate this is to say that relationships between persons and property took precedence over relationships between persons. In other words: Western individualism is at the base of Western society (if, indeed, the West can be said to have a "society"; in Dumont's view that is a moot question, cf. his "Ontologically, the society no longer exists" [Dumont 1980: 9]), and it is also the foundation not only of economics but also, to Dumont more crucially, of sociology. Recall that simple, profound question, so often put before introductory classes in sociology and anthropology, "How is society possible?" (see Simmel 1910–11). Dumont's point is that only in the West does such a question make intuitive sense; after all it is a natural corollary to what we cannot not think. How could anyone in the West doubt the existence and the presence of individuals?—it is rather the ontological (and hence epistemological) status of society that would seem to represent a challenge. Given Dumont's position that the situation in India—and probably elsewhere—is the reverse, he insists that any analysis of India cannot begin with the individual, because there "on the level of life in the world, the individual is not" (Dumont 1960: 42). In short, the Western and the Indian societies are based on different premises, and a sociology that derives its foundational concepts from properties of the former has no purchase in the analysis of the latter. We think this methodological point is insufficiently recognized: Because Western social science is so embroiled in Western value systems—indeed, it is one of their products—its possibility for accurately assessing what is really at stake in other social systems is nil. Unless, that is, it rethinks its ontological presuppositions.[12]

Paradoxically, perhaps, bearing in mind what we just noted, one of the main charges against Dumont's analysis of India is that it has a destructive, ethnocentric bias. For, as we have pointed out already, in the eyes of some scholars, the India that Dumont portrays is an India that is "other" in an Orientalist sense: Dumont's India is the India of the British Empire. Dumont's is the India so different from societies in the West that it cannot be juxtaposed to them, except—unfavorably so—as their Orientalist antithesis. In effect, Dumont has allegedly given us an India with whom Westerners cannot speak (see Dirks 1987, 2001; Inden 1990). This, ironically, is an argument that in one sense mobilizes Dumont's thinking (though not of course his argument) against himself: From this perspective, India would seem to be encompassed by the West—that is, by the West's warped version of Brahmin essentialism as its polar opposite (again, see Gupta 2005 for an up-to-date variant). The flip side of this paradox is that analysts who have managed to dodge Dumont's Orientalist spell—and who can therefore still claim to see clearly that all sociocultural configurations, and especially the Indian, are sites of unequal struggles between the powerful and the deprived—these analysts do not really have to know much about matters Indian in order to arrive at their conclusions. At any rate, these arguments also actualize that perennial problem in anthropology: translation and, with it, the problem of comparison.

Contrary to those of Dumont's critics who think his works merely propagate Orientalism, our own opinion is that his radical and relentless comparativism—one he learnt from Mauss—is perhaps his greatest achievement.[13] Let us be clear: We see the merits of the Dumontian perspective as it applies to his analysis of India, and we support his insistence that a truly comparative sociology cannot be based on categories internal to societies of one particular type. One might object that Dumont here seems to grope for an Archimedean point. But our view is that he aims instead to analyze the West by way of Indian categories, not—and this should be obvious—thereby claiming that these categories are untainted by time and place. Until such timeless, value-free concepts have been arrived at (and given the nature of language one would wonder for how long such concepts would remain pristine), one must proceed without them; it cannot be thought illegitimate to employ a terminological apparatus external to the object of study. Not, at least, while simultaneously claiming that the sociological apparatus developed in the West is eminently suited to the same task.[14]

Getting to Know India

The force of ethnography is that it always has the potential for challenging existing concepts and knowledge about social settings. We will now move on to indicate briefly ways in which Dumont's concept of hierarchy has been challenged by more recent advances in Indian ethnography. For the purpose of understanding hierarchy in India these contributions have been more useful than the criticism of the Orientalism, the Exotism, and the Holism of Dumont—which have been raised more on historical and moral than on ethnographic grounds, in our view. There has been a vast number of articles and books published, which we cannot touch upon here (among them Burghart 1978; Madan 1982; Barnes, De Coppet, and Parkin 1985; Fuller 1988; Cort 1991), but which have managed to nuance the image of Indian social life.

One of these has been Gloria G. Raheja's *The poison in the gift* (1988a), which describes in great detail the relationships between the landholding *jajman* in relation to the various village castes in North India. Building on Marriot's transactionalist approach, Raheja presents an account of how hierarchy works as a social movement through an emphasis on the sacrifices made by landowners:

> The cultivator is the *jajman*, the "sacrificer," and he stands at the conceptual center of village ritual organization; the Barber, the Sweeper, the Brahman, and many other castes of the village carry out virtually identical roles in relation to the *jajman*, particularly in their acceptance of *dan*. These recipients of *dan* take upon themselves and "digest" the sin, the evil, and the inauspiciousness of the *jajman*, his household, and the village (Raheja 1988a: 248).

Raheja here proposes that a center-periphery model of North Indian village society works better than a model based on Dumont's concept of hierarchy. In this *jajmani* system—a system of allotting customary shares of the harvest to members of the various service castes—landowners stand at the center of the system, not only of lands and power, but also of sacrifice and ritual.[15] Landholders, and not priests, hold the central functions of society. Furthermore, she makes clear how the gift of *dan*—gifts from the landowners to other castes that take away inauspiciousness—do not work on a model of purity and impurity. Her argument is that purity and impurity are relevant to the system as a hierarchy, but *on the level of social interaction and transactions*, inauspiciousness is much more important:

> [F]orms of impurity have little if any relevance for more generalized well-being or auspiciousness. Ill-health, lack of prosperity, failure to produce sons, death, madness, family discord, poor harvests, and many of the other misfortunes about which villagers are concerned and that receive much ritual attention are never attributed to impurity or hierarchical consideration of any sort (1988: 46).

We learn that inauspiciousness is the main focus of the ritual system of sacrifice, but not as a system that posits permanently one caste or another as superior. Gifts of *dan* crosscut divisions of caste. Raheja points out that in the case of the villages studied, Brahmans were in fact often landholding *jajmans*, and they would then also give *dan* to other Brahmans or other castes. It is hard to find in her ethnography the centrality of the priestly castes that Dumont proposed. In fact, in the context of a marriage ceremony, wife-givers give daughters as *dan* to secure their own auspiciousness and wife-receivers are obligated, among other things, to receive the wife as one variety of *dan*—*kanya dan* (literally, the gift of a virgin) (1988: 118–21). This underplays the important role of the Brahman in Dumont's model, and Raheja's analysis goes in the direction of suggesting that hierarchy is only a superficial ideology in Indian society.

Raheja thus brings back into relevance Hocart's material on the king and the village *jajman*—the chiefly cultivator—not only as positions of political power, but also of ritual maintenance and sacrifice. Raheja argues for a closer attention to village level interaction—where power and ritual are more intermingled than Dumont would be willing to admit. Importantly, Hocart was a predecessor in the field of radical comparison who had inspired Dumont. In his highly original *Kings and Councillors* (1936) and *Caste* (1950), Hocart argues that the basis for comparison between societies is the way they organize life, growth, and reproduction through ritual forms. Thus he also traces the origin of government in Western state forms to ritual organization:

> [T]he functions now discharged by king, prime minister, treasury, public works, are not the original ones; they may account for the present form of these institutions, but not for their original appearance. These were originally part, not of a system of government, but of an organization to promote life, fertility, prosperity by transferring life from objects abounding in it to objects deficient in it (Hocart 1970 [1936]: 3).

Even though Hocart forwards the Durkheimian idea that all social institutions have religious roots, his views more clearly give preeminence to ritual and sacrifice in the study of human sociality. Hocart's emphasis on ritual as constitutive for social formations had a lasting influence on Dumont. On the basis of his study of Indian society, Dumont, however, would go against the overly generalist assertions that Hocart made. Whereas Hocart implied that there would be a straight continuity between previous evolutionary stages of ritual societies and modern state government, and that all cases would be reducible to the same principle, Dumont introduces radical difference into the comparison of societies. In Hocart's view the figure of the king would already be implied in any performance of ritual, and through examples from all over the world, he implicates this figure as a common denominator in ritual, even among the most "primitive" of societies. Here the ritual leader holds the role of ancestor-god and takes on the world through imitation, so that he becomes one with nature and society. He becomes therefore the merger between nature and society in order to produce fertility and growth (Hocart 1970: 46–47).[16] To Hocart this is already evidence that the encompassing function and hierarchical institution of the king is present in these societies, and that royal sacrifices are direct extensions of this function. And it is interesting that, in a sense, Raheja recycles Hocart's point in her critique of Dumont. Whereas Hocart would speculate on kingship as the very ritual origin of society through various forms of royal sacrifice, Dumont would later reorient Hocart's emphasis on ritual, to state that, in the Indian case, historically the king had become subservient to the ritual supremacy of the priest through these sacrifices to the priest by the kings or landholders (see Dumont and Pocock 1958; Raheja 1988b: 504; Scubla 2002). But Dumont would also grant that Hocart's theory on caste was correct—but only *"for Ceylon,"* to which India "exported quasi-caste rather than caste proper" and where the king "has remained the centre both of group religion . . . and of political and economic life" (Dumont 1980: 216, original emphasis). Marriott's scrutiny of transactions and reciprocity on the Indian village level (Marriott 1969, 1976) had indeed given us the nondualistic—"monist" in Dumont's own gloss (1980: xxxii)—version of Indian ideology that Raheja calls for, where also the alleged "secular" castes would be submitted to the religious values and practices of Hinduism.

A diversity of strategies and transactions replaces Dumont's dualism of values. Of course, at this point we are also beyond the problem of what constitutes the caste system as such, the question that Dumont wanted to answer through the concept of hierarchy. In the center-periphery model that is proposed by Raheja, it is hard to realize the constitution of the different castes—other than their being in service to the landowners. It is also difficult to understand from her account how and why, in cosmological and ontological terms—for example, a house becomes inauspicious when death occurs in it and when birth occurs; and what might be the reason for inauspiciousness in the grain at harvest time. As pointed out in a review, Raheja's book does not work altogether as a critique of Dumont's theory of hierarchy either, since it does not deal with hierarchy in social contexts where hierarchy would make itself relevant: "[T]his exhaustive treatment of ritual exchange, at the expense of other facets of village life, does make it hard to understand the argument. The author's focus on ritual prestation does not allow us to see the extent to which the hierarchical model of caste does obtain in other social contexts" (Bonner 1989: 224). However, if we then take into account the ethnography of Jonathan Parry, who has also analyzed the *dan* prestations extensively (see

Parry 1979; 1980; 1986), we become aware of the benefit in this upgrading of ethnographic knowledge. In his article about Benares funeral priests, Parry, like Raheja, is determined to enhance our understanding of the role of the Brahman, and to confront Dumont more directly:

> The priest's status is highly equivocal; and he is seen not so much as the acme of purity as an absorber of sin. Just as the low caste specialists remove the biological impurities of their patrons, so the Brahman priest removes their spiritual impurity by taking their sins upon himself through the act of accepting their gifts. . . . Since he cannot really "digest" the sins he accepts, so far from being a paragon of purity, he regards himself as a cess-pit for the wickedness of the cosmos (Parry 1980: 89).

The importance of both these contributions is their negation of Dumont's presumed essentialisms regarding hierachical status and the immobility of the social system. Raheja and Parry actually both insist on the processual character of hierarchy, which in their view is working against any strict or formal categorizations or identities. Brahmans can be landowners; hierarchy can be relativized—between the parties in marriage, for instance; and he who is pure in one moment can be impure in the next; kings and landowners suddenly stand at the center of religious offerings, and so on.

We can, then, benefit from these cases and mobilize them for a better understanding of hierarchy. They actually present us with evidence of how any transaction in Indian society actually calls for hierarchization. By this we mean a social motion that continually demands for sins and inauspiciousness to "be passed on" in certain directions according to a cultural grammar of donors and recipients (see Raheja 1988a: 71, 92). Through these ethnographic accounts, we get a detailed view of how the gift works as a social principle for securing religious reproduction. This is also clear from Parry's account of funerary rites: "For the successful conclusion of the rites [the funeral priest] must be satisfied with the gifts he is offered. 'His belly must be full' and he must ungrudgingly bestow his blessing" (Parry 1980: 95). When the Mahabrahmans (funeral priests and Brahmans) of Benares receive *dan* at the mortuary ceremony and services, they not only take on the sins of the *jajman*, they also take upon themselves the identity of the deceased: they *become* the deceased (Parry 1980: 96). We then also realize that beyond the descriptions of the Brahman as having varying status with regard to purity, with regard to the landholder at the center—even operating at the same level as the so called secular castes—the Brahman *is* an encompassing figure in his role as "vessel" of sins. The gift of *dan* is itself embodying hierarchization in the way it transfers qualities from person to person. The "taking out," "transferring," "ingesting," and "passing on" of negative influence through the prestations of *dan* all demonstrate how sociality itself is the moving force, the agent of these transformations between different statuses. The Brahman is not receiving the gift for himself, but as a duty to this social form, just as all castes provide their services on behalf of social transformation itself. The role of *dan* for removing inauspiciousness and the role of the priests as "vessels" for transporting evil underline the explicit indigenous social theory of totalization that we see as crucial for our effort of defining hierarchy as a social form. In turn, this realization can lead us toward a better understanding of hierarchy as process and social movement.

Thus far, we have presented Dumont's concept of hierarchy, its relation to individualism, and its reception in the anthropology of India. In the next section we will attempt to assess further some of the wider implications of Dumont's theories for the anthropological debate about totality before we propose a change of language circumscribing the social.

The Problem with Totality and the Social

In the foregoing we have perceived how totality has been seen, first and foremost, as a property of ideology, and secondly as a property of society. Of course, if we consider the possible scale of a totality, it is easy to imagine the relevance of an ideology as a totality. Ideology consists of ideas that can spread; they can be taught and learned; and they are liable to be picked up in practice. Values find their existence in people. In our ontology of the social, on the other hand, society does not so easily adhere to a logic of totality. People move out of society; they create conflicts; they ignore its boundaries and regulations; there are ruptures in issues of belonging, contestations in terms of stratification, and so on. Society is no viable concept for totality, and this is why society was not the primary analytical frame for Dumont either. Values were his interest, and therefore he had problems "selling" his concepts to the British audience, who conceived of society and interaction as the primary and often exclusive stuff of anthropology (see Dumont 1986a: 235).[17] And there is reason to be sensitive to the use of expressions and metaphors here. As pointed out later by Marilyn Strathern, in her notion that the concept of society be "despatched as obsolete" for analytical purposes (1996: 66), the problem with the concept of society is not only its unitary composition vis-à-vis other units "out there"—and the way the concept creates in our imagination an artificial awareness of events either working *for* or *against* society—but most importantly the way the concept of society has become interchangeable with the concept of the individual. She complains about how social relations and social structures have vanished from sight in contemporary Britain, and how what remains are only discrete individuals and discrete aggregates of individuals (states, corporations, families, and so on). And this, she claims, goes for all voices from that of Margaret Thatcher—who profited from this denial of social forces—to those of social scientists who are thus making themselves more and more peripheral in the market of knowledge about society. In short, the language of individualism has invaded the language of society, rendering society unthinkable outside the rhetoric of individualism. This corresponds well to the way Dumont was constantly arguing for an alternative understanding of the social. Working with values instead of interaction and totality instead of fragments, he wanted to accomplish a way around the complex implications of thinking through individuals.

A crucial issue in the forthcoming discussion, and a constant source of misunderstanding, is the degree to which a totality demands closure. From Iteanu (in this volume, p. 340) we learn that:

> Hierarchy is a relation between a part and a totality. However, here again, the notions both of totality and of part do not posses their usual meaning. In the usual Western sense, a totality is an entity which leaves nothing outside of itself. This is not the case in hierarchic ideologies, where each element is in relation to a larger context, and each totality needs another totality to encompass it. Totalities are, therefore, not closed, but open.

Here Iteanu's and Dumont's sense of hierarchy could be compared to Arthur Koestler's concept of *holon*—i.e., that which is simultaneously part and whole—and the idea that in the very logic of natural hierarchies all levels would be both encompassing lower levels and encompassed by higher levels (see Koestler 1967: 45–58):

> Parts and wholes in an absolute sense do not exist anywhere. The living organism and the body social are not assemblies of elementary bits; they are multi-levelled, hierarchically organised systems of sub-wholes containing sub-wholes of a lower order, like Chinese boxes. These sub-wholes—or *holons*, as I have proposed to call them—are Janus-faced entities which display both the independent properties of wholes and the dependent properties of parts. Each *holon* must preserve and assert its autonomy, otherwise the organism would lose its articulation and dissolve into an amorphous mass—but at the same time the *holon* must remain subordinate to the demands of the (existing or evolving) whole. "Autonomy" in this context means that organelles, cells, muscles, nerves, organs, all have their intrinsic rhythm and pattern of functioning, aided by self-regulatory devices; and that they tend to persist in and assert their characteristic patterns of activity. This "self-assertive tendency" is a fundamental and universal characteristic of *holons*, manifested on every level, from cells to individuals to social groups (Koestler 1972: 111–112).

Although useful, to us these analogies between the natural world and the social world have their clear limitation. In the realm of the social, imagination and ideology are the crucial forces and not the relationships of the kind possibly existing between the elements of organic bodies. Values regulate the social world so that not only are things and relationships given their direction through values, but also the social movement itself is given its direction through these same values.

In this regard Dumont's search into the ontology of the social in many ways converges with the philosopher-psychoanalyst Cornelius Castoriadis, who oriented much of his work toward the imaginary status of society. In his attempts at grasping society in its own terms, he points out the fallacies in two current ways of thinking society. One is the functionalist idea that society is the self-perpetual organism that satisfies the needs of the human organism and exists for that reason. As an extension of this, theories of "desire" that set up society as either fulfilment of desire or repression of desire are equally tautological. The second fallacy is what he calls the "logistics type" (1997: 200). Currently inherent in structuralist analyses, this approach sets up society as a combination of discrete elements that "unquestionably take for granted both the finite set (*ensemble*) of elements on which the operations are performed and the oppositions or differences it postulates between them" (1997: 200). Note the difference here from Maussian "total social facts" and the "keeping totality within view"—a perspective that seems to have been abandoned in Lévi-Straussian structuralism. Further, Castoriadis goes on to argue that, "Society presents itself immediately as the coexistence of a host of terms or entities of different orders. What is available to inherited thinking in order to think coexistence and the mode of being-together of a diversity of terms?" (1997: 205). Not being content with society as a composite of relations or ensembles, and being equally uncomfortable with ideas of organic wholes, the claim is the same as Strathern's that our greatest obstacle is that we cannot control our language of society:

> We are able to name only things, subjects, concepts, and their collections and unions, relations, attributes, states and so on. However, the unity of a society . . . cannot be analysed into relations between subjects mediated by things, since every relation between subjects is a social one between social subjects, every relation to things is a social relation to social objects, and since subjects, things, and relations are what they are and such as they are here only because they are instituted in the way they are by the society concerned (Castoriadis 1997: 208).

And it does not help us if we then instead resort to a language of the organism, because this "is to speak of a system of interdependent functions determined by an end; and this end is the conservation and the reproduction of the same, the affirmation of permanence across time and accidents, of essence, *eidos* (aspect/species)" (1997: 208). Even though this has been part of the criticism of Dumont's study of hierarchy, we find that the direction in Dumont's treatment of wholes actually rescues him from such a definition of society. As pointed out by Iteanu (in this volume), Dumont's India is not teleologically and self-perpetually reproducing itself. It is simply working on its own "logic-ontology," to follow Castoriadis. For Castoriadis, the question of society boils down to realizing the "ontological genesis" in social formations. Society is the "magma of magmas" and a "nonensemblizable diversity" (1997: 211): "Society institutes itself as a mode and a type of coexistence: as a mode and type of coexistence in general, with no analogue or precedent in another region of being, and as *this* particular mode and type of coexistence, the specific creation of the society considered" (1997: 210). Importantly, he adds that, "The organization of society redeploys itself each time in a different way, not only in as much as it posits different moments, sectors, or domains in and through which it exists, but also in as much as it brings into being a type of relation among these moments that can be new and even that is always new in a nontrivial sense" (1997: 210). These attributes make society a unique category in the human world, as the creation of creations, as an unthinkable and unnameable category that we can only approach in unsatisfactory ways. This is why the effort of rethinking hierarchy in India for Dumont was also "at the heart of the unthought of modern ideology" (1980: xvi).

But what does it entail that we term a social system "holist"? According to Dumont, what is holist is "an ideology that *valorizes* the social whole" (Dumont 1986a: 279, emphasis added). We have then to imagine an ideology or a set of values—made manifest in the actions of all the Indians and Indian scriptures—that accords all social beings a value after their placing in an imaginary, always potential, totality. Hierarchy is an ideology in motion that constantly melts down categories and substances, things, ideas, and people that come under its totalizing sway and transforms them, that gives them value according to its own social universe. Values represent a totalizing movement—an "ontological genesis" in Castoriadis's terms—that draws into its own movement all social events, and, as such, values always indicate the presence of hierarchy: "To adopt a value is to introduce hierarchy" (Dumont 1980: 20; see also Hoskins in this volume). If Dumont's claims are sound, then every Indian person at a given time in history would not only act with his or her own perspective in mind, but would also operate with a kind of intentionality toward such an undefined and only potential whole. The acts of each and every Indian would be the simultaneous instantiations of multiple agency and the agency of the ideology. For Dirks, as we noted above, this sort of thing would be impossible to imagine without the context of the colonialist project (Dirks 2001). The claim of an agency of totality would be a mystification of the Indian, in the paradigm of Orientalism, which would make him a slave to religiosity. Dirks's point is that this was how the apparatus of the British Empire wanted the Indian to be perceived. And allegedly Dumont went along with that. But this represents a rather narrow reading of the social, one that refuses to admit the possibility that a totalizing social formation could exist outside of a state apparatus such as that of the British. If we consider the Indian ethnography that we have just surveyed—the constant attention to ceremony and ritual prestations at every level of village life, the constant movement of inauspiciuousness and evil through gifts of *dan*—it is hard to see how this motion and intentionality toward fulfilment of religious values could be attributed entirely to the colonial system. We believe that, in the encounter with such practices, we should use them instead for confronting our concepts of the religious and the social.

Dumont's analytical framework, therefore, does not restrict itself to the Indian case, and this is the strength of his relentless comparativism. The bottom line of the argument is that all social formations are given their direction from their paramount values, not only in Hindu ideology but also in what he calls Individualism. Here the argument comes very near, of course, to biting its tail. For how, then, is individualism not also another version of hierarchy? Could we not perceive it as an ideology where the paramount value is the singular in encompassing opposition to the plural, the homogenous in encompassing opposition to the heterogeneous, equality in encompassing relation to the inequal? (see Tcherkézoff in this volume). But as we have already pointed out, individualism is an ideology that denies its own existence as a social ideology. Westerners operate within a paradigm of sociality based on "the absolute distinction that lets *facts* be considered independently of *values*" (Dumont 1980: 244). Values are only accorded a place on the outskirts of reality.

If we were to suggest a value that is paramount to systems of individualism, it would be *change*, and not the individual itself as a category or an essence. The individual is only valued if in states of transformation. Mobility, reformation, renewal, and creativity are some of the characteristics that go along with freedom. This is not a freedom to stay the same, to remain immobile, to uphold inertness. In itself, democracy is based on the morality of always seeking change in social systems. Lévi-Strauss pinpointed this in his distinction between "hot" and "cold" social systems. Whereas "cold" societies value points of origin and mythological beginnings, and continually structure the present after these beginnings, "hot" societies instead value change in itself and always keep looking for transformations and new beginnings to celebrate.

We believe this also implies that there is in individualist society a motion set out to demolish values. The absolute value of change is always trying to encompass—through destruction—values that uphold permanence. And wherever these opposite values tend to manifest themselves, they are neutralized or destroyed. Iteanu's example (in this volume) of the religiously manifested value of the veil in France is a timely example. Within an individualist sociality such as there is in France, the veil became illegal in French schools as soon as it became a symbol of religious values. Another recent example came in January of 2006 when Scandinavian newspapers published caricature drawings of Mohammed. Mohammed is an absolute sacred value among Muslims, and even depicting Mohammed's face is prohibited in the Muslim world. These drawings then immediately aroused aggression and violence in Muslim societies, whereas in the European countries there was a mobilization around the defence of the right of "freedom of speech." Initially we could see this "human right" as a value in and of itself, closely related to the paramount value of the individual. However, this is not how these values articulate themselves. We would argue that these values upheld around the individual—of freedom and equality especially—actually do not work as values, but are articulated in a social movement against religious values. In Norway and Denmark, intellectuals, politicians, and artists stood up for their right to be provocative and especially to attack religious values. In this way individualism not only submits values to facts, but as a social movement, characteristically, also turns against values; and change itself is the motor of this movement. Whereas values under a hierarchical society are encompassed and totalized by opposite values, individualist society tends to exile them to a forced dispersal. The status of the social then also becomes ambiguous.

We could here refer to Kapferer's comparative analysis of Australian egalitarianism and Sri Lankan hierarchy, respectively (Kapferer 1988), a book that proposes to adopt Dumont's framework of comparison, but that brings important corrections to it. With regard to these two value systems, Kapferer describes how in them, violence operates in different ways. In the holist Sinhalese Buddhist state any attack on the Sinhalese identity (by Tamils) is an attack on the state, and conversely any attack on the state's organs is also an attack on the Sinhalese person: "In their violence they are oriented to the reassertion and restoration of the hierarchy of the state, of their power, and of the integrity and wholeness of their persons" (1988: 101). Violence is then itself a totalizing act that brings the state and the person into relation as totalities with exchangeable identities. Violence strikes toward evil as a reincorporation of evil *in* hierarchy—and evil is always both a potential of the state and of the person. In the context of the egalitarian Australian nation state, state violence takes a different expression. Through an analysis of the myths and rituals inherent to the image of Australian identity—of Anzac and male bonding—Kapferer's point is that the nation state's attacks on religion are brought about through the "sacralization of the political" (1988: 136). The political arena of the nation and its history forms the communal platform for the individual—and individuals in the sum of their achievements stand forward *as* the nation: "This is not merely the idea that the individual is prior to society or the atom, with which the wider structures of society are eventually built. It is the notion that the ideals of a perfect society are already embodied within the individual, the Australian male individual" (1988: 161). The state or social totality is only an artefact of what individuals do, and is as such unnecessary. The sacralization of the political is then ultimately the sacralization of the individual, and violence takes place when the naturalized autonomy of the individual is threatened. Since the natural equality of man is a given in this ideology, aggression is directed toward everything that indicates difference, or that resists the free movement of the individual—aggression against Islam, aggression against what is seen as artificially hierarchical corporations, aggression toward immigrant populations that are culturally hierarchical. Even though Kapferer argues that this form of individualism is as much based on ritual and religious values as is the case with Sri Lanka, it is important to note that as a social movement, individualism takes a quite different form.

We would claim, put simplistically for the sake of argument, that whereas hierarchy is typically gaining movement and momentum from values (for example, purity or auspiciousness) totalizing social matter (persons, things, ideas, and so on), individualism is driven by social matter (individuals, corporations, states, and so on) totalizing values—unmasking them, dispersing, or destroying them. This is also how anthropology can account for the existence of this last value system itself in analytical terms. We will suggest that we term these two different social forms *totalizing* and *detotalizing* social formations. Even science, in its effort to totalize the world by making it all known to man must, in its very analytical mode, compartmentalize objects under study and thus disperse and unmask the world of values. As André Celtel describes individualism: "No longer is one's identity inextricably bound up with the social whole, no longer is one conceived, ideologically, as a social person. Each now appears as an individuum of the human species, a substance existing in and of itself, an ideologically self-contained whole" (Celtel 2005: 94). In that way the world is divided into an infinite and unknown number of social entities, a mass that can be counted, regulated, or manipulated in various ways. Detotalization becomes another form of totalization, a new form that begins wherever the individual, science, bureaucracy, or media comes into contact with social phenomena. We will expand on this topic below, after a short review of arguments pertaining to the problem of individualism as equality.

Individualism and (In)equality

Another issue that emerges from this treatment of society under individualism is the vexed notion that what individualism "entails" is primarily, and definitionally, equality (see also Tcherkézoff in this volume). Here we think that Béteille (1986) has put his finger on an important point: Is not Western individualism by definition coupled with competition? And does not competition produce inequality? It seems to us that the kind of individualism extolled especially (but not of course exclusively) in the United States is willy-nilly an individualism of both competition and inequality—despite the overt celebration of "equal opportunity" for individuals to pursue their "happiness." But, as noted by Iteanu (in this volume), Western forms of stratification actually involve a power play between "legal equals." Again Dumont's response is that Béteille's (1987) definition of the individual differs from his own. Already in the paper mentioned above (1970b, first published in 1967)—its core points are repeated almost verbatim in the first chapter in *From Mandeville to Marx* (1977: 8) and elsewhere (see for example the Glossary in *Essays on Individualism* (1986: 279)—Dumont differentiates between two meanings of "individual":

> Individual here designates a mental construct, not a physical phenomenon. On the whole, we have two persons in one: the empirical subject of speech, thought and will, *indivisible* sample of mankind, and the independent, autonomous moral being as found first of all in our own ideology of man and society. The latter conception of man as an Individual is as peculiar in the range of known societies as its economic and political concomitants: "free enterprise," "liberty and equality," "the rights of man" *et al.*, and, underlying them, the autonomy of Economics and Politics. The society that invented this—actually a new type of society—has for centuries believed in a personal immortality guaranteed by an omnipotent and unique God come down to earth as man, apparently the first Individual, being at the same time man and the absolute. This should never be forgotten because the normative, the value content of "the individual" is too easily hidden behind its empirical aspect.

> I submit that, unless we disentangle these two aspects, the empirical as a general but infra-sociological datum and the ideological and normative as a characteristic

of our own type of society, we remain within our society: we succumb to *sociocentricity*. We are unable to study other societies without superimposing an alien and fundamentally unfit ideology or to see ourselves objectively. All the time we take as a constant of human nature what is in fact a particular, an exceptional pattern (Dumont 1970b: 135, original emphasis).

To dispel any remaining doubt as to the nature of the object Dumont constitutes, let us just quote him again. What he refers to as "individualism" is embodied in the second meaning of the term: "the independent, autonomous, and thus (essentially) non-social *moral* being, as found primarily in our modern ideology of man and society" (1977: 8, original emphasis).

What the disagreement between Béteille and Dumont boils down to is, first of all, the former's concentration on post–independence India and the pressing political and economic challenges it faces, while Dumont's interest lies in the *longue durée* of entrenched values. These, we submit, are each legitimate concerns, and the prospects of reconciling one with the other would not seem imminent. The disagreement between the two scholars derives from a fundamental difference in general outlook: whereas Dumont is a self-professed "holist" (his Maussian legacy), Béteille resists "the temptation of taking either the Indian or the Western tradition 'as a whole'" (1986: 133).[18]

But there is another aspect of the discussion in *Current Anthropology* we just drew upon that we wish to stress. In the Comments section to Béteille's paper, Tim Ingold remarks that there are in fact "traditional," "holistic" societies where individual autonomy is highly valued, and where equality is also highly valued: those of hunter gatherers (Ingold 1986: 129–130). Now while Ingold here cites Woodburn (1982) to good effect, we draw instead on Signe Howell's article on Chewong classification (1985). Unlike Woodburn's piece, it is not only informed by but also directed against precisely a central tenet in Dumont's work.

Howell begins by fixing attention on a Dumontian axiom, namely that "it is only by a perversion or impoverishment of the notion of order that we may believe contrariwise that equality can by itself constitute an order" (Howell 1985: 167, citing Dumont 1982: 238). Dumont's dictum here is based on his position that "equality" is a modern, Western notion inextricably linked to "the individual," itself also a modern, Western notion. In his view, the kind of "order" that a disingenuous adherence to this notion of equality would produce would be a true perversion; for example, the "order" of racism (Dumont 1982: 239).

The Chewong, a small group of hunter gatherers in Peninsular Malaysia (see also Howell 1984), much like the mainly African hunter gatherers Woodburn discusses (the !Kung, the Hadza, the Mbuti, and we might add

North American ones such as the Naskapi described by Henriksen 1973), place great emphasis on equality and individual autonomy and industry:

> there are no lineages, clans, or other formal groups . . . there are no structural principles that underlie the formation of any group or individual social relationships . . . there are no leaders of any kind; the nuclear family is a self-sufficient, self-determining unit which works alongside other such units . . . [t]he task of maintaining and re-creating society as a whole rests ultimately with the individual . . . there is a virtual refusal to acknowledge differences in abilities within the same activities . . . adults are said to be equally proficient in their performance of the various traditional tasks . . . instances of manifest superior competence, including hunting, are conspicuously ignored (Howell 1985: 170–171).

Combined with a Chewong predilection for uniquely naming each child ("it is explicitly forbidden to give a child the same name as someone else—alive or dead" [171]), it is easy to concur with Howell that the Chewong show us that it is indeed feasible to distinguish persons and activities—of separating each person and each activity from any other—while simultaneously "refusing to order these in terms of relative value" (171). So, if order is established but relative value shunned, what kind of order is it? Without the space here for rehearsing the empirical evidence Howell marshals, we must content ourselves with the conclusion: The polar oppositions (as in "a:b") of the Chewong hardly ever contain valuations in the sense that "a" is accorded greater value than "b" (or, obviously, vice versa.) "Hardly ever," but not never: Howell notes a significant departure from the common state of affairs with respect to the hot/cool distinction. Its importance becomes especially clear in the work of the shaman, who forays into a number of supernatural realms—assuming the perceptual capabilities of the beings who inhabit them—in order to be able to rectify human's transgressions and the illnesses they consequently have inflicted (on themselves or on others). To the Chewong it is of utmost importance to keep phenomena in the several realms separate from each other. Any traffic between them—above all uncontrolled traffic—is fraught with danger. And whereas "cool" (the enviable attribute of nonhuman realms) is generally accorded greater value than "hot" (the despicable characteristic of the world of human mortals), it is in the acquired nature of the shamans to be able to assume nonhuman form and hence to have access to beings and resources in those other, superior realms. In fact, it is only after the shamans have prepared the human realm—by making it as cool as possible—that the benevolent beings of those other realms can visit the human realm without creating the cataclysmic havoc were the two realms to interact *without* the mediation of the shaman.

Thus Howell can conclude that the Chewong (and we are tempted to suggest that her analysis can be applied to other hunter gatherers) are able to operate a fully functioning society on the principle of equality as a value, and when—as in the case of the shaman just noted—hierarchy encompasses equality as a value and an ordering principle, it does so at a subordinate level. To put this in algebraic terms: Whereas the dominant principle in Chewong society can be formulated as "a:b = b:a," the subordinate principle can be formulated as "a>b ≠ b>a." Thus when the latter relationship is articulated, it is as an exception to the rule.

One might think that the individualism and autonomy so valued among the Chewong is the same individualism and autonomy as one finds in the West, the genesis of which Dumont devoted years of research to understand. But of course the foundation of Western individualism is utterly different from that among the hunter gatherers, as is the sociological (and demographic, economic, historical, political, and technological) contexts in which the two individualisms occur. Importantly, Chewong *society*—as an entirety—would seem to offer a major challenge to any comparativist insofar as, from the Chewong's own point of view, it consists not only of human beings but also of what Howell calls "personages"—an indeterminable number of nonhuman, sentient, conscious beings equipped, as are humans, with morality. Chewong sociality "is directly engaged in relationships with other conscious beings as well as with the parts of the forest that are not envisioned as personages" (Howell 1996: 136). To this must be added the complication that "non-human personages may appear in human bodies . . . thus expressing the fundamental equality between all species or personages" (139)—evidence leading Howell to assert that "their social world consists only superficially of the 350-odd individual human beings, but must be extended to be coexistent both with the forest and with their cosmos" (136). Whether or not Chewong social practice is totalizing (totalization being a theme we shall return to) is a question, the answer to which is not obvious. However, given the modest development of collectivizing institutions, the absence of notions of leadership, the negligence of individual prowess, and the thoroughgoing lack of interest in other people's affairs, we would speculate that sociality works along axes of morality that constantly subject humans to the whims of alternative forms of beings. What appears to be a form of individualism is thus at the same time a striking encompassment of this interconnected world of forest creatures. What appears to us as a world of individuals and autonomous agencies is on closer inspection tightly interwoven with other sorts of agencies and the totality of this multiple cosmos.

We are not the first to highlight what one might call Howell's counter case. Joel Robbins presented an extensive analysis of Dumont's discussion of the problem of equality, drawing in part precisely on the Chewong material, in an earlier paper (1994). We consider his extended treatment of equality as a value to be highly useful. Robbins, too, sees the kinds of equality cherished in what Dumont consistently called "non-modern societies" as of a qualitatively different type than the equality valued in modern ones, but also notes that Dumont's own treatment of equality is not as clear as one might have hoped: "discussions which begin with equality very often end up being with individualism" (Robbins 1994: 61 n.6). While Dumont's notorious slippage from equality to individualism is regrettable, it is simultaneously instructive because it reveals that he saw equality as internal to the constitution of the individual. The one simply does not manifest without the other. And here precisely is the rub. Robbins's analysis shows how the inescapable problem with the equality/individualism linkage lies in the polysemous nature of equality: Is it equality of opportunity or of outcome? If the latter, what happened to the individual's right to be different? Thus (to truncate an intricate and incisive analysis, see Robbins 1994: 30–36): The equality of initial opportunity can only—in the West—manifest itself as difference in outcome, because the very purpose of securing equality of opportunity for all is that each individual be granted the liberty to develop his or her (putative) uniqueness. Any move to secure equality of outcome would stultify such development. Moreover, the Western brand of equality is geared exclusively to the individual's relationship to the State—the State assumed to be the guarantor of such equality as well—not, and this is crucial, to individuals' relationships to each other (see also Kapferer 1988). Here is where Robbins turns to Melanesian ethnographic materials, where—in contrast to Western individualism—ideologies of equality are centered precisely on interpersonal relationships, in their well documented manifestations as relationships of exchange, something which Robbins terms "relationalism." The Western spectre of equality as (ultimate) individual similarity here gives way to composite persons ("dividuals"), whose sum total of interpersonal exchange relationships, each of which, often with great effort, is achieved and construed as "equal" and balanced, nevertheless renders them different from each other: "One is similar in different ways to different people through different exchanges, and thus no assumptions about the overall homogeneity of people need be made" (Robbins 1993: 57). Thus, in Melanesia, "equivalence is demonstrated in particular relationships, but the result of each such relationship of equality in no way defines the totality of the person" (Robbins 1993: 58).

We leave Robbins's paper at this point, but note that further theorizing on the complicated links between notions of equality and individualism— be it in the West or elsewhere—cannot afford to disregard it. Robbins's ideas on how Melanesian societies are differentiated in ways that Dumont has referred to as "beyond or outside the opposition individualism/holism" (Dumont 1986a: 215–216)—thus outlining at least one alternative to hierarchy—are in our view especially useful, and he expands on them in his contribution to this volume.

Coming back to India with these issues in mind—posed in different ethnographic regions and under different theoretical considerations—we will adress yet another question relating to the status of the individual in Dumont's analysis of India as it unfolds in *HH*.

Even if we grant that Dumont has a point when he insists on the pre-eminence of the whole over the part, and even if we concur with him when he differentiates between two distinct senses of "individual" already referred to: one, the empirical subject in any society; the other, the independent, autonomous moral being of Western ideology, there remains in his analysis what to us is a troubling lacuna. It consists in his failing to consider the analytical status of individual action—not individual action as the "social action" figuring so prominently in the Western sociological apparatus from Weber onward, but individual action as it has been thematized within Hindu thought over the last two and a half thousand years. In *HH*, Dumont draws heavily on what in this regard are the relevant scriptures, but he is rather partial in the topical aspects he selects from them. Thus he is very explicit (if not very thorough) in outlining the Hindu notion of *dharma* (as the "law of the whole")—and Hindu totality is nothing if not the doctrine of *dharma*. But, as Jaer (1998) has pointed out in a major comparative exercise, the putatively eternal dharmic strictures of the whole have their transitory counterpart in the law of *karma* that applies to each individual. Now one searches in vain in *HH* and elsewhere for Dumont's understanding of the concept of *karma* (or for any analysis of the Hindu understanding of it) as providing, so to speak, the empirically social content of the whole. To repeat, we do not castigate Dumont for the reasons that motivate the objections forwarded by Béteille, Dirks, Inden, and others, more or less in unison—these scholars seem to us to insist that "individuals" in India have everything in common with individuals anywhere and everywhere and, thus, these individuals and their actions can be satisfactorily comprehended within the already established, Western sociological conceptual apparatus. On the contrary, we insist that the logic underlying actions of caste Hindus cannot be reduced to that of the Western individual. Rather, the logic—including motivations and justifications—of Hindu action is deeply internal to Hindu ideology; *karma* is thus the caste specific, and simultaneously individualized, ongoing realization of timeless *dharma*.

Without going into the complex details of Jaer's argument (most of which are found in *Capital and Karma* [1998], chapters 7 and 9, and in an appendix [pp. 159–164]), we will outline its thrust. The first point to note is that *dharma* has two aspects, the holistic aspect (which is what Dumont implicitly refers to), called *varnashramadharma*, and the individualistic aspect, *svadharma*. Their common basis is the doctrine of universal causality: all events in the cosmos are linked in causal chains. Actions, however, do not produce all their effects immediately; *karma* produces a residue (*apurva*) assumed to accumulate in each person. "The sum total of these residues constitutes the *karma ashraya*, the karmic ballast of the person, which determines his future destiny" (Jaer 1998: 73); that is, with regard to reincarnation. The second point is that good acts and bad acts produce favorable and unfavorable results, respectively, and that the positive or negative balance of such acts determines whether the person will be reborn in a higher or a lower caste (or as something not human). Acts, therefore, are considered in an ethical perspective; acts have consequences not only in the world, but also for the actor. The third point is what has been assumed already: the doctrine of rebirth (*punarjanma*). All of existence is understood to consist of a total caste system composed by various species (*jati*)—the term also used for the caste groups—the etymology of which (from the root *jan*) signifies existence brought about *by birth*. Scriptures have it that there are 8.4 million species into which a soul can be reborn—3,000 of them human—and as long as the soul is burdened with karmic ballast, it will be reborn in a new body in order to live out that ballast. The fourth point is the fundamental problem: How can this apparently eternal cycle of rebirth come to a halt? How can one attain a state of such purity that one ceases to be reborn? The answer is: through ritual.

Now Dumont, as we stated above, is concerned with the whole from the point of view of *dharma* and, given that "the individual is not," has omitted not only any consideration of *svadharma*, but also of *karma*. We have no doubt that the caste Hindu is enmeshed in the karmic cycles and thus always and inescapably in "action mode"—perhaps even more so, if for fundamentally different reasons, than the average Westerner. It is therefore striking that when Dumont does find an individual in India, it is the renouncer, the individual-outside-the-world: "By renunciation, a man can become dead to the social world, escape the network of strict interdependence which we have described, and become to himself his own end as in the theory of the West, except that he is cut off from the social life proper" (Dumont 1980: 184–185). But, Jaer points out, there is a fallacy here: Dumont fails to recognize that the renouncer's purpose is not to become an end to himself, as in the theory of the West; rather the renouncer's goal is to decrease his self "towards the final extinction of individuality in the Absolute. It is indeed the individual as his own end which the renouncer should struggle to conquer" (Jaer 1998: 161).

Our conclusion at this point must be that impressive as Dumont's analyses of matters Indian are, those aspects that deal with Indian totality are most convincing. The Hindu *Homo* is indeed—*pace* Appadurai—*hierarchicus*, but to stop short of analyzing him as also inextricably enacting *dharma* through his karmic obligations, is to stop short of completing the picture of the Hindu person.[19] Again, this does not deny the hierarchical nature of Hindu society—this is not tantamount to saying that the totality is "the sum of" what individuals "elect" to do; there is no appeal here to methodological individualism, its voluntarism, and its aggregates. The point is simply that individual caste Hindus incessantly manifest the whole as an effect of their own, internalized *svadharma*, and that they do so as moral beings with Hindu souls—the fate of which is subject to the law of *karma*.

Hierarchy, Holography, and Totalization

In the following we will suggest a rethinking of these issues, a rephrasing of the language, in order to bring in some realism again to the foregoing discussions about individualism and hierarchy. We want to elaborate on the conceptual pair of *totalization* and *detotalization* in order to escape some of the difficulties connected to the pair individualism/holism, in an attempt to convey an alternative vision of social processes that can crosscut essentialized views of regionalist and evolutionist character. We want to discuss how social process can be both totalizing and detotalizing—the first being a movement drawing in social matter, the other distributing it, dispersing it. This implies, in a sense, a reintroduction of the social to the discipline of anthropology.

A reason for doing this is that we need to avoid confusion about what the object of analysis is. As we have already pointed out, it is becoming harder and harder for anthropology to conceive of sociality beyond interaction and individuality. What we apparently deal with in our field studies are individual people—engaging us as one body after another, one household after another, one society after another, and so on—assumed to be finite figures distributed in an infinite world. We have indicated how we carry around a whole conceptual apparatus implementing these terms, and we have hinted at how Dumont's approach has problematized this ontological problem in a fruitful way (but see also Kapferer 1976, 1988, 2005). In the arguments advanced by Howell, Robbins, and Jaer, we realize, however, that we are still left with a problem when we cannot account for the sorts of individualization that we encounter in holistic settings. This demonstrates again the awkwardness in this kind of conceptual apparatus:

it creates its own stumbling blocks. In the post–Dumontian approaches, authors have tended to rush directly to the question of whether societies without individuals could be possible. Alternatively they have tended to search for ultimate values in societies, as a measure of how right or wrong Dumont was and as a criterion for finding hierarchy (for Oceania, see Mosko & Jolly 1994; for Indonesia, see Fox 1994; for Southeast Asia, Micronesia and Polynesia, see Fox & Sather 1996; for Western societies, see Melhuus 1990). In our view we should instead be searching for the mode in which society manifests itself in actions, in agencies, and in socialities—in what way social process moves people and other social materials in certain directions.

Holography in Melanesia

We will now recapitulate and try to convey some examples of how we think totalizing and detotalizing social movements work, and how they can be realistically described. For the case of totalization—as an extension of Dumont's analysis of India—we will mention how the argument can go for one kind of ethnographic setting. Much ethnography of Papua New Guinea has made manifest the well-known figure of the "big man" (see Sahlins 1963; A. Strathern 1971; Godelier 1986; Godelier and Strathern 1991). Drawing on the points Howell raised with respect to the Chewong situation, we suggest that the case of the interpersonal realm of the New Guinea Highlands can also be perceived as one where equality does constitute an order. As has been argued by Feil in his analysis of the relationships between exchange partners in the Tee exchange, the competitive arena of the exchange works on the strict premise of its taking place among equal exchange partners (see Feil 1984). On the surface of things, what you encounter when arriving in New Guinea is in fact an excessive emphasis placed on personal autonomy, glorious entrepreneurial cunning, and individual wit. You will see one big man after another exchanging and competing. In later modeling of the societies in question, theorists have nuanced that image of the "big man" by introducing that of the "great man." In order to conceptualize the difference, we quote M. Strathern:

> Big men are produced in systems that promote competitive exchanges, the transfer of women against bridewealth, and war compensation procedures that allow wealth to substitute for homicide. Great men, on the other hand, flourish where public life turns on male initiation rather than ceremonial change, on the direct exchange of women in marriage and on warfare pursued as homicide for homicide (Strathern 1991: 1).

In short, whereas the great men societies seem to posit an absolute value on the vital substances of life—that cannot be substituted for, that are inexhaustible, and that have to be instilled in people through ritual—the big men societies tend to value first and foremost absolute equality, free substitution of persons for things, and entrepreneurial skills. We could be tempted to call the first kind of sociality hierarchical, and the other individualist, but such use of comparative language has yet to be attempted in these analyses. And a problem seems to be that these analyses have been cast within a transactionalist frame; societies have been analyzed on the basis of the character of their exchanges. When Pierre Lemonnier (1991) describes the process where a transformation takes place—when a great man logic turns into that of a big man system—he identifies a few central aspects: war turns into exchange, ritual functions turn into political functions, and pig rearing goes from being qualitatively estimated to becoming quantitatively valued. Here, too, we realize the obvious parallel to theories of the transformation from hierarchy to individualism under state forms.

But what Lemonnier also discovers is that the driving social process in both of these systems is a principle of a finite pool of life substance. This finiteness generates exchange only as an artefact of a system intended for the reproduction of life forms—issued through the idioms of blood, semen, and growth. Even in the big men systems the individual is submitted to being part of larger assemblages of such substance. As he points out, "In the patrilineal systems of the Highlands, a child belongs to his agnates. They must therefore 'compensate' his maternal kin for that part of the female life principle contained in him; if this is not done, maternal kin may and sometimes do cause him harm" (Lemonnier 1991: 13). Further, when Marilyn Strathern tries to rethink the role of the Mount Hagen big man, she, too, ends up with a similar claim (Strathern 1988). In this prototypical area of the big man she concludes that what we encounter as the autonomous, entrepreneurial individual is really a composite being, who in his person totalizes and "eclipses" social relationships on a large scale (see also Eriksen in this volume). More than being the generator of social relations, he is a visible manifestation of the social relationships that he encompasses—he is their outcome, their effect. The big man is what sociality produces. The infinite terms of the many become finite terms of one singular person after another. As Strathern writes, "The Hagen big man presents the entire clan as a homogeneous collectivity. He is its capacity for unity" (M. Strathern 1991: 211) and "it is not that the big man concentrates within his person diverse functions that among the Baruya are distributed among many. All that is concentrated, so to speak, is the will to act. And that can only exist in the singular. The big man represents no group; the group exists in the fact that many wills are seen to have composed one will, one action, and thus one man" (1991: 212). And so, just as among the Chewong, it is in fact insisted that there is no society articulating itself beyond singular persons. Instead there is a strong argument among these ethnographers for how sociality as a relentless process creates these singular totalities as persons.

In his contribution to Godelier and Strathern's volume, Roy Wagner demonstrates his perspective on this in a cognate analysis that the great man of New Ireland really works as an imagery of totality which he can only make manifest in his own partiality (Wagner 1991). Again we encounter the argument that what is at issue is not the creation of society through exchange and ritual, instead the issue is how the social reveals itself in different forms. In order to convey the indigenous Melanesian version of the great man, Wagner resorts to an imagery of "the fractal person"—he who is "neither singular nor plural" (1991: 162). Through various examples from the region he demonstrates that the big man and the great man both stand forward ultimately only as the singular face of the multiple transactions that ritual and exchange engender in the various settings. This personality stands forward as the social equivalent of the holographic design. Wagner explains:

> A holographic or self-scaling form thus differs from a "social organisation" or a cultural ideology in that it is not imposed so as to order and organise, explain or interpret, a set of disparate elements. It is an instantiation of the elements themselves. . . . When a whole is subdivided in this way it is split into holographs of itself; though neither the splitting nor its opposite amount to an "ordering" function. What we call an "order" belongs to the world of partibility and construction (1991: 166–167).

Here we seem to be back to Mauss's idea of the "total social fact" or "privileged phenomenon," where the hologram is also a figure that manages to reveal simultaneously its inherent totality in its very existence as a partiality. In New Guinean societies it seems that the prototypical "total social fact" is first and foremost the person standing forward as either great or big.

We suggest that we learn from these attempts at coming to grips with the big man/great man problem in Melanesian societies when we take on the quandaries of hierarchy versus individualism. If we deploy this image of social process as holography heuristically, as a "mode of understanding," as suggested by Wagner (1991: 170), we might arrive at a useful rethinking also of Dumont's issues. Wagner again:

> The task of the great man, then, would not be one of upscaling individuals to aggregate groupings but of keeping a scale that is person and aggregate at once, solidifying a totality into happening. Social form is not emergent but

immanent. If this calls to mind Louis Dumont's powerful evocation of holism in the Hindu caste system, it also resonates with Marriot's concept of the "dividual" person—the person, like the society, that is whole and part at once (1991: 172).

What we are dealing with in these holistic societies is "holographic totalization" (Wagner 1991: 171), a process similar to Indian hierarchy in that it provides for a constant recasting of statuses, things, and events in accordance with their own being as *holons*, wholes contained within larger wholes. If a caste Hindu purifies her kitchen by smearing it with cow dung, it is a social act that transports the kitchen into the larger ideological imagery of purity—manifesting it as pure. The kitchen then becomes a singular, but also total (that is, holographic), image of the absolute purity that on another level is referred to as the fundamental Brahmin value. However, this totality is not India or Hinduism, it is always an emergent potentiality that social matter and social acts strive for. By moving our attention from totality and over to totalization as social process, we become able again to study these processes.

In fact, what Wagner demonstrates is that Melanesian sociality—from the indigenous point of view—is founded on cyclic processes of constituting wholes and taking them apart again; that is, of building up singular identities such as individual men and other produce through work and other kinds of relational exchange (sexual relations, ceremonial exchange), as well as—and subsequently—distributing these singular identities out onto relationships through gifts and especially rituals that again make singular identities "incomplete" (see Strathern 1991, 1993). Employing a Dumontian vocabulary we might say that social process here is always working toward manifesting the totalizing value of the relation (see also Robbins in this volume) on an ever larger scale—and thus concretely generating the objectifications of this value through exhibiting and displaying great men, great pigs, and great heaps of wealth. The crowning measure of this process is achieving totality—through producing holographic images. We believe the ultimate anthropological account of such holographic totalization is Mimica's description of the Iqwaye counting system (Mimica 1988). Here counting is conducted on the extremities of the body. The number twenty amounts to one, since what is then counted is one body (ten fingers and ten toes). Accordingly, numbers counted always lead toward the—composite—number of one, since twenty times twenty also equals one, according to a fractal logic of the body total, and further, so that high numbers also always approach one since the whole cosmos was originally crafted by one man; the creator Omalyce. In this way the practice of counting is itself a form of totalization that draws in the world's multitude and elevates it into totality, a "one." Each instance of someone counting is then, from a phenomenological point of view, an intimation of the original creation. This is the kind of sociality that we would try to frame within the extension of the concept of hierarchy. Totalization is the social motion that draws in social matter in order to construe images that are composed in recognizable unitary designs. In such a social world, each entity is an infinite being in a world that is a finite being, that is, a hierarchical situation quite opposite to the individualist assumption that the world is made out of finite beings in an infinite world.

Knut Rio, in an analysis referring to Mimica's material, has identified this kind of sociality as paradigmatic also in the islands of Vanuatu in Central Melanesia (Rio 2007). The concept of power on the island of Ambrym is conceptualized as "seeing-understanding." In practices of constructing marriage diagrams out of the ongoing flow of women moving here and there, we encounter the same indigenous concern with totalization. The figure that Rio terms "the third man"—the persona that sees-understands relationships and intervenes in them from the point of view of their totality—constantly draws sociality into recognizable patterns (see also Rio 2005). Each and every person then also perceives himself or herself as being totalized by these singular men who are seen to survey the routes of marriage. Rio has also drawn attention to how sorcery in Melanesia is a question of thirdness in an even more direct way, in which relationships are under constant evaluation and destruction by the sorcerer (see also Rio 2002; Stephen 1996).

But how would the Melanesian themes now alluded to correspond to the concept of hierarchy as proposed by Dumont? What becomes clear is that, whereas in Dumont's India hierarchy implemented itself through the constant presence of the value system in Hindu cosmology, the regulations of this religious totality and the internalization of these regulations in the agency interior to each and every person and event, Melanesians are instead busy giving a face and personality to totality—in even more immediate and concrete ways than do the Brahmins in Indian society. In the image of the equal and free big man, Melanesian totality is installed as a "will to act," and the singular subjects are only providing vehicles for totality. In the image of the individuated sorcerer, the negative side of this totality is implemented through a much more destructive intervention in relationships than by the big man (see also Mosko 1994). From these examples we begin to realize how sociality can be a totalizing force by absorbing social materials into its own movement. We see how totalization takes place not only in the drama of ritual and sacrifice (as the classic accounts prepare us for), but also in more everyday events of exchange of wealth and life-substance, and even in situations when people are drawn into kinship systems. In these societies people are always caught up in agendas beyond their immediate control. They are aware of this, however, and invest their lives into the grander motions that they perceive themselves ultimately to take part in (for a cognate example from Indonesia, see Smedal in this volume).

If we move on to the region of Polynesia we might see also here how totalization works as ongoing social process, although of course, in quite a different way than described for Melanesia (see Valeri 1985; Sahlins 1985a; 1985b; 2004). Even though, in contrast to Melanesia, one has been accustomed to seeing Polynesian systems as rigid, authoritarian kingdoms, in the anthropological literature there has been reference to the dynamism and openness of these kingdoms in practice. For the case of the Tongan status system, Irving Goldman writes: "The state of balance is, we need hardly say, as unreal as a single still photograph is as a statement of an energetic process. Status is by definition an energetic condition" (Goldman 1970: 304). This tendency of Polynesian hierarchy has also been attested to by Aletta Biersack (1990; 1996). In her analysis she emphasizes that the Tongan kingdom and its structural character was achieved as much through choices in marriage as through given descent (see also Valeri in this volume). But more importantly for us, she insists on shifting the attention from structure to *structuring*, a structuring through practice, in order to understand in what way the kingdom is perceived as a totality. Turning to the process of totalization understood indigenously, she explains:

> Tongans themselves speak of such activities in terms of *fa'u*. As a verb the word means "to bring into existence; to make, construct, put together; to build . . . ; to found, institute; to formulate, draw up, making, bring in (a law, etc.)" (Churchward 1959: 147); and as a noun the word means "bringing into existence, constructing, etc.; plan, measure, or institution; thing formed or constructed" (ibid). These words accent the activity of construction rather than its product; they call attention to a certain kind of agency. . . . Whether the action maintains the *status quo* or encourages change, in either case the hierarchy of titles is generated through marriage as a *fa'u* or artefact of historical practices (Biersack 1996:269–70).

Here totalization is seen as a social process that can be estimated and judged as materialized artefacts, but without the materialization being a hindrance to further change or the openness of the structuring process itself.

Moving from this level of royalty and into the general value system, we can perceive how this structuring process takes place even in the minutest practice. In the branch of Austronesian languages that we can call Proto-Oceanic, the *mori-mora* pair contains the opposition of values related to back-front, past-future, base-top, senior-junior. This pair is a key hierarchical conceptual device and a "foundational model" in Polynesian societies (see Shore 1996). In Tongan conceptions of strength, authenticity, beauty, order, and efficacy, for example, the *mu'i-mo'a* axis is a complete parameter for ranging all important substances such as food and social relations between juniors and seniors and men and women. When a ceremonial meal is arranged, not only the participants, but the items of food as well—down to every single tuber of taro—are arranged along the long stretch of tapa cloth placed on the ground in order to create a beautiful and abundant feast (see Perminow 2001). So even though the precolonial supreme powers of the chiefs as described by Valeri and Sahlins have been transformed into quasi-democratic institutions under state forms (see Tcherkézoff in this volume; Hoëm in this volume), the effect of totalization is still absolute in certain mundane arenas. Totalization of social substance is an ongoing process that collects food, people, and appearance into cosmic unification under these Polynesian hierarchies.

These examples from Melanesia and Polynesia are meant to draw attention to what we believe to be universal—the social totalization of social materials to create certain structures, forms, or artefacts that we (and they) can then relativize and term, "cultures," for instance. We have exemplified social forms that work to draw together social materials, and which present their artefacts (number, kinship, big men, or kingdoms) on the form of the hologram (simultaneously part and whole, process and structure).

We will now elaborate on individualism as a different logic of totalization. Here social process draws in social matter only to leave behind an indefinite sum of parts. This does not present itself as a "culture," or even as a set of values, but merely extends as an ongoing social force and, on a certain level, counteracts these other forms of totalization that we have seen. Several of the next chapters analyze how this takes place in concrete settings, and we will here elaborate on the form that individualism takes socially.

Individualism, Seriality, and Detotalization

These instances of implicative sociality we have reviewed are drastically different from individual totalization and the tradition inspired by Heidegger, in which the *Dasein* structure of being-in-the-world is a holistic unity that extends practice to everything within its grasp. Consciousness, practice, and intentionality are as such always totalizing activities, from the child searching for its mother's nipple to people engaging with the world as they burn a plot of land for planting, plow a field, watch television news, are caught up in traffic, and so on. Being-in-the-world is about taking in the world—wrapping consciousness around it; constituting it as meaningful through acts of intentionality. But the ethnographic examples we discussed above demonstrate to us that totalization is not only (or not even necessarily) a question of subjects taking in and totalizing the world; what we see in operation in these events is sociality itself as totalizing. The creation of great men in Papua New Guinea and the efforts at achieving auspiciousness or purification in the Indian context reflect how society—not reducible to social relations—becomes a force that continues to give things value. However, also in the context of individualist society, we should not become blind to the possibility that society is very much present in the articulation and destruction of values.

As we have already clarified, we can also see processes of individuation in the discussion about the inworldly individual and the outworldly individual. We come back to the way the Hindu renouncer gives Dumont the answer to how the development of hierarchy in India is different from the development of hierarchy into individualism in early European history:

> The renouncer is self-sufficient, concerned only with himself. He has abandoned the social world—a "yawning gap" exists between him and it—since distance from this world is a prerequisite of spiritual salvation . . . In forsaking the world, the renouncer ideologically relativises worldly existence . . . The *sannyasa* thinks of himself as an individual not a social being and this brings him closer to the ideological construct of the West, with the one important difference . . . : While those in the modern West are individuals-in-the-world, "inworldly" individuals, the renouncer is an "outworldly" individual—outside-the-world (Celtel 2005: 96–97).

To become "outworldly" is the only way to become individualized in a holist world. In the West individuality is given by the social. Accordingly, Tyler (1973) has speculated, interestingly, that the Hindu renouncer in India has his counterpart in "the mad" in the Western world, since this character has abandoned the being-in-the-world and can no longer have reference points in the real social world. The mad one is a person who loses his individuality and thereby loses the social. We have could mention other examples of individuation in nonindividualist societies: the sorcerer in the Melanesian world and the sultan in the historical Ottoman world (see Fosshagen in this volume). These characters all embody the institutionalized force of the outside perspective on society and social relations. It is through the eyes of these characters that each and everyone comes to see how the social world is really constituted. This modality of individuation, which works in opposition to and complements the social, stands in sharp contrast to the kind of sociality that we term detotalizing. Here the model of the individual is also the model of society, and aggregate social assemblages take on the form of the individual. We see this clearly explained in Kapferer's account of Australian nationalism, where he documents how the nation is constructed as a unitary construct composed of similar parts: "Thus as the nation is an autonomous person equivalent to other nations, so the nation is an internal amalgamation of autonomous individuals, which are interrelated according to a principle of consensus equivalence, in such a way as not to threaten individual autonomy" (Kapferer 1988: 185).

Of course, this brings us back to the problem we have in the Western world with attributing any ontological status to a concept of the social. Instead, we tend to construct for ourselves finite wholes, which are autonomous and independent of their social outsides. Children are "socialised" and absorb outside influences into their autonomous persons as grown adults. New nations in "the third world" similarly must build an apparatus of democracy, law, and order in order to contain themselves internally. Thus, unlike the totalizing social movements that we see exemplified in this volume—from Melanesia, Polynesia, in historical Turkey and Mongolia, where sociality works to confer things and people with relational, holographic identities within potentially finite social frames—this Western form of detotalization leaves behind a field of closed, finite identities that are infinitely distributed in social space.

In the many attempts by social scientists to comprehend society and group formation, Jean-Paul Sartre's work has been sadly underestimated. His subject-centered philosophy in *Critique de la raison dialectique* (Sartre 1976) represents first and foremost a project of grasping social assemblages as totalizing praxis. This philosophy has valuable clues for how to understand the status of the group in human history and praxis. In order to theorize any collective social formation in the individualized Western world, he developed the concept of "seriality." His prime example of this is a collection of people lining up in a queue at a bus stop. These people are not related in any way, they merely exist side by side in a "plurality of isolations" (1976: 256)—"in terms of the forces of disintegration which the social group exerts on individuals" (1976:257). Sartre identifies this particular social form as conditioned by the emerging totalization, so that "isolation becomes, for and through everyone, for him and for others, the real, social product of cities. For each member of the group waiting for the bus, the city is in fact present as the practico-inert ensemble within which there is a movement towards the interchangeability of men and of the instrumental ensemble" (Sartre 1976: 257). Due to scarcity—that is, the limited number of seats available or, in general, the limited number of whatever each member in the series corresponds to—seriality is a kind of social formation that is determined by each person being an equal other to all others:

It matters little if the commuters are biologically or socially differentiated; in so far as they are united by an abstract generality, they are identical as separate individuals. Their identity is their future practico-inert unity, in so far as it determines itself as *meaningless separation*. And since all the lived characteristics which might allow some interior differentiation lie outside this determination, everyone's identity with every Other is their unity elsewhere, as other-being; here and now, it is their common alterity. Everyone is the same as the Others in so far as he is Other than himself (Sartre 1976: 260, original emphasis).

This is what the city does to you, and this is how modern capitalist society works generally. Increasingly, society constructs serial movements set up around scarcity and individuation as a form of total alienation that brings each and everyone into the realm of the material "practico-inert." When you draw a ticket, you not only become other to all others, you become other also to yourself through that ticket's material existence as one among many. Seriality is therefore a kind of social group, stripped down to the barest minimum, that is first and foremost a material reality—forcing sociality itself to become material, too. Here Sartre insists on taking Marx's *Capital* seriously as an analysis of our social forms. To recognize this serial form of sociality is fundamental to any understanding of individualist society, and Sartre extends the analysis to the example of taking on a serial identity such as being a Jew. Being a Jew under anti-Semitic conditions is about being subject to the social unity of a field where one is in danger, exposed to others over whom one has no power. Sartre thus demonstrates the fundamentality of seriality in different modern social institutions. When tuning in to a radio broadcast, for example, listeners constitute an indefinite gathering: they are an infinite series of isolated subjects in front of the radio voice. Precisely for this reason the radio broadcast became especially potent in the mobilization of the dispersed masses in front of Hitler or Churchill.

The concept of seriality also became useful in Sartre's analysis of class relations, and his concerns here converge with Dumont's own concern with Individualism in *Essays on Individualism*, despite the lack of any similar convergence in their basic perspectives. Dumont had noted earlier that the problem of the "totalitarian disease" was "the attempt, in a society where individualism is deeply rooted and predominant, to subordinate it to the primacy of the society as a whole" (Dumont 1977: 12). He pointed out how both Marxism and National Socialism were founded on the awkward mating between the principle of individual equality, liberty, and freedom on the one hand, and on the other, a utopian idea of holism as a total sum of parts. Both movements constructed for themselves finite social wholes around the individual at the bottom of the hierarchy, then class or race respectively, and finally the state. The aim was to erase the intermediate levels of class and race through state-initiated violence. But in contrast to Stalinism, the Nazi movement had no explicit ideology apart from pursuing a vision of humanity as part of nature, a pursuit based in turn on an implicit naturalized creed, in which the values of struggle, action, and violence were primary. So on the different levels of the social scale, individual was set up against individual, race (or *Volk*) against race, and state against state (as Nazism versus Bolshevism) in what was to become a constant condition of struggle and violence. Nazism's final utopian goal was to subsume the state and the rest of the world under the Aryan *völkischer Staat* (Dumont 1986a: 165) as a new holist order. In outlining the major features of Hitler's *Mein Kampf*, Dumont argues that despite Hitler's romanticizing of the hierarchical and holistic dimensions, he led a movement that in fact encompassed the value of economics by the paramount value of politics (as "relations between men" [1986a: 166]), upholding a principle of egalitarianism through the "atomisation" of the mass in front of the leader, and implementing a view that force and "the most brutal struggle" (1986a: 171) themselves were propelling the movement. Importantly, against the facile assumption that the movement could be holist, Dumont finds in it "an intervening heterogeneous element" (1986a: 169)—an element definable through Hitler's difficult relationship with egalitarianism. On the one hand, Hitler conceived of egalitarianism as the basis for the evil Jewish forces and, of course, the competing movement of Marxism, but his ideal of political struggle through "the survival of the fittest" necessarily introduced the same kind of individualism as he was fighting: "It is hence very likely that, because of the symmetry that set them in opposition, Hitler projected onto the Jews the individualism that was tearing him apart. At bottom the extermination of the Jews appears as a desperate effort on Hitler's part to rid himself of his own basic contradiction" (Dumont 1986a: 176).

So in this historical social movement Dumont identifies certain features, some of which the central figures were aware, while others lay more in the spirit of contemporary German society. The most basic tendencies stemmed from the view of society as unnecessary from nature's perspective. The resistance against the presumed artificiality of ideology, of social groups, and economic regulations gave the Nazi movement its strength. By directing all efforts of the state apparatus at the individual, the movement installed itself as a natural movement—simulating principles of natural selection; and, as Dumont adds, "the real subjects (or at any rate the main ones) are the biological individuals" (1986a: 172). There would not be even a possibility of the encompassment of the contrary: lesser values would instead be removed. The inferior races would be cleansed away, as impurity could not be sustained within the system. Hence the movement also developed the notion of race as the only aggregate of this individual struggle. The concept of race became an artefact of individualism as a struggle of all against all. Note the important transition here, from concepts of nation, state, or even community into a language of individual faithful followers, *Volk* and race. The result was a pure individualist ideology that arranged people as equal, similar, natural bodies implanted with the naturalized urge to become dominant.

We believe this event in European history is the prime example of what we term a detotalizing social process. The atomization of people and race through Nazism is perhaps the clearest incident of an individualist social order installing itself that we have seen. But whereas we have tended to think of individualism first and foremost in relation to State structures, that is, the infinite distribution of individuals through Human Rights, citizenship, and other interrelations between State and subject—for instance in Althusser's concept of "interpellation" or in Foucault's concepts of "subjectification" and "governmentality"—what comes out of this study of Nazism is in fact that "the State would be merely a means in the service of race" (Dumont 1986a: 178). Once the logic of individualism is installed as a natural order, detotalization as a social process tends to uphold itself merely on the natural grounds laid out for it by this very ideology—by installing a principle of nature into every entity that it constructs as an entity given as itself only, and not in relation to any other. The Italian philosopher Giorgio Agamben speaks about the "animalization" of man in terms very similar to those of Dumont:

> It was in some ways already evident starting with the end of the First World War that the European nation states were no longer capable of taking on historical tasks and that peoples themselves were bound to disappear. We completely misunderstand the nature of the great totalitarian experiments of the twentieth century if we see them only as carrying out the nineteenth-century nation-states' last great tasks: nationalism and imperialism. The stakes are now different and much higher, for it is a question of taking on as a task the very factical existence of peoples, that is, in the last analysis, their bare life. Seen in this light, the totalitarianism of the twentieth century truly constitutes the other face of the Hegelo-Kojevian idea of the end of history: man has now reached his historical *telos* and, for a humanity that has become animal again, there is nothing left but the depoliticization of human societies by means of the unconditioned unfolding of the *oikonomia*, or the taking on of biological life itself as the supreme political (or rather impolitical) task (Agamben 2004: 76).

This is also why we think that we are obligated as anthropologists to treat Western social formations as radically different and radically new in the history of humankind. It is of crucial importance that we provide analyses of the modern social movement in a comparative framework that brings out its contrasts to other globally extant social forms. The trend in the critique of Dumont and his radical comparative project has been the recurring idea that human societies are everywhere more or less the same because they grow out of human nature. By advancing that sort of argument one is already deeply committed to a conceptualization of society as a natural aggregate of individual behavior, once again opening oneself to racism, legitimate violence, and political maneuvering of difference and inequality (see also Béteille 1986; Gullestad 2002).

It is not difficult to expand our argument of detotalization as a crucial social movement under the ideology of individualism, but two examples will have to do. A rather recent occurrence that comes very close to the mechanisms of the Nazi movement are the so-called "reality shows" of modern television. Interestingly, these televized entertainment offerings started out in the 1980s with "back to nature" concepts—with the audience attraction being to watch what happens to people when they are returned to "natural" conditions. Groups of carefully selected individuals were transported to Pacific or Southeast Asian islands where they were stimulated to engage in competition and intrigue. As the show progressed from week to week, audiences witnessed how a harsh natural environment, starvation, primitive sanitary conditions, boredom, annoying bugs—and the even harsher struggle of human nature, of one pitted against another—took the toll they were meant to take: those who failed to stand up to the pressure were eliminated from the show in various ways. More recently we have seen other versions of reality shows, but every time what is on display is "human nature." The shows in fact make the claim to their audiences that human nature is a given, as if competition, equal opportunities, and entrepreneurial maneuvering were the most basic of human qualities. And, of course, these shows can only attract billions of television viewers if this premise by and large is agreed upon. From week to week, the shows construct miniature recollections of the Nazi experiment, and we would be naïve if we did not see some correspondence between these popular shows and the way social process works on the other side of the screen. If we think of this as a mirror of tendencies we currently encounter also in the social sciences, the shows also work on the very premise that "society is obsolete" (see Ingold 1996).

Some three decades before these reality shows became the staple of commercial television, Robert Sheckley wrote a short story that anticipates what they may one day turn into: the assault of many against one. The hero of "The Prize of Peril" (originally published in 1958) is a man who solves his financial troubles by taking increasingly greater personal risks—all televized—until he accepts an offer that, if he survives, is the final solution to his problems. In a society that has passed a Voluntary

Suicide Act, trained killers are granted temporary immunity; hired by the network they go after the hero, who wins the prize if he manages to stay alive for a full week in New York City with the gang of trigger happy sociopaths chasing him. The hero, "an average man" as the show's host proclaims—"he is *the people*," he "can count on the aid and goodhearted-ness of *the people*"—is, when we meet him, five hours from winning the prize, and the situation is critical. He is trapped in a vacated building, bullets are flying, and if he is indeed sometimes aided by *the people* that same *people* (is it *das Volk?*) are just as often giving him away. "Yes, *the people* had helped him but they had helped the killers, too . . . 'Here he is,' the children screamed. 'Here he is'" (Sheckley 1975: 338–339, original emphases). In this account, the hero finds economic salvation if he suc-ceeds. But if he fails, he risks not merely expulsion from the reality show setting, that is, social death; he also risks physical obliteration. In this account, society has been detotalized into killers and survivors, helpers and traitors, and social life is reduced to enacting the putative universals "power" and "greed." Only this remains: economy and survival—the grim reality of Agamben's (1998) "bare life."

The Essays

In this introduction we have laid the ground for some of the issues that are discussed in the essays that follow—we have not attempted to exhaust the material in each chapter. Nor have we tried to impose the language of totalization and detotalization on these contributions. This chapter is merely intended as an auxiliary to the further reading, as well as being a suggestion for the general audience of how we can extend further the discussion about hierarchy. We have sought to establish certain inescap-able themes as they emerge from the writings by Dumont and others on value, hierarchy, holism, individualism, equality, and society, and to pur-sue some of the issues that extend from them. This chapter as such stands for itself.

The following contributions mark the efforts by regional specialists in engaging these concepts of value and totalization—in relation to their eth-nography. The principal objective throughout is to provide ethnographic evidence as it is conveyed in local traditions of thought and action and to bring back again into review the concept of hierarchy—with respect to emerging movements inspired by Christianity throughout the world (see Robbins, Eriksen, and Hoskins); with respect to the ideological concepts of equality and egalitarianism, and their manifold consequences when employed with inattention to ethnographic realities (see Tcherkézoff,

Sneath, and Hoëm); and with respect to the concepts of power and value in social systems (see Smedal, Fosshagen, Valeri, and Iteanu). We have chosen to emphasize persistence and transformation in the title of our book, and we believe the essays demonstrate in various ways how social and cultural change implies transformation as well as persistence of socio-cultural forms. Realizing—or so we hope—the potential of seeing ethnographic material through the specter of values, as the contributors to this volume do, readers can also begin to realize how anthropology here has a tool for comparison that can differentiate types of change; perhaps even enabling practitioners of the discipline to distinguish between significant changes and insignificant ones.

It follows from what we have said so far that we see hierarchy as a particular kind of social dynamic, one that essentially can be working in competition or in parallel with other kinds of social forms. This recognition is crucial in our reopening of the problem, and in the essays by Joel Robbins (chapter 2), Annelin Eriksen (chapter 3), and Janet Hoskins (chapter 4), we see different ways in which the individualism inherent in modern religious movements recreate social structures. As we have discussed above, Dumont saw in Christianity in Europe the emergence of the Individual-in-the-world, mankind as humanity composed of individual and essentially equal beings lined up before God, each with individual responsibilities toward himself and toward the next man in a serial (after Sartre) social formation. In these three essays the question is how and to what degree such modern individualist movements engender social and cultural change in environments formerly based on other kinds of values.

Joel Robbins attacks directly approaches that see the conversion to Christianity as merely blending in with "traditional" values, in "syncretism" or in "hybrid" forms. Robbins employs Dumont's analytical apparatus to great effect in addressing radical cultural change; he understands "value" as Dumont conceives of it to be exactly the stuff that culture is made of. He describes how the Urapmin of the Mountain Ok area of Papua New Guinea—through their radical break with relations to ancestors and the spirit world, and their rapid conversion to charismatic Christianity—have by and large adopted the individualist values that appear to be intrinsic to Christianity in any form, charismatic or not, with its stress on individual salvation. These values contrast starkly to the relationalist values the Urapmin adhered to until they embraced Christianity, but what Robbins finds is that the new, individualist values have infiltrated the overall value system only up to a point. Christianity has won the battle over the Urapmin souls, one might say, but has not managed to fully subsume Urapmin relationalism under itself. Thus the current situation is in many respects a standoff between two sets of values or, more accurately, between competing processes of totalization: Christianity has succeeded in this with respect to the religious sphere, but relationalist values are still dominant in the social sphere. So far, this struggle is inconclusive.

Although approaching Christianity from a different angle, Annelin Eriksen presents a parallel case from the island of Ambrym in Vanuatu. She focuses on two coexisting and structurally complementary social forms—one personified and hierarchical and functioning mainly through the male ritual society, and the other nonpersonified, lateral, and functioning through marriage and ceremonial exchange. She shows how the Presbyterian Church has brought about a radical transformation in the relation between these social forms. Whereas in its early period of colonialism, the Church was brought into the all male ritual arena, it only acquired force when it later became an arena for women and men who were operating laterally and not hierarchically. Eriksen also transfers her view of these competing social forms to the national level, where she identifies the nationalist Christian movement leading up to the Independence of Vanuatu in 1980 as a movement that also had the character of laterality, cross sex relations and communal values. Whereas Robbins argues that the church has brought about a completely new value, that of individualism, Eriksen insists that the value transformation taking place in Vanuatu can be understood as an inversion of the pre–Independence order of values.

Within a quite similar historical context of colonialism and religious conversion, Janet Hoskins's chapter describes the twentieth century Vietnamese religion called Caodai. Caodai offers a new religious interpretation of the colonial encounter with France, and the meaning of the fall of Saigon and the exodus of the boat people to California, Australia, and elsewhere. Hoskins writes about a hierarchical religion—its social organization is modeled on that of the Catholic Church, with a Pope, cardinals, and archbishops—which blends Eastern philosophy (Taoist spiritism and Buddhist ideas of self realization) with Western literary (Victor Hugo as an important saint of the religion) and political doctrines of humanism and national independence. The re-creation of this religious organization in exile in California, and the revision of its teachings to create a theodicy in which the Vietnamese diaspora assumes a new leadership role in global spirituality, present for us a case wherein the issue emerges of how individualism transforms social movements. From its start in Vietnam this religion has in a sense been totalizing the modern world—dragging into its theology teachings of Jesus, Moses, Buddha, Confucius, Lao Tse, and Victor Hugo; but through its various stages of being outlawed and exiled, this totalization has worked as a centrifugal force that makes the religion appear throughout the entire world. Its muted center is, in an interesting way, refinding its values in distributed things; distributed so far in time and space as to Paris, Rome, and California. Through these distributed teachings Caodai communicates its own values with each and every individual follower throughout the diaspora communities, but through the individuated social form taken on as modern humanism.

In the next two essays we move to other regions of the world and other perspectives on hierarchy—posing a challenge to Dumontian ideas. It was Dumont's achievement to insist on a comparative historical perspective on structural and cosmological differences. In Dumont's view, in most (non-Western) societies, religion provides the point of entry to the whole, and in these societies the political domain is only relatively autonomous from religion, in contrast to the situation in the modern West. In the essays by David Sneath (chapter 5) and Kjetil Fosshagen (chapter 6), these assumptions are tested in the context of two quite different social settings, the nomadic state structures of the historical Mongol empire of Inner Asia (Sneath) and the Ottoman empire in the Middle East (Fosshagen). In these settings the question of hierarchy emerges not only with respect to Dumont's model, but also in relation to assumptions about the nature of "tribal society" and, more recently, the extension of "the tribal" in Deleuze and Guattari's work on "nomadology" and the "war-machine." Sneath demonstrates how both the European colonial order and the Qing Imperial order recognized certain relations as hierarchical, but not others, and how ethnographically inspired notions of "kinship society" were used to present a sort of naturalized notion of "homo equalis." Sneath provides documentation to demonstrate how the enduring dualisms in conceptualizing social organization—as state versus tribal, territorial versus kinship based, egalitarian versus hierarchical—have led us to completely false assumptions about nomadic state organization.

In many ways Fosshagen's paper is complementary to, and to some degree in conflict with, Sneath's abandonment of the tribal model. Here we see how historical Ottoman society challenges the European individualist model of hierarchy as a stratified chain of command. It can, however, also challenge Dumont's definition of hierarchy as essentially reducible to "hierarchical opposition" within a holistic cosmology. In Dumont's Indian case, the Hindu king holds political power, but he is subordinate to the authority of the Brahman in the holistic cosmology. In the Ottoman case, the power of the sultan was not submitted to nor authorized by religious leaders, but may be said to be an unrestricted pure power outside the social order. As Fosshagen explains, the social order was divided into two estates: the military and bureaucratic elites were classified as "soldiers"; the rest were producers. Outside the centralized, hierarchical, and rationalist state apparatus stood the sultan—a figure of formally unrestricted power, operating in the structural dynamic of a war machine, through personal ties in a flattened space. Here we see Deleuze and Guattari mobilized in a reading that is different from the one proposed in Sneath's critique. Whereas Sneath criticizes the notion of tribal, antiterritorial movements in the Mongol empire, Fosshagen capitalizes on the concept of the war machine for the Ottoman empire. This further suggests that the cosmology of the State is perhaps not (at least not always) the clue to understanding hierarchies in different societies; rather one must identify the structural dynamics of different ensembles within a society. Whereas Sneath provides evidence for a headless state and a hierarchical nomadic structure where state subjects were regulated through rank and rights in land, Fosshagen describes the Ottoman empire from the point of view of the sultan as a sovereign (we might say as a stateless head) achieving his power not from fulfilling religious duties but instead from his transcendence from society as an unrestricted and personalized force. In both cases totalization in social process was carried out by ancient forms of bureaucracy as redistributive systems—collecting people into relations of dependence, not through ritual requirements but secular duties such as war service or taxation.

The three essays that follow take us to relatively much smaller societies: in Hawaii and Tokelau in the Pacific and Flores in Eastern Indonesia. In these three contributions, also from the Austronesian speaking world, we get deeply into ethnographic settings where we see exemplified the processual and dynamic character of hierarchy— through issues of marriage, sacrifice, and gifts. Valerio Valeri's article (chapter 7), based on historical materials, deals with the ways in which hierarchy was expressed in marriage rules, and the political impact of dynastic politics in Hawaii. The argument began as an article published in *L'Homme* in 1972 and was subsequently expanded by Valeri in 1996 with new historical materials. What is presented here is one of the last unpublished works he prepared before his death in 1998.[20] Crucially for our understanding of Polynesian hierarchy, Valeri puts kinship as exchange back in the center, and his model of "horizontal hierarchy" is interesting for its focus on the dynamics of marriage as crucial to the hierarchial formation. The problem that Valeri sets himself is how rank (especially high rank) was conceptualized and transmitted in Hawaii in the precolonial and early colonial periods—as effects both of filiation and alliance. In a "kinship system" that was basically cognatic in orientation, there were clear differences in how qualities of rank were understood to devolve from the matrilateral and patrilateral sides respectively. In other words, transmission of rank and representations of gender were tightly interwoven. In consequence, so were strategies of marital alliance. Valeri demonstrates that the straightforward "reciprocity" between equals often taken to be an axiomatic quality of marital alliance in cognatic systems (at least at the structural level) simply does not exist in the highly stratified Hawaiian context. Instead, every marriage is *ipso facto* a marriage between unequals. Given that there are a great number of ways in which one's genealogy can be determined (a cognatic feature) and thus one's rank (a Polynesian feature) it becomes immediately clear that one's rank is a function of the marriage of one's parents. The competitive struggle to generate children of high rank is therefore, Valeri concludes, a characteristic of Hawaii that precludes any stable order of alliance, symmetric or asymmetric.

Departing explicitly from highly influential previous research that stresses the temporal discontinuities between Polynesian social forms as they have evolved throughout known history, Ingjerd Hoëm (chapter 8) instead focuses on that ubiquitous regional institution, social exchange. Through three illustrations taken from various points in Tokelau history, she explores the dynamics that allow the Tokelau *inati* exchange system to manifest as mirroring markedly hierarchical relationships under certain conditions, and at other times as mirroring egalitarian relationships. The first example shows how the *inati* is a system of tribute (from the vanquished to their overlords) within a context of what Goldman (1970) described as typical traditional leadership. The second example shows how the *inati* works as a system of generalized reciprocity, geared toward a leveling of social differences. The third illustration shows how the *inati* has become a model—a metaphor—for viable political interaction in relation to emerging nationhood. Through these examples Hoëm investigates the forms of sociality and the conceptions of hierarchy and egalitarianism that allow for such plasticity in actual manifestation. Thus she proposes that the dynamics involved be understood as relations of ascendancy within a framework of an encompassing and constant value, the collective. This conception implies that an individual or a group is consistently seen as representing—in the holographic vein we outlined above—a larger totality: a family, a village, or even society as a whole. Importantly, there is no evidence that these patterns of identification disappear in the increasing confrontation with other ways of life. The inbuilt, fundamental flexibility in the kind of dynamic field of interaction Hoëm identifies here provides, we think, a fruitful example of how the nature of the relationship between hierarchical and egalitarian modes can be studied.

While Valeri's and Hoëm's chapters deal with marriage and exchange as an entry to understand historical formations of hierarchy, Olaf H. Smedal (chapter 9) turns to contemporary field material and the crucial role of sacrifice. Returning to the point about persistence in hierarchical forms, he notes that in a general way peoples of what was once known as the tribal world are now "modernizing"—more often than not by forsaking crucial aspects of a "traditional" value system. The obvious and immediate outcome of such modernization processes are the frequently observed attempts at coming to terms with State and transnational strategies on education, resource exploitation, market adaptation, political ideology, religious practice, social system, family life, and so on. Even so, attitudes, practices, and especially principles of the past often persist, providing mental and political spaces where modernized rationality has little purchase.

Drawing on extensive field investigations in Eastern Indonesia among the Ngadha ethnic group (in central Flores), Smedal provides a semiotically inspired analysis of one such space. It is constituted, he argues, by cosmological convictions, sacrificial practices, matrimonial strategies, bridewealth items, moral injunctions, and notions of social stratification. A common denominator in these diverse phenomena is blood—a substance with profound signifying properties. In empirical terms, the chapter explains why certain bridewealth items may be substituted with money while others cannot. Here Smedal capitalizes on his identification of a "privileged phenomenon": one that encapsulates an entire complex of social values in one corporeal form, that of the water buffalo. In theoretical terms, the chapter provides first of all a case for understanding how and why time honoured hierarchical deliberations embedded in local institutions are made to take precedence over the more expedient notions and routines of modernity. But there is more than the trivial opposition between the protection of traditional values and the pragmatic considerations of the market at work here; Smedal contends that the "hierarchy of value" he identifies is less an example of Dumontian "encompassment" by one value of another, the two values thus retaining their position also as contraries; it is more a case of one (superior) value obliterating another, rendering it irrelevant, thus reigning supreme as unassailable totality.

In the final two contributions, these questions are discussed by two French researchers who themselves were part of Dumont's *equipe* at the CRNS in Paris. They now take up what we think has always been the strength in Dumont's work—his relentless, thoroughgoing comparativism, and how anthropology needs more than ever to readdress the problems that Dumont raised. One deals with the legacy of Dumont universally and independently of ethnographic setting, and the other places it firmly in the ethnography of one concrete region. Serge Tcherkézoff (chapter 10) starts this evaluation of Dumont by outlining how hierarchy and equality as organizing principles are antithetical to one another, and quickly proceeds to provide examples from the Polynesian context. These examples demonstrate that the study of social hierarchies as advocated by (Western) anthropology implies a comparative decentering between, on the one hand, a notion of general inequality that is familiar to it as stratification and, on the other, specific forms of inequality operating according to sacred values such as are found in Samoa. The chapter addresses, in particular, certain approaches to Polynesian sociality—exemplified by the works of Bradd Shore and Margaret Mead—that Tcherkézoff asserts have mistaken one kind of inequality for the other. As Dumont made clear, the European individualist ideology and its theory of hierarchy—which equates hierarchy with inequality as a stratified chain of command—can obscure our understanding of non-Western forms of hierarchy and of what hierarchy essentially is. André Iteanu (chapter 11) discusses how Dumont used the notion of hierarchy in an unusual comparative sense, separating it explicitly from any notion of a "chain of command." This novel usage, Iteanu stresses, allows the concept—first devised with a view to analyzing Indian society—to be extended to other societies thought of as equalitarian, such as those of Papua New Guinea. His chapter explores explicitly the Dumontian definition of hierarchy, its methodological implications and its actual or potential extensions to different societies deprived of instituted political authority and social ranking.

As should be obvious from these summary remarks the essays that follow do not constitute one single argument, nor do their authors subscribe to one single theoretical vision. But the highly disparate empirical materials they have analyzed have compelled them to rethink the commonplace sociological ontology that pits "individuals" against "society." Thus, by engaging with a specific theoretical apparatus (employing notions such as value, hierarchy, equality, holism, individualism, and so on) they demonstrate, we think, the poverty of more conventional analyses.

We do not know if tomorrow's events will alleviate the anxiety that many now have about the future. But we think that the essays below provide conceptions of social reality that deviate profoundly from the West as we know and fear it. And if these conceptions resonate with the insight contained in the lines by Leonard Cohen we have used as an epigraph for this introduction, they also evince kinds of experience that differ from the nightmare (or is it?) that Bob Dylan once described:

> Everybody's having them dreams.
> Everybody sees themselves walkin' around with no one else.
>
> Bob Dylan, from "Talkin' World War III Blues," on
> *The Freewheelin' Bob Dylan*, 1963

Notes

1. In a rare interview Dumont, alluding to a well-known anthropological classic (Hertz 1909) made this point—that status is categorically separated from power—by analogy: "The right hand is superior to the left hand, but it does not have power over the left hand" (Delacampagne 1981: 5).

2. Of course, apart from the numerous articles on India that Dumont published before writing *HH*, he was also able to draw on his own monograph, based on two years' fieldwork (1949–1950): *Une sous-caste de l'Inde sud* (1957). This book was soon reviewed in *American Anthropologist* (Tyrner 1959), and made some stir in Anglo-American circles. Thus in 1966 it was reviewed by eleven scholars in a "Symposium" (see *Current Anthropology* 7: 327–346). Long after the second Chicago edition of *HH* was in print, *Une sous-caste* was issued in English (Dumont 1986b) and the *American Anthropologist* review that followed (Kolenda 1988) ends by calling it a "deserved-to-be-classic work," the reviewer thanking Dumont for having made it available in English.

3. Other legacies inherent in the efforts at understanding Indian hierarchy have been discussed and debated (see especially Appadurai 1988, Parry 1998), but we can see clearly how Robert Hertz's essay on "the pre-eminence of the right hand" (1909) influenced the way Dumont came to comprehend oppositional categories as belonging to religious regimes constituting conceptual wholes (see Parkin 2003).

4. Such as for instance Berreman's claim that this view of hierarchy would only be true inside a perspective of the superior castes (Berreman 1971; Dumont 1980: xxi).

5. In the same way Marilyn Strathern's (1988) more recent effort at investing the region of Melanesia with its own social parameters for ontological categories, such as person, gender, and productivity, has met with massive protests on both epistemological and empiricist claims (see Josephides 1995; Thomas 1991; Carrier 1992).

6. For example, one contemporary review of *HH* begins: "This book is one of the most talked about works in South Asian anthropology. The 1966 French edition was subjected to lengthy reviews in the *American Anthropologist* and *Man*, and 1971 American Anthropology meetings devoted an entire session to a critique of Dumont's views. This attention is deserved" (Ames 1972: 439).

7. There are other explicit notions in Dumont's work, too, that contribute to the Anglo-American reserve, such as the axiom that value reversals signal shifts between levels (see Eriksen in this volume; and Iteanu in this volume; cf. Barraud 1985) and not merely changes of context (see Barnes et al. 1985), or that any relation of complementarity is always and necessarily hierarchical. We return briefly to those below.

8. One parallel was the debate between Sahlins and Thomas about the *kerekere*, or "begging" as a precolonial institution in Fiji (see Sahlins 1993; Thomas 1993).

9. The "or anywhere else" refers to Berreman's opinion that caste is just a variant of social stratification, little different from class or race-based inequalities as they are found in the United States—in other words, that it is mistaken to think that specific ideologies (in India or in the West) shape and make meaningful social formations. On this issue we agree with Barnett's assessment: "Berreman does not seem able to grasp Dumont's point that if equalitarianism is the stressed aspect of American ideology, far from limiting the understanding of racism, it illustrates its unique form: the nature of the justification of inequality in the American setting" (Barnett 1982: 142).

10. The page reference to *HH* is puzzling: here Dumont is simply in the middle of discussing the emergence of *ahimsa* (the doctrine of nonviolence) and the origin of vegetarianism among Buddhists and Jains.

11. The perhaps surprising conclusion Dumont draws in his reading of Marx is precisely that Marx is no sociologist proper; that Marx was caught up in the enlightenment adulation of freedom and equality—that is, *individual* freedom and equality—epitomized in the slogans of the French and the American revolutions and carried to their current extreme in ever broader global sweeps.

12. An opposing view—that one might begin equally well, or even better, with "personal histories," and analyze them from, say, a social-psychological perspective, as Mines put forward (1988) on the basis of data from Tamil Nadu—would be dismissed by Dumont as all but mindless empiricism. A fair converse to Miner's approach would be to ask average (Western) wage earners if they adhered to Marx's theory of labor, and conclude, if the answers were largely negative, that no exploitation takes place.

13. "Practically, or methodologically, Mauss teaches us always to maintain a double reference—to the global society on the one hand and, on the other, a reciprocal reference of comparison between the observer and the observed" (Dumont 1986a: 5).

14. For all its breathless, faddish hype, Restrepo and Escobar's call (2005) for "other anthropologies" and "anthropologies otherwise" seems to us puny and disappointingly parochial in contrast to Dumont's immense and drastically radical project.

15. In referring for the sake of convenience to these practices as the *jajmani* "system" we follow a usage that has been critiqued for some time, see Good (1982, 1996) and Fuller (1989).

16. Through examples from Uganda, Australia, and New Guinea we are given glimpses of how the leader in rainmaking ceremonies imitates the system that the ritual is sought to have an effect on. The principal *becomes* thunder; he *becomes* the sky; he *becomes* water; and Hocart mentions that in Uganda he becomes a cloud to the degree that if rain fails, people would cut open the rainmaker because he was withholding the rain inside his body (1970: 55).

17. Anthropology, perhaps especially the British tradition, has gone through a phase where "society" has been under consideration (Kuper 1992; Ingold 1996). To the French school following Dumont, society has kept its strong analytical importance (see especially de Coppet 1992; de Coppet & Iteanu 1995; Barraud, de Coppet, Iteanu, and Jamous 1994; also Tcherkézoff in this volume).

18. This point was recently stressed by Bastin: "Many years ago, Béteille generously gave me his time and suggested that, in his view, Dumont could not confront the shocking immediacy of contemporary India and so was driven into a romanticized construction in which the fundamental holism is developed as a means of glorifying an Indian past" (Bastin 2005: 90).

19. We note with interest Jaer's suggestion that rather than basing the comparative study of Hinduism and the West (in Jaer's terms: Capitalism) on analyses of the individual, one should begin with "action": "Action/structure as a theoretical framework, and karma/Dharma as the concrete structuring principles in the Hindu context, provide a better basis for an interpretation of Hindu society and its ideology" (Jaer 1998: 163).

20. As is acknowledged in the piece itself, it was originally written in French, subsequently translated by Aletta Biersack and Janet Hoskins, and finally edited down by Rio and Smedal from more than twice its current size. Although the original manuscript contained much detail, especially on alliance between specific kin groupings, that there was simply no space for in this collection, we are confident that the paper as it now appears retains its theoretical force. As we worked on Valeri's manuscript, we consulted Hoskins repeatedly. We wish to acknowledge here the assistance she kindly extended to us and to note that she reported her relieved satisfaction with the final product (personal communication, 19 June 2005).

We should make it clear that since this chapter is a posthumous publication, any possibility to raise factual or analytical issues with the author was precluded. Given the topic of the present volume this is somewhat regrettable: Valeri's use of the concept "hierarchy," for example, is clearly different from that of Dumont, as Valeri makes plain in *Kingship and Sacrifice*, chapter 3 (Valeri 1985). Rather than peppering the chapter with editor's comments whenever relevant, we simply note this fact here.

References

Agamben, Giorgio. 1998. *Homo Sacer: Sovereign Power and Bare Life*. Stanford: Stanford University Press.

———. 2004. *The Open*. Stanford: Stanford University Press.

Ames, Michael M. 1972. "Review of Louis Dumont: Homo Hierarchicus: An Essay on the Caste System." *Pacific Affairs* 45 (3): 438–440.

Appadurai, Arjun. 1986. "Is Homo Hierarchicus?" *American Ethnologist* 13 (4): 745–761.

———. 1988. "Putting hierarchy in its place." *Cultural Anthropology* 3 (1): 36–49.

Barnes, R. H., Daniel de Coppet, and R. J. Parkin, eds. 1985. *Contexts and levels: Anthropological Essays on Hierarchy*. Oxford: JASO.

Barnett, Steve. 1982. "Review of Louis Dumont: Homo Hierarchicus: The Caste System and its Implications" (Complete revised English edition), and Gerald D. Berreman: Caste and Other Inequities: Essays on Inequality." *Pacific Affairs* 55 (1): 140–142.

Barraud, Cécile. 1985 "The Sailing-boat: Circulation and Values in the Kei Islands, Indonesia." In *Contexts and Levels: Anthropological Essays on Hierarchy*, ed. R. H. Barnes, D. de Coppet, and R. J. Parkin. JASO Occasional Papers 4. Oxford: JASO, 117–130.

Barth, Fredrik. 1992. "Towards Greater Naturalism in Conceptualizing Societies." In *Conceptualizing Society*, ed. Adam Kuper. London: Routledge, 17–34.

Bastin, Ronald. 2005. "Death of the Indian Social." In *The Retreat of the Social: The Rise and Rise of Reductionism*, ed. Bruce Kapferer. Oxford: Berghahn, 89–103.

Berreman, Gerald. 1971a. "The Brahmanical View of Caste." *Contributions to Indian Sociology* n.s. 5: 16–23.

———. 1971b. "Review of Louis Dumont: Homo Hierarchicus." *Man* 6 (3): 515.

Béteille, André. 1986. "Individualism and Equality." *Current Anthropology* 27 (2): 121–134.

———. 1987. "On individualism and Equality." *Current Anthropology* 28 (5): 672–677.

Biersack, Aletta. 1990. "Blood and Garland: Duality in Tongan History." In *Tongan Culture and History*, ed. P. Herda, J. Terrell, and N. Gunson. Canberra: Department of Pacific and Southeast Asian History, 46–58.

———. 1996. "Rivals and Wives: Affinal Politics and the Tongan Ramage." In *Origins, Ancestry and Alliance. Explorations in Austronesian Ethnography*, ed. J. J. Fox and C. Sather. Canberra: Department of Pacific and Southeast Asian History.

Bonner, Jeffrey. 1989. "Review of Gloria Raheja: The Poison in the Gift." *American Anthropologist* 91 (1): 224.

Bourdieu, Pierre. 1977. *Outline of a Theory of Practice*. Cambridge: Cambridge University Press.

Burghart, Richard. 1978. "Hierarchical Models of the Hindu Social Systems." *Man* (n.s.) 13 (4): 519–536.

Carrier, James, ed. 1992. *History and Tradition in Melanesian Anthropology*. Berkeley: University of California Press.

Castoriadis, Cornelius. 1997. "The Social Imaginary and the Institution." In *The Castoriadis Reader*, ed. D. A. Curtis, Oxford: Blackwell.

Celtel, André. 2005. *Categories of Self*. Oxford: Berghahn Books.

Cort, John E. 1991. "The Svetambar Murtipujak Jain Mendicant." *Man* (n.s.) 26 (4): 651–671.

David, Kenneth, ed. 1977. *The New Wind: Changing Identities in South Asia*. The Hague: Mouton.

De Coppet, Daniel. 1992. "Comparison, a Universal for Anthropology: From 'Re-presentation' to the Comparison of Hierarchies of Values." In *Conceptualizing Society*, ed. A. Kuper. London: Routledge.

Delacampagne, Christian 1981. "Louis Dumont and the Indian Mirror." *RAIN* 43: 4–7.

Deleuze, Gilles and Felix Guattari. 1983. *Anti-Oedipus: Capitalism and Schizophrenia*. Minneapolis: University of Minnesota Press.

Descartes, René. 1962. *The Meditations; and Selections from the Principles*. La Salle: Open Court Publishing Company.

Dirks, Nicholas B. 1987. *The Hollow Crown: Ethnohistory of an Indian Kingdom*. Cambridge: University of Cambridge Press.

———. 2001. *Castes of Mind: Colonialism and the Making of Modern India*. Princeton: Princeton University Press.

Dumont, Louis. 1957. *Une sous-caste de l'Inde du sud: Organisation sociale et religion des Pramatai Kallar*. Paris: Mouton.

———. 1960. "World Renunciation in Indian Religions." *Contributions to Indian Sociology* 5: 20–43.

———. 1970a. *Religion, Politics and History in India: Collected Papers in Indian Sociology*. Le Monde d'outre-mer passé et présent, Première série, Études XXXIV. The Hague & Paris: Mouton.

———. 1970b. "Religion, Politics and Society in the Individualistic Universe." *Proceedings of the Royal Anthropological Society of Great Britain and Ireland* 1970: 31–41.

———. 1977. *From Mandeville to Marx: The Genesis and Triumph of Economic Ideology*. Chicago: The University of Chicago Press.

———. 1980. *Homo Hierarchicus: The Caste System and Its Implications*. Chicago: The University of Chicago Press.

———. 1982. "On Value" (Radcliffe-Brown Lecture 1980). *Proceedings of the British Academy*, vol. LXVI: 207–241.

———. 1986a. *Essays on Individualism: Modern Ideology in Anthropological Perspective*. Chicago: The University of Chicago Press.

———. 1986b. *A South Indian Subcaste: Social Organisation and Religion of the Pramalai Kallar*. New York: Oxford University Press.

———. 1987. "On Individualism and Equality." *Current Anthropology* 28 (5): 669–672.

Dumont, Louis and David Pocock. 1958. "A. M. Hocart on Caste," *Contributions to Indian Sociology* 2: 45–63.

Evans-Pritchard, Edward Evan. 1954. "Introduction." In Marcel Mauss's *The Gift*. London: Cohen & West.

Feil, Daryl K. 1984. *Ways of Exchange: the Enga Tee of Papua New Guinea*. St. Lucia: University of Queensland Press.

Fox, James J. 1994. "Reflections on 'Hierarchy' and 'Precedence'." In *Transformations of Hierarchy: Structure, History and Horizon in the Austronesian World*, ed. M. Jolly and M. S. Mosko, 87–108.

Fox, James J. and Clifford Sather, ed. 1996. *Origins, Ancestry and Alliance: Explorations in Austronesian Ethnography*. Department of Anthropology, Research School of Pacific and Asian Studies, Canberra: Australian National University.

Fuchs, Martin. 1992. "Le paradoxe comme méthode: La structure antithétique de la théorie sociale de Louis Dumont." *Recherches Sociologiques* 23/2: 19–42.

Fuller, C. J. 1988. "The Hindu Pantheon and the Legitimation of Hierarchy." *Man* (n.s.) 23 (1): 19–39.

Galey, Jean-Claude 2000. "Louis Dumont (1911–1998): A Committed Distancing." *American Anthropologist* 102 (2): 324–328.

Godelier, Maurice. 1986. *The Making of Great Men: Male Domination and Power among the New Guinea Baruya*. Cambridge: Cambridge University Press.

Godelier, Maurice and Marilyn Strathern, ed. 1991. *Big Men and Great Men: Personifications of Power in Melanesia*. Cambridge: Cambridge University Press.

Gofman, Alexander. 1998. "A Vague but Suggestive Concept: The 'Total Social Fact.'" In *Marcel Mauss: A Centenary Tribute*, ed. W. James and N. J. Allen. Oxford: Berghahn Books, 63–71.

Goldman, Irving. 1970. *Ancient Polynesian Society*. Chicago and London: The University of Chicago Press.

Gullestad, Marianne. 2002. "Invisible Fences: Egalitarianism, Nationalism and Racism." *Journal of the Royal Anthropological Institute* 8 (1): 45–63.

Gupta, Dipankar. 2005. "Caste and Politics: Identity over System." *Annual Review of Anthropology* 21: 409–27.

Henriksen, Georg. 1973. *Hunters in the Barrens: The Naskapi on the Edge of the White Man's World*. Newfoundland Social and Economic Studies 12. St.John's: Institute of Social and Economic Research, Memorial University of Newfoundland.

Hertz, Robert. 1909. "La prééminence de la main droite: etude sur la polarité religieuse." *Revue Philosophique* 68: 553–80.

Hocart, A. M. 1936. *Kings and Councillors: An Essay in the Comparative Anatomy of Human society*. Cairo: Printing Office Paul Barbey [reissued by The Chicago University Press, 1970].

———. 1950. *Caste: A Comparative Study*. London: Methuen & Co.

Howell, Signe. 1984. *Society and Cosmos: The Chewong of Peninsular Malaysia*. Singapore: Oxford University Press.

———. 1985. "Equality and Hierarchy in Chewong Classification." In *Contexts and Levels: Anthropological Essays on Hierarchy*, ed. R. H. Barnes, D. de Coppet, and R. J. Parkin. JASO Occasional Papers 4. Oxford: JASO, 167–180.

———. 1996. "Nature in Culture or Culture in Nature? Chewong Ideas of 'Humans' and Other Species." In *Nature and Society: Anthropological Perspectives*, ed. P. Descola and G. Pálsson. London and New York: Routledge.

Inden, Ronald B. 1986. "Orientalist Constructions of India." *Modern Asian Studies* 20 (1): 1–46.

———. 1990. *Imagining India*. Oxford: Basil Blackwell.

Ingold, Tim. 1986. "Comment on Andre Béteille's 'Individualism and Equality.'" *Current Anthropology* 27 (2): 129–130.

Jaer, Øyvind. 1998. *Capital and Karma: Hinduism and Capitalism Compared*. Bangkok and The Institute for Comparative Research in Human Culture, Oslo: Orchid Press.

James, Wendy. 1998. "'One of Us.' Marcel Mauss and 'English' Anthropology." In *Marcel Mauss: A Centenary Tribute*, ed. W. James and N. J. Allen. Oxford: Berghahn Books, 3–28.

Jolly, Margaret and Mark Mosko, ed. 1994. *Transformations of Hierarchy: Structure, History and Horizon in the Austronesian World*. Special issue of *History and Anthropology*, vol. 7(1–4). Canberra: Australian National University.

Josephides, Lisette. 1995. "Replacing Cultural Markers: Symbolic Analysis and Political Action in Melanesia." In *Cosmos and Society in Oceania*, ed. D. De Coppet and A. Iteanu. Oxford: Berg, 189–213.

Kapferer, Bruce. 1998. *Legends of People, Myths of State: Violence, Intolerance, and Political Culture in Sri Lanka and Australia.* Washington, D.C.: Smithsonian Institution Press.

———, ed. 1976. *Transaction and Meaning: Directions in the Anthropology of Exchange and Symbolic Behavior.* Philadelphia: Institute for the Study of Human Issues.

———, ed. 2005. *The Retreat of the Social: The Rise and Rise of Reductionism.* Oxford: Berghahn Books.

Kirkpatrick, John. 1985. "Review of Louis Dumont: Essais sur l'individualisme: Une perspective anthropologique sur l'idéologie moderne." *American Anthropologist* 87: 168–170.

Koestler, Arthur. 1967. *The Ghost in the Machine.* London: Hutchinson.

———. 1972. *The Roots of Coincidence.* London: Hutchinson.

Kolenda, Pauline. 1988. "Review of Louis Dumont: A South Indian Subcaste: Social Organisation and Religion of the Pramalai Kallar." *American Anthropologist* 90: 463.

Kuper, Adam, ed. 1992. *Conceptualizing Society.* London: Routledge.

Lemonnier, Pierre. 1991. "From Great men to Big men: Peace, Substitution and Competition in the Highlands of New Guinea." In *Big Men and Great Men*, ed. M. Godelier and M. Strathern. Cambridge: Cambridge University Press.

Lévi-Strauss, Claude. 1987. *Introduction to the Work of Marcel Mauss.* London: Routledge and Kegan Paul.

Madan, Triloki N., ed. 1982. *Way of life: King, Householder, Renouncer: Essays in Honour of Louis Dumont.* New Delhi: Vikas.

Marriott, McKim. 1969. "Review of Homo Hierarchicus by L. Dumont." *American Anthropologist* 71: 166–75.

———. 1976. "Hindu Transactions: Diversity without Dualism." In *Transaction and Meaning: Directions in the Anthropology of Exchange and Symbolic Behavior*, ed. B. Kapferer. Philadelphia: Institute for the Study of Human Issues, 109–142.

Melhuus, Marit. 1990. "Gender and the Problem of Hierarchy." *Ethnos* 56 (3–4): 151–168.

Mimica, Jadran. 1988. *Intimations of Infinity.* Oxford: Berg.

Mines, Mattison. 1988. "Conceptualizing the Person: Hierarchical Society and Individual Autonomy in India." *American Anthropologist* 90 (3): 568–79.

Mosko, Mark S. 1994. "Junior Chiefs and Senior Sorcerers: The Contradictions and Inversions of Mekeo 'Hierarchy.'" In *Transformations of Hierarchy*, ed. M. Jolly and M. S. Mosko. Canberra: Australian National University, 195–222.

Parkin, Robert. 2003. *Louis Dumont and Hierarchical Opposition.* Oxford: Berghahn Books.

Parry, Jonathan P. 1979. *Caste and Kinship in Kangra.* London : Routledge & Kegan Paul.

———. 1980. "Ghosts, Greed and Sin: The Occupational Identity of the Benares Funeral Priests." *Man* (n.s.) 15 (1): 88–111.

———. 1986. "The Gift, the Indian Gift and the 'Indian Gift.'" *Man* 21 (n.s.) (3): 453–473.

———. 1998. "Mauss, Dumont and the Distinction between Status and Power." In *Marcel Mauss: A Centenary Tribute*, ed. Wendy James and N.J. Allen. Oxford: Berghahn Books,151–175.

Perminow, Arne Aleksej. 2001. "Captain Cook and the Roots of Precedence in Tonga." *History and Anthropology* 12 (3): 289–314.

Radcliffe-Brown, Alfred Reginald. 1957. *A natural Science of Society.* Glencoe, IL: The Free Press.

Raheja, Gloria G. 1988a. *The Poison in the Gift*. Chicago: The University of Chicago Press.
———. 1988b. "India: Caste, Kingship and Dominance Reconsidered." *Annual Review of Anthropology* 17: 497–522.
Restrepo, Eduardo and Arturo Escobar. 2005. "'Other Anthropologies and Anthropologies Otherwise': Steps to a World Anthropologies Framework." *Critique of Anthropology* 25 (2): 99–129.
Rio, Knut M. 2002. "The Sorcerer as an Absented Third Person." In *Beyond Rationalism*, ed. B. Kapferer. Oxford: Berghahn Books, 130–154.
———. 2005. "Discussions Around a Sand-drawing: Creations of Agency and Sociality in Melanesia." *Journal of the Royal Anthropological Institute* (n.s.) 11: 401–423.
———. 2007. *The Power of Perspective: Social Ontology and Agency on Ambrym Island, Vanuatu*. Oxford: Berghahn Books.
Robbins, Joel. 1994. "Equality as a Value: Ideology in Dumont, Melanesia and the West." *Social Analysis* 36: 21–70.
Sahlins, Marshall. 1963. "Poor Man, Rich Man, Big Man, Chief: Political Types in Melanesia and Polynesia." *Comparative Studies in Society and History* 5 (3): 285–303.
———. 1985a. *Islands of History*. Chicago: Chicago University Press.
———. 1985b. "Hierarchy and Humanity in Polynesia." In *Transformations of Polynesian Culture*, ed. A. Hooper and J. Huntsman. Auckland: The Polynesian Society, 195–217.
———. 1993. "Cery Cery Fuckabede." *American Ethnologist* 20 (4): 848–867.
———. 2004. *Apologies to Thycydides*. Chicago: The University of Chicago Press.
Sartre, Jean-Paul. 1976 [1960]. *Critique of Dialectical Reason. Volume 1: Theory of Practical Ensembles*. Trans. Alan Sheridan-Smith, ed. Jonathan Rée. London: Verso.
Scubla, Lucien. 2002. "Hocart and the Royal Road to Anthropological Understanding." *Social Anthropology* 10 (3): 359–376.
Sheckley, Robert. 1975 [1958]. "The Prize of Peril." In *The Robert Sheckley omnibus*, ed. Robert Conquest. Harmondsworth: Penguin.
Shore, Bradd. 1996. *Culture in Mind: Cognition, Culture, and the Problem of Meaning*. New York: Oxford University Press.
Simmel, Georg. 1910–11. "How is Society Possible?" *American Journal of Sociology* 16: 372–391.
Stephen, Michele. 1996. "The Mekeo 'Man of Sorrow'": Sorcery and the Individuation of the Self," *American Ethnologist* 23 (1): 83–101.
Strathern, Andrew. 1971. *The Rope of Moka: Big-men and Ceremonial Exchange in Mount Hagen*. Cambridge: Cambridge University Press.
Strathern, Andrew, ed. 1979. *Ongka: A Self-account by a New Guinea Big-man*. New York: St.Martin's Press.
Strathern, Marilyn. 1988. *The Gender of the Gift*. Berkeley: University of California Press.
———. 1991. "One Man and Many Men." In *Big Men and Great Men*, ed. M. Godelier and M. Strathern. Cambridge: Cambridge University Press, 197–214.
———. 1993. "Making Incomplete." In *Carved Flesh, Cast Selves*, ed. V. Broch-Due, I. Rudie, and T. Bleie. Oxford: Berg Publishers, 41–51.
———. 1996. "The Concept of Society is Theoretically Obsolete." In *Key Debates in Anthropology*, ed. T. Ingold. London: Routledge, 60–67.
Thomas, Nicholas. 1991. *Entangled objects: Exchange, Material Culture and Colonialism in the Pacific*. Cambridge, Mass.: Harvard University Press.
———. 1993. "Beggars Can be Choosers." *American Ethnologist* 20 (4): 868–876.
Tyler, Stephen A. 1973. "Review of Louis Dumont: Religion, Politics and History in India." *American Anthropologist* 75 (2): 381–385.

Tyrner, Alice G. 1959. "Review of Louis Dumont: Une sous-caste de l'Inde du sud: Organisation sociale et religion des Pramatai Kallar." *American Anthropologist* 61: 1125–1126.

Valeri, Valeri. 1985. *Kingship and Sacrifice. Ritual and Society in Ancient Hawaii*. Chicago: The University of Chicago Press.

Wagner, Roy. 1991. "The Fractal Person." In *Big Men and Great Men*, ed. Maurice Godelier and Marilyn Strathern. Cambridge: Cambridge University Press.

Woodburn, James. 1982. "Egalitarian Societies." *Man* (n.s.) 17: 431–451.

CHAPTER 2

Conversion, Hierarchy, and Cultural Change

Value and Syncretism in the Globalization of Pentecostal and Charismatic Christianity

Joel Robbins

The study of cultural change, particularly radical change, has always been something of a secondary topic in cultural anthropology.[1] If sociology and history have been disciplines in large measure defined by their attention to issues of discontinuity and change (Patterson 2004), anthropology has staked its claim on elucidating such presumably enduring objects as traditions, cultures, and systems of belief. This is not to say, of course, that anthropologists have never discussed or described cultural change. Rather, the point is that cultural change has rarely been theorized in its own terms. Even today—after a decade and a half of attention given to such matters as practice theory, globalization, and modernity—the discipline does not have any widely agreed upon frameworks for approaching the topic. What I want to suggest is that Dumont's notion of hierarchy provides an important starting point for developing an analytically useful definition of radical cultural change and opens up productive avenues for exploring its dynamics.

In introducing the concept of hierarchy, I have in mind Dumont's use of it to refer to the way values organize the relations between elements in a culture. Values are determinations of the relative importance of elements of a culture (beliefs, ideas, things, and so on) and as such always serve to produce hierarchies of more or less valued elements. The ways elements are arranged in such hierarchies can be further specified by referring to Dumont's idea that the more valued term of a pair encompasses its contrary: that is, in some contexts the more valued term can stand both for itself and for its contrary, as in English the lexeme "man" can stand for both "man" and "woman," or "goods" can stand for both "goods" and "services" (Dumont 1977, 1980). Furthermore, drawing on other parts of

Dumont's work, one can suggest that encompassment is just one aspect of the way values organize cultural elements. It is also the case that more valued elements tend to be more elaborately worked out, more rationalized as one might put it in Weberian terms, and to control the rationalization of less valued ideas such that they can only be worked out to the extent that they do not contradict more valued ones.[2] Finally, it is only in less valued contexts that less valued ideas are able to approach full expression. As an example of these last two aspects of cultural organization, one can consider how, within cultures marked by Western liberalism, highly valued ideas of liberty as the right to differ control the rationalization of less valued ideas of equality; such that ideas concerning equality of opportunity—which support the achievement of individual difference—are fairly well worked out, while those of equality of outcome—seen to promote the creation of similarity—are less so. Equality of outcome is in fact only seriously pursued in less valued, private contexts such as the family (where all children, even as their abilities to differ from one another should be fostered, should be loved and treated equally). (These ideas are more fully developed in Robbins 1994.)

One of the great advantages of Dumont's understanding of the way values articulate hierarchical organization within culture is that Dumont sees value as something internal to culture—not as a matter of subjective appraisal. In a Dumontian framework, one reads values off of the organization of a culture, by looking at relations of encompassment and limitation between elements. Where such relations occur, it is clear that there is a value in play. As is the case with linguistic markedness, which clearly served as a model for Dumont's ideas about hierarchy and encompassment, value is understood to be part of the structure, not something people add to structure by virtue of their subjective responses to it (Battistella 1990). Values can be understood, then, as that part of culture that structures the relations between other parts. The argument I want to pursue here is that, given this understanding of the central role values play in structuring cultures, radical cultural change should be understood to have taken place only when values have changed—either because new values have been introduced or because the relations between traditional values have shifted.[3]

I have been motivated to open my discussion of cultural change in such abstract terms by what I see as a problematic tendency in the anthropological approach to change in general, and to Christian conversion in particular. Committed as they tend to be to looking for continuities in culture, those who study Christian conversion often deploy concepts of syncretism that support the notion that nothing much has changed. The rhetoric that surrounds studies of syncretism is familiar: Christianity is just a thin veneer overlaying traditional culture; what looks like change is just a case of people pouring old wine into new skins as they seize on elements of Christianity that are similar to elements of their traditional culture; people feign conversion to get the material benefits the mission has to offer, but it is their traditional beliefs that are still most important to them (as the well known "rice Christian" argument has it). What such approaches have in common, beyond their obvious investment in demonstrating cultural continuity, is that they encourage those who use them to take an elemental approach to matters of cultural change. That is to say, they lead people to look at a culture as a collection of disparate items, and then in essence to count up how many items are new and how many are old—and as long as a substantial number are old, then it is possible to analyze the culture as one that remains to a significant extent traditional. An approach to change focused on matters of value and cultural hierarchy works against this tendency, for it insists that one not count up old and new elements to determine if change has taken place, but rather examine if new values, or new relations between old values, are structuring most influentially the relations between elements (both old and new) in a culture. If the question is whether the culture of Christian converts has changed, then the answer has to be sought by asking if Christian values—particularly the value placed on individual salvation—have become the primary values organizing the relations between elements. No simple enumeration of how many new ideas people have versus the old ones they retain will suffice.

Such an approach to cultural change is particularly valuable when looking at the globalization of Pentecostal and charismatic Christianity. These are forms of Christianity in which all believers are thought to be able to receive the gifts of the Holy Spirit (although not all believers do receive such gifts, it is believed that all of them are capable of doing so). They constitute the fastest spreading branches of Christianity worldwide, and are growing particularly rapidly in Asia, Latin America, and Africa (Jenkins 2002; Martin 2002). Some estimate that there are currently as many as 525 million Pentecostal and charismatic Christians worldwide (Barrett and Johnson 2002: 284), and even conservative estimates put the number at about 250 million (Martin 2002: xvii). From the point of view of issues of cultural change, what is most interesting about the spread of these kinds of Christianity is that analysts have found it difficult to decide whether to see them as particularly open to indigenization, and hence as a force for cultural preservation, or as perhaps the most successful example of a globalizing Western form that holds its shape as it spreads around the world and homogenizes all that it touches. Both points have been argued quite vigorously in the literature on Pentecostal and charismatic Christianity, and little work has been done to settle the paradoxical picture which readers are left with from these contradictory accounts (Robbins 2004a). An approach to cultural change focused on values and hierarchy can clarify the cultural dynamics of Pentecostal and charismatic growth in a way that does precisely that.

The paradoxical picture arises in the first place because globalizing Pentecostal and charismatic Christianity are unusual among forms of Christianity in that, while they demand that people adopt new ideas about the spiritual world, they simultaneously accept as real the spiritual ontologies of those who convert to their faith. Pentecostal and charismatic Christianity do not dismiss traditional gods and spirits as illusory, but rather affirm them as real. On the basis of this affirmation, those who convert to Pentecostal and charismatic Christianity remain deeply involved with important figures of their traditional religions. For this reason, they appear to have indigenized Christianity quite thoroughly, and it is easy for analysts to imagine that their traditional cultures have survived very much intact.

Yet if one looks closely at the way in which traditional spiritual figures are understood in the cultures of Pentecostal and charismatic converts, it is clear that major changes have taken place by virtue of the fact that, in the religious realm at least, the hierarchical arrangement of elements has been radically transformed. In the vast majority of cases, traditional spirits have been demonized, have come to be seen as evil figures, allied with Satan, whom believers have to fight against with the help of the Christian God and Holy Spirit (Meyer 1999). By preserving traditional cultural figures, only to define them as beings believers must constantly struggle against, Pentecostal and charismatic Christianity set up their own values related to individual Christian salvation as the primary ones in the cultures they create, and in classic Dumontian terms they allow those values to encompass and limit the expression of the indigenous ideas that remain. The rituals by which converts carry on their battles with traditional spirits—rituals of prayer, healing, exorcism, and so on—tend to look very similar around the world, and they give Pentecostal and charismatic Christianity its homogenized appearance. Even more important as a homogenizing force, however, is the shared commitment to the value of individual salvation, a value that everywhere sets up a similar dynamic of at once preserving and demonizing key elements of traditional culture.

It is only by understanding how Pentecostal and charismatic Christianity enshrine their own values as paramount that we can adequately specify the ways old and new mix in the cultures of their converts. Once we recognize the dynamic of preservation and encompassing demonization that these forms of Christianity regularly set in train, however, the character of their global spread loses its paradoxical quality. Tradition, with its ontology of spiritual beings, is there, but only in its place—a subordinated place of limited elaboration.[4] The homogenizing qualities of Pentecostal and charismatic Christianity, then, are not mere veneers or covers for an enduring tradition. Cases of conversion in which this dynamic occurs must be understood as cases of genuine cultural change.

The account of the cultural dynamics of Pentecostal and charismatic conversion that I have just presented has of necessity been quite schematic. It is meant to be widely applicable, including to many cases in Asia, the Pacific and elsewhere (see, for example, the discussions of Asia in Martin 2002; and of the Pacific in Robbins, Stewart, and Strathern 2001). In order to flesh it out, and to illustrate more concretely the general approach to change as a matter of value that I am proposing here, in the rest of this chapter I will look at one case in some detail. This is the case of the Urapmin of Papua New Guinea, a group with whom I carried out fieldwork in the early 1990s. I will first indicate the ways in which the Urapmin case fits the more general model of Pentecostal and charismatic conversion, and show how change in their case can be analyzed as a matter of values. I then go on to discuss in some detail aspects of their traditional religion that remain quite important, showing how, even in such hard cases, the model of change as changes in value can help us analyze this case without resort to an undue emphasis on continuity. I conclude by exploring the nature of the individualism that charismatic Christianity has enshrined as the core religious value in Urapmin and consider the ways in which this value has encompassed traditional ones in the religious domain.

The Cultural Dynamics of Charismatic Conversion among the Urapmin

The Urapmin are a group of 390 people living in the West Sepik Province of Papua New Guinea. They are one of what is known as the Min groups and are speakers of a Mountain Ok language. Located in an area that is remote even by Papua New Guinea standards, the Urapmin were never directly missionized by Western missionaries. In the early 1950s, the Australian Baptist Missionary Society set up a station in Telefomin, a rough, half-day walk across the Sepik gorge from Urapmin. Relatively quickly the Urapmin began to send some of their young people to be educated at the mission, and the latter brought back news of the Christian religion. Throughout the 1960s and early 1970s, the Urapmin continued to send young people to become students at schools the mission had begun to operate in parts of their region that had airstrips. While many of these students became devoted Christians, and found a niche in the changing, post–contact Min region by acting as paid evangelists to other groups, they were unable to make a significant number of converts at home. As late as the mid 1970s, the bulk of Urapmin, even as they tolerated the turn of some younger members of the community to Christianity, continued to practice their traditional religion.

The situation changed radically in 1977. During that year, a series of charismatic revivals (rebaibal)[5] swept through Papua New Guinea (Flannery 1983a, 1983b, 1983c; 1984). They were carried out by local people but introduced a form of charismatic Christianity recognizably Western in origin. Several young men who had been studying at a Min regional bible college brought the revival to Urapmin, and in short order people began to be possessed by the Holy Spirit. They shook when the Spirit "kicked" them and watched as some among them became healers or seers, able to discern sins that were causing problems in the community. Those touched by the Spirit and those who simply watched others receive charismatic gifts became convinced of the existence of God, and by 1978 all adult Urapmin had converted. Since that time, the Urapmin have conceived of themselves as living in a completely Christian community, and the successful conduct of what they call "Christian lives" (Kristin laip) is their primary shared goal—a goal they pursue in regular church services (at least three times a week and often far more), home prayer sessions, quiet bible study, and numerous Christian rituals designed to deliver people from sin. By 1991, when I first visited the Urapmin, Christianity was clearly the dominant theme in their public culture and in their private lives.

The questions of why and how the Urapmin converted so unanimously and intensively to Christianity are ones I have taken up elsewhere (Robbins 2004b). In the context of this chapter, the more important issue is the nature of the cultural formation in which their conversion has resulted. What I will show in some detail is that it has resulted in precisely the kind of cultural formation that I argued above is typical of Pentecostal and charismatic convert cultures: one in which traditional spirits still play an important role in people's lives, but in which they and the values they represent have been encompassed by Christian spiritual beings and the values they embody.

The dynamic of acknowledging the traditional spirits while also demonizing and rejecting them came into play in Urapmin as soon as people began converting in large numbers during the revival. Converts vowed to stop relating in any positive way to the spirits, making all possible efforts to chase them from the community and its land. People gave up the paraphernalia by which they had approached ancestors for help in hunting, gardening, and pig raising. Individuals took their magical seeds and other charms (*serap*) and the bones (*kun*) of close relatives that they had kept for use in entreating the ancestors and threw them into the forest, or burnt them, or discarded them down toilet holes. Working in more systematic fashion, leaders of the revival took it upon themselves to remove from the most important men's houses the bones of more distant ancestors (*alowal*), those who had been responsible for prospering gardens throughout the community and region and for helping boys grow into warriors. In a move that neatly indicated the extent to which the Urapmin still recognized the existence and power of the spirits to which these bones were attached, those who removed them from the cult houses put them in sheltered environments such as caves or the hollow parts of trees. They remained there while people planted gardens to see if they would still grow and watched to see if boys would still become men. When these things did come to pass, people determined that the power of the Christian God was stronger than that of their spirits, and they left the bones where they lay and ceased to perform their duties toward their ancestors. As they say now, when revival came we "threw out" (rausim) the ancestors.

Contemporary Urapmin talk little about the ancestors. They believe that the ancestors still exist as spirits, but they also say they could never return to their traditional religion because the ancestors, after how the Urapmin have treated them, would never have them back. To the extent that they pay the ancestors any heed, it is to acknowledge that they are evil spirits occasionally capable of causing sickness. They perform no rituals especially for them, and it is fair to say that their charismatic Christianity has almost wholly eliminated the force of the ancestors in Urapmin life.

The same cannot be said for the other major class of spirits that inhabit the Urapmin world. These are spirits connected with specific parts of the environment that the Urapmin understand them to own. They are called *motobil*, and all significant parts of the environment—trees, large rocks, streams, pieces of land, animals, and so on—are owned by one or other of them. For the most part, these spirits let the Urapmin use the resources they own. But when *motobil* feel they have been disturbed, as when people violate taboos (*awem*) that *motobil* have set in place about not eating certain animals, or not speaking loudly or laughing while gardening or hunting, they make people sick. Most illnesses of any severity are thought to be caused by *motobil*, and they are also the cause of all infant deaths.

The behavior of *motobil* spirits and the problems they cause are topics of constant discussion in contemporary Urapmin. As Urapmin understand Christianity, one of its primary injunctions is that believers should not follow any traditional taboos. People should trust God to protect them from the spiritual punishments that follow from taboo violations, and thus to honor a taboo is to demonstrate a lack of faith. People have little trouble disregarding most taboos put in place by the ancestors. They find it a bit more difficult, however, to violate the taboos connected with the *motobil*, for the sicknesses that still beset them demonstrate the *motobil's* continued capacity to cause harm. The power of the *motobil* is therefore a constant worry, and very often people's prayers include petitions to God to keep the *motobil* from causing them trouble.

Whenever people are sick, their activities turn toward finding ways to address the *motobil*. Friends and relatives pray to God to chase these spirits from the afflicted. More serious illnesses are treated by a class of female ritual specialists called Spirit women (<u>Spirit meri</u>), who first arose at the time of the revival. They become possessed by the Holy Spirit, who tells or shows them which *motobil* are causing an illness. They then pray over their patients, asking God to deal with the *motobil* who is causing the trouble. Sometimes they also engage in more elaborate rituals aimed at chasing the spirits from villages or other areas in which many people have been sick. During these rituals, several Spirit women will go into trance in the area to be cleansed of spiritual inhabitants. They call on God to chase out the nature spirits and bind them in hell. Once they have prayed in this way, they plant small wooden crosses in the ground at the openings to the village or other area they have cleansed, in this way erecting a spiritual fence to prevent the *motobil* from returning to reoccupy their land.

None of the activities of the Spirit women that I have discussed thus far are controversial, although the rites that aim to cleanse whole areas of spiritual presence are undertaken relatively rarely. There is, however, one aspect of the practice of the Spirit women that is a subject of some controversy. Sometimes, in cases in which infants are ill or adults are suffering lingering illnesses that have not responded well to treatment by prayer, Spirit women will say that the Spirit has ordered the afflicted person's relatives to sacrifice a pig *(kang anfukeleng)* to the *motobil* who is the cause. In the sacrifice, which is carried out by one of the few traditional ritual specialists who knows the proper spells, the *motobil* will be encouraged to release the person whom they are making sick in return for the smell, and sometimes the blood, of the pig. Most Urapmin feel ambivalent at best about pig sacrifice. Jesus, they say, is supposed to have been the last sacrifice, and in any case no one is supposed to have such positive exchange relations with the *motobil* as those represented in sacrifice; rather spirits are to be battled against with God as an ally, not to be cooperated with in exchanges which repair one's relationship with them. Some even suggest that when Spirit women call for sacrifice, they may be possessed not by the Holy Spirit but by an evil spirit *(sinik mafak)* who is impersonating it. Yet even in the face of these ambivalences, people do resort to sacrifice, especially when children are sick (since children, unlike adults, can be killed by *motobil*), and they recognize sacrifice as the one traditional ritual they still practice somewhat regularly and publicly.

The whole complex of beliefs and behaviors surrounding *motobil* is quite prominent in Urapmin life, and as we have seen important parts of Urapmin Christian belief and practice are addressed to it. Looked at from the perspective of an elemental view of cultural change, or from that of the standard models of syncretism with which such a view is often allied, the importance of the *motobil* in contemporary Urapmin life represents the continuing influence of tradition, and suggests that to characterize their conversion as a case of radical cultural change would be inaccurate. In their concern with these spirits the Urapmin seem, after all, quite regularly to be preoccupied with traditional matters.

From the point of view of a model of change as constituted by shifts in values and the hierarchical arrangements of cultural elements that they produce, however, it is difficult to read the Urapmin case in terms of the persistence of tradition. As the model of change I laid out earlier would predict, in post–revival Urapmin ideas about traditional spiritual powers have been greatly reduced in importance and have been restricted in their elaboration. In explaining how less valued cultural elements come to be reduced and restricted in this way, I argued that they are only elaborated to the extent that they do not contradict more valued elements, and that their greatest elaboration comes in less valued contexts. Both of these factors are evident in the way traditional spiritual ideas are handled in Urapmin. Furthermore, a process like that described in Dumont's classic model of encompassment has also taken place, whereby traditional spiritual ideas appear only against the ground of more valued Christian conceptions.

Take first the restriction on the elaboration of less valued ideas when they conflict with more valued ones. One of the key planks of Urapmin Christianity is the claim that God is the sole creative power in the universe. God made everything, the Urapmin regularly say, and in their prayers they often repeat that it is he who has real power. If we take Urapmin spiritual ideas as a single corpus—one that includes ideas about the ancestors as well as those about *motobil*—it is clear that those traditional ideas the elaboration of which is centrally concerned with matters of creative power in essence have been abandoned. There is little talk of ancestors now, and no elaboration of ideas about their creativity or positive ways to approach them, because any elaboration of ideas about their creativity contradicts more valued ideas about the all-encompassing reach of God's power. The rather residual state in which ideas about the ancestors exist is caused by the inability of the Urapmin to find a way to elaborate those ideas without threatening now central Christian values.

A second concern has to do with traditional ideas that are more fully elaborated, but only in less valued contexts. This explains how the *motobil* have come to be represented and understood. Ideas about the *motobil* are elaborated primarily in the domain of illness, for Urapmin tend to disregard the *motobil* until they become ill, and it is only in the context of illness that they discuss issues of the spirit ownership of pieces of the natural environment.[6] Such elaborations dwell primarily on the possessive quality of *motobil*—their refusal fully to give what they own to the Urapmin—and their desire, when angry, to possess the Urapmin themselves, since it is their rapacious clinging to their victims with their clutching tails, hands, and feet that make people sick. For all that the Urapmin talk about *motobil*, then, they imagine them in what remain quite limited terms: as far as human beings are concerned, they are able only to cause illness and are led to do so by their single-minded dedication to the task of possession. Such elaboration of ideas about the efficacy of the *motobil* as causes of trouble does not contradict any more valued ideas about God's powers, for God does not cause illness or other harms, and ideas about *motobil* spirits play the role in Urapmin theodicy that ideas about the satanic and demonic often play in Christianity elsewhere. Confined to such a limited context and elaborated only in the terms that are suitable to it, the *motobil* fit comfortably within the world as it is understood by Urapmin Christianity, and it is on this basis that they are the one part of the traditional Urapmin spiritual world that remains highly relevant today.

Finally, it is worth considering how encompassment looked at in classically Dumontian terms has served to shape the way the *motobil* are handled in post–conversion Urapmin culture. Even as Urapmin Christianity gives ideas about the *motobil* only the constricted and negatively valued context of illness in which to flourish, it also manages to encompass them, such that they are only understood in relation to God and the Holy Spirit, who are figured as their opposite number. When Urapmin think about how to respond to the *motobil*, it is to the Christian God and Holy Spirit that they turn. Indeed, the entire domain of the spiritual is now defined by God, who can stand for the whole domain, much as the lexeme "man" stands for the domain of gender in English. Those *motobil* that still cause problems are simply those that God has not yet banished from Urapmin and bound in hell. And in the Christian future the Urapmin imagine will come after Jesus returns, the *motobil* will be completely irrelevant. They are good to think about in the present only to the extent that one has Christian ways of addressing the problems they cause.

This analysis in terms of encompassment is for the most part supported by the rise of the Spirit women as the most important ritual specialists that people turn to for help in responding to the spirits.[7] Spirit women are explicitly Christian figures, whose powers derive from the Holy Spirit. People understand them to be effective to the extent that they are able to direct God to control particular spirits who are causing problems. Almost all of their techniques—possession, prayer, the planting of crosses—are, as the Urapmin understand them, Christian and therefore serve to contain people's responses to the spirits within the realm in which the Christian God is preeminent and (as I will show later) Christian values are paramount. The one seeming exception to this claim is the Spirit women's resort to sacrifice. Their turning to a traditional ritual to address problems with traditional spirits appears to be the one case in which Spirit women allow traditional spiritual ideas and practices to find elaboration unencompassed by Christian ones. Granted, as discussed above, it is only in the negatively valued sphere of illness that traditional ideas are able to do this, but it remains true that in the case of sacrifice the *motobil* seem to be addressed only in their own, traditional terms. This is surely one reason why sacrifice is so marked and controversial in contemporary Urapmin.

Even as we can acknowledge the uniqueness of sacrifice in relation to our argument that traditional spiritual ideas are restricted and encompassed in contemporary Urapmin culture, it is also true that a close look at how the ritual unfolds suggests that Urapmin work hard to model the Christian encompassment of the ritual iconically in the practice of the rite itself. This modeling is accomplished first by having the rite be called for by a Christian ritual specialist (a Spirit woman), and then by beginning the rite with a Christian prayer that seeks to explain it in wholly Christian terms. The analysis of an example of such a prayer makes clear the encompassing intent of this way of framing the rite.

The prayer I will present here was performed before the sacrifice of a piglet for a young girl about four years of age. The pastor who performed this prayer began by reading out James 5: 13–16. Translated from the Tok Pisin Bible the Urapmin use, this reads as follows:

> Is there amongst you a brother who has a problem (lit. "a heavy")? Then he must pray to God. Is there a brother who is happy? Then he must sing God's praises. Is there a brother who is sick? He must call for the leaders of the church. In the name of God they must put oil on his body, and they must pray to God to help him. If they believe in God and they pray, then God will heal this sick man and put him back on his feet. And if he has committed some sins, then God will completely take away these sins. So you must confess your sins to your brothers. And you must pray to God to help your brothers, and then God will make all of you well. The prayer of a good man has strength, and is truly enough to help a man.

It is striking that the pastor reads these verses just before beginning his prayer for the sacrifice, for these verses are precisely the ones pastors always read before they perform formal healing prayers aimed at seeking God's help in removing spirits from a person (see Robbins 2004b). The pastor will refer back to the language of these verses in the middle of his prayer. By reading the verses and then making reference to them in his prayer, he works to assimilate the upcoming sacrifice to a Christian healing ritual of the kind that will in all cases have preceded it (and the failure of which to cure the patient will have led the Spirit woman to call for sacrifice). Even before the prayer has begun, then, the Christian encompassment of the sacrifice is underway.

After reading the verses, the pastor continues [in what follows, I have put occasional explanatory remarks in brackets; I've also numbered each paragraph for ease of reference in the subsequent discussion]:

[1] This is what James chapter 5, verses 13 to 14 and 15 say. I read only those [in fact he read verse 16 as well] and now the Spirit woman can jump up and down with happiness [become possessed]. She can do her work with the piglet.

[The pastor moves toward the sick child and says "pray strongly" and begins to pray.]

[2] God, you! God. Holy God. I pray to you now. As you can see, the daughter of my younger sister and her husband has been sick. We family are gathered here.

[3] Please God, you have power. God you have strength. God you have glory. You are the God of mercy, the God of peacefulness. I am praying in your name. You must heal this daughter of mine.

[4] My child Kiki [the sick girl's father] and my younger sister, this couple's daughter, Jesus you appear to her. Come down to her and bring your heavenly, sharp knife and chop off the tails and the hands of the spirits. Send away the spirits of Alal [a place], spirits of Lalip [a place], spirits of the Wim Tem cave, spirits of Delolbikma [a place], Spirits of Bantok [a place], and the bad animal spirits, like those of the Belulumin species of flying fox.

[5] Only you Jesus have power. It's like when people are sick, when they have a problem. That's what they said in James, chapter 5 verses 13, 14, and 15. It said that "if your friend has a heavy, like he has become sick, you must go see him and you must put him . . . the church leaders can come, like the pastor or deacon, Spirit women and men [there is one Spirit man in Urapmin]. You strong Christians should come and stay with your friend like that and pray for him and I will hear it. I will heal your friend who is sick. And if your friend sins, if he has become heavy with his sin, I will heal him, I will take back his life, or put back his life. I will heal him." This is what you have said and so my child's child, Jesus you! You—we brothers and sisters are people but you are holy and clean—we pray to you.

[6] We say you will heal this child and so she has come and I am praying. And also, we will kill a good, small young piglet in order to . . . to kill it and then

we must cook it. That's the way we can heal her with the piglet. She has brought it and we family want to kill it.

[7] Bad spirits, ghosts, hidden people, she [this can refer to the Holy Spirit, who is grammatically feminine, as well as to the Spirit woman] will throw them all out. She will throw out all the spirits.

[8] Jesus, you were a good lamb that died to bring our lives back to us. That's what you did and we too bring a young, child pig and kill it and do a ritual about this [The Tok Pisin word translated here as "do a ritual" is singsing; at least by way of connotation, it would refer to a traditional ritual since "singsing" is rarely used to refer to Christian practice.]. This is what we will do and so God you look at us. God send down only your strength. It's just meat, so we will kill it and eat it and so God send down only your strength and holiness and heal this child.

[9] Please, I have said this and God, you! God you are merciful, you are peaceful, you are happy and so I pray to you. Please look carefully at this child and heal her. Chop off the hands and feet of the poison snake spirit, the dog spirit, the cassowary spirit, the echidna spirit, whatever kind of spirit-like things, residents of the trees, any kind of man [a way of referring to spirits], any kind of man, snake spirits, any kind of man, send him away to his own house. You take him and step on him and crush him and, please, heal this child.

[10] I send her to you Jesus, to your realm of life. Resident of Nazareth, she comes to your holy presence. Please appear and heal her.

[11] My child's child has been sick. I pray for her but I am a sinful man. Some have not come to see her, I have not, so holy God please appear and heal her of this. Jesus, only you can heal my child's family's daughter. We father's and mother's brothers are just men, so Jesus please you yourself [must do this]. Jesus, I send her to you. I have said enough and it is true [this is the formulaic conclusion used with most prayers].

The Urapmin lay out their theological conceptions most articulately in their prayers (Robbins 2004b). This prayer contains many themes that are central to that theology, most notably in the way it opposes God's power to human weakness. But as befits its nature as a prayer that opens a sacrifice, it can also be seen to give voice to a theology of the Christian encompassment of the traditional spirit world. In it, particularly in paragraphs 6 and 8—the key paragraphs in which the pastor addresses sacrifice directly—sacrifice is described as something people do, as opposed to something God does. It is something people are capable of doing (paragraph 6), but in the end the sacrifice is "just meat" and has no real power (paragraph 8). The actual healing of the child will have to be carried out by God. Furthermore, the pastor suggests that in performing the sacrifice people are only acting on the model of Jesus' sacrifice—a line of thought he does not develop very far, but which clearly points to the Christianization of the sacrificial rite. Both of these moves in paragraphs 6 and 8 are encompassing ones. The identification of the sacrifice of the piglet with Jesus' death suggests that sacrifice may in fact be a Christian ritual, and in any case the suggestion that it is merely something humans do serves to indicate that any real efficacy it has must rest on the power of God. The explicit content of these paragraphs thus articulates a model of the kind of encompassment the pastor is working to effect.

As much as the explicit content of the prayer works toward encompassment, so too important aspects of its structure actually perform such encompassment: that is to say, they bring it about as they are enacted. This is true in several respects. First, in a number of ways the prayer presents itself as akin to a standard healing prayer. I already mentioned that the verses from James 5 that the pastor read at the outset were those that would be read at a healing prayer. Beyond this, paragraphs 2–5 and 9–11 are made up of kinds of statements that are common in healing prayers. Enumerations of the kinds of spirits that might be causing the sickness, along with calls to God to chop off the hands and legs of the spirits, to crush them, to send them away, all of these are standard fare in healing prayers. Appearing here, they serve to suggest that this ritual itself is in effect a healing prayer, and that the real efficacy of the rite will follow from this prayer being made, rather than from the sacrifice. In fact, the performance of the prayer virtually turns the rite into one of Christian healing. A second aspect of the prayer further allows its performance to enact the encompassment of sacrifice. This relates to its structure, which is in essence an icon of encompassment as Dumont represents it, with one term surrounding and thus both absorbing and providing the ground for another. In this prayer, sacrifice appears only in the middle section. In the beginning and end the focus is squarely on God and his power, and the suggestion is that it is he who ultimately heals. This structure accurately represents the way the Urapmin currently construe the spiritual realm as one that is thoroughly Christianized and in which non-Christian spirits appear only as they can be construed and controlled in Christian terms.

I have paid such close attention to sacrifice here because it is a hard case for the model of change, which I have been arguing accounts for the current situation in Urapmin. In that model, a shift toward Christian values has determined that those traditional ideas that remain are elaborated only to the extent that they do not contradict Christian ideas, and confine themselves to appearing in domains that Urapmin culture defines as less valuable. Moreover, I have argued that these ideas are thoroughly encompassed by Christian ones, such that they never appear without indicating the Christian ground against which they are defined. When the Urapmin turn to sacrifice, however, they appear to respond to traditional spirits in traditional ritual terms, and thus to have preserved an area of their culture in which Christian ideas and practices have no purchase, and in which traditional ones are allowed full elaboration. The foregoing analysis has shown that this appearance is deceiving. Sacrifices are called for, and in important respects (albeit not all respects) carried out by Christian ritual specialists (Spirit women and pastors). They are also hedged around with Christian prayers designed to assimilate them to Christian rituals and to critique their pretense to possess their own efficacy. In the case of sacrifice, we see that the techniques of restriction and encompassment that everywhere limit the elaboration of traditional spiritual ideas in Urapmin are brought into play quite explicitly, a recognition on the part of those who use those techniques of the need to deploy them vigilantly in this marked case.

My argument thus far has focused on the process by which Urapmin conversion to charismatic Christianity has led to a situation in which Christian values serve to structure Urapmin culture. I have suggested that they structure it in a way that has not eliminated traditional ideas but has decisively influenced how they are understood and acted upon. I have also delineated some of the formal ways in which the structuring power of Christian values has expressed itself—through restricting the elaboration of traditional ideas, relegating them to less valued contexts, and encompassing them as subordinate to Christian ideas. This analysis has drawn extensively on Dumont's model of the way values structure cultural elements. In the next section, I examine the paramount value Christianity introduces into cultures that take it up, and consider the how the substance of that value conflicts with the value that is traditionally paramount in the cultures of Melanesia.

Paramount Values and Cultural Change

In Dumont's model of culture, every culture is dominated by a paramount value that delineates its structure in its broadest outlines. The vast majority of his work rests on a view of the world that differentiates between two kinds of cultures: those in which holism is the paramount value and those that are governed by individualism. Holist cultures, as Dumont describes them, are ones in which it is the social whole that is valued, and elements are evaluated on the basis of their contribution to the creation of a successful whole. Individualist cultures, by contrast, are those in which individual elements (including most notably human individuals) are valued, and elements are evaluated on the basis of their contribution to the flourishing of individuals. There is in Dumont a bit of a "West and the rest" tinge to the individualist/holist opposition, and to the extent that his own writing has focused on cultural change, it has primarily taken up the question of how holist cultures sometimes become individualist ones.[8] It is thus not surprising that most readers have assumed that Dumont understands individualism and holism to exhaust the kinds of paramount values that exist among the cultures of the world.

Yet despite that fact that Dumont himself did not identify any paramount values beyond those of individualism and holism, he did note that the cultures of Papua New Guinea appeared to him to be governed by some other principal value (Dumont 1986: 215–216). I have elsewhere argued at length that this value should be understood as one of relationalism (Robbins 1994, 2004b). In cultures in which relationalism is the paramount value, it is social relations that are valued most highly, and other elements (including both persons and things) are evaluated on the basis of their ability to help create and maintain such relations. This does not mean that one never finds holist or individualist representations in Melanesian cultures, only that these are not the most highly valued ones and hence not the most fully elaborated (Dumont 1980: 420 fn. 118d; see also 237). To borrow a term of art from Munn's (1986) theoretical perspective, one that is in many ways quite compatible with Dumont's, the notion of relationalism argues that what Melanesians most generally aim to produce are relationships, and that representations focused on individuals and wholes generally have to find places for themselves in processes of value transformation that overall are oriented toward relational goals.

There is no space here to rehearse in full the argument for relationalism as the Melanesian paramount value, which I have made elsewhere, anchored in important ways in the work of Wagner (1977, 1981), Gregory (1982), and Strathern (1988). One quick way into the argument in terms that will be helpful for my analysis here is to note that a major part of what it intends to comprehend is the central importance of various kinds of exchanges in the cultures of Papua New Guinea—exchanges that ethnographers have time and again explained as serving primarily the purpose of fostering, reinforcing, and transforming relationships rather than that of shaping up social life so that it fits a pre-existing model of the social whole. While one can discern the force of relationalism in many aspects of Melanesian cultures (Robbins 2004b), it is most clearly articulated by the exchange of objects and substances between persons and groups (Robbins 1994).

Given the centrality of relationalism as a value in the traditional cultures of Melanesia, questions about the nature of conversion are at least in part questions about how Christian values and relational ones interact. In order to study this interaction, one also has to define the paramount value that structures Christianity. For Dumont, Christianity is primarily individualist, and its rise has been central to the processes by which Western cultures developed in an individualist direction (Dumont 1986). Christianity's individualism is evident in its focus on the salvation of the individual, a salvation guaranteed by the state of the individual's own soul and often achieved by some measure of withdrawal from the social world. While one may find holist representations in Christian cultures—particularly in some forms of high church ecclesiastical arrangements—they ultimately take their place as parts of value transformation processes that have the salvation of individuals as their goal. Given this, in Dumont's terms we would expect conversion in cultures like those found in Melanesia to be best understood as a shift from a paramount value of relationalism to one of individualism.

As I have discussed elsewhere, in Urapmin culture as a whole the struggle between the paramount values of individualism and holism has been protracted and inconclusive (Robbins 2004b). The conduct of social life in Urapmin depends upon people's adherence to aspects of their culture that continue to be structured along relationalist lines and that cannot be replaced unless individualist institutions for structuring social life, most importantly the market, come to be prominent in Urapmin (Robbins 2004b: 311). Thus one cannot argue that Urapmin culture as a whole has, in the wake of the conversion of the Urapmin, come to be structured solely by the value of individualism. In this chapter, however, my goal has not been to argue for such a thorough going triumph of this new value. Instead, I have worked to show that representations in the religious domain are predominantly structured along individualist lines. This, I would suggest, should be a minimal criterion for arguing that Christian conversion had radically changed a culture at the level of values.

In order to show how individualism has struggled against relationalism in the religious domain in contemporary Urapmin, I want to argue that the confrontation between traditional spirits (both the ancestors and the *motobil*) and the Christian God and Holy Spirit, which I discussed in the last section from the point of view of issues of encompassment, restriction, and elaboration only in subordinate contexts, can also be seen as a struggle between representations that embody relationalism and those that embody individualism. In considering the kind of evidence that would support this argument, it is helpful to borrow Rio's (2005) notion of totalization, which has been significant in the framing of this volume. In important ways, representations of spirits, and of the value transformation processes into which those representations are organized, totalize the value of relationalism, in the sense that they make the value explicit and encourage reflection upon it. In similar ways, the Spirit women's practices of healing through possession and prayer (that is, their practices of healing that do not involve sacrifice) constitute a totalizing representation created from the perspective of individualism. This argument assumes that totalizations do not always have to result in representations of a social whole structured along holist lines, rather, they can be defined as clearly elaborated images representing social life from the point of view of any paramount, or would-be paramount, value. If that value is individualism, for example, then the totalization will represent social life as composed of individuals entering into relations of their own choosing, rather than as taking the form of a structured social whole. If we understand totalization in this way, the struggle that emerges around the practice of the Spirit women—a struggle between possession and prayer, on the one hand, and sacrifice, on the other—can be viewed as a struggle between totalizations of the two paramount values that are competing to structure Urapmin religious life.

It is not difficult to make a case for the ancestors as totalized embodiments of relationalist values. Ancestors are genealogically related to those who worship them, and worship primarily consists of carrying out those actions understood to maintain one's relationships with them on good terms. The work the Urapmin undertook during the revival to break with the ancestors is work they quite consciously understood as aiming to destroy rather than enhance relations. Such destruction left them, as they say, "free" (*fri*), unencumbered by any of the taboos their former relationships saddled them with. On their own account, individuals feel themselves liberated by throwing away their relations with the ancestors, and they often speak of the present as "free time" (*fri taim*), a phrase that in their usage has distinctly individualist connotations.

The case for the *motobil* as embodiments of relationalist values is a bit more complex, but it too can be made. The *motobil* less obviously represent relationalist values because the Urapmin appear not to value relations with the *motobil* very much *qua* relations; they only engage with the *motobil* ritually when things have gone wrong and otherwise tend to disregard them, not counting their relations with them as a particularly positive feature of their lives. Yet if we take relations with the *motobil* as symbolic of relationships with human beings (Gardner 1987; Robbins 1995), then the way the Urapmin conceptualize those relationships carries a very clear relationalist message. In effect, the *motobil* evidence all of those qualities that make the maintenance of relationships difficult. They are selfish, possessive, and vindictive when they feel their interests have been disregarded. When confronted with beings of this type, people's impulse is to ignore them completely. But the process of becoming ill and sacrificing to the *motobil* to effect a cure is a powerful representation of the futility of that strategy of withdrawal. It says, in effect, that one needs relationships even if they are difficult to maintain. This is, of course, a key relationalist truism.[9] The fact that one of the ways it is most forcefully expressed in Urapmin is through representations concerning the *motobil* is what renders them an important representation of the relational thrust of Urapmin culture.

It is in the idea and practice of sacrifice that representations of the *motobil* most clearly realize their potential to totalize the Urapmin value of relationalism. Most of the time, people relate to the *motobil* through avoidance. They aim to leave them undisturbed and neither exchange material goods nor speech with them. Since relations are articulated through material exchange in Urapmin, the gift of a pig that is at the heart of the sacrifice is what gives people's relations with the *motobil* their substance. It is at the moment of sacrifice that the relational emphasis of spirit representations is laid out most clearly.

The Christian attack on sacrifice in Urapmin, and the attempt to replace it with possession and prayer as the most important healing techniques, are thus a direct assault on the last stronghold of relationalism in the contemporary religious domain. Christian prayers for the sick call for relations to be severed rather than reaffirmed—the *motobil* are to be sent away, removed from the Urapmin world. The afflicted give the *motobil* nothing. Rather, they ask God to loosen the ties that bind these spirits to them. The imagery people deploy in their prayers of the severing of holding, grasping relations neatly inverts the exchange that is the key act of sacrifice and that affirms and repairs the relationships people have with the *motobil*.[10] In doing so, the imagery of healing prayers helps people imagine a life given over more fully to individualist values: one in which they can make their own decisions without regard for (spiritual) others whose primary concern, unlike that of the Christian God, is not with their personal development.[11] For this reason, the routine practice of the Spirit women, the healing rituals they perform focused on possession and prayer aimed at driving *motobil* away from their victims, can be taken as a totalizing epitomization of the individualism of Christianity.

When Spirit women find prayer to be insufficient for healing a patient and call for sacrifice, they make a move to substitute a totalization of relational values for a totalization of individualist ones. It is the threat of this substitution that the actual practice of sacrifice and the prayers that encompass it work to prevent. In the previous section, I showed how the prayers people perform prior to sacrifice accomplish, among other things, the reframing of the rite as something akin to a healing prayer. The importance of this reframing as an anti-relationalist move becomes even more evident when it is considered in contrast to the frames sacrifices more usually evoke. Sacrifices to the *motobil* in important respects closely resemble what is perhaps the primary ritual embodiment of the value of relationalism in Urapmin culture. This is the ritual of *tisol dala-min* ("exchanging wealth"). *Tisol dalamin* rituals involve the exchange of exactly equivalent goods between parties whose relationship has in some way been damaged. People resort to them following all kinds of disputes, and they also lend their form to rituals carried out after death (Robbins 2003). They are the most explicit and formalized moments of relation-ship maintenance in Urapmin life. Sacrifices resemble *tisol dalamin* ritu-als to the extent that they involve the gift of material goods to repair a relationship that has been damaged. They are not precise analogues of *tisol dalamin* exchanges, since the spirits do not give back equivalent goods (what they give back is the afflicted person him or herself, and in this way they also resemble bridewealth exchange rituals in which goods also move against people). But in their relationship-repairing intent and overall architecture, sacrifices to the spirits resemble the more regularly practiced *tisol dalamin* rituals closely enough that it is clear that the latter provide the frame in which the former is most readily understood. For this reason, when those carrying out a contemporary "Christian" sacri-fice explicitly reframe the rite in terms of healing prayers that are based on individualist ideas, they are working in very direct ways to attenuate its relational force. Here, then, we see a further example of the ability of individualism to construct itself as the paramount value in the contem-porary religious domain.

The contest between individualist and relationalist values in Urap-min cultures is unlikely to be fully settled any time soon. As long as relationalism continues to hold sway in many social domains, Christi-anity will be unable to fully encompass it (although it tries to do so by counseling withdrawal from social relationships as the most reliable path to salvation, Robbins 2004b). Yet in the religious domain, individualism has emerged as the more powerful value. Its preeminence has been at the heart of the cultural dynamics of change I described in the previ-ous section. Those dynamics explain in formal terms how the religious domain is structured in contemporary Urapmin culture. The discussion of individualism and relationalism as paramount values in this section has indicated some of the substance of the goals these values set before those who live their lives under their influence, and the way these goals shape concrete ritual practices.

Conclusion

In this chapter I have argued for a model of cultural change based on Dumont's theoretical contributions to our understanding of the way values organize culture. The study of cultural change is hampered by an anthropological tendency to emphasize cultural continuity. This tendency is supported by models of syncretism that look at change as a matter of cultural elements to be tallied, such that the continuing presence of traditional elements indicates that little change has taken place. I have argued that one way anthropology can get beyond its entrenched habit of continuity thinking is to move to the center of discussions of change a model based on Dumont's understanding of values and the structured hierarchies of cultural elements they produce. On this model, changes occur when new values or new rankings of values create new arrangements of cultural elements, some of which are traditional but none of which retain the same hierarchical places they once had. Transformations in kinds of intracultural relationships between elements first theorized by Dumont—those such as encompassment, restricted elaboration, and confinement to subordinate contexts—are what give value-transformative change its impact. It is when this kind of change has occurred that anthropologists can talk about radical cultural change.

This model of change is particularly appropriate to the analysis of cultures that have been transformed by Pentecostal and charismatic Christianity. These kinds of Christianity do not define away traditional spiritual beings as unreal, and for this reason analysts are often led to imagine that they are not powerful forces for change. Yet everywhere they are seriously taken up, they radically transform cultural values and thereby set in motion processes by which traditional spirits and the values they represent are encompassed, have their elaboration restricted, and are confined to less valued contexts. In this chapter I have developed this claim through the analysis of a single case, that of the Urapmin of Papua New Guinea. But my more general claim is that what has happened in the Urapmin case has happened in many other places as well (Robbins 2004a).

If one looks at the topics that preoccupy anthropologists at the moment—topics such as globalization, modernity, migration, hybridity, and so on—one might be forgiven for imagining that radical cultural change was one of the few unifying topics in an increasingly fragmented discipline. Yet in imagining this, one would be wrong. In the absence of any clearly worked out theory of radical cultural change, the topic is rarely taken up explicitly, and no dialogue uniting the disparate work that in fact addresses it has begun. Dumont's theoretical work, I have argued, can serve as the basis of a theory of radical cultural change that could support such a dialogue. Ever since Bourdieu's vogue in the late 1980s, the times have not been kind to major theoretical projects in anthropology. Given this, it is not a surprise that Dumont's work is less and less read these days. What I have wanted to do here is remind people of the force of his thought, and indicate how acknowledging its widest theoretical ambitions can help us reconceptualize processes of radical cultural change that are central to social life in all parts of the world today.

Notes

1. A version of this chapter was presented as a paper at the International Workshop, "Power and Hierarchy: Religious Conversions, Ritual Constructions, and Cosmological Belief Systems in Asia and the Indo-Pacific," organized by Dr. Pamela J. Stewart, Prof. Andrew Strathern, and Dr. Pei-yi Guo, and held at the Institute of Ethnology, Academia Sinica, Taipei, Taiwan, 30 May–1 June 2005. I thank the organizers and participants at this conference for their comments on the paper.

2. I think the extent to which Dumont's ideas can be brought into fruitful dialogue with those of Weber has yet to be explored and this issue represents an important frontier in the development of Dumont's approach (Robbins 2004b: 11–13; for Weber as an influence on Dumont, see also Allen 1998: 3).

3. This chapter looks at changes brought about by the introduction of a new value. Eriksen's paper (2005) is very similar in spirit to what I put forth in this chapter, but it focuses on how the introduction of Christianity in North Ambrym, Vanuatu transformed the relations between traditional values, and studies the effect this transformation has had on people's ritual lives and social lives more broadly.

4. By limited elaboration I do not mean that no attention is paid to traditional spirits. Very often the opposite is the case. Rather I mean that discussion about and reasoning on the basis of traditional spirits is constrained only to dwell on their negative qualities and the evil that they cause (sickness, undue desire, death, and so on). Christian values leave no room for exploring any ambivalent or positive qualities they may have formerly possessed in their various cultures.

5. In this chapter, terms given in Tok Pisin, the most prevalent lingua franca in Papua New Guinea and an important language for Urapmin Christianity, are underlined. Terms in the Urap language are given in italics.

6. The one exception to this general claim involves ideas about the ways *motobil* may be causing the failure of mineral prospecting in Urapmin. These ideas, which revolve around the idea that the *motobil* are holding gold they own and refusing to release it to prospectors, has led to some innovations in the practice of sacrifice (Robbins 1995). Yet these ideas are as yet inchoate, and I do not treat them here. They do not, in any case, contradict the general arguments about the restricted contexts in which ideas about *motobil* find their elaboration, and in their emphasis on the possessiveness of the *motobil*, they follow lines very similar to those taken in discussions of illness (see below in the main text).

7. I say most important here because in the early stages of an illness people will often pray with their pastors, or even simply with relatives, to entreat God to chase the spirits from themselves or their children.

8. Dumont's emphasis on change has often been missed by those who read him primarily as a high structuralist, but it is very much present in his work (see especially Dumont 1994; see also Ortner 1994: 381).

9. In comparative terms, it might be mentioned that the Kaluli *gisaro*, as discussed in Schieffelin's (1976) well known account, can be read as conveying this truism as well. In the face of the ultimate threat to relationship constituted by death, the *gisaro* unfolds a series of agonistic interactions that resolve into a final statement of the value of exchange and relationship building.

10. It is worth noting in this context that the Urapmin often use the verb "to hold" (*kutalfugumin*) in a positive sense to refer to supportive relationships between people, as in one person saying to another, "I will hold you" to indicate steadfast support.

11. Pentecostal and charismatic healing and deliverance rituals in many places around the world aim at severing relations people have, both with kin and with traditional spirits (Robbins 2004a). In this respect they often stand in contrast to traditional healing rituals aimed at repairing damaged relations.

References

Allen, N. J. 1998. "Obituary: Louis Dumont (1911–1998)." *Journal of Anthropological Society of Oxford* 29 (1): 1–4.

Barrett, D.B. and T.M. Johnson. 2002. "Global Statistics." In *The New International Dictionary of Pentecostal and Charismatic Movements*, ed. S. M. Burgess and E. M. van der Maas. Grand Rapids: Zondervan, 283–302.

Battistella, Edwin L. 1990. *Markedness: The Evaluative Superstructure of Language*. Albany: State University of New York Press.

Dumont, Louis. 1977. *From Mandeville to Marx: The Genesis and Triumph of Economic Ideology*. Chicago: University of Chicago Press.

———. 1980. *Homo Hierarchicus: The Caste System and its Implications*. M. Sainsbury, L. Dumont, and B. Gulati, trans. Chicago: University of Chicago Press.

———. 1986. *Essays on Individualism: Modern Ideology in Anthropological Perspective*. Chicago: University of Chicago Press.

———. 1994. *German Ideology: From France to Germany and Back*. Chicago: University of Chicago Press.

Eriksen, Annelin. 2005. "The Gendered Dynamics of an Inverted Hierarchy in North Ambrym, Vanuatu." Paper presented at the ESfO conference, Marseilles 2005.

Flannery, Wendy. 1983a. "Religious Movements in Melanesia Today (1)." In *Point* No. 2. Goroka: The Melanesian Institute for Pastoral and Socio-Economic Service.

———. 1983b. "Religious Movements in Melanesia Today (2)." In *Point* No. 2. Goroka: The Melanesian Institute for Pastoral and Socio-Economic Service.

———. 1983c. "Religious Movements in Melanesia: A Selection of Case Studies and Reports." Goroka: The Melanesian Institute for Pastoral and Socio-Economic Service.

———. 1984. "Religious Movements in Melanesia Today (3)." In *Point* Series 4. Goroka: The Melanesian Institute.

Gardner, Don S. 1987. "Spirits and Conceptions of Agency among the Mianmin of Papua New Guinea." *Oceania* 57 (3): 161–177.

Gregory, Chris A. 1982. *Gifts and Commodities*. London: Academic Press.

Jenkins, Philip. 2002. *The Next Christendom: The Coming of Global Christianity*. Oxford: Oxford University Press.

Martin, David. 2002. *Pentecostalism: The World Their Parish*. Oxford: Blackwell.

Meyer, Birgit. 1999. *Translating the Devil: Religion and Modernity among the Ewe in Ghana*. Trenton: Africa World Press.

Munn, Nancy M. 1986. *The Fame of Gawa: A Symbolic Study of Value Transformation in a Massim (Papua New Guinea) Society*. New York: Cambridge University Press.

Ortner, Sherry B. 1994 [1984]. "Theory in Anthropology Since the Sixties." In *Culture/ Power/History: A Reader in Contemporary Social Theory*, ed. N. B. Dirks, G. Eley, and S. B. Ortner. Princeton: Princeton University Press, 372–411.

Patterson, Orlando. 2004. "Culture and Continuity: Causal Structures in Socio-Cultural Persistence." In *Matters of Culture: Cultural Sociology in Practice*, ed. John Mohr and Roger Friedland. Cambridge: Cambridge University Press.

Rio, Knut M. 2005. "Discussions Around a Sand-Drawing: Creations of Agency and Society in Melanesia." *Journal of the Royal Anthropological Institute* 11: 401–423.

Robbins, Joel. 1994. "Equality as a Value: Ideology in Dumont, Melanesia and the West." *Social Analysis* 36: 21–70.

———. 1995. "Dispossessing the Spirits: Christian Transformations of Desire and Ecology among the Urapmin of Papua New Guinea." *Ethnology* 34 (3): 211–224.

———. 2003. "Given to Anger, Given to Shame: The Psychology of the Gift among the Urapmin of Papua New Guinea." *Paideuma* 49: 249–261.

———. 2004a. "The Globalization of Pentecostal and Charismatic Christianity." *Annual Review of Anthropology* 33: 117–143.

———. 2004b. *Becoming Sinners: Christianity and Moral Torment in a Papua New Guinea Society*. Berkeley: University of California Press.

Robbins, Joel, Pamela J. Stewart, and Andrew Strathern. 2001. "Charismatic and Pentecostal Christianity in Oceania." *Journal of Ritual Studies* [special issue] 15 (2).

Schieffelin, Edward L. 1976. *The Sorrow of the Lonely and the Burning of the Dancers*. New York: St. Martin's Press.

Strathern, Marilyn. 1988. *The Gender of the Gift: Problems with Women and Problems with Society in Melanesia*. Berkeley: University of California Press.

Wagner, Roy. 1977. "Analogic Kinship: A Daribi Example." *American Ethnologist* 4 (4): 623–642.

———. 1981 [1975]. *The Invention of Culture*. Chicago: Chicago University Press.

CHAPTER 3

Gender and Value

Conceptualizing Social Forms on Ambrym, Vanuatu

Annelin Eriksen

In this chapter I give "gender" as an analytic category a status beyond that of gendered identities and gendered bodies.[1] My focus will be on gender as a social and structural category. I claim that social "forms," or social "structures," can be gendered. By this I mean that in some societies, gender is a primary category for conceptualizing the dynamics of society. I will show that on Ambrym, an island in the young nation state of Vanuatu in the Southwest Pacific, there are two opposing social forms working to counteract each other, and operating in different contexts historically. When analyzing the impact of colonialism, mission history, and Christianity, it is the relation between these gendered forms, which I focus upon. I apply Dumont's theory on hierarchy and discuss whether gender can be dealt with in terms of encompassing and encompassed values by drawing upon Strathern's model of "the gendered gift" (1988).

In much of Dumont's work the contrast between Indian and European sociality and cultural organization is basic. In this contrast between the West and India, the extreme differences enable us to perceive the value foundation of the two social systems, the individual and the social whole respectively. However, the question becomes: is the hierarchy of India the only alternative model to Western individualism? Are other social systems from other parts of the world only variations of the hierarchical model we find in India? I suggest a slightly alternative structural analysis, deviating from a language of opposite values, and instead focus on *opposing social structuration* in the course of the last fifty to a hundred years of Vanuatu history and the deeper social implications of change in the relation between forms of structuration.

Notes to this section begin on page 109.

Dumont in the Austronesian World

Before entering into my own ethnography, I will outline the broader framework of the Dumontian conceptual apparatus as it has been used in the Austronesian speaking world. I will not outline Dumont's notions of hierarchy and value, as this is already done very thoroughly in the introduction to this volume. Rather, I will point out how his theory has been applied and criticized from the perspective of the Austronesian region. Much of the critique against Dumont from the Austronesian speaking areas of Southeast Asia and the Pacific has circled around his notion of levels (Fox 1989, 1994; Mosko 1994; Jolly 1994). The notion that a reversal of opposing values only takes place at an inferior level implies that there is always only one encompassing value, and that this never alternates equally with the opposite value, only unequally. Through an analysis of Dumont's early writings in comparison with his later, post *Homo Hierarchicus (HH)* writings, Mosko (1994) has argued that it was Dumont's replacement of the pure–impure distinction for the sacred–profane distinction that influenced his model of hierarchy in general. His early writings (Dumont and Pocock 1957; Dumont 1959; etc.) were based on the sacred–profane distinction as the primary distinction and were in this sense within the Durkheimian tradition. Durkheim's argument, in *Elementary Forms of Religious Life* (1915), was that the sacred–profane distinction was a universal and absolute distinction. But, the way Mosko reads him, this distinction was in its nature alterable and reversible; the profane could, for instance in initiation rites, become the sacred. As Dumont's work develops, however, he alters the original Durkheimian notion of the sacred–profane distinction, as well as his own sense of it in his early writings, according to Mosko (1994). As the pure–impure distinction was emphasized at the cost of the sacred–profane distinction, the irreversibility of the hierarchy emerged, because pure–impure, in Dumont's analysis of the Indian material, had this character to a greater extent than the sacred–profane distinction. Mosko points out that Dumont argues the following in relation to levels: "Hierarchy consists in the combination of these two propositions concerning different levels. In hierarchy thus defined, complementariness and contradiction is contained in a unity of a superior order" (1980: 24). This implies that there is no reversal in Dumont's model of hierarchy, where the inferior can become the superior without change of level, and "there is just a single axis of categorical opposition" (Mosko 1994: 45). However, there is an ambivalence in Dumont's work and in the Postface, Dumont expressed it differently, according to Mosko:

Hierarchy assumes the distinction of (two) levels. . . . As soon as we posit a relation of superior to inferior, we must become accustomed to specifying at what level this hierarchical relation itself is sustained. . . . Hierarchy thus offers the possibility of reversal: that which at a superior level was superior may become inferior at an inferior level. The left can become the right in what might be called a "left situation" (Dumont 1980: 244, in Mosko 1994: 46).

Mosko points out that this notion of "levels" is different from the first definition of hierarchy. The inferior level is a different axis, or a second dimension, and Mosko argues: "I suggest therefore that reversals, rather than indicating changes of level or presupposing relations of encompassment, point to inversions or transpositions of the relations between complementarily or asymmetrically opposed terms in accordance with changes of context" (1994: 48). Then Mosko arrives at the following definition of hierarchy as an alternative to the categorical opposition:

Hierarchy consists simply in the complementary or asymmetrical relation between two contrary and mutually opposed terms or categories as composing a single universe of discourse . . . each opposition may serve as the axis upon which the asymmetry of the other may be reversed or inverted so as to produce differentiations among contexts (1994: 49).

This definition, he argues, is more suitable to use in the Austronesian speaking worlds where, "In all such hierarchical systems there are ways in which hierarchy is con–strained and contested, by co-existing egalitarian values, by alternative sources of power" (1994: 10).

It is worth noting that Iteanu (1990) has comparable analyses of Durkheim and Dumont, where he, as does Mosko, takes the difference between the pure–impure and the sacred–profane distinction as his point of departure. Contrary to Mosko, Iteanu argues that it is the sacred-profane distinction, the way it has been analyzed by Durkheim, which is problematic rather than the pure–impure distinction the way Dumont has analyzed it. Whereas Mosko sees the pure–impure distinction as changing the initial dynamic character of the sacred–profane distinction, Iteanu sees the pure–impure distinction as a solution to the internal contradiction inherent in the sacred–profane distinction. Iteanu argues that Durkheim faced a problem because when he compared two Australian totemic religions in *Elementary Forms of Religion*, he argued on the one hand that the sacred and the profane are absolutely distinct and comprise two distinct parts of the social order. On the other hand, in rituals of initiation for example, the profane becomes sacralized as the candidates become more sacred, and this, according to Iteanu, shows that the distinction between the sacred and the profane is not absolute, but rather a matter of degree. Iteanu compares Durkheim's model to Dumont's and argues that by recognizing the hierarchical nature of the concept pair, the paradox is solved. Through a comparison of the pure–impure distinction as outlined by Dumont, Iteanu argues that just as the pure–impure concept pair creates two hierarchies, this is the case for the sacred and profane as well. It is the bidimensional character of the hierarchy that makes the profane become the sacred, at another level. At the level of the profane, the profane may become the sacred, because this is at an inferior level.

This different reading of Durkheim and different evaluation of Dumont can be said to be caused by the evaluation of the fruitfulness of seeing variation in a society as limited by one axis of differentiation. Through an analysis of historical transformations of hierarchy in Vanuatu, Jolly (1994) has argued that there is not *one* value more prominent than others that can be seen as structuring hierarchy in this region. She focuses on three hierarchical oppositions in northern Vanuatu, implied in rank, gender, and place, and compares these to historical hierarchical principles in Fiji. She criticizes Sahlins (1985) for privileging the distinction between chief and commoner as a gendered distinction, and applies Toren's (1990) model of how hierarchy on Fiji works. Toren points out that there is no generalized hierarchy between man and woman, but that there is one between wife and husband, between older and younger, and so on. Jolly argues that Toren (1990) "sees the intersection of these oppositions not as contained within an overarching totality but as constantly generating ambiguities and contestations" (Jolly 1994: 157). In other words, there is no dominant difference to which other differences are related as parts to wholes, in the Dumontian sense. Jolly criticizes Sahlins for taking a position where he puts himself in a privileged place, as a transcendental subject, where he is able to see this totality. There is no such place, according to Jolly, or rather, as she puts it (1994: 161), "I am rather nervous in the face of this monstrous specter of an overarching intellectual sovereignty and would prefer a location which is more partial." No opposition is primary according to Jolly, neither in the Fijian case nor in that of Vanuatu. She argues that there is a range of different axes on which hierarchy is developed, and not only according to one difference.

Values and Gendered Social Forms

In other words, according to the scholars just referred to, the question of whether Dumont's work can be applied to the Austronesian world has become a matter of whether or not we can conceptualize one ultimate value, and whether variation on this value might be regarded as just another context among other kinds of values, or whether this variation must be related to a notion of inferior levels. I will discuss this broad question by drawing on ethnography from one small Melanesian island, Ambrym, in Vanuatu. I will show that in order to understand Ambrym's social organization and cultural system, Dumont's model of a hierarchy organized on an ultimate value is useful. However, although I find a structuring value in this society, it has other implications than the one we find in India. Furthermore, Ambrym hierarchy varies significantly between ritual and everyday contexts. These contexts are interdependent but reveal contrasting dimensions of the social system. They display what I call a logic of "gendered forms" because they are related to male and female ways of relation making. In using these concepts I operate with a fundamental distinction between relations that create what Strathern (1988) has called "personification," and those relations that create "substitution." Strathern has outlined a processual model for social relations in Melanesia where she argues that there are mainly three outcomes of a relationship: personifications, substitutions, and objectifications. I will look more closely at the first two. By personification she refers to a person who is able to represent relationships through his or her person. In other words, one person becomes the representation of a relationship, or many relationships. One might imagine this model as resembling the Russian nesting dolls, the Matryoshka, but without a beginning or an absolute end, and with several stops. At any particular moment, one of the dolls stands out as the representation of every doll, containing many others within her and herself capable of being encompassed. However, the relationship able to create this momentary stop, in which a single person becomes the representation of a whole cosmos of relations, is of a particular kind. This is what Strathern calls "mediated exchanges." Mediated relations are those based upon a gift, in which the giver, being the superior party, takes it upon himself to represent the relationship. An "unmediated relationship" does not take the form of a gift transaction at all, but works as a directly productive relation, in which the object given is typically labor or bodily fluids (semen or mother's milk). We might conceptualize unmediated relationships as work relations in which there is not an explicit giver and receiver and where the outcome does not highlight one of the persons in the relationship, but produces a representation of the whole relationship—a child or an agricultural crop—a "substitution."

I will here take inspiration from Strathern's framework and this distinction between different modalities of relationships and argue that on Ambrym, one of these modalities, the "personification," has traditionally been the dominant mode of relation making. It has also been a mode of relation making connected to manhood. Before returning to the relationship between these two modalities in social process, I will give an outline of the traditional hierarchy on Ambrym: the male secret society. I will argue that we can look on the social activities in these ceremonies as a "distilled" version of "personification." I will then contrast this social form to the social form of everyday life by showing how the latter is driven by a logic of mutual and cooperative work relationships, which does not create the kind of "personifications" that we find in ritual contexts. In order to understand Ambrym hierarchy we need not only understand the internal dynamics of the secret male cults, but we also need to understand how this form relates to the contrasting form it was suppressing and encompassing. In other words, I argue for the usefulness of relating contexts to a notion of levels, supporting the notion of an absolute value. However I will also show that over the last decades, the church has become the main representation of the social form of everyday life. As a consequence, this previously encompassed value of work relations has gained a ritual context for its expression, implying the subordination of the previously highly respected "'personified" form and the traditional ritual context. This has implied a reversal of the value hierarchy, and I thus argue for a perspective on hierarchy that opens for historical change and a reversal of levels diachronically.

The Graded Society

The graded society and ritual hierarchy on Ambrym, a secluded male cult where men buy rights to ceremonial grades, has been in decline over the last decades. Today only a handful of men still take grades and can claim to have rights to the grades of this society. The Ambrym ritual hierarchy was a version of a wider regional phenomenon in north central Vanuatu that has been described for several of the islands (Deacon 1927; Layard 1942; Patterson 1976; Allen 1981; Bonnemaison, Kaufmann, Huffman, and Tryon 1996). Comparing this literature to my own findings during fieldwork in 1995, 1999, and 2000, it is safe to argue that the Ambrym graded society—called locally the *mage*—was at its peak in early colonial times, but was an important social institution up until the late 1970s. Theirs was a society organized in the men's house, where men of the same grade prepared and ate their meals together at the same "taboo fire" (*feangkon*). The cult was regulated by avoidance behavior, and eating with someone of a higher grade could be dangerous, the men's house being ordered along a line of different *feangkon* inward in the building. Although I never witnessed a ceremony on the *mage* myself, I will try to make a short account of what this society was and how its important ceremonies were conducted.

Guiart (1951) described the preparations and performance of a grade taking ceremony on North Ambrym. In 1949 a man from the village Linbul wanted to buy the rights to a graded name, the *mage ne hiwir*, from one of the most renowned men of the *mage* society in Ambrym called Tainmal, who was living in the neighboring village of Fanla. Guiart describes the transactions and exchanges that took place in the days before the ceremony. Pigs were exchanged and work on the ceremonial ground began. In order for the ceremony to be realized, specific elements had to be in place. Among the most important objects was a tree fern image, the *bwerang*. The fern log was erected on the ceremonial ground some days in advance, so that a skilled carver could design a proper image on the tree fern before the ceremony began. This image, of a manly figure with his hands meeting in front of his genitals, represented the specific grade that was going to be achieved during this ceremony. Another grade would be represented by another image. After the payment of pigs to Tainmal, the man from Linbul who was to perform the ceremony had the right to take a new name, as well as the right to erect his own personal grade statue. When the image was completed, a platform was erected above it, almost like a small house for the figure. This platform was beautifully decorated with leaves of croton, cordiline, and water lilies. The ground around the image and the platform was decorated by whitish, sticky water from the breadfruit tree. On the day of the performance, the Linbul man, who was painted in the appropriate colors of black and red, and with rooster feathers in his hair, joined other men who were to achieve other grades purchased from other men in the same graded society. At the end of the ceremony, when a dance had been performed in front of the platform, the candidates concluded by killing one tusker pig for each man from whom a new name was bought. As they clubbed the pigs on top of the platform, the candidates also shouted out their new names.

In general the *mage* consisted of thirteen to fifteen individually named grades (also see Patterson 1981; Rio 2007). Each grade involved payment in the form of pigs, live and dead. For the highest grade, of which there existed three variants all referred to as *mal*, forty pigs were required. Tree fern images or stone dolmens were carved for each grade, and roofs were erected above the statues for every ceremony. When the candidate climbed up on the roof, he literally climbed the *mage*. It was generally known on Ambrym that *mage* was a ritual concept introduced relatively recently, and Patterson (2002) estimates the arrival of the *mage* in Ambrym between the seventeenth and eighteenth century. In the early twentieth century men from Ambrym still travelled to Malekula in order to be initiated into grades in the *mage*. However, according to Patterson (1981, 2002), before the introduction of the *mage*, another variant of the graded society existed on Ambrym, which was to a greater extent part of the kinship structure, building on the principles of paying tribute to the mother's place, and compensating for the blood one has received from this place.[2] These ceremonial institutions were called *bwerang yanyan* and *fenbi*. The ceremonies involved ritual "shooting" of the father and the father's father, who were mourned by the spectators, and payments were made to the "deceased's" mother's place. This was a way of securing regeneration of life and the continuity of kinship structures. When the ceremonial "killer" compensated for the blood that was lost by killing boars for the mother's place, focus was placed on women as carriers of blood and on the importance of attributing offerings of food and pigs to the mother's natal group. By doing this, the "path" was opened for the next generation, and intermarriage between the two places could continue. Because the shooting was only pretended, and the father "turned" back to life, one might claim that the rite made the "candidate" realize that the relation to the mother's place was life giving. According to Patterson, these ceremonies also involved grade taking, killing of pigs, and erection of tree fern statues. The last aspect of this ceremonial complex makes Patterson argue that, "Far from secular, these rites in North Ambrym were the creative basis of ontological and cosmological ideas as well as the means of status differentiation between individuals and groups" (2002: 128).

The Male Social Form

Allen (2000) has recently argued that there is a strong correlation between the structure of society and the kind of male initiation they perform. He has pointed out that ritualized homosexuality for instance mainly occurs in societies with a great man structure (Godelier 1986). This implies direct sister exchange, lack of bridewealth and no competitive exchanges. These societies tend to turn in on themselves instead of seeking social alliances outward to other groups. In these societies men reproduce themselves through inseminating what Allen (2000: 146) calls "cooperative" women, and then later reassuring their reproductive capabilities by inseminating the boys in order to turn them into proper males. In societies with a more outward oriented social structure, we do not find this kind of ritualized homosexuality, according to Allen. Here men seek to create alliances through women from other areas. These women are then potentially dangerous and deceptive, and not necessarily "cooperative." In order for men to reproduce manhood they need to rid their boys of female characteristics, namely blood. Therefore, Allen argues, one finds in these societies a greater degree of penis bleeding in initiation ceremonies, and not ritualized homosexuality. On Ambrym the traditional male cults were of the latter kind. Boys where initiated through penis bleeding ceremonies, called *malyel*, and the focus was on the return of the female blood, as was revealed in the *bwerangyanyan* and the *fenbi* ceremonies. Although I am not sure whether Allen's very general model holds for all societies in Melanesia, I do think he has pointed to an important feature in many Melanesian societies, namely the production and reproduction of gendered forms. Initiation ceremonies create gendered persons and gendered relations by attaching and detaching male and female elements. In the boys' circumcision ceremony on Ambrym, the *malyel*, boys get rid of their remaining female elements, and become men. Through other such rituals throughout their youth—as in the *bwerangyanyan* and the *fenbi* ceremonies—they emphasize their ability to "pay back" blood to various relatives, and thus transcend the female qualities. When as grown ups they were to be initiated into the *mage*, they were already men. The focus was no longer on the return of blood but on the purely male qualities: the competitive aspects and the ability to become a big man, or rather, a "personification" of relationships on a larger scale. The female qualities of boys were totally encompassed. Symbolically the yam on Ambrym is connected to manhood, and at least the rumor has it that small baby boys who were meant for the ritual society of the famous *mage* men, should only eat dry, roasted yam and not be breastfed.

The powers that were achieved in the *mage* seem to have gone beyond any everyday matter. The ceremonies of the *mage* were not part of the kinship payments, as was the case with the *malyel*, *berangyanyan*, or the *fenbi* ceremonies, but existed as a separate sphere of ceremonial exchange. The concerns in the *mage* were not related to the concerns of kinship, namely repaying maternal blood. Rather the purpose of the *mage* was to glorify the performer who reached a new level of fame. The special character of the *mage* ceremonies in contrast to the general ceremonial economy on Ambrym was emphasized by the secrecy it entailed, and the way the ceremonies were conducted in places secluded from female witnesses. It was almost as if the participants had to hide to perform these ceremonies because of their shameless full attention to the male form and their glorification of one person.

I hence suggest that the graded society had as its prime goal to create men who had the ability to represent relationships, and the highest graded men became representations of the society as a whole in their containing capacity. The aim of this grade system was to become the last of the Matryoshka dolls, the absolute "encompasser." Achieving social capacities of this kind also signaled great social skills and magical potency. This was also a dangerous thing to do, and a person with such an enormous encompassing ability could become too potent, and had therefore to eat by himself and live by himself, secluded from the rest of the community (Layard 1949; Patterson 1976; Rio 2007).

Going back to the distinction between different modalities of relationships from Strathern's (1988) analysis, I will argue that, through the graded society, men sought to "stop" or "freeze" the image created in the process of personification. This becomes especially obvious when the ceremonies in the graded society are compared to other ceremonies. Then we clearly see how the process of personification is "purified." Even though the process of personification is most prominent in the men's graded society, it is not limited to this context only. In kinship ceremonies—such as weddings, circumcision ceremonies, or death ceremonies, we find the same effort by one man to stand out as the prime representation of the relationship, in other words as a "personification." However, in ceremonial contexts outside of the *mage*, the process of personification is only momentary. It never lasts. In the next moment, the personifier becomes part of a new relationship in which he is submerged by other relations and new personifiers and substitutions.

In a payment of bridewealth, for instance, the groom and his father spend a number of weeks collecting resources from relatives to whom they themselves have contributed in a previous marriage ceremony. Based on this form of generalized exchange, on the day of the wedding, the father of the groom can present an impressive amount of pigs, yams, and also, in some cases, money. Usually on Ambrym, the ceremonial ground in the village has been decorated and prepared. There are several heaps of yams and other vegetables, and pigs fastened to poles are orderly lined up. People stand around this spectacle on the outskirts of the ceremonial ground. Only the groom and his father and brothers are allowed on to the ceremonial ground. In the act of giving, the father of the groom becomes the personification of all those who have contributed to the payment. This representation is only momentary, however, because in the next instance the ceremony highlights the many relationships that have been vital for the formation not only of the bridewealth, but also in the creation of the bride herself. When the bridewealth has been handed over to the bride's family, the money and pigs are immediately subdivided into different shares. Not only is the bride's agnatic family compensated when she marries, but the bride's maternal family also receives a share of the payment. The bridewealth that is shared out among many makes manifest the concept that the bride is a result of multiple relations. The emphasis is shifted from the personification of the bride's father to the bride herself as having resulted from many relationships. This alternation between different modalities of the relation is common in kinship-based ceremonies. It is only in the *mage* that the image of the personification is not interrupted by the next stage of the relational development. As we saw from the description based on Guiart above, the ceremonies end with the candidate shouting out his new name. After the ceremony the tree fern figure remains on the ceremonial ground as a representation of the man, his new name, and his new taboo fire.

As I have pointed out, on Ambrym this personified form of the relation is gendered. It is male. It is male not because it is usually associated with men's practices. It is the very idea of personification that is male. This does not imply that women do not create personifications. There are in fact many examples of women who do. Layard (1949), for example, describes what he calls the women's *mage* (or *maki*) on Malekula, Ambrym's neighboring island. After having outlined in detail the different stages of the low and high grades of the *mage*, he describes the ceremony in which women buy rights to names and grades in the *mage* as well. This is done at the end of the period of seclusion, which follows from the highest grade in the men's *mage*. Wives of men who have achieved that grade are initiated into the hierarchy. Layard had limited data on this matter, and points out that "women's rites need much fuller investigation" (1949: 454). However, he does point out that the women who entered the graded society took the names of their brothers along with their new titles. In other words, it was only wives of the highest graded men who entered and, when they entered, they took the names of their brothers, thus associating themselves with the male line of their natal place. I will suggest that the few women who entered the graded society took on male qualities. They engaged in a male performance and thus received male names. On Ambrym I have also heard the account of the wife of a man of *mal* rank, the highest grade in the *mage*. She received the grade name after her husband had appropriated a particular grade. To my knowledge, she was the only woman initiated into the *mage* on North Ambrym in recent history. People told many stories about her, and all of these stories reflected the enormous prestige and respect people felt toward her and her husband. These stories also reflected that particular woman's transition from embodying female qualities to male ones. On Ambrym only men are considered sorcerers.[3] After her initiation, however, this woman became capable of sorcery, according to people's stories. Furthermore, whereas it is the normal role of a woman on Ambrym to care for children, this woman became dangerous, especially for children. People on North Ambrym today who tell stories from their childhood remember avoiding the house and the area of this woman. In other words, in spite of the graded society being open for some women, and in spite of women being able to take part in personified forms of social relations, I claim that the personified form on Ambrym is a male form. Furthermore, I will argue also that the *mage* purified form is an alternative form, and not the social form most relevant for ordinary everyday life.

The Male Form and the Social Form of Everyday Life

Harrison (1985) has argued that the male hierarchical cult among the Avatip on the East Sepik of New Guinea operated on a different cultural logic than the secular society. Harrison argues for the existence of two different sociocultural domains, one ritual and the other non-ritual, everyday, and secular. In non-ritual contexts, in matters of kinship for instance, the fundamental ideology was one of equality. The male ritual worked as its antithesis. Instead of talking about different domains, such as the political domain of the male cult and the domestic domain of gender relations, for instance, Harrison argues that these are different forms of social action. The social action that dominates production, for instance, is one of equality. On Ambrym as well, gardening, to take one example, involves cooperation between the spouses. Husband and wife work together, clearing, planting and harvesting. The hierarchy of the male cult does not affect the egalitarian principles that govern productive work. High-ranking men have no coercive power or any other ways of influencing younger men or women in relation to production. About the Avatip, Harrison states that the only power achieved by men in these hierarchical cults is the "power to constitute, occasionally and for limited periods, an altered social reality in which women and junior males are subordinate to them" (1985: 419). Similarly, the "frozen" personification of the *mage* was not achievable outside of the *mage*. However, the *mage* did represent a social form that was highly valued. Although not achievable in its absolute form in everyday life, the personified social form was of ultimate value on Ambrym. The personified form of the *mage* implied a kind of metaphysical power. Layard (1949) describes the Malekula *maki* as a spiritual journey, where the different grades in the secret society represented different stages on the journey to the afterlife. The highest grade involved access to the last "station" of the ancestor spirits, the volcano. We can imagine a society where men, with their grades in the secret initiation society, sought to control the cosmological forces of the world. They sought to create a name that not only was echoed in the here and now but forever.

Anette Weiner (1976) has described a similar gendered contrast between male and female world makings from the Trobriand Islands. The Trobriand women already control the transitions between life and death, through birth and also through control of the mortuary exchanges in the *dala* matrilineage. Men seek to create renowned names through the famous Kula exchanges. Creating names as representations of themselves through the Kula objects becomes their way of transcending the barrier between life and death. The *mage* men achieved this as well, and the metaphysical power they gained became dangerous to other people. The men of the *mage* achieved a transcendental status that made it hard for the most renowned of them, those holding the highest titles, to take part in everyday life. They became *kon*, or "taboo." This implied that they could not eat with others but had to cook on their own fire outside the hamlet. Although sitting there, in solitude, in front of their ceremonial houses and erected fern images, they became representations not only of the society they were secluded from, but also of the afterlife and the ancestral spirits. In their singular person they represented society as a whole. Their ability to create the "frozen" image of themselves, an image that was not deconstructed in the next moment, gave them this position. It was not a position of political power but one of cosmological power. By leaving ordinary society and joining this alternative society, they had disconnected themselves on the one hand from ordinary social life, but on the other had become the ultimate representation of it—a sacred status above ordinary social life.

Understanding Ambrym hierarchy then implies an understanding of two forms of encompassment. First, through the grade taking ceremonies, men in the *mage* became personifications of relations, as total "encompassers." Second, this pure male social form, although an alternative and mostly ceremonial form, was the most highly valued. Thus, the male social form encompassed the other relational forms that did not create stops and personifications. These latter forms were mostly work relationships of the unmediated kind and did not confer status the way in which the personified relations in the *mage* did. Thus, although the cooperative relationships were most prominent in the everyday context, while the personified form was in the background, the personified form was nevertheless the most valued social from, taking place in a context emphasizing cosmological forces. Everyday life was an inferior context, or a subordinated level, in Dumont's words. Let us now have a look at these other kinds of relationships in which substitutions rather than personifications were created.

The Church: a New Ceremonial Form

When describing the prototypical unmediated relationship, Strathern (1988: 199) refers to the Hagen couple who raise pigs, which the husband uses in a Moka exchange.[4] The Moka exchange is only between men. The husband-wife relationship is prior to the Moka exchange, in the same way that the productive relations are prior to the *mage* on Ambrym. The relationship between husband and wife results in products (food, pigs, children, and so on) which Strathern calls "substitution" (Strathern 1988: 183). In the male ceremonial institution, where the husband exchanges the pig, the pig comes to stand for the previous cross sex union, which engendered it. Following Strathern's analysis, and Gell's reinterpretation of it (Gell 1999), the unmediated relationship is composed of a woman doing female work—for instance, feeding the pig—and the man doing male work—for instance, making gardens. When extracted from the cross sex relationship, the grown pig is a substitution, or a manifestation, of the unmediated relation between the husband and the wife.

When the church was established on Ambrym almost a hundred years ago, the male ceremonial form was challenged by a new ceremonial form that did not play on the structure of personification. When the missionaries first arrived on Ambrym, high graded men from the *mage* sought to establish the church as yet another representation of their greatness. This was hard, however. First, it was hard because the missionaries denied the high graded men from the *mage* the right to exclude women, young men, and children from the church (see also Eriksen 2005, 2006). Second, because the church did not welcome the kind of grand and materialist ceremonies the *mage* represented. Traditional objects and representations were not allowed in the church. Gradually another social logic came to dominate the church, wherein expressions of the product of relationships more than the personifications of them became primary.

The social form of the church echoed the cooperative form. This is particularly evident today in the fundraisings frequently arranged by the church: people contribute food, garden produce, and handicrafts, sell them between each other, often sharing a communal meal, and contribute the money to the church. Individual labor is here transformed into relational products through the church, without taking on a personified, mediated form. People pool and share, on fundraisings for instance but also during one of the most important church based ceremonies today, the New Yam. I have described elsewhere (Eriksen 2005) how New Yam was transformed, as it became a church based ceremony, from a personified social form into a social form no longer focusing on singular persons but on the product of relationships. The first Ambrym missionary, Murray, described in his diary a first fruit ceremony he witnessed in North Ambrym in 1889 (see Eriksen 2005). Here the ceremony is described as a male matter. No woman was allowed on to the ceremonial ground. Paton (1979) has also described an early version of the New Yam ceremony:

> When all seemed ready, the men took the yams and bananas into the centre of the enclosure, and placed them in a heap, yams resting against the bananas. Hanlam took in his hand a small bundle of sticks called *muju*, which represents yam. With the *muju* in his left hand, he moved to the further side of the *hara*, enclosure, and made passes with the *muju* in various directions. He was said to be thinking about the yam in all the surrounding villages, and, in a sense, to be "praying for a good crop for all." He then turned full on to the gathering of men, and gave the sign for the climax of the ceremony.
>
> One man, squatted in front of the two drums (*atingting*), heartily began to beat a specific rhythm. . . . Being specific rhythms significant of the New Yam ceremonies, they carried the message to the surrounding villages, where other drums began to beat and spread the message further. . . . The rhythm was said to represent the sound of rainwater. . . .
>
> During all these proceedings the women stood watching from beyond the stone walls of the enclosure.
>
> At the same time as the vigorous beating of the drums, the conch shells were blown, and all the men shouted and cheered, and threw oranges out beyond the enclosure, mainly in the direction beyond the spot where Hanlam stood during his part in the ritual. They were said to be chasing away the old year, or the old yam.
>
> To end the formal proceedings, the food is piled in little heaps, much care being taken to divide it equally or fairly equally; and the piles are then distributed, as free gifts, among all the men (Paton 1979: 42).

We see here that large walls of palm leaves were raised in order to seclude the event from the sphere of women. Men blew in the conch shell, danced, sang, and exchanged yams. Single men represented the heaps of yams they piled up for the ceremony and held speeches. Women were only allowed to peek from behind the enclosure. Today the structure of the ceremony is inverted in North Ambrym. Women are almost the only ones present, and men are the spectators. The main part of the ceremony involves women bringing yams to the church, praying for the yam, and then redistributing them. Furthermore, the focus is now on a communal meal that is cooked by the end of the ceremony and shared by all agnatic relatives. The New Yam has become a church based ceremony and the focus is on the communal production and the sharing out of the surplus harvest. The social form of the church is thus about creating unmediated relationships based on generalized exchanges and work relations.

Others have argued that the church might represent a new arena for big men to develop their authority, and thus, in Strathern's conceptual apparatus, create personifications (see, for instance, Allen 1981). There are positions in the church which seem to create a hierarchy of authority, such as, for the Presbyterian Church on Ambrym: priest, elder, and deacon. To some extent, I think these are positions that stand out from the rest of the congregation. Those in these positions have a more formal connection to the church than do the other villagers. However, based on my experience in North Ambrym, I do not think they create the kind of status the graded society did. Although the priest holds a position where he can confront the congregation, talk, and, for instance, lead fund raisings (as in fact the elder and the deacon can also), he does not take the leading role in exchange relationships. His position in the church does not separate members of the congregation from one another as a result of how they operate in relations. However, as I have argued elsewhere (Eriksen 2004), the priest's position in the church might give him an advantage in other contexts, for instance in national politics. In recent Ambrym history there is evidence for arguing that the church can create leaders for other contexts, such as representatives for regional or national assemblies. However, this is a position outside of Ambrym. When these leaders return home, they are confronted with the egalitarian and cooperative mode of the church and everyday life, and do not hold a special kind of authority. As my reference to some of the important ceremonies in the church suggests, the focus is on the contribution from the community as a whole, and not from specific persons. Furthermore, the church on Ambrym has become the framework for communal work. Whenever there is a need for organized communal effort, for instance fixing the local road, clearing up the village after a hurricane, and so on, this will be organized in the church.

It is also interesting that, except for the role of a priest, in the Presbyterian Church on Ambrym, these positions are gender neutral. Both men and women become elders in the church. Both men and women can talk to the congregation. Thus the focus is not on exclusiveness. The church is not an arena for particular persons, but for cooperation. The social form of the church on Ambrym creates social wholes.

Although Strathern (1988) herself usually refers to relations on microlevels—relations between husband and wife, and relations between exchange partners—I use her model of mediated and unmediated relations on a different scale. I suggest that on Ambrym, the church is a substitution for unmediated relationships, as it stands for the totality of relations in the church. When people give yams to the church during church service on the morning of the New Yam ceremony, for instance, every household, usually represented by a woman, contributes a yam to the church, placing it in front of the altar. The yams that have been pooled by various households are then sold and the money kept in the church. This event involves, first, the donation of the yams to the church by the women representing different households (or cross sex relationships), and then the buying of the yams by the women. The same woman who first gave a yam then buys a yam, although a different one. I will argue that this is not an exchange, but rather "work." By the concept "work" here, I invoke the content of unmediated relations the way Strathern uses the concept (Strathern 1988, see for instance p. 183). The outcome of the relation then is not a personification (as in exchanges) but a substitution. This is comparable to the prototypical cross sex relationship between the husband and wife in Strathern's model outlined above, in which the wife feeds the pig by giving it sweet potato (female work) which the man has grown in their garden (male work). This relationship is unmediated because it involves "work" and not "objectifications." The relationships between the different households, represented through women in female-female relationships, which involve first the "work" of donation and then the "work" of buying, produce the church as a representation of the relationship between the households, just as the pig is a representation of the fruitful relationship between the married couple. The church then is unmediated in its form.

The Inverted Hierarchy

The church is a relatively new social institution, whereas the *mage* has longer historical roots. However, the church has grown as a social movement, whereas the *mage* is in decline. This has had implications for the form social relations take on Ambrym today. Whereas the *mage* represented the competitive male personified form, the church represents relations without personifications, what I have called an unmediated social form. Men, who seek to succeed and manage the former social form, are thus not so interested in the church. Ceremonies in the church, such as the "New Yam," blessings, and services take on an unmediated form that cannot result in personifications. The churches on Ambrym today are manifestations of social communities, and of "social wholes." The church cannot be manifestations of one man as an isolated person. With Strathern's conceptual apparatus, I suggest that the church cannot create "relations which separate" (Strathern 1988: 191). Strathern has argued that an exchange creates separation between the involved persons. This separation is necessary for the process of personification. Separations between persons are created in order to differentiate between them. In relations where separations are not created, the focus on the whole is reinforced. Within the church there is no room for separations through exchanges. There are no objects referring back to only one person's achievement, as there were in the men's graded society, the *mage*. During the *mage* ceremonies, the pigs that were killed, as well as the tree fern statues that were erected, pointed to one man and his greatness. The church, on the other hand, both in contexts such as fund-raising events and markets, as well as in ceremonies, does the opposite. I have outlined how men in traditional exchange contexts sought to eclipse the social whole in order to emerge as the one person who performs an exchange. Traditional ceremonies opened for these kinds of performances, and the ceremonies of the *mage* in particular highlighted individual men's performances. Church based ceremonies, such as fundraising events and New Yam distributions, do not make room for these male practices. One might claim that the old ceremonies in the graded society focused on one particular person and thereby eclipsed the total social whole, whereas the church does the opposite. In the church based New Yam ceremony, specific work relations are eclipsed, and the total social whole is focused upon. This is a radical transformation of the social form of the ceremonial economy on Ambrym, caused by a shift from a male to a female form of expressing social relations. Ceremonies are today to an increasing extent performed and enacted within the framework of the church. The female form, then, has gained a ceremonial context for its expression, and I will argue that this has caused a reversal of the value hierarchy. We can understand the implications of Christianity on Ambrym as a process where an earlier sub-ordinated value (the female social from) has gained a context (the church). This context has challenged the existing value (the male social form, the personification), and forced it into the background.

Understanding Change

The personified form was the dominant form in the past. It was through the personifying ceremonies in the *mage* that men achieved status and metaphysical power. This is not the case today. Rather it is through the egalitarian institution of the church that both men and women manage to influence the community. Through work that is channeled through the church, which might be fundraisings or different kinds of develop-ment projects, the social form of the unmediated exchange has gained a new significance. Hierarchy on Ambrym has changed in two senses. First, the graded society, where men literally climbed the hierarchy and achieved degrees of cosmological power, is in decline. Second, today the relational form of this hierarchy, the personified form, which in the past had an encompassing position, is realized to a lesser degree. The unmediated form, what I have also called the "work" relations, has gained a new significance also in the ceremonial domain. It is clear, then, that Christianity on Ambrym has affected radically the social intuitions of this society; not by introducing a completely new value, however, but rather by foregrounding a value that had been of lesser significance in the past.

Robbins (in this volume) has shown that Christianity led to a much more dramatic kind of change among the Urapmin in the Mountain Ok region of the western highlands of Papua New Guinea. He argues that Christianity brought along the idea of the individual as the ultimate value and that this value was incompatible with the already existing value, that of relationships. It was primarily the need for individual salvation that prevented the relational form from persisting. Salvation is always an individual matter, and Robbins has shown elsewhere (2002) the problems that occurred for the Urapmin as they tried to make sense of the content of Christianity, especially the concept of salvation, in terms of their preexisting value system. One of Robbins' informants stated: "My wife can't break off part of her belief and give it to me." Salvation is not a relational phenomenon. It is the individual belief that on the last day will save the soul. The belief in the imminent return of Jesus and the day of Judgment made it necessary for the Urapmin to deal with the problem of salvation. The unit of salvation is the individual and not the relationship.

On Ambrym, as we have seen from my analysis above, Christianity did not transform the relational value into the value of individualism. Presbyterian Christianity, as it has gradually developed there for over a hundred years, did not create that notion of individual salvation. In the church ceremonies on Ambrym, as well as when people talk about the church in general, the idea of moral behavior is more central than individual salvation. Moral behavior—such as not drinking, smoking, dancing, and not spending all the money on consumer items for oneself, is compatible with the value of maintaining social relationships. However, the relational value on Ambrym had several forms, one encompassing the other. Christianity led, as we have seen, to the inversion of this hierarchical relationship between the relation forms. Why did Christianity there not bring about the value of individualism the way it did among the Urapmin?

In order to answer this, the specific colonial situation in the Papua New Guinea Highlands must be compared to another, different colonial history in Vanuatu. Whereas the Urapmin had their first colonial visit in the late 1950s, and Christianity, specifically Pentecostal Christianity, arrived most forcefully in the 1970s, Vanuatu and Ambrym have had well over a hundred years of colonial experience. Christianity was introduced to plantation migrants already around 1860, and people in these islands came into regular contact with missionaries from 1880. Whereas the Urapmin's encounter with colonialism and Christianity was intense and shocking, people on Ambrym had a very gradual accommodation to the colonial regime and Christian ideas. Robbins has described the Urapmin encounter with the Christian worldview as "humiliating" (Robbins 2004). He argues that a period of rapid change took place after the colonial patrol station was set up in the Ok area. Living at the bottom of a valley, the Urapmin had difficult access to the administrative center. They thus had limited access to trading Western goods and gaining knowledge about the new worldview. Their neighbors, mainly the Telefolmin, were much more privileged. They had easy access to the new resources. As a consequence, the precolonial intergroup system was influenced more by the new elements, and the Urapmin did not gain the upper hand. This new economic and political shift in combination with other factors, such as the patrol officer's effort to control the Urapmin and introduce new laws, led to an intense feeling of humiliation among the Urapmin. This humiliation was also enhanced by the feeling that their cultural system, their way of thinking about the world, could not make sense of what was happening. They lacked an explanation. The belief in their own sinfulness became one such explanation. They needed new laws to govern them. They needed new ideas to make sense of the world. Christianity and the value of the individual provided this.

On Ambrym the value of relationships was never challenged in the forceful way it was among the Urapmin. The relational system was also developed in a very complex way on Ambrym. The two relational forms, the male and the female, were clearly and institutionally separated. The ritual hierarchy contributed to this development where the gendered forms became so distinct. It was the internal hierarchy between the two relational forms that was affected when the church as a social system and Christianity as a value system were introduced. Thus, returning to the problem of levels and contexts with which I started this chapter, one cannot understand hierarchy on Ambrym by focusing on single contexts. Hierarchy cannot be understood partially. The development of the church must be seen in opposition to the *mage*. Different contexts, such as the church and the *mage*, must be related to each other in order for a view of the total social system to emerge. Understanding social life on Ambrym implies not only an understanding of the principles ordering the different contexts and situations, but also how these are related to each other, and the reason that one value emerges in one context and not in another. When Mosko (1994) argues that hierarchy must be contextual and cannot be based on one categorical opposition, he is arguing for several equal value systems existing synchronically. Jolly (1994), as well, as I pointed out in my introduction, cannot imagine a value that unites all differentiating mechanisms. She argues that hierarchy must be contextual, and that there is not one value but several, which can organize differences. For Ambrym, a partial understanding of hierarchy—for instance an analysis of the social form of the church without a parallel analysis of the *mage*, would miss the way these contexts are related to each other. However, the Ambrym case also shows that, although contexts are ordered according to an absolute value, this value might not be stable over time. This implies that change of value does take place, not only at an inferior level. Both the Urapmin and the Ambrym cases show that ultimate values are reversible, not synchronically, but through historical transformation.

Notes

1. This chapter is based on doctoral work from Ambrym Island, where I did fieldwork between 1996 and 2000. This material is also part of my monograph *Gender, Christianity and Change in Vanuatu* (Eriksen 2008). I thank the editors for valuable comments, and I am also grateful to Fred Damon for a thorough reading and valuable comments.
2. Ambrym social organizations are based in principle on three places: the place of the agnatic line (*wuruen*), one's mother's agnatic line (*mukuen*), and one's wife's agnatic line (*gemalsul*) (see Patterson 1976, Eriksen 2004, chapter 2, for an outline and discussion of this).
3. Women might be the victims, and sometimes the innocent vehicles, of sorcery, but seldom the agents of sorcery (see also Patterson 1976; Rio 2002).
4. Strathern builds extensively on her own ethnographic material from Mount Hagen in the Papua New Guinea Highlands.

References

Allen, Michael, ed. 1981. *Vanuatu: Politics, Economics and Ritual in Island Melanesia*. Sydney: Academic Press Australia.

———. 1981. "Innovation, Inversion and Revolution as Political Tactics in West Aoba." In *Vanuatu: Politics, Economics and Ritual in Island Melanesia*, ed. Michael Allen. Sydney: Academic Press Australia, 105–135.

———. 1984. "Elders, Chiefs and Big Men: Authority, Legitimation and Political Evolution in Melanesia." *American Ethnologist* 11: 20–41.

———. 2000. *Ritual, Power and Gender: Explorations in the Ethnography of Vanuatu, Nepal and Ireland*. New Delhi: Sydney Studies in Society and Culture (Manohar).

Bonnemaison, J., C. Kaufmann, K. Huffman, and D. Tryon, ed. 1996. *Arts of Vanuatu*. Bathhurst: Crawford House Publishing.

Deacon, Bernard. 1927. "The Regulation of Marriage on Ambrym." *Journal of the Royal Anthropological Society* 57: 325–42.

———. 1934. *Malekula: A Vanishing People in the New Hebrides*. London: Routledge and Kegan Paul.

Dumont, Louis. 1959. "Pure and Impure." *Contributions to Indian Sociology* 3: 9–39.

———.1979. "The Anthropological Community and Ideology." *Social Science Information* 18: 785–817.

———. 1980. *Homo Hierarchicus: The Caste System and its Implications* (complete revised English edition). Trans. M. Sainsbury, L. Dumont, and B. Gulati. Chicago: The University of Chicago Press.

———. 1986. *Essays on Individualism: Modern Ideology in Anthropological Perspective*. Chicago: The University of Chicago Press.

Dumont, Louis and D. F. Pocock. 1957. "For a Sociology of India." *Contributions to Indian Sociology* 1: 8–22.

Durkheim, Emile. 1961 [1915]. *Elementary Forms of Religious Life*. Trans. J. B. Swan. New York: Collier.

Eriksen, Annelin. 2004. "Silent Movement: Transformations of Gendered Social Structures in North Ambrym, Vanuatu." Dissertation for the degree of Dr. Polit., University of Bergen.

———. 2005. "The Gender of the Church: Conflicts and Social Wholes on Ambrym, Vanuatu." *Oceania* 75 (3): 284–301.

———. 2006. "Expected and Unexpected Cultural Heroes: Reflections on Gender and Agency of Conjuncture on Ambrym, Vanuatu." *Anthropological Theory* 6: 227–247.

———. 2008. *Gender, Christianity and Change in Vanuatu: An Analysis of Social Movements in North Ambrym*. Aldershot: Ashgate.

Gell, Alfred. 1999. *The Art of Anthropology: Essays and Diagrams*. London: Athlone Press.

Godelier, Maurice. 1986. *The Making of Great Men: Male Domination and Power among the New Guinea Baruya*. Cambridge: Cambridge University Press.

Guiart, Jean. 1951. "Société, Rituels et Mythes du Nord Ambrym." *Journal de la Société des Oceanistes* 7: 5–103.

Harrison, Simon. 1985. "Ritual Hierarchy and Secular Equality in a Sepik River Village." *American Ethnologist* 12 (3): 413–426.

Iteanu, André. 1989. "Sacred and Profane Revisited: Durkheim and Dumont Considered in the Orokaiva Context." *Ethnos* 55: 169–183.

Jolly, Margaret. 1994. "Hierarchy and Encompassment: Rank, Gender and Place in Vanuatu and Fiji." *History and Anthropology* 7: 133–167.

Kapferer, Bruce. 1988. *Legends of People, Myths of State: Violence, Intolerance, and Political Culture in Sri Lanka and Australia*. Washington, D.C.: Smithsonian Institution Press.

Layard, John. 1942. *Stone Men of Malekula*. London: Chatto and Windus.

Mauss, Marcel. 1990 [1925]. *The Gift: The Form and Reason for Exchange in Archaic societies*. Trans. W. D. Halls. London: Routledge.

Mosko, Mark S. 1994. "Transformations of Dumont: The Hierarchical, the Sacred and the Profane in India and Ancient Hawaii." *History and Anthropology* 7: 19–87.

Paton. W. F. 1979. *Customs of Ambrym*. Pacific Linguistics series D-22. Canberra: The Australian National University.

Patterson, Mary. 1976. "Kinship, Marriage and Ritual in North Ambrym." Ph.D. dissertation. University of Sydney.

————.1981. "Slings and Arrows: Rituals of Status Acquisition in North Ambrym." In *Politics, Economics and Ritual in Island Melanesia*, ed. M. Allen. Sydney: Academic Press Australia.

————. 2002. "Moving Histories: An Analysis of Place and Mobility in North Ambrym, Vanuatu." *The Australian Journal of Anthropology* 13 (2): 200–218.

Rio, Knut M. "The Sorcerer as an Absented Third Person: Formations of Fear and Anger in Vanuatu." Social Analysis 46 (2): 129–154.

————. 2007. *The Power of Perspective: Social Ontology and Agency on Ambrym, Vanuatu*. New York and Oxford: Berghahn Books.

Robbins, Joel. 2002. "My Wife Can't Break Off Part of Her Belief and Give It to Me: Apocalyptic Interrogations of Christian Individualism among the Urapmin of Papua New Guinea." *Paideuma* 48:189–206.

————. 2004. *Becoming Sinners: Christianity and Moral Torment in a Papua New Guinea Society*. Berkeley: University of California Press.

Sahlins, Marshall. 1985. *Islands of History*. Chicago: The University of Chicago Press.

Strathern, Marilyn. 1988. *The Gender of the Gift*. Berkeley: California University Press.

————. 1996. "Cutting the Network." *Journal of the Royal Anthropological Institute* 2: 517–535.

Toren, Christina. 1990. *Making Sense of Hierarchy: Cognition as Social Process in Fjii*. London School of Economics Monographs on Social Anthropology 61. London: Athlone Press.

Weiner, Annette B. 1976. *Women of Value, Men of Renown: New Perspectives in Trobriand Exchange*. Austin, Tex.: University of Texas Press.

CHAPTER 4

Can a Hierarchical Religion Survive without Its Center?

Caodaism, Colonialism, and Exile

Janet Hoskins

The new religion of Caodaism has been described both as a form of "Vietnamese traditionalism" (Blagov 2001) and "hybrid modernity" (Thompson 1937). It has been seen both as conservative and outrageous, nostalgic and futuristic. This paper explores that meddling of different oppositions in a religion which Clifford Geertz has called *"un syncrétism à l'outrance"*—an excessive, even transgressive blending of piety and blasphemy, respectful obeisance and rebellious expressionism, the old and the new. These apparently contradictory descriptions of Caodaism revolve around its relation to hierarchy, and in particular the ways in which its new teachings have played havoc with the hierarchy of the races in colonial Indochina, the hierarchy of the sexes in East Asian traditions, and the hierarchy of religion and politics in French Indochina, the Republic of South Vietnam, and the postwar Socialist Republic of Vietnam. Since the fall of Saigon in 1975, the exodus of several million Vietnamese has brought Caodaism to the United States, Canada, Australia, and Europe, with the largest congregations in California. Separated from religious centers in Vietnam, which were largely closed down for about twenty years, overseas Caodaists have had to consider how to revise the hierarchies of their faith in a new land, and whether to focus on diasporic virtual communities or evangelizing a global faith of unity.

The new forms of hierarchy which emerged in French Indochina in the 1920s were born in the context of anticolonial, nationalist resistance, which created an alliance between former mandarins trying to restore Vietnam's cultural heritage and young civil servants interested in poetic experimentation, spiritism, and social revolution. Seeking to go beyond the limits imposed on them by colonial society, they made contact with Cao Dai, the Supreme Being, who was at the same time the Jade Emperor of Taoist tradition and the father of Jesus. Evoking the new spiritual power of an activist, monotheistic faith that combined Confucian, Taoist, and Buddhist teachings, this doctrine was perceived by French colonial officers as profoundly transgressive. In a structural sense, transgression consists of a negation of difference between two hierarchical positions (Valeri 1985: 164). The transgressor of hierarchical taboos does not recognize the distinctions that constitute the society that he is part of, and so endangers the entire social order as it is constituted. Following transgression, the whole society suffers the disaggregating effects of possible undifferentiation.

The first role of the successful transgressor, therefore, is to erect a new hierarchy, but one that inverts certain key positions and reorders the society on his own terms. This is more or less what the founders of Caodaism did, in creating a hierarchically ordered religion which seemed in some ways to present a pastiche of Roman Catholic social organization, with its own Pope, female Cardinals, Bishops and Archbishops, and so on. What was different about this new hierarchy and new pantheon was that, while Jesus and Moses were included, they were hierarchically encompassed by Asian spiritual leaders like Buddha, Confucius, and Lao Tse. And they were led by a spiritual Pope who was the epitome of Chinese literary culture: the Tang dynasty poet Ly Thai, who reestablished Chinese literature after it own period of destruction and chaos in the sixth century c.e.

The birth of Caodaism in 1926 has been interpreted as a response to the cultural dislocations of the colonial encounter, described by the paramount spirit medium Pham Cong Tac as a *bouleversement total* of all prevailing forms of order, a topsy-turvy inversion of all established values. Its rebirth on foreign shores, in communities stretching from California to Montreal, from Sydney to Paris, followed a situation of even greater trauma—loss of the country, massive arrests and internments, and dangerous escapes in boats, which produced almost as many victims as survivors. The challenges that Caodaism first faced in the early twentieth century—healing the wounds of colonialism, restoring the vitality of Vietnamese heritage—were made even more intense by the conditions of refugee resettlement and global dispersal. The hierarchies of the early age of revelations were called into question and rethought in the new world, where members of the overseas community have struggled to achieve consensus.

Caodaism's eclecticism has fascinated many visitors and writers, but it has also attracted an almost unparalleled series of attacks on its credibility and integrity, from an early description by Norman Lewis of its Holy See in Tay Ninh as "the most outrageously vulgar building ever to have been erected with serious intent" (1951: 44) to the recent account by Carsten

Jensen (2001: 220) of the faith as the creation of the "half-educated" and "half integrated" who turn to superstition as opposed to religion. In probing the reasons for the passion behind these attacks, I suggest that they erect a category defined by the intersection of "good taste" and "devout faith," which is deliberately calibrated to exclude the transgressive mixtures of a cosmopolitan spirituality, particularly when that spirituality is based on an Asian synthesis of religious elements rather than a Western one. While the patronizing attitude of these commentators is presented as a defense of civilized European aesthetics against the "grotesque forms" (Lewis 1951: 44 and Jensen 2001: 221) of those less educated than themselves, in fact these authors betray their own continuing colonial mentalities in a rather raw and unmediated form.

Old Hierarchies and New Ones: Caodai Syncretism

In a séance held on the island of Jersey 29 September 1854, "Death" spoke to Victor Hugo and gave him some excellent publishing advice: "In your Last Will and testament, space out your posthumous works, one every ten years, one every five years . . . Jesus Christ rose from dead only once. You can fill your grave with resurrections. . . . You can have an extraordinary death; you can say while dying, you will awaken me in 1920, you will awaken me in 1940 . . . in 1960 . . . in 1980, you will awaken me in the year 2000" (Chambers 1998: 178–79). The purpose of these reawakenings was to "be able to talk to posterity and tell it unknown things which will have had time to ripen in the grave" (Chambers 1998: 178), so that Hugo's death itself "would be a formidable rendezvous arranged with the light and a formidable threat launched against the night" (Chambers 1998: 179). Hugo followed this advice, and published fifteen works posthumously, extending his publishing career from 1822 to 1951. Hugo described the spirit séances as "those works willed by me to the twentieth century" (Chambers 1998: 180); "probably the basis of a new religion," and noted that by the time they appeared, "it will be discovered that my revelation has already been revealed" (Chambers 1998: 180). Transcripts of the séances were not published until 1923, in Gustave Simon's *Chez Victor Hugo. Les tables tournantes de Jersey* (Paris: Conrad 1923).[1] Hugo also produced a series of ink paintings based on his visions, including one (*Soleil d'Encre*) not published until 1985, which bears an uncanny resemblance to Caodai temple images of the Eye of God.

The new religion called Caodai was announced in a séance in Saigon on Christmas Eve 1925, but visions of the divine eye had—as Hugo predicted—already been revealed to Ngo Minh Chieu, the governor of the island province of Phu Quoc. God announced to his disciples that this new faith was a syncretic product of a global age of communication:

> Formerly people lacked transportation and did not know each other. So I founded five branches of the Great Way-Confucianism, ancestor worship, the worship of saints, immortals and Buddhas, each based on the customs of its respective race. But people do not live in harmony because of religious differences, so I have now come to unite all religions back into one, restoring their primordial unity (séance in January 1926, Bui and Beck 2000: 14).

This new religion emerged as a response to the crisis of modernity and particularly of literacy—the Supreme Being made his first appearance as the first three letters of the Romanized Vietnamese alphabet (a á ae). It was born, as it has been argued, as nationalism was also born, in the context of the new possibilities opened up by print capitalism (Anderson 1983), and it is expanding now through an online network, where the divergent branches and orthodoxies are best identified by their Web sites.

Caodaists worship a pantheon of nine deities, beginning with the Left Eye of God, whose radiant light shines out from the top of every one its temples and cathedrals. Below that stands Buddha, flanked by Lao Tse on his right and Confucius on his left, then Li Tai Pe (the famous Chinese poet from the Tang Dynasty), flanked by the female Bodhisattva Quan Am, and the terrifying red faced warrior Quan Cong, followed by Jesus Christ on the third level showing his bleeding heart, and Khuong Thai Cong on the fourth level, representing East Asian traditions of venerating heroes, spirits, and ancestors.

The saints of Caodaism—who famously include figures like Sun Yat-Sen, Mohantas Gandhi, Vladimir Lenin, Joan of Arc, Shakespeare, Descartes, La Fontaine, and Louis Pasteur—are not the products of a bureaucratic canonization process as in the Catholic Church, but are instead the spirits of great men and women who chose to reveal themselves to Caodai spirit mediums and engage in a conversation with sages of all ages about the proper direction that the new religion should take. The main scriptures of Caodaism—its sutras or sacred texts—are derived from 169 spirit messages (selected from many thousands of others) received by Tay Ninh mediums from Christmas Eve 1925 until 1935, and these spirit messages instructed the original twelve disciples on how to build their churches and cathedrals, which prayers and offerings to make, and how to lead a religious movement which should eventually establish peace and harmony between all peoples, races, and religions. Victor Hugo is, among all these saints and sages—the vast majority of them Asian—the spiritual head of the overseas mission, and his spirit is thus particularly important to those missionaries who are now trying to spread the faith in the New

World. They are all, in the broadest sense, the "spiritual sons of Victor Hugo," and also his students in the great "school for spirits" that Victor Hugo described in séances in 1929 and 1930.

Vietnam went through rapid linguistic transformations at the beginning of the period of French domination, characterized by a historicist feeling of living in totally novel times after a thousand years of a deliberately traditional society, which was perceived as remaining relatively unchanged. The effect of French language schooling was to create a Eurocentric cosmopolitanism: "Within a single generation not only were the most educated Vietnamese unable to read Chinese or Japanese, but they were incapable of reading anything that any Vietnamese had written during the previous two millennia. . . . Intellectually ambitious members of the interwar elite were left with little choice but to immerse themselves in the literary traditions of France and its European neighbors" (Zinoman 2002: 11). The reliability of language in general came into question, as did the unstable relationship between knowledge and power.

Caodaism appealed to a new generation educated in French but still loyal to elements of Vietnamese tradition. Converts during the first few decades of its existence were drawn to it because it was a religion where they could find a spiritual home. One man who converted to the religion in mid life remembered its appeal this way:

When I was young, I was on a quest to find the right faith. My family was Buddhist and worshipped ancestors, but they did not have much to say about the modern world. I went to a Catholic boarding school, and my French teachers wanted me to convert. But they taught me that our ancestors were really evil spirits. I could not accept that, I wanted something more inclusive. The Christians say they have a universal faith, but it seemed to exclude Asian traditions and to teach feudal values. Buddhism has idealistic values, but it did not help people in the time of French colonialism. When I found Caodaism, it was like coming home: The rituals and altars were familiar, but the message was more universal. It was a way to worship one God, but to see him as the father of all. . . . Kipling said, "East is East and West is West and never the twain shall meet." In Caodaism, we are proving that he was wrong.

Many of the Vietnamese civil servants who founded Caodai were graduates of the finest *lycée* in the colony (Chasseloup Laubat), and held stable, responsible jobs as in the offices of taxation, public works, or the railroads. But "in relation to their mostly French superiors, they were no more than simple servants. The democracy, equality, fraternity and liberty they had been taught as vague notions on their school benches were simply dead words in a textbook. Living estranged from the colonial community and separated from the mass of their own compatriots who looked at them with suspicion and distrust, they suffered from the moral solitude of a subaltern.

Their life, at a certain moment, seemed blocked to them. Those who had natural poetic gifts had recourse to the imaginative escapism of words, often in exchanges of verses at evening meetings where young people of both sexes gathered to celebrate the lyric muse." (Tran Thu Dung 1996: 40, translation mine).

These young intellectuals were also reading the work of European spiritualists like Flammarion and Alain Kardec. Kardec's *Le Livre des Esprits*, first published in 1857, was particularly influential in establishing a new technology for contacting the invisible world. Table turning (the method Victor Hugo used on the island of Jersey) was supplemented by the beaked basket. Kardec received spirit messages telling him to fit a pencil to a small basket. "This basket, placed on a sheet of paper, was then to be set in motion by the same invisible force that moved the tables. The pencil would trace letters that formed words, sentences, and entire discourses on philosophy, ethics, metaphysics, and psychology, writing as quickly as the human hand" (Kardec [1860] 2002: 8). In Saigon, the beaked basket was known as the "greater tool" (*grand appareil*), while another small board with the letters of the alphabet on it (called a *planchette*) was the "smaller tool" (*petit appareil*). On 3 January 1926, God instructed his disciples in Saigon about the method, which had also been used by Taoist occultists of the Tang dynasty period in China (Smith 1970, part 3: 20):

> The spirit is your second body. It is very difficult for the spirit of a human being to transcend the physical body. The spirits of Saints, Immortals, and Buddhas are very marvelous and immortal. The spirit of an enlightened person may transcend the body and even travel the universe. Only the spirit may approach Me. When the basket with beak is used in spiritism, if the person is unconscious, the spirit may then leave the physical body, hear My instructions, and have the body transcribe the messages. If the interpreter's reading is incorrect, the medium's spirit will not agree with the interpretation. They will be obliged to write again. In the other form of spiritual contact known as automatic writing, or inspired writing, I will come to you and make your spirit unstable for a while. During that time, your spirit will be able to listen to Me. Your hand will obey and write. In this form of spiritual contact, I cooperate with you so that you can reach Universal Truths.

Caodaists were aware of intersections between ancient Chinese spiritist techniques and the modern vogue for table turning in France. For them, Victor Hugo's séance transcripts provided a "magic mirror in which Oriental readers met the political and religious thoughts of Buddhism and Taoism" (Tran Thu Dung 1996: 190). It was shock of recognition—seeing notions of reincarnation and communication between the living and the dead being embraced by a great French intellectual—that proved exciting and inspiring. Since Caodai was from its conception a religion with global aspirations, the selection of Hugo was also strategic: he embodied the sweeping oceanic vision of French romanticism, and by adding the exotic appeal of the colonies, created a combination that was to fascinate—although also at times to repel—a great many people who visited Caodai temples and cathedrals. The reaction of Westerners was mixed. French authorities kept a close eye on the new religion, afraid that it could become the basis for a form of "cultural nationalism," which would fuel anticolonialist revolt. Some Western observers, like the American Virginia Thompson, called it "the one constructive indigenous religious movement among the Annamites" (Thompson 1937: 475). She admired the tolerance preached by the new religious leaders and the "Gandhiesque flavor about creating a community which is economically self-reliant" (Thompson 1937: 474), as the religious complex at Tay Ninh came to be surrounded by hospitals, schools, printing presses, and weaving centers all identified with the new religion. She described its character as eclectic—"a compromise between old and new, a reconciliation of Eastern and Western concepts" (Thompson 1937: 474).

The new religion also received support from French Free Masons, who recognized a kinship between Masonic ideas of universal brotherhood and even their emblem of the all seeing eye and Caodai practices. Free Masons and Jews were targeted for persecution by the Vichy government and its colonial annexes, so they shared the same enemies.[2] Caodai is worshipped under the sign of the left eye of God, while Free Masons—and Americans who enshrine the eye of Providence on that most sacred of objects, the one dollar bill—are said to worship the right eye of God. The left eye is identified with the heart, morality, and the Orient, while the right eye is by opposition allied with the brain, science, and the Occident. In the Sino-Vietnamese tradition, the left is the side of yang (*duong*), the east, the sunrise, and positive, male energy, while the right is the side of yin (*am*), the west, the sunset, and negative, female energy. This is an inversion of the Indo-European associations we are most familiar with, but appears to be a consistent feature of Taoist thought in East Asia.

Caodaism shares with Free Masonry the idea of a fraternity where all secular ranks are suspended, even if there is also a separate system of religious ranks. The lure of a spiritual brotherhood which transcends race, gender, and class was crucial to attracting over a million converts in the first decade of the religion's existence. In this way, the religion destabilized existing hierarchies and brought people of opposing classes—landlords and peasants, illiterates and intellectuals—into the same moral universe.

> Among Caodaists, we call each other brother and sister. We have ranks, but we do not address anyone except God as "Your Excellency." Even the Pope is simply the eldest brother. I have been called "Your Excellency" in my civil life,[3] but among my co-religionists I am just the elder brother. When I call

someone my elder brother, I have a duty to respect him. When I call someone my younger brother, I have a duty to help him. Every brother has to go through a process of self-correction before he can serve the religion. You must convert yourself first before you convert others (Do Van Ly, interviewed 3 April 2004).

Reversing the Hierarchy of Race in Colonial Indochina

Race was a significant category in Caodai religious teachings because of the argument that, since God had chosen to reveal his message of the unity of all religions in Vietnam, the Vietnamese people (*dân tôc nguoi Viêt*) were the "chosen people" who had a spiritual mission to show the world the shared origins of all faith. In early messages, there was some discussion of both the "French race" and the "Vietnamese race" being selected to reveal this message, but from 1940 onwards it became increasingly clear that, since the French had not responded to this message, it was the Vietnamese alone who would incorporate Western prophets and messiahs into the more encompassing vision of Buddhism and Taoism.

Through the spiritual agency of Victor Hugo, Cadoists presented a moral critique of colonialism. They argued that the only way to escape the hypocrisy of a colonial government, which taught them the value of *"liberté, égalité, fraternité"* but failed to deliver on these values in practice, was to speak directly to one of the great Frenchmen of the nineteenth century. While some commentators have suggested that Victor Hugo was selected as a sly propaganda tool,[4] reading the messages themselves reveals that a more complex process was at work: Hugo presents himself as schoolmaster lecturing, not only the Vietnamese but also the French, on the ethics of their behavior. His most quoted poem is this one:

L'univers est donc une école pour les esprits	The universe is a school for spirits
Qui la fréquentent pour être encore plus érudits	Who attend to become more erudite
Ceux qui font souvent l'école buissonière	Those who cut their lessons to play hooky
Doivent doubler leurs années et reprendre leurs matières.	Must repeat a grade taking each subject again
Toutes les âmes espèrent lire ce livre éternel	All the souls hope to read the book of eternity
Qui contient le secret à se faire immortel.	Containing the secret of immortality.

(Séance night of 21–22 April 1930, 11 o'clock, in Tran Thu Dung 1996: 275.)

The metaphor of life as a great school, even—as Tran Quang Vinh argued in a famous speech in 1945—a graduate school of the highest spiritual wisdom—is particularly poignant when we recall that it was used to address a generation of Vietnamese students taught exclusively by French professors, who offered lessons to their native charges by drawing on the great works of French literature. In effect, spirit mediumship was utilized to cut out these professors as the middlemen, and to show that great literary figures can speak for themselves—and would, in fact, speak out against the inequities of colonialism if they could be summoned directly. This was the students quite literally turning the tables on their professors, and applying the "lessons" of French literature to the daily life of French Indochina.

The critical message is even clearer in a spirit message received in December 1931:

Nous sommes en Indochine sous le pouvoir des potentats	We in Indochina are under the tyranny of potentates
Méfions-nous qu'au regard des lois	Watch out that in the eyes of the law
L'on ne nous traite de forçats	We may be treated as convicts
Je ne parle pas de la foi	I do not speak of faith
Le gouvernement colonial s'abaisse	The colonial government loses its dignity
Sous la férule catholique	Under its dependence on the Catholics
Notre nouvelle religion se laisse	Our new religion is becoming
Corrompre par des procès souvent publics	Corrupted by the often public trials
Des droits de liberté	Of the rights to freedom of conscience
De conscience, tant de fois annoncés.	So often announced
Par la France Humanitaire	By a Humanitarian France
De par le monde qu'elle prétend assez chers.	To a world that pretends to cherish them.
Fils d'une telle nation,	As a son of that nation, which I love,
Que j'aime, quoique je n'y compte que pour une vie.	Although perhaps only for one lifetime
J'ai pu connaître vraiment à fond	I have been able to know deeply
Comme est son idéal trahi.	How her ideals have been betrayed.

(Séance at midnight 30 December 1931, at the home of Thai Tho Thanh, in the presence of Pope Le Van Trung and Tran Quang Vinh.)

Hugo is "indigenized" as a schoolmaster and father figure, taking the paternalistic stereotypes of colonial rhetoric and giving them a new twist, in which the Vietnamese sons of the great French literary figure emerge as the true champions of his prophetic ideas of humanism and emancipation, while his European descendants are criticized for their hypocrisy. This séance—one of the most quoted passages of the Caodai scriptures or sutras—was received by the famous spirit medium Pham Cong Tac and recorded by Tran Quang Vinh, the reincarnation of Hugo's son François. The two of them were to remain two of the most celebrated, charismatic, and controversial figures in the religion. Tac, baptized as a Roman Catholic before he was called by spiritism to Caodai, became the most prominent spiritual leader of the faith, its Master of Mysticism and Supreme Head of the College of Mediums, and is often misidentified in English language histories as its Pope.[5] Tran Quang Vinh, in contrast, became a temporal and even military leader, who came to epitomize the movement's anticommunist activism.

Vinh began his career as the general secretary of the Musée Albert Sarraut, the museum of Cambodian arts that tangled with André Malraux in his scams to sneak Cambodian antiquities out of the country. Vinh was sent to Paris in 1931 to attend the *Exposition Coloniale de Vincennes*, where he represented the protectorate of Cambodia. Secretly, spirit séances before his departure revealed that his official French mission was a cover for the more important spiritual mission given to him by God, which was to spread the new religion to metropolitan France. In Paris, he converted the French philosopher and novelist Gabriel Gobron and his wife Marguerite. Gabriel Gobron later published a book on the history and philosophy of Caodaism, and Marguerite a photographic essay on its rituals and costumes (G. Gobron 1947; M. Gobron 1949).

One Frenchman, M. Latapie, was appointed in spirit séances to the position of bishop in the overseas mission, and another, Paul Monet, the prominent critic of colonial exploitation, was asked to be a delegate to the Universal Congress of Religions.[6] Several French people were attracted to the new faith and attended séances, but the movement was also heavily scrutinized by the Sureté police. In the early 1930s, the colonial government accused Caodaists of mixing religion and nationalist politics. The Interim Pope Le Van Trung was imprisoned in 1933 for fiscal irregularities which he perceived as persecution of the religion. He reacted by angrily turning in the ceremonial ribbons of the *Legion d'Honneur* medal he had received a decade earlier as a prominent political figure in the French colonial regime. He was released, but soon fell ill and died.

Divisions within Caodaism appeared at the time of the death of Pope Le Van Trung. On 20 November 1934, Caodaists at Ben Tré voted to establish a "reformed" branch under the leadership of Cardinal Nguyen Ngoc Tuong. The election was held when Le Van Trung was known to be ailing, but in fact it coincided exactly with the day of his "disincarnation." Members of the Holy See saw this as an extreme sign of disrespect, while others interpreted it as a sign that the succession was legitimate. But when Cardinal Tuong came to the Holy See to attend the funeral of the first Pope, he was not allowed to enter. Pham Cong Tac presided at a séance where the spirit of Victor Hugo appeared and supported these actions. Refusing to believe that these and other messages were legitimate, Tuong and his followers in the Ben Tré group renounced spiritism completely, arguing that it only served to feed "egotism, dissidence, and sectarianism" (Tran Thu Dung 1996: 236). None of the séances since July 1927 were recognized, and even those dignitaries who had once conversed with the spirit of Victor Hugo now refused to recognize him as a saint or the head of the foreign mission. While Tay Ninh continued to commemorate Hugo's death each May 22 with an annual festival in his honor, no such event appears on the sacred calendar of the Ben Tré group, which was then and remains the second largest Caodai congregation (Blagov 2001: 169).

Tay Ninh never had another Interim Pope, but Pham Cong Tac received spirit messages saying that the religion could continue under the guidance of its Spiritual Pope (giao tong vo vi) Ly Thai Bach, who was in direct communication with Tac. Caodaists in other denominations criticized this move, arguing that Tac took over both the executive and legislative functions of the faith, and was in effect the Acting Pope, a position that he should not assume while still serving as the Ho Phap or Master of Mysticism and Guardian of Religious Law. By 1940, there were three rival Popes: at Ben Tre (Ban Chinh Dao), Tiên Thiên (nearby on the Mekong Delta, with its own spiritist traditions) and Minh Chon Ly (at My Tho), and the religion appeared to take on the character of competing revitalization movements led by charismatic leaders whose spiritual differences could not be reconciled.

In 1941, the Pétainist French colonial government accused the Tay Ninh mediums, and Pham Cong Tac in particular, of being pro-Japanese, since he had received spirit messages which government agents interpreted as prophesying the eventual triumph of the Japanese in Indochina. The French army invaded the Holy See at Tay Ninh and arrested Pham Cong Tac, exiling him and five other members of the college of spirit mediums to Madagascar.

Vinh escaped arrest at the time since he was working for the French colonial government in Phnom Penh. Guided by a spirit séance that told him it was time to fight back, he approached the Japanese, who offered him support and military training to form the Caodai Army. Caodai forces helped the Japanese in the March 1945 coup that captured French soldiers and police, and declared Vietnam an independent state under emperor Bao Dai. When the Japanese were defeated in August and Ho Chi Minh issued another declaration of independence in Hanoi in September, most Caodaists rejoiced. The Caodai army, allied with the separate militia of the Buddhist reformists Hoa Hao, controlled more of southern Vietnam than any other force, including the Viet Minh, and seemed poised to share power in a new government of national unity (Fall 1955: 239). But since the religious leaders were still in exile, there was no consensus. Military leaders appointed by the new government in Hanoi did not want to share power, and Viet Minh political prisoners released from French prisons attacked Caodai communities, killing not only soldiers but also civilians. A monument erected in Quang Ngai in 1956 commemorates the deaths of 2,791 Caodai priests, women, and children in a series of killings beginning in August 1945, and this date is still commemorated in religious ceremonies mourning "Caodaists martyred for their religion."

Alienated from their former comrades in arms by these attacks, Caodaists were then courted again by the French, who realized that if they were to return to reconquer Indochina, they would need at least some indigenous collaborators. On 6 June 1946, Tran Quang Vinh was captured by French forces, tortured, and forced to agree to a truce. In return for his promise not to attack the French army, he was able to negotiate for the return of Pham Cong Tac and the other exiled leaders from Madagascar. The French General Latour announced dramatically that the Caodaists had "rallied to the national cause," and a military convention was signed with the French High Command in which Caodaists promised "loyal collaboration" with the French (Dutton 1970: 19). The French benefited immensely from this agreement, since it gave them "control over wide areas of south Vietnam which they could never have hoped to conquer militarily" (Fall 1955: 297), while the Viet Minh suffered a setback because of their brutality in dealing harshly with Caodaists and other nationalist groups who would normally have been their allies.

When Pham Cong Tac returned from exile, he accepted the political conditions which had made this possible, and stated that a continued French presence might be "necessary" for a few more years. Some leaders of dissident denominations in My Tho and Ben Tre remained in French prisons, but the mother church in Tay Ninh functioned openly, and the Holy See was reopened as well as thousands of temples in Vietnam and Cambodia (Blagov 2001: 94). Caodai soldiers saw themselves as a defensive force, primarily concerned with protecting their own religious centers, but they served as a home guard throughout the south, allowing the French to concentrate on waging war against Ho Chi Minh's armies in the north.

The Viet Minh saw this alliance as a betrayal and continued to kill Caodai dignitaries and their followers from 1945 to 1954, in a slaughter that Caodai historians estimate at 10,000 people. From 1948–49 Vinh was Minister of Defense of South Vietnam, commanding not only the Caodai army but also the militias of the Buddhist revivalists Hoa Hao and the Saigon based Binh Xuyen. In 1951, after conflicts over who would lead Caodai forces, he was kidnapped by the renegade General Thé and held hostage at Black Lady Mountain. After he was freed (and General Thé was assassinated), Vinh spent ten years in France recovering from this ordeal, and writing a history of Caodaism (published posthumously as Tran Quang Vinh 1997).

In 1953–54, Pham Cong Tac gave a series of press conferences praising both Bao Dai and Ho Chi Minh and calling for national union. When the French were defeated at Diem Bien Phu in 1954, he called for a reconciliation of the southern nationalists with the northern communists. Tac believed that his religion of unity would provide the ideal setting for negotiations to bring Vietnam's different political groups together, and he hoped for French and American backing for this to proceed. The U.S.-backed Ngo Dinh Diem regime, however, moved to consolidate all armed forces into the South Vietnamese Army. In October 1955, Diem ordered Caodai General Commander Phuong to invade the Holy See and strip Pham Cong Tac of all his temporal powers. Three hundred of the Tay Ninh papal guardsmen were disarmed, and Tac became a virtual prisoner of his own troops (Blagov 2001: 147). Tac's daughters and a number of other religious leaders were arrested, but he himself managed to slip away. He made contact with his followers several weeks later from Phnom Penh, and lived out the last three years of his life in exile in Cambodia. Tac's body was placed in an elaborate tomb in Phnom Penh, protected by a special mandate from his former classmate King Sihanouk, who allowed him to rest in Cambodia until the day that Vietnam would be "unified, peaceful and neutral."

His associate, Vinh, returned to Vietnam in 1964, reassumed his religious duties, and served as Vice President of the Chief Council of national government in 1965 and Vice President of the Legislative Council in 1965.[7] During this period he continued to receive spirit messages from

Victor Hugo, who provided guidance to his spiritual son and advised the Caodaist hierarchy on missionary activities. After the fall of Saigon, Vinh, then 77, was imprisoned in a communist "reeducation" camp. His relatives were told that he died in detention in January 1977, but other sources claimed he was executed in September 1975 (Blagov 2001: 152).

Unsettling Hierarchies of Gender in Traditional Asia

Although Caodaists have become famous for being innovative in having female Cardinals and religious dignitaries, the emphasis on liberation has been more focused on national and religious goals than on sexual equality. The tensions between hierarchy and egalitarianism were evident from the syncretistic beginnings of this religious movement. Its Confucian elements celebrated the literary achievements of an elite, its Taoist occult practices focused more on the relation of man to nature rather than to society, and its esoteric tradition was primarily Buddhist in inspiration. What was novel about Caodaism, however, was that in contrast to all three of Vietnam's "great teachings," it fostered a more personal and direct contact with God. While Confucianism can be described as an ethical system, Taoism as a metaphysical one, and Buddhism as a philosophy of self realization, what Caodai added to the mix was a more personal relationship to a monotheistic deity. Caodai spirit mediums have direct conversations with God and the various saints, and the goal of Caodai meditation exercises was to study directly from the spiritual entities themselves. The "personal relationship with Jesus" which is advocated by some Protestant groups was expanded to include a much wider Asian pantheon of spirits, and a more cosmopolitan spirituality.

The direct and activist form of religious communication influenced the new religion's orientation to the world and to sexual politics. Both men and women have served as spirit mediums, and young female mediums emerged as particularly important in the 1960s and 1970s in Saigon during the American war. Caodaism is unusual in world religions in seeking parity—equal numbers of male and female dignitaries at religious ceremonies—and in allowing women to hold high ranking positions. Women's greater longevity and many years of service in the religion (uninterrupted by military service or prison camp) have often made them the only guardians of Caodai temples during stressful times. As a result, membership in some temples—like the one in Hanoi—has been "feminized," with many more women attending ceremonies than men, perhaps because they are less likely to suffer the social censure that being religious may bring to professionals and civil servants in Vietnam today.

The *Tan Luan* or New Code of Conduct is Confucian in its prescriptions for women to honor their fathers, husbands, and sons, and also in its tolerance for divorce, or a husband's taking a second wife if his wife has not produced a male descendant. Veneration of the Mother Goddess and of female saints and deities like Quan Am, Joan of Arc, and the Virgin Mary appeal to followers of feminist spirituality, but rules pertaining to marriage, divorce, and the family have seemed to reassert traditional sex roles rather than displacing them. Divorce can be requested by a woman only in cases of desertion, offending the inlaws, or infertility, but in practice many allowances have been made for different cultural contexts. The highest ranking Caodai dignitary at a 2004 retreat in San Martin, California was a female archbishop Ngoc Tuyet Tien, and temple Thien Ly Buu Toa was founded by her and the female spirit medium Bach Dien Hoa as one of the earliest Caodai temples in the United States, and the only one to receive and distribute spirit messages since 1977.

Women are active in California temples in fundraising, organizing youth groups, hosting religious ceremonies with good food, and attending international conferences. Caodai's innovation in defining a new way to "live a religious life" (*song tu*), not only in the monastery but also in the family home, has certainly opened doorways to greater female participation in religious leadership than was the norm in Buddhism or Roman Catholicism.

Grappling with Hierarchies of Religion and Politics in California

Two million Vietnamese now make America their home, and after initial sponsorship by Church groups throughout the United States (and some heavily pressured baptisms), the Caodai community has reconstituted itself in California, alongside other Vietnamese congregations. Caodaism's earlier goals of healing the wounds of colonialism and bringing the "gods of Asia" into dialogue with the "gods of Europe" have been rearticulated into current projects of preserving Vietnamese heritage in the United States and offering a spiritual alternative to Americans whose lives were marked by the Vietnam War. Spirit messages from 1926 predicted that "people from the north and from the south" would travel overseas at the time that Vietnam was reunified, and many Caodaists have thus seen the exodus as predestined, a part of God's plan to place disciples of the new religion all over the world, where they would learn foreign languages and be able to spread the faith to new audiences.

Refugees who fled Vietnam after 1975 suffered the loss of their country in military defeat, and then the dangers of traveling by boat, fighting off pirates, and the lack of food or water. Over a million people who remained in the country were arrested and interned in reeducation camps, where they served indefinite terms of many years at hard labor. More than a thousand Caodai religious leaders were interned in specialized camps, but it was younger men who had served the South Vietnamese government in military or civilian positions who often became more committed to religious ideals as a result of this experience. Just as the colonial prison formed an earlier generation of revolutionaries, the communist reeducation camp produced prisoners of conscience who found solace in meditation, religious discipline, and secret study groups to counter their forced indoctrination. In 1985, the Humanitarian Transfer Act allowed many former prisoners to emigrate to the United States, and many of them came to occupy positions of leadership in American Caodai temples.

Trauma and dislocation initially produced a fragile consensus that allowed Caodaism to be reconstituted on American soil without attention to sectarian divisions, focusing instead on the shared message of peace, harmony, and love that has always been the basis of the new religion's teachings. Do Van Ly, the most senior Caodai leader in California, formed a congregation in Los Angeles in 1979–1990 which was based on a unified vision of the faith and not affiliated with any specific branch. But the history of Caodaism in Vietnam and its troubled relationship to hierarchy later made this unity in exile more problematic.

Hierarchy and Diversity:
Sectarian Divisions and Political Trials

Caodaism in Vietnam is divided into about a dozen different denominations, each with its own set of spirit messages or scriptures. In Caodai oral tradition, the twelve original disciples were eventually scattered among twelve separate "churches," although the historical evidence suggests a more fitful sequence of defections and returns, including twenty-three separate branches (Do Van Ly 1989), with ten specific branches or *Phái* now officially recognized by the government. Tay Ninh, the "mother church" has 500 out of 1,300 temples, and retains about half of all those Vietnamese citizens who identify themselves on census forms as Caodai (about 2.5 million). It is often referred to as the "Vatican" of Caodaism, or its "Rome," in contrast to the esoteric branch of the founder, Chiêu Minh, which is sometimes called the "Bethlehem" of the religion, or the center of early prophecies and apocalyptic traditions. Tiên Thiên, a third branch, considers itself the "Jerusalem." The new ecumenical teaching organization, the Institute of Caodai Teachings (Co Quan Pho Thong Giao Ly), draws its membership mainly from urban elites, and has been described as the "Jesuit" branch of the religion and its intellectual center.

The Institute was founded in Saigon in 1964 by Tran Van Que, in response to a spirit message to found a center focusing on the shared doctrines and meditation techniques of the religion, rather than on rank, ritual, or recruitment efforts. Not affiliated with any specific Holy See, the Saigon Institute offers courses to students and residents, drawing in many educated professionals. Its idealistic vision of how the shared teachings could overcome sectarian differences brought in many new members, and created an intellectual infrastructure, which was to have a great impact on overseas communities. Institute leaders sponsored spirit séances in a nondenominational format, and the popularity of these séances reinvigorated Caodai doctrine, which had seemed to stagnate a bit after the death of the inspirational but divisive Pham Cong Tac.

Do Van Ly received a spirit message calling him to join the Institute after serving as the Ambassador to the United States and head of diplomatic missions to India and Indonesia. Renouncing politics to travel throughout South Vietnam opening up new temples in an increasingly war torn country, he saw Caodaism as a way to liberate the Vietnamese people from the legacy of colonialism and forge a new national consensus based on shared spiritual values. Returning to Vietnam after many years of schooling and diplomatic service overseas, he helped organize a more cerebral, reflective religious practice, which incorporated the cosmopolitan orientation of a new generation of city dwellers. While he and many of the young men and women who took classes at the Institute escaped in 1975, a core of members remained in Saigon, and the Institute remained open after the fall of Saigon.

The Holy Sees in Tay Ninh, Ben Tre, My Tho, and Soc Trai did not fare as well: Communist troops seized forty out of the forty-six buildings in Tay Ninh, arrested 1,291 Caodai religious leaders, killed thirty-nine of them in clashes, and sentenced nine to death (Blagov 2001). Tay Ninh Caodaists in the United States have tried to maintain a state of purity in exile by usually refusing to collaborate with the present communist-appointed management committee and emphasizing ways in which the religion was constrained and paralyzed under communist control. The other Mekong Delta denominations seemed to have made their peace with the new regime in another way, as they now display large portraits and busts of Ho Chi Minh.

The Saigon Institute, in contrast, was led after 1975 by an opposition party leader, Dinh Van De, who decided to work with the new regime to assure that Caodaism would remain a national presence. Noting that during the many years of civil war, Caodaists were found on both sides of the ideological struggle, he explained to me in 2004 that this political division ultimately helped the faith to survive: "The Caodaists who supported the communists have given us some room to move in relation to a regime which opposes all religious organizations. They have helped to create a place for us to place our feet in the new Vietnam, and since 1990 we have been able not only to survive in the shadows but even to come out again on the national stage."

In the period since 1990, Caodaism—like the famous magical phoenix bird that is one of its favorite religious icons—has raised itself up from the ashes both in Vietnam, where it finally received official recognition in 1997, and in North America, where it is now building new temples and establishing the largest community in exile. But this amazing rebirth has not been without costs: The religion is only allowed to operate in Vietnam under strict government controls that do not permit spirit séances for the promotion of new leaders to the higher ranks. As a result, the leadership appears "decapitated," with no one over the rank of archbishop currently alive.

In September 2004, the U.S. Department of State designated Vietnam as a "country of particular concern" under the International Religious Freedom Act, for particularly severe violations of religious freedom. The most high profile groups lobbying for this designation were Protestant evangelical churches in the highlands, and expatriate members of the banned Unified Buddhist Church, but it was noted that some Caodai leaders had been imprisoned or placed under house arrest. The designation was prompted in part by a new Ordinance on Belief and Religion, passed by the National Assembly on 18 June 2004 in which the government reserved the right to control and oversee religious activities, including the training of clergy, the construction of new temples, public speaking (now defined to include Internet postings), and evangelizing. Religious organizations are encouraged to engage in charity work, but their participation in the public sphere is tightly monitored.

It will be many years before Caodaists in Vietnam can have the same public and even political profile that they had in the 1940s and 1950s, but the resurgence of interest in religion in the Post Reformation Period—combined with the fact that Tay Ninh is now the second largest tourist destination in South Vietnam—have helped Caodaists to renovate their churches, refresh the paint on their brightly colored facades, and gain new adepts among the new generation. In 2005 and 2006, Tran Quang Canh, the son of Tran Quang Vinh, visited Vietnam as the head of the Tay Ninh Overseas Mission, and met with Hanoi government officials to discuss ways to increase religious freedom under the current regime. In November 2006 the body of Pham Cong Tac was brought back to Tay Ninh and Vietnam was dropped from the list of countries of particular concern because of religious freedom.

Diaspora Versus Global Community

The diasporic perspective is strongest among refugee groups who migrated in circumstances of persecution or civil war, and for these very reasons many Vietnamese who came to the United States after years in reeducation camps share some of the political conviction of Holocaust survivors and Cuban exiles. While some, particularly older, members of the Caodai community are most concerned with defending freedom of religion in the homeland, others, many of them now American born, are trying instead to build a larger understanding of the religion in the wider American public.

I use a narrow definition of diaspora developed by Hans von Amesfoot in a discussion of Moluccans in the Netherlands: "A diaspora is a settled community that considers itself to be 'from elsewhere' and whose concern and most important goal is the realization of a political ideal in what is seen as the homeland" (Amesfoot 2004: 151). Under this definition, the two most important diasporic communities of Vietnamese Americans are without doubt the "Little Saigon" in Orange County, California, and the "Littler Saigon" of the Bay Area around San Jose. In Orange County, some members of the 135,000 Vietnamese American community have supported special "anti-communist zone" ordinances in the cities of Westminster and Garden Grove, which require prior notice for Vietnamese government delegations to visit and discourage official contacts with Vietnam. They also protested for months in 1999 when a video store displayed a photo of Ho Chi Minh or raised the Vietnamese flag. In January 2004 a State Department sponsored visit by Hanoi officials to Little Saigon was cancelled when Westminster officials refused to ensure their safety.

In the Bay Area, by contrast, San Francisco has had a sister city relationship with Ho Chi Minh City since 1994, and a Vietnam government consulate since 1997. The Bay Area is home to about 100,000 Vietnamese Americans, and since December 2004 it has also established the first direct air service between the United States and Vietnam in nearly 30 years (Moore and Tran 2004: 1). For many years a number of Vietnamese American leaders discouraged contact with Vietnam, including doing business there or even traveling to visit family members, since they saw all contact as offering implicit support to the communist government. In 1993, when the United States normalized diplomatic relations with Vietnam, the number of Vietnamese Americans who returned to visit their homeland increased significantly, and in the first nine months of 2004 about 10,000 people flew to Vietnam from the United States to visit friends and family, according to the U.S. Department of Commerce (Moore and Tran 2004: 1). Vietnamese Americans make up about 10 percent of all foreign tourists to Vietnam, in a rapidly expanding industry that recently topped the million mark.

Among those returning for visits were Caodai religious officers, bringing funds to rebuild the Caodai Sacerdotal Center (Hoi Thanh) in Binh Dinh that was destroyed during the American war. Others have returned to arrange for the shipment of Caodai altars, gongs, and religious icons to California, to give courses at the Caodai Institute in Saigon, and to consult with religious leaders in the homeland.

Hierarchy and the Future of Caodaism

Hierarchy is part of the "Asian traditions" which Caodaism honors, but events over the past half century have made its ranked system of spiritual titles and delegated authority hard to maintain. Scholars have argued that the disciplined hierarchical structure of Caodaism has allowed it to expand and grow over an eighty year period, providing a sense of stability and tradition that many other millenarian new religious movements have not managed to maintain (Werner 1976). But Caodaism has now become a religion where the center cannot speak, and only those on the periphery are allowed to converse with God and the various saints. The tensions between a ranked leadership and a dispersed membership have grown ever more evident as Caodaists have been spread all over the globe, and as refugees forced to adapt to a series of new cultural contexts.

For those Vietnamese Americans who are growing up in the shadow of Disneyland, worshipping the left eye of God may suggest Indiana Jones and the Temple of Doom rather than solar energy, lunar calendars, and Oriental morality. Do Van Ly suggests that the future of Vietnam depends on making good use of these contrasts: "We are the two peoples in the world to worship under the sign of the eye. We Vietnamese worship the left eye of God, you Americans worship the right. There is an Arab proverb that says: 'The two eyes are very close but they cannot see each other.' This shows how wrong the Arab world can be. My lifelong goal of liberating my people will be achieved when the American educated Vietnamese return to their country to bring them Western democracy with an Eastern ethical orientation."

This articulation of the "diasporic perspective"[8] sees Caodaism as a religion in exile whose members are all striving for political changes in the homeland so that they can return. It contrasts with another view—perhaps more common among younger members and those who are American born—of a "global religion reinventing itself in the new world"—in which ties to non-Vietnamese converts become more important, and the religion can receive new revelations on American soil. Dr. Hum Dac Bui, a California physician who has coauthored the only book in English by a Vietnamese Caodaist, Caodai: Faith of Unity (2000), describes his perspective in this way: "Now, Americans are beginning to discover the value of the original esoteric form of CaoDai, with its practices of meditation, vegetarianism and emptying the mind to open the way for conversations with God. In much the same way as Tibetan Buddhism has attracted many Western disciples, CaoDai has begun the process of disseminating its valuable and closely held esoteric information to the West. The first temple to open itself to the influx and acceptance of Westerners is underway in Riverside, California. Its leaders have the desire to relate their teachings in English to Americans (both Vietnamese and non-Vietnamese) so that the first and main message received from the Supreme Being, that we are all One and must reunite under The One Nameless Divinity, can be delivered and that a path of esoteric practice toward that end (reunification of the self with the Supreme Being) may begin" (Bui and Beck 2000: 28–29).

The efforts begun in 2000 to build a more encompassing temple in Riverside were doomed, however, to some disappointment. After a very promising beginning, in which Caodaists of all denominations took part and contributed funds, quarrels began about which specific architectural and liturgical traditions would be followed. Not everyone was willing to go along with a bold new conceptualization of the faith, which seemed to sever ties with precedent and establish its own clergy. Some promised contributions failed to materialize, and the project itself is stalled for the moment, awaiting a greater consensus of American Caodaists.

In 2006, construction began on a Tay Ninh affiliated Caodai temple in Garden Grove, California, in a residential neighborhood close to the business district of "Little Saigon." Although there was concern about the relationship between an American-built temple and the stagnant hierarchy in Vietnam, the successful example of a new Tay Ninh affiliated temple in Sydney, Australia, was enough to carry fundraising forward. The temple was finished in 2007, and became a landmark for tourists and school groups. While some have wondered how such a great enterprise could be guided without spirit séances from the "Vatican" in Tay Ninh, others have argued persuasively that the temple will be a visual guide to the esoteric teachings of the faith, and should attract converts as well as curious visitors (Biederman 2006: 2).

Spirit séances have also been held in California, although they remain extremely controversial. The Court of Heavenly Reason Temple (Thien Ly Buu Toa) near San Jose has had a female spirit medium since 1977, and she has received hundreds of spirit messages, which they have published as "new volumes of the Caodai Bible" (*Dai Giác Thánh Giáo Pháp*). The first volume had fifty-four messages, including fourteen from Caodai (Ngoc Hoang Thung De, the Supreme Being, also called the Jade Emperor), six from Jesus Christ, two from Buddha (Thich Ca Mau Ni Phat), two from Quan Cong (Quan Thanh De Quan), one from the Virgin Mary (Duc Me Maria), four from the founder of Caodai Ngo Minh Chieu, two from Ly Thai Bach (the spiritual Pope), one from the Mother Goddess (Dieu Tri Kim Mau), one from Noah of the Old Testament, and one from an American spirit—Joseph Smith, the founder of Mormonism.

Joseph Smith is appreciated because his revelations from the Angel Moroni are seen as part of a tradition of spiritism that includes Caodai, and Smith's own background as a Free Mason caused him to include many Caodai symbols (like the all-seeing eye, the moon and stars, and so on) on the outside of Mormon temples. It is perhaps significant that several non-Vietnamese Caodaists, like Stephen Stratford and Ngasha Beck, came from Mormon backgrounds, but renounced Mormonism as racist and patriarchal, and have come to find Caodaism a more welcoming spiritual home.

On 9 November 2003, a new medium in San Jose, Hue Tanh, received a message stating that, since after 1975 the sacred centers in Vietnam (Hoi Thanh) could not communicate with Caodaists overseas, they should now listen to the direct spiritual guidance of Ly Thai Bach, the Spiritual Pope, and seven of its most important twentieth century leaders (including Pham Cong Tac and the founder Ngo Van Chieu): "We immortals are happy to see you going overseas and carrying the Caodai messages to new people. God created the religion to save the Vietnamese and also all of humanity. His blessings will go to the good and penalties will go to those who oppose God's will. Look at the example of the past and learn from it in order to spread the teachings in the future. When we immortals were alive, we were sometimes separated by divisions, so you should not follow that example but learn to work together more effectively.... You need to unify to become the lighthouse of the Western world (*sáng chói o Tây Phuong dê*) so that people can find peace, salvation and happiness."[9] This call for unity is an effort to transcend the tensions between hierarchy and egalitarianism, between a respect for the authority of religious leaders in the homeland now paralyzed by government restrictions and the leaders of refugee communities who need new messages of spiritual guidance for the new world. It speaks both to the glorification of ancient traditions and the innovations forced by the present moment.

In informal discussions with Caodai leaders in California, several of them noted that over the past thirty years they have tried to learn from the forms of religious organization they saw in the United States: "On the one hand, we see the Catholic Church, which has retained a strict hierarchy, but is plagued by scandals about priestly celibacy, women in the religion, and birth control. On the other hand, we see a great many Protestant churches that divide and form new congregations everyday.

There are new Baptist preachers all over the place, and any one who can get a following can become an evangelist. In many ways, the egalitarian Baptist model seems to work better here" (Kham Bui, interviewed 23 April 2005). Since Caodaism proposed itself initially as an alternative to the racist teachings of French colonial Catholicism, its historical organization was similar to that of the Vatican, but now—on new terrain—the mixture of anarchic individualism and shrewd public relations marketing exemplified by many American churches presents an appealing new form of organization. Denominational differences had already been eclipsed in the organization of Caodai congregations because of low numbers, so the de facto organization of the California community was, in effect, a set of groupings centered on a few charismatic spiritual leaders—not unlike the splintering of the followers of the first disciples in the 1930s.

Caodaism and the Postcolonial Critique of Hierarchy

Caodaism as a new religion created in the colonial context has been represented by its founders as both a force for modern national liberation and the revival of Asian traditions. While it has deliberately violated certain hierarchies, it has done so by creating new ones, and the vicissitudes it has suffered over its eighty years of history have created new forms of organization and collaboration. How does its complex history in Vietnam and California shed light on the controversies over the colonial construction of notions of Asian hierarchy?

Dumont's *Homo Hierarchicus* (1980) sparked a series of discussions about holism, difference, hierarchy, and race that have remained central to questions of how to interpret what is often called "Asian traditionalism." Hierarchy is, in Dumont's sense, not so much an expression of power differences, as of worldview. His famous statement that "to adopt a value is to introduce hierarchy, and a certain consensus of values . . . is indispensable to social life" (1970: 36) was an effort to explain a commitment to unifying values that the modern world has lost, and an effort to use that commitment to differentiate East from West.

Since Caodaism was, from its very beginning, an effort to fuse East and West, it would seem to deny both Dumont's notion of hierarchy—motivated as it may have been by a peculiar Western form of nostalgia—and the idea that hierarchy is a necessary component of Asian religiosity. Dumont's hierarchy implies the regular ordering of a phenomenon on a continuous scale "such that the elements of the whole are ranked in relation to the whole" (Dumont 1980: 66). It is thus a ritual hierarchy (and that is why Dumont sees it as "true"), which is dependent upon a state of mind and is not influenced by secular forces of economics and politics (see Dumont 1980: 19, 34, 66). More recent critics (Appadurai 1986, 1988; Dirks 2001) have argued that hierarchy is not an enduring ideological disposition but instead the "precipitate" of the colonial encounter: "Hierarchy, in the sense of rank or ordered difference, might have been a pervasive feature of Indian history, but hierarchy in the sense used by Dumont and others became a systematic value only under the sign of the colonial modern" (Dirks 2001: 5). Many of the features they identify as characteristic of British colonial rule—shoring up a local aristocracy and using them to sustain a very particular form of indirect rule—were at least as true of the French colonial presence in Indochina, "the pearl of the Orient," as they were of the British in India, "the jewel in the crown."

Vietnam differs from India, however, in being a much more homogeneous state, where nationalist forces could draw on three already fused Asian spiritual traditions and marry them to the organization of the Catholic Church, creating a new and more encompassing religious order under a monotheistic God. The Caodai leader Pham Cong Tac was at times compared to India's Gandhi (Thompson 1937) because of the way he combined religious ideals with a struggle for political independence, but the two countries were divided in very different ways: for India, partition came because of deep divisions between Hindu and Muslim nationalists, while in Vietnam, many religious groups shared nationalist aspirations, but cold war struggles between the United States and China imposed a partition which became an ideologically charged civil war. Caodaism proposed a syncretistic model of ritual unity that argued directly that Vietnamese nationalists could use Jesus' message of shared humanity and fuse it with Buddhist ideas of equality, Taoist metaphysics, and Confucian universal citizenship. Caodaism spread through a social organization that was both egalitarian (a fraternity of brothers and sisters morally bound to assist one another) and hierarchical (in proposing ranks of religious office, with promotion based on a combination of seniority and spiritual approval). While the Holy Sees which were the sacred centers of each denomination are now cut off from their diasporic disciples, new forms of organization have emerged through the more anarchic structure of the Internet, through which each individual temple remains in contact with others in a virtual community with no clear leader or coordinated system of ranks.

During its initial "age of revelations" (1925–1934), Caodaism was totalizing and hierarchical in a Dumontian sense, in that it sought to encompass all the world's religions within itself, promoting a single, oceanic vision of shared teachings and spirituality. But it is the differentiating, historicizing aspects of hierarchy in practice, which produced (as Dirks and Appadurai might have predicted) a splintering of this initial consensus and competing denominations led by charismatic leaders, each of whom claimed his own forms of divine inspiration. In Indochina as in India, colonial governments sought both to domesticate and reproduce local hierarchical structures. Caodai doctrines emerged as a response to the displacements of the colonial modern, and the sense that the country had been "lost" to the French (as many early nationalists argued). The more recent and complete "loss of country" experienced by refugees after 1975 opened up older wounds, and forced a new reevaluation of ways in which Eastern spirituality could be wedded to Western modernism. The educated young men and women of 1925, whom their parents found already "too French," found themselves with children and grandchildren in California, who seemed to them to be altogether "too American"—and in even more desperate need of traditional moral values.

Caodai's Critics and Contemporary Neocolonialism

In spite of its lofty ideals of interracial cooperation, Caodaism has been dismissed by many European commentators, who use vivid descriptions of its temples to form the comic relief chapters in travel books on Southeast Asia. There were relatively few historical materials available to visitors in the 1950s, like Norman Lewis and Graham Greene, so they can perhaps be forgiven for siding clearly with French colonial powers and dismissing Caodaists as "no longer naïve and charming but cunning and unreliable" (Greene 1991: 240). Greene in particular had been attracted to the new faith since it combined echoes of Catholicism with Asian spiritual aspirations, but concluded that the Caodaists were bad allies to the doomed French and therefore untrustworthy. Carsten Jensen visited Tay Ninh in the 1990s, shortly after the Great Temple had been allowed to reopen after decades of persecution. He seems to have read little since Greene's and Lewis' descriptions half a century before, treating it as "an ersatz religion," which "provided a standpoint for those who never took a stand on anything, renegades caught between two worlds, their own Vietnamese world, which they considered themselves to have risen above, and that of the French, which they could never hope to attain. . . . Its imagination owed its inspiration to choreography and set design as opposed to theology. It provided its devotees with costumes, symbols and physical rituals; gave them an easy answer to who they were, which they needed, since they no longer belonged either to the East or to the West" (2000: 220–221).

This patronizing condemnation of Caodai's religious hybridity would seem come straight from the colonial apologists, and includes no mention of the ways in which this religion survived the exodus of over a million

Vietnamese, reeducation camps, and the banning of spiritism, as well as the dissolution of its original constitution. Caodaism has not provided "an easy answer" to modern Vietnamese, but rather a difficult one that has required a lot of sacrifice and suffering to keep its dream of eventual reconciliation alive. Jensen alludes briefly to the many Euro-American "spiritual seekers" who seem to shed partners and philosophies with equal ease, seeking exoticism perhaps as much as wisdom. But he fails to see that Caodaism has shown much greater staying power than many New Age spiritual fashions. After so many years of war, its message of peace and reconciliation has become particularly poignant because it originated in a land torn by violence.

Caodaism is now a transnational religious movement, although there are deep and significant differences between the way it is perceived and lived in the Socialist Republic of Vietnam and the New Age-influenced communities of California. But it is precisely because of these differences that a study of efforts to revitalize this "faith of unity" is especially important and significant today. Eighty years ago, Caodaism came into being to provide Vietnamese intellectuals in a modernizing world with a form of spiritual and religious activism, using the principles of Buddhism and Taoism in a much more "this worldly" organization. Today, it is being reconceptualized as a way to heal not so much the lingering wounds of colonialism but the continuing inequities of a globalized society. This new vision of bringing the Left Eye of God to the Western world brings an Eastern perspective on universal religion to the land illuminated by the right eye on the dollar bill.

Notes

1. They have now been republished in English in Chambers, *Conversations with Eternity* (1998).
2. A French dissertation on Caodaism in Cambodia (Bernardini 1974) published a photograph of an altar in Phnom Penh erected in 1955 with Victor Hugo on the left, Le Van Trung in the center, and Sun Yat Sen on the right. The temple in Phnom Penh, destroyed once in 1954, and again in 1975 by the Khmer Rouge, was rebuilt in 1990 in Tay Ninh style next to the tomb of Pham Cong Tac, and now features many images of Tac but none of Victor Hugo.
3. The speaker, Do Van Ly, has served as the Vietnamese ambassador to the United States, India, and Indonesia; so as an ambassador he was addressed in Vietnamese as Duc Dai Su, "Your Excellency the Ambassador," but he did not use this title when he was with members of his religious brotherhood. He argues that he treats his coreligionists as equals, although in his diplomatic work he had to respect hierarchical protocols.

4. "But one cannot dismiss the possibility that the main reason why early Caodaists mentioned Hugo so frequently in talking with Europeans was a desire to impress them with their high degree of loyalty to French culture, and perhaps thereby to cover up the more essential features of their cult. For men like Ngô Minh Chiêu and Nguyen Ngoc Tuong, Vietnamese and Chinese spirits must surely have been more important than those of any Frenchman" (Smith 1970: 20).

5. Pham Cong Tac held the position of Ho Phap, or "Guardian of Religious Law," and was the head of the Hiêp Thiên Dai, or legislative branch of the religion, which received laws from spirit séances and also administered justice (including possible excommunication) to those who violated religious law. Pham Cong Tac published the Religious Constitution of Caodai (Pháp Chánh Truyên), which was inspired by spirit messages, but after 1938 members of other denominations charged that he violated the separation of powers described in this constitution by assuming executive as well as legislative powers. Tac never formally held the title of Pope, but he was addressed by Tay Ninh followers as "His Holiness" and recognized in a painting with shifting perspectives as the spiritual successor of Buddha and Jesus Christ (in the Tay Ninh Holy See).

6. Captain Paul Monet (1884–1934) was a soldier who served in Indochina and in World War I, then returned to Hanoi and established a dormitory for Vietnamese students, publishing a bilingual journal and joining "Confucius," the first Free Mason lodge to admit Vietnamese members. He wrote books critiquing racial exclusion in the colony: Francais et Annamites (1926), Entre Deux Feux (1928), and Les Jauniers (1930), which argued that the exploitation of peasant labor was a "yellow slave trade" in which uneducated workers were duped into signing lifelong contracts. While Monet was known as an "Annamatophile," he wanted to reform colonialism rather than end it all together. In a séance on 15 December 1926, the Spiritual Pope of Caodai, Li Thai Bach spoke directly to Monet, who attended the séance in Tay Ninh: "You have tried to create a moral relationship in this country between the two races of the French and the Vietnamese, so that they can live together in a community of shared lives and interests. Your wishes will be realized. . . . You will later be one of my most fervent disciples, preaching peace and harmony to the world."

7. Caodai religious leaders were also been prominent members of the opposition party in the national government of the Republic of South Vietnam. After Vinh retired in 1965, he was replaced by Dinh Van De (one of the founders of the Caodai Institute in Saigon) as Vice Chairman of the National Assembly. De, who I interviewed in Saigon in the summer of 2004, explained that since he was seen as a critic of corruption in the Republic, he was not confined in a re-education camp but simply asked to follow courses from his home in Saigon. He retired from politics, and his teaching of meditation and esoteric mysticism at the Institute was heavily monitored by security personnel.

8. I use a narrow definition of diaspora developed by Hans von Amesfoot in a discussion of Moluccans in the Netherlands (2004: 151–174): "A diaspora is a settled community that considers itself to be 'from elsewhere' and whose concern and most important goal is the realization of a political ideal in what is seen as the homeland" (151). This diasporic perspective was developed by Zionists, but is also found among Cuban exiles in Miami and among many refugee groups who migrated in circumstances of persecution or civil war.

9. The Vietnamese transcript of this spirit message was handed to me when I attended a Caodai retreat at Thien Ly Buu Toa on August 30, 2004. It was translated with the assistance of Judy Vy-Uyen Cao, who attended the retreat with me, and a copy of the translation was sent to the temple for them to review. Many spirit messages received at Thien Ly Buu Toa are archived at the website www.thienlybuutoa.org.

References

Amesfoot, Hans von. 2004. "The Waxing and Waning of a Diaspora: Moluccans in the Netherlands, 1950–2002." *Journal of Ethnic and Migration Studies* 30 (1): 151–174.

Appadurai, Arjun. 1986. "Is Homo Hierarchicus?" *American Ethnologist* 13 (4): 745–761.

Bernardini, Pierre. 1974. *Le Caodaisme au Cambodge (Thèse du troisième cycle)*, Université de Paris VII, Directeur Jean Chesnaux.

Biederman, Patricia Ward. 2006. "Cao Dai Fuses Great Faiths of the World." In *Los Angeles Times*, California section, January 2006: 2.

Blagov, Sergei. 1999. *The Cao Dai: A New Religious Movement*. Moscow: The Institute of Oriental Studies.

———. 2001. *Caodaism: Vietnamese Traditionalism and its Leap into Modernity*. New York: Nova Science Publishers.

Bui, Hum Dac. 1996. *God Has Come: Messages from Vietnam*. Bilingual compilation in English and Vietnamese. Santa Ana: Caodai Overseas Mission.

Bui, Hum Dac and Ngasha Beck. 2000. *Cao Dai: Faith of Unity*. Fayetteville: Emerald Wave Press.

Buttinger, Joseph. 1967. *Vietnam: A Dragon Embattled. Volume 1: From Colonialism to the Vietminh. Volume 2: Vietnam at War*. New York: Praeger.

Đại Đạo Tam Kỳ Phổ Độ [The Great Way of the Third Revelation]. 1982. *Pháp Chánh Truyền* [The Religious Constitution of Caodaism]. Trans. Lucy Davy. Sydney: Caodaist Association of Australia NSW Chapter.

Dirks, Nicholas. 2001. *Castes of Mind: Colonialism and the Making of Modern India*. Princeton: Princeton University Press.

Do, Merdeka Thien-Ly Huong. 1994. *Cao Daism: An Introduction*, California, Centre for Dai Dao Studies.

Dong Tan. 2000. *Tim Hieu Dao Cao Dai*. Victoria, Australia: Nha Xuat Ban Cao Hien.

Dutton, Thomas E. *Caodai History, Philosophy and Religion*. MA Thesis in Oriental Religions, submitted to John A. Hutchinson at the University of California, Berkeley, 1970. Found on the website http://caodai.org.au/pdf/.

Dumont, Louis. 1980. *Homo Hierarchicus*. Chicago and London: The University of Chicago Press.

Fall, Bernard. 1955. *The Political-Religious Sects of Vietnam*. Pacific Affairs, XXVII: 235–53.

———. 1963. *The Two Viet-Nams: A Political and Military Analysis*. New York: Praeger.

———. 1967. *Vietnam Witness 1953–66*. New York: Praeger.

Gobron, Gabriel. 1949. *Histoire et Philosophie du Caodaisme: Bouddhisme rénové, spiritisme vietnamien, religion nouvelle en Eurasie*. Paris: Dervy.

Goborn, Marguerite. 1949. *Images du Caodaisme*, Paris: Dervy.

Greene, Graham. 1955. *The Quiet American*. London: William Heineman. Reprinted in the Viking Critical Library with additional texts and criticism selected by John Clark Pratt (1996). New York: Penguin Books.

Hartney, Christopher. 2004. "A Separate Peace: Cao Dai's Manifestation in Australia." Ph.D. thesis in Religion submitted to the University of Sydney, Australia.

Hickey, Gerald C. 1964. *Village in Vietnam*. New Haven: Yale University Press.

Jensen, Carsten. 2000. *I Have Seen the World Begin: Travels through China, Cambodia and Vietnam*, trans. Barbara Haviland. New York: Harcourt.

Meillon, Gustave. 1962. "Le Caodaisme." In *Les Messages Spirites de la troisème Amnistie de Dieu en Orient. Tay Ninh, Sainte Siège du Caodaisme*, ed. Tran Quang Vinh. [This article first appeared in 1955 in *La revue des membres de la Legion d'Honneur "le Ruban Rouge."*]

Moore, Solomon and Mai Tran. 2004. "Vietnam Flight to Make History." Article in 9 December 2004 Los Angeles Times, California Section, page B1 and B9.

Oliver, Victor L. 1976. Caodai Spiritism; A Study of Religion in Vietnamese Society. Leiden: E. J. Brill.

Phái Chieu-Minh. 1950. Le Grand Cycle de l'Esoterisme. (Spirit messages in French from the founding branch of Caodai esoterism). Saigon: Cénacle de Chieu-Minh.

Phan Truong Manh. 1950. La Voie du Salut Caodaique. Saigon: Imprimerie Ly Cong Quan.

———. 1951. Qu'est-ce que le Caodaisme? J'éclaire et J'unis. Saigon: Revue Caodaiste, Cao Dài Giao Ly No. 1–20, Saigon 1930–1932. Revived under a new editor, 1949–50. Photocopies of bilingual journal received from the files of the Co Quan Pho Thong Giao Ly Dai Dao, Ho Chi Minh City 2004.

Savani, A.M. 1952. Le Caodaisme: Notions Sommaires. Saigon: Imprimerie de la Sainte Siège, Tay Ninh.

Sherry, Norman. 1994. The Life of Graham Greene, volume 2: 1939–1955. New York: Viking.

Smith, Ralph B. 1970. "An Introduction to Caodaism." Bulletin of the School of Oriental and African Studies, University of London, XXXIII, vol. ii and iii.

Tac, Pham Cong. 1953. Ho Phap La Constitution Religieuse du Caodaisme. Paris: Dervy.

Tai, Hue-Tam Ho. 1983. Millenarianism and Peasant Politics in Vietnam. Cambridge, MA and London: Harvard University Press.

Thiên Lý Bửu Tòa [Court of Heavenly Reason Temple]. 1986. Đài Giác Thánh Kinh & Kinh Thánh Giáo Pháp [New Spirit Messages: Scripture and Method]. San Jose: Papyrus Press.

Thompson, Virginia. 1937. French Indochina. New York: Macmillan Company, American Council Institute of Pacific Relations. Reprinted New York: Octagon Books, 1968.

Tran Quang Vinh, ed. 1961. Les Messages Spirites de la trosième Amnistie de Dieu en Orient. Tay Ninh: Sainte Siège du Caodaisme.

Tran Quang Vinh. 1977. Hoi Ky Cua Phoi Su Thuong Vinh Thanh 1867–1975. The Diary of Archbishop Tran Quan Vinh. Tay Ninh: Toa Thanh Tay Ninh.

Tran Thu Dung. 1996. "Le Caodaisme et Victor Hugo." (Ph.D. diss. submitted to the Dept. of French Literature, University of Paris VII.)

Valeri, Valerio. 1985. Kingship and Sacrifice: Ritual and Society in Ancient Hawaii. Chicago: The University of Chicago Press.

Vo, Kim Quyen. 1950. Prières aux Quatre Heures Canoniques. Ben Tre, Vietnam: Ecole Nam Phuong.

Werner, Jayne. 1976. "The Cao Dai: The Politics of a Vietnamese Syncretic Religious Movement." (Ph.D. diss., Cornell University 1976.)

Werner, Jayne. 1981. Peasant Politics and Religious Sectarianism: Peasant and Priest in the Cao Dai in Vietnam, New Haven: Yale University Southeast Asia Studies.

Woodside, Alexander. 1971. Vietnam and the Chinese Model: A Comparative Study of Nguyen and Ch'ing Civil Government in the First Half of the Nineteenth Century. Cambridge MA: Harvard University Press.

Woodside, Alexander. 1976. Community and Revolution in Modern Vietnam. Boston: Houghton Mifflin.

Zinoman, Peter. 2001. The Colonial Bastille: A History of Imprisonment in Vietnam, 1862–1940. Berkeley: University of California Press.

Zinoman, Peter. 2002. Introduction. Dumb Luck: A Novel by Vu Trong Phung. Trans. Nguyen Nguyen Cam. Ann Arbor: University of Michigan Press.

CHAPTER 5

The Headless State in Inner Asia

Reconsidering Kinship Society and the Discourse of Tribalism

David Sneath

Although the concept of "tribal society" as an evolutionary stage preceding state-organized society continues to have wide currency (Earle 1994: 944–5), the pejorative, colonial baggage of the term "tribe" and its entanglement with nineteenth century evolutionist theory caused most anthropologists to avoid it by the late twentieth century.[1] Critiques such as Fried's (1975) *The Notion of Tribe* and revisionist works such as Vail's (1989) *The Creation of Tribalism in Southern Africa* helped establish the view that "tribalism" was a product of colonial classification and administration. A now common view, as Fried put it, is to see the

> tribe as a secondary sociopolitical phenomenon, brought about by the intercession of more complexly ordered societies, states in particular. I call this the "secondary tribe" and I believe that all the tribes with which we have experience are this kind. The "pristine tribe," on the other hand, is a creation of myth and legend, pertaining either to the golden ages of the noble savage or romantic barbarian, or to the twisted map of hell that is a projection of our own war-riven world (1975: 114).

However, this critique has not seriously undermined the application of the model of tribal society to Inner Asia, or indeed much of the Middle East, where the institutions of "the state" date back to the beginning of recorded history. Historians and anthropologists continue to apply all or parts of the tribal society model, despite anthropological work by Kuper, Schneider, and others, which has successfully critiqued the theories of kin-organized society that actually underpin the concept. While accepting that in sub-Saharan Africa modern tribalism does not represent indigenous

---

political systems, for example, in *The Dictionary of Anthropology* R. B. Ferguson reproduces the classical association between pastoralism and tribalism. "In the Middle East, unambiguous tribal identities are well known among *pastoral nomads* who have mobile bounded groups and a very long history of interaction with states" (1997: 476).

The relative equality of tribal society is still central to this description, although the difficulty of sustaining this assumption in the face of the evidence of stratification is evident. "Most tribal leaders are noncoercive consensus managers, often working in formal councils. However, tribes of the Middle East and Central and South Western Asia have chiefs and even khans" (Barfield 1993 cited in Ferguson 1997). The continued application of the notion of tribal society to "pastoral nomads" in Asia reflects anthropology's longstanding preoccupation with evolutionary kinship theory, and its entanglement with notions of stratification and equality.

Tribe, Evolution, and Visions of the Kinship Society

It was only with the sixteenth-century expansion of Europe into the Americas and Africa that the association of tribes with a more primitive order of mankind began, and only with the Enlightenment of the eighteenth century that this was formalized into that concept of progress, which set tribal people outside the pale of civil society. It was then supposed that the natural course of human development was a progression to higher levels of social, economic and political organization, which could be equated with civilization; and that those people who remained grouped in tribes represented an earlier, lower form of life, left behind by the march of history and destined to be redeemed and refashioned by the intervention of superior forces. The epithet most commonly found in association with the word "tribe" was "savage" (Yapp 1983: 154).

The notion of the tribe as a descent group stretches back to the original thirteenth century appearance of the Latin word *tribu* in English, when it was used for the thirteen divisions of the early Israelites.[1] By the fifteenth century it was being used in nonbiblical contexts in a way that overlapped with later notions of lineage and clan, and was, for example, applied to Irish groups having the same surname (Murray et al. 1933: 339). However, the association between the notion of the tribe and kinship society was given a particular form in nineteenth century evolutionist notions of primitive society and sociocultural evolution. Maine, who grounded his work on primitive society in studies of classical Greek and particularly Roman sources, wrote: "The history of political ideas begins, in fact, with the assumption that kinship in blood is the sole possible ground of community in political functions" (1861: 106). Like Marx, McLennan, and Morgan he saw extended ties of kinship as forming the basis for early society, and only later giving way to territory as the basis for social organization. This fundamental opposition between societies based on kinship (that is, membership of clans—*gens* in Latin) and those based on territory was mapped onto the dichotomies of primitive and civilized, pre-state and state. Morgan writes: "all forms of government are reducible to two general plans. . . . The first, in the order of time, is founded upon persons, and upon relations purely personal, and may be distinguished as a society (societas). The gens is the unit of organization. . . . The second is founded upon territory and upon property, and may be distinguished as a state (civitas)" (1877: 6–7 cited in Kuper 2004: 81). This "gentile society" based on kin-groups was a democratic and egalitarian system. "Liberty, equality, and fraternity, though never formulated, were cardinal principles of the gens" (Morgan 1877: 634). This vision fitted well with both liberal and socialist philosophies which were concerned with such notions as the original natural liberty of man, or in the Marxist variant, the idea of property-as-theft in the light of the universal sharing claimed for "primitive communist" society. The notion that without the state people organize themselves into descent groups and that these tend to be nonhierarchical became deeply ingrained in the Western social sciences. Durkheimian sociology conceived of clan-based society as a stage in the evolution of more complex systems, and saw this as a special case of "segmental organisation," that is, "societies based on repetitive parts which joined together simply through a sense of mutual resemblance" (Kuper 2004: 81). Evans-Pritchard's model of the Nuer segmentary lineage system fitted so perfectly with this thinking that one is tempted to feel in retrospect that if such a society had not existed it would have had to have been invented. Despite numerous subsequent critiques of the ethnographic basis of Evans-Pritchard's representation of the Nuer (e.g., Gough 1971; Beidelman 1971), the segmentary kinship model remained enormously influential in work on tribal and pastoral societies. The general frame into which it fitted remained so strong that Ernest Gellner continued to see segmentary society as the major predecessor and rival to "the state" as late as 1994.

Well into the late twentieth century, the dominant view in both Western and Soviet anthropology was to regard tribes as "survivals" of earlier stages of political evolution.[2] As such the tribal continued to act as the primitive counterpoint to self descriptions of "Western civilization," narratives dominated by the discourse of class, kinship, territory, and function, where the Hobbesian brute contended with the Rousseauian noble savage. For example, Sahlins writes:

> Tribes occupy a position in cultural evolution. They took over from simpler hunters; they gave way to more advanced cultures we call civilizations. . . . the

contrast between tribe and civilization is between War and Peace. A civilization is a society specially constituted to maintain "law and order"; the social complexity and cultural richness of civilizations depend on institutional guarantees of Peace. Lacking these institutional means and guarantees, tribesmen live in a condition of War, and War limits the scale, complexity, and all-round richness of their culture. . . . Expressed another way, in the language of older philosophy, the U.S. is a state, the tribe a state of nature. Or, the U.S. is a *civilization*, the tribe a *primitive society*" (1968: 4–5, original emphasis).

Despite some disquiet, the notion of tribal society as organized primarily by kinship rather than territory was retained, although it was acknowledged that there was rather little ethnographic evidence that clearly illustrated this.[3] The idea of tribal social organization as kin-based crystallized into a particular model by which the units generated by kinship form nested series of descent groups. "The tribe presents itself as a pyramid of social groups, technically speaking as a 'segmentary hierarchy.' . . . The smallest units, such as households, are segments of more inclusive units such as lineages, the lineages in turn segments of larger groups, and so on" (Sahlins 1968: 15).

Chiefs and Chiefdoms

Anthropology inherited the term "chief" from a colonial order in which civilizations were governed by monarchs and aristocrats, and more primitive "tribal" societies were ruled by chiefs and paramount chiefs. Although the most powerful African rulers were regarded as royalty, such as the monarchs of Dahomey, Benin, Ashante, and the Zulu, in general local rulers were described as chiefs rather than kings, lords, or some other noble title. For all the salience of the capitalist economy of colonialism, aristocracy still commanded great prestige in Europe, and the use of titles had important political and diplomatic implications.[4]

The colonial usage was later rationalized by structural functionalist modeling of many African political systems as smaller in scale, less centralized, and territorially looser than "the state." But as the true grounds for the term had always been to distinguish civilized from barbaric societies, this terminology did not correspond to descriptions of any European forms of leadership since the Dark Ages. Each one of the hundred or so petty rulers of seventh century Ireland was termed a king, for example, despite the fact that they governed a few thousand persons at best. The hereditary ruler of the Bemba, however, governing some 140,000 aristocrats and commoners was termed a Paramount Chief (Richards 1940).

The chiefdom was fitted into the evolutionary scheme of development. "Tribes present a notable range of evolutionary developments. . . . in its most developed expression, the chiefdom, tribal culture anticipates statehood in its complexities. Here are regional political regimes organized under powerful chiefs and primitive nobilities" (Sahlins 1968: 20). The distinguishing feature of "primitive nobilities" was, needless to say, the circular argument that they existed in chiefdoms or "primitive states." As an evolutionist concept the characteristics of the chiefdom had to conform with the theory of change from egalitarian kinship society to impersonal class society. It was said to be made up of descent groups that were simultaneously communities, and could not be *really* stratified, as that was thought to be a characteristic of a later stage.

> A chiefdom is a ranked society. The descent and community groups of a segmentary tribe are equal in principal, but those of a chiefdom are hierarchically arranged, the uppermost officially superior in authority and entitled to a show of deference from the rest. A chiefdom is not a class society. Although a stage beyond primitive equalitarianism, it is not divided into a ruling stratum in command of the strategic means of production or political coercion and a disenfranchised underclass. . . . One particular type of chiefdom organization, developed on exactly such distinctions of kinship grade, is so often called to anthropological mind it has come to epitomize the class . . . The conical clan system" (Sahlins 1968: 24).

As Kuper notes, the conical clan model, originally proposed by Paul Kirchhoff in 1955, was used to try and explain the coexistence of descent models and stratified social systems. Sahlins explains it thus:

> The conical clan is an extensive common descent group, ranked and segmented along genealogical lines and patrilineal in ideological bias. . . . Here clanship is made political. Distinctions are drawn between members of the group according to genealogical distance from the ancestor: the first-born son of first-born sons ranks highest and other people lower in the measure of their descent, down to the last born of last-born sons—everyone's commoner. . . . the chiefdom as a political unit is constructed on the clan as a ranked descent unit (1968: 24).

But the ethnographic basis for these ideal types began to dwindle on close inspection. Sahlins claimed the conical clan was widespread in Central Asia and parts of Africa, but he describes it as the "Polynesian type," considering it to be most common and perfectly manifested in that region. Subsequent ethnography from Polynesia suggested that in fact residential communities did not match descent groups, and status need not depend on descent at all (Kuper 2004: 91).

As early as 1961 Leach had suggested that the supposed structure of unilineal descent groups might be a "total fiction" (Leach 1961: 302).

The ethnographic evidence for the segmentary kinship model had always been rather slight, and what there was faded away in the light of more critical later studies. As Kuper writes, "in the end even the Nuer, Tiv, and Talis cannot be said to have 'true segmentary lineages'" (2004: 93). He concludes that "the lineage model, its predecessors and its analogues, have no value for anthropological analysis. . . . First, the model does not represent folk models, which actors anywhere have of their own societies. Secondly, there do not appear to be any societies in which vital political or economic activities are organized by a repetitive series of descent groups" (2004: 93). Indeed, as Goody notes, it is doubtful if even the original classical Roman agnatic descent group, the *gens*, was ever the dominant organizational form that Morgan supposed (2000: 18).

Without its grounding in a distinctive form of kinship organization, the characteristics that are supposed to distinguish the chiefdom are reduced to the idea that societies termed tribal, ruled by chiefs, represent a "pre-state" stage in political evolution.[5] This, however, is equally problematic. The Weberian definition of the state—a political community possessing a monopoly of the use of the legitimate use of force within a given territory—was actually devised to distinguish the "modern" state, but was used by the structural-functionalist theoreticians to underpin the notion that the chiefdom was at least one "evolutionary stage" behind "the state." In retrospect this approach seems limited historically and culturally, and poorly suited for application beyond Weber's original subject. Applied to the medieval world, for example, this Weberian definition would rule out almost every kingdom in Europe, as the Roman church retained independent judicial jurisdiction over significant parts of many kingdoms until well into the sixteenth century.

Evans-Pritchard and Fortes used the term "primitive state" for the evolutionary step after the chiefdom, a category into which they placed the majority of precolonial African polities. The working definition of this sort of state was a polity in which "a ruler who is recognised as supreme makes his authority effective through territorial agents chosen by himself . . . [and] The collection of tribute . . . is characteristic of all states" (Mair 1972: 124). This test of statehood is a hard one to pass for most early modern European states, in which the powerful aristocracies that controlled much of the territory can hardly have been said to have been chosen by the ruler. In the colonized world the most centralized and autocratic precolonial polities were considered primitive states, but everything else was, by default, tribal. The idea that England or Portugal should be regarded as tribal chiefdoms until—say—the Elizabethan or Imperial periods, reveals the residual ethnocentric evolutionism of the term. Europe had "passed that stage,'" it had entered "historical time," whereas polities in much of the rest of the world were examples of earlier stages, particularly in areas without systematic written histories to contradict the models projected onto them by the theorist.

Service (1975: 82) provides a typical justification for keeping Europe out of the evolutionary scheme imposed on "the rest." "European feudalism, then, was historically of a very complex, and perhaps unique sort. For this reason it cannot be considered a stage in evolution, or even a usual case of devolution." Without the mass of complicating historical detail available for Europe, societies in other parts of the world could be read more easily as evolutionary stages.[6] Although an earlier generation of scholars of Africa such as Rattray and Nadel had used the term "feudal" to describe precolonial African states, this terminology lost ground to the structural-functionalist scheme, which presented itself as a less particularistic classification of political society (Service 1975: 137). Similarly, Vladimirtsov's 1934 study of Mongolian society had described it as "nomadic feudalism," but this approach gave way before the advance of the tribal discourse of Radloff, Barthold, Fletcher, Kazanov, and Krader. The attention of political anthropologists has drifted away from these wranglings to join sociologists and others in remarking on the distinctiveness of the "modern" state, the Weberian, Marxist, and Foucauldian characterizations of which seemed more promising academic subjects. But this left the remnants of the language of an older political anthropology in widespread use—utilized by historians and regional specialists as well as anthropologists themselves.

Orientalism and Nomadology

The segmentary kinship model for nonstate society is evident in the work of Deleuze and Guattari, for example, who reproduced it in their own account of social form. Their work is highly functionalist, in that they describe social form in terms of machine systems. In *Anti-Oedipus* they write: "it is in order to function that a social machine must not function well. This has been shown precisely with regard to the segmentary system." While they accept from Engels the notion that only the State truly territorializes society in that it "substitutes geographic organization for the organization of *gens*" (Deleuze and Guattari 2004: 160), they also imagine that nonstate society, which they call "the primitive machine," was "the only territorial machine in the strict sense of the term." This is because its organization subdivided people (in the form of lineages) on the indivisible body of the earth "where the connective, disjunctive, and conjunctive relations of each section are inscribed along with other relations."

They adopt the standard narrative in which segmentary opposition prevents the stratification required for state formation: "the segmentary territorial machine makes use of scission to exorcise fusion, and impedes the concentration of power by maintaining the organs of chieftainry in a relationship of impotence with the group: as though the savages themselves sensed the rise of the imperial Barbarian, who will come nonetheless from without and will overcode their codes" (Deleuze and Guattari 2004: 167).

In *Nomadology* Deleuze and Guattari build on this approach to elaborate a theory of nomad society, which they call "the war machine," reflecting the abiding vision of the warlike tribe.

> Primitive, segmentary societies have often been defined as societies without a State, meaning societies in which distinct organs of power do not appear. . . . Clastres goes further, identifying *war* in primitive societies as the surest mechanism directed against the formation of the State: war maintains the dispersal and segmentarity of groups . . . just as Hobbes saw clearly that *the State was against war, so war is against the State*, and makes it impossible. It should not be concluded that war is a state of nature, but rather that it is the mode of a social state that wards off and prevents the State . . . the war machine is realized more completely in the "barbaric" assemblages of nomadic warriors than in the "savage" assemblages of primitive societies. In any case it is out of the question that the State could be the result of war in which the conquerors imposed through their victory a new law on the vanquished, since the organisation of the war-machine is directed against the State-form, actual or virtual (Deleuze and Guattari 1986: 10–14, original emphasis).

States may acquire military institutions, but these are anomalous and remain a potential threat to it.[7] "*The state has no war machine of its own*; it can only appropriate one in the form of a military institution, one that will always cause it problems" (Deleuze and Guattari 1986: 9, original emphasis).

There is no space here to discuss Deleuze and Guattari's general theory of war as the antithesis of the essentialized state, except to note that scholars such as Carneiro (1981) and Patterson (1991) argue convincingly that war is a fundamental ingredient in state formation. The concept of the nomad war machine, however, reflects both the tendency to exoticize mobility as a characteristic of an entirely different mode of society and thought, and the association with war that has been such an important element of European representations of steppe "nomads" since Marlow's dramatic portrait of the Mongol warlord Tamberlane.

Deleuze and Guattari argue for an "eccentric science" that stands opposed to "State science." They call this "nomadology"—concerned with "becoming and heterogeneity as opposed to the stable, the eternal"

(1986: 18). The "savant" of this nomad science is caught between "the war machine that nourishes and inspires him and the State that imposes on him a rational order" (1986: 20).

In this scheme the notion of the nomad is made to stand for a sort of essentialized liberty, a fundamental antistate form. But Deleuze and Guattari also seek to identify general structural forms, based on the actual histories of particular societies. They propose, for example, the numerical organization of society as one of three basic modes of social organization and an essential feature of the war machine:

> Tens, hundreds, thousands, myriads: all armies retain these decimal groupings. . . . For so peculiar an idea—the numerical organization of people—came from the nomads. . . . Everywhere the war machine displays a curious process of arithmetic replication or doubling. . . . For the social body to be numerized, the number must form a special body. When Genghis Khan undertook his great composition of the steppe, he numerically organized the lineages, and the fighters in each lineage, placing them under a cipher and a chief (groups of ten with decurians, groups of one hundred with centurions, groups of one thousand with chiliarchs). But he also extracted from each arithmetized lineage a small number of men who were to constitute his personal guard, in other words a dynamic formation comprising a staff, commissars, messengers and diplomats ("antrustions") . . . the war machine would be unable to function without this double series: it is necessary both that numerical composition replace lineal organization, and that it conjure away the territorial organization of the State. . . . Tensions or power struggles are also a result of this: between Moses' tribes and the Levites, between Genghis' "noyans" and "antrustions." . . . it is a tension inherent in the war machine, in its special power, and in the particular limitations placed on the power (puissance) of the "chief" (Deleuze and Guattari 1986: 63–71).

This part of Deleuze and Guattari's work reveals several of the problems with the standard narrative of segmentary society and the State. Firstly, it draws upon a largely discredited structural-functionalist account of "segmentary societies." Secondly, "the state" is treated in a highly essentialized way in which the particularities of certain European centralized polities are taken as its necessary and eternal features. By accepting the "territorialization" notion of State formation, and imagining that nomads have liberty of movement, Deleuze and Guattari immediately locate them outside the State and opposed to it. The argument becomes circular: how do we know nomads do not have States? Because the State must be territorial in a properly sedentary way, and nomads must *a priori* have a different sort of territoriality. Using this approach Deleuze and Guattari are bound to reject the application of the same terms for political organization to both "nomad" and "sedentary" societies. Feudalism, for example, is a "properly sedentary category," so they are bound to seek other terms to describe nomadic society.[8]

In fact, the historical record shows that steppe polities had a series of features commonly used to characterize feudalism, including a warrior aristocracy, vassalage, taxation, and the granting of land by the sovereign. Deleuze and Guattari recognize this but try to explain it away.

> There is no doubt that nomad organization and the war machine deal with these same problems [as sedentary states], both at the level of land and that of taxation. . . . But they invent a territoriality and a 'movable' fiscal organization that testifies to the autonomy of a numerical principle: there can be a confusion or combination of the systems, but the specificity of the nomadic system remains the subordination of land to numbers that are displaced and deployed, and of taxation to relations internal to those numbers (1986: 74).

Having decided that the numeric principle is essentially nomadic, it is used to explain away the existence of taxation and land allocation, rather than used to describe the form that these practices take.[9] The fundamental characteristics of the state that they mention, "*territoriality, work or public works, taxation*" (Deleuze and Guattari 1986: 115), were all present in "nomadic" steppe polities in Mongolia and elsewhere. Rather than reproducing the reified sedentary-nomad dichotomy, we must recognize that the practices we refer to when we use terms such as "taxation" and "land allocation" take different forms in different political economies and property regimes—be they pastoral or agricultural.

In general, Deleuze and Guattari offer their version of the common nineteenth century myth of political evolution, but with the State cast in negative, monstrous terms. They project an idealized, timeless notion of nonstate society onto actual historical societies about which they know very little, fastening on a few exotic features.[10] Although the civilized state is targeted and the nonstate "other" romanticized in the best Rousseauian tradition, the approach cannot but echo the orientalizing discourse of colonialism.[11] Recent ethnographic studies of "nomadic" societies show that rather than being defined by their mobility, actual steppe pastoralists have a variety of ways in which they make use of movement as a technique, to a greater or lesser extent depending on circumstances (Humphrey and Sneath 1999).

The Egalitarian Nomad and Pastoral Society as an Ideal-Type

Structural-functionalist anthropology treated "pastoral nomadic society" as an ideal-type with general characteristics to be discerned from the whole range of actual pastoral societies. As Asad notes, the segmentary lineage system model helped bolster the widespread assumption that, left to its own devices, pastoral nomadic society tended toward equality (1979: 421). Irons summed up the received wisdom:

> Among pastoral nomadic societies, hierarchical political institutions are generated only by external political relations with state societies, and never develop purely as a result of the internal dynamics of such societies . . . in the absence of relatively intensive political interaction with sedentary society, pastoral nomads will be organized into small autonomous groups, or segmentary lineage systems. Chiefly office with real authority will be generated only by interaction with sedentary state-organized society (1979: 362–72).[12]

Pastoral specialists, such as Dahl, argued that the ecological constraints of pastoralism tend to prevent the accumulation of wealth necessary for stratification (1979: 261–280). Others, such as Burnham, saw the spatial mobility of the pastoral nomad as also being a political mechanism that inhibited centralization and class formation (1979: 349–360). This environmentally deterministic reasoning deduced these characteristics "from first principles" rather than by close examination of particular historical cases. Surely, the argument went, nomads are bound to be egalitarian, as they could just move away from oppressive rulers? The counterarguments do not appear to have been seriously considered—that the rulers were also mobile and had political relations with neighboring power holders, that the rolling steppes might appear empty but were almost entirely divided between the various seasonal pastures governed by some powerful authority or other, or that there were numerous examples of historical pastoral societies with vast inequalities of wealth.

The segmentary kinship model was enthusiastically applied to Asian societies, with particular vigor in the case of groups thought of as "nomadic." Despite a notable lack of evidence, the practice that Andrew Strathern called the "background use of the segmentary model" retained a firm grip on ethnography of the region (1983: 453).

In his treatment of Afghanistan, for example, Hager advocates the "distinction between tribe, based on descent, and state, based on control of territory" (1983: 83). As ideal-types, he argues, "power in the state is monopolized by a central government, while in tribes such as the Pashtuns it may typically remain distributed among persons who adhere to the tribal law or who may occasionally be consolidated within various levels of latent tribal hierarchy" (Hager 1983: 86). This theoretical distinction, however, is of debatable value. State power operates through its distribution among persons adhering to state law, and state citizenship is also generally based on descent.[13]

Descriptions of the purest segmentary or conical clan systems are generally found in accounts of historical "tribal" societies, rather than contemporary ethnographic accounts (for example, Krader 1968; Garthwaite 1983; Barfield 1989). When such claims are made for a contemporary society, the clan system is usually in the process of being displaced or transformed as a political system by the state, so that its characteristics are never fully found.[14]

Ironically enough, one of the reasons for the persistence of this model of the pastoral nomadic tribe was that it happened to fit with arguments made by critics of the notion of the "pristine" tribe. Fried, for example, uses the long history of interaction between steppe powers and recognized states, such as China, as evidence that every group described as a tribe is in fact a product of the "secondary tribalism" generated by contact with states (see Fried 1975: 72). This is part of his argument, *contra* Sahlins—that small scale, aggressive societies are created by contact with states and reflects his own notion of egalitarian "prestate" society as a sort of human "starting point," which, Fried all but admits, is a matter of personal speculation and conjecture (1975: 71).

Fried reproduced Owen Lattimore's (1940) argument that Inner Asian pastoralists developed hierarchical formations as part of long historical relations with the Chinese state (see Lattimore 1940: 381). This provided an appealing reversal of the colonial trope whereby savage tribes were civilized by states. In Inner Asia it seemed that some of the most famous predatory tribes, such as the Xiongnu, Mongols, and Manchu were created by states. Jagchid and Hyer (1979: 261) reproduce this argument, and even the otherwise well-informed Gledhill is taken in by this appealing narrative: "the nomad chiefdoms [of Inner Asia] were organized into a structure of clans whose segments were ranked. Although the power of the chiefs was limited in peacetime, the hierarchical order of a chain of command was present in embryo in this political organization . . . it enabled the nomads to achieve rapid consolidation of administrative control over the territory they conquered" (1994: 43–44).

One of the reasons for the widespread reproduction of this vision of Inner Asian pastoral society is the work of Lawrence Krader, who is Sahlins's principle source on the subject. In his 1968 work *Formation of the State*, Krader gave a description of Mongolian pastoral society that fitted the dominant model of tribal political organization perfectly. "An ordinary pastoral village in Mongolia is usually arranged in the form of either a circle, or an arc, of tents. The basis of village organization is the extended family, composed of a patriarch and his sons, and their wives and children. Since families in the village are related, a kin community is formed. Typically the entire village is descended from a common founding ancestor" (Krader 1968: 86–87).

Krader explains this contemporary social organization as the remaining, irreducible building block of the grander clan and tribal systems of the past. "The history of the formation of these kin communities is directly related to the history of herding in Mongolia. . . . Villages were grouped into clans, and clans further into confederations, all still related by bonds of descent from a common ancestor. Thus all male members of a clan or confederation were related, even if only distantly; emperor and subject might be tenth or twentieth cousins in the male line. Each clan had a body of ritual which was special unto itself: ceremonies venerating clan ancestors, clan spirits, territorial spirits, the natural forces and phenomena of the territory" (Kader 1968: 87).

In fact Krader is wrong in almost every detail of this description. There is nothing like the relation between kinship and residence that Krader postulates, no evidence of different bodies of ritual special to "clans" (whatever he means by this term in the Mongolian context), and no genealogical scheme relating nobles with their commoner subjects.[15] Such a clan or lineage social organization was no more apparent in the early twentieth century, as the work of ethnographers such as Simukov (1933) and Vreeland (1962) make clear.[16] In fact, there is no reason to believe that anything like this structure of kin villages grouped into clans ever existed in Mongolia.[17]

Krader's next step, to claim that clans were grouped into confederations, could have been read directly from Morgan's original pattern for primitive society. "The plan of government of the American aborigines commenced with the gens [clan] and ended with the confederacy. . . . In like manner the plan of the government of the Grecian tribes, anterior to civilization, involved in the same organic series" (Morgan 1878: 66 cited in Fried 1975: 93). In the conventional treatment of pastoral nomads, the confederation became the natural political aggregate formed by tribes.

The Tribe in Inner Asia

Historically the steppelands of Inner Asia have given rise to a series of imperial powers, including the Xiongnu, early Türk, Manchu, and the vast Mongol empires. Scholars of Inner Asia have made much of the apparently incongruous phenomena of nomadic tribes periodically establishing vast and powerful states. Dominated by the notion of pastoral nomadic society as an ideal-type, these accounts commonly graft received wisdom regarding segmentary tribes onto their descriptions to fill the gaps left in the historical record.

Thomas Barfield, one of the best known anthropologists of Inner Asia, generalizes: "Inner Asian nomadic states were organized as 'Imperial confederacies' . . . They consisted of an administrative hierarchy with at least three levels: the imperial leader and his court, imperial governors appointed to oversee the component tribes within the empire, and indigenous tribal leaders. At the local level the tribal structure remained intact, under the rule of chieftains whose power was derived from their own people's support, not imperial appointment" (1989: 8).

Barfield offers a description of a timeless, essentialized steppe nomadic society that could have been written by Krader or Sahlins:

> Throughout Inner Asia historically known pastoralists shared similar principles of organization alien to sedentary societies. . . . Patrilineal relatives shared common pasture and camped together when possible. . . . Tribal political and social organization was based on a model of nested kinship groups, the conical clan . . . an extensive patrilineal kinship organization in which members of a common descent group were ranked and segmented along genealogical lines. . . . Political leadership was restricted to members of senior clans in many groups, but from the lowest to the highest, all members of the tribe claimed common descent. . . . When nomads lost their autonomy to sedentary governments, the political importance of this extensive genealogical system disappeared, and kinship links remain important only at the local level (Barfield 1989: 24–26).

The lack of historical evidence of segmentary kinship system was explained away by assuming that contact with, or conquest of, state systems caused them to decay. In any historical description, the argument went, one would only expect to find elements, remnants of the complete system of the past. The thirteenth century Mongol state founded by Chinggis Khan (Genghis Khan), for example, created a rich fund of historical materials, particularly Chinese and Persian sources. It is clear from these that this was a hierarchical society with a powerful pastoral aristocracy ruling common subjects, and the richer historical sources of the fourteenth century show that the *lack* of a segmentary lineage structure dates back to at least this time.[18]

So the essentialized tribal society is envisaged as existing before the Chinggisid state, at a period for which we have almost no historical material. Barfield writes: "At the time of Temüjin's [Chinggis Khan's] birth the steppe was in anarchy. Segmentary opposition was the basic form of political organization: opposing tribes or clans would unite against a common foe, only to separate and continue fighting one another when the common enemy was defeated" (1989: 189). Most of what is known about the pre-Chinggisid period not written by outsiders is provided by a single source—the *Mongqol-un niuca tobca'an*, the *Secret History of the Mongols*, which was almost certainly authored by one or more members of Chinggis Khan's court in the thirteenth century.[19] The *Secret History of the Mongols* includes some genealogical data, and some of the named groups in it appear to trace descent from common ancestors. However, on closer inspection these genealogies are not "segmentary."[20] There is no reason to suppose that the society was composed of territorial kin groups and what little evidence we have on political alliances suggests shifting pragmatic alliances between powerful nobles with little or no respect for genealogical proximity, the most bitter warfare often breaking out between close aristocratic relatives.[21]

At the time of Chinggis Khan's birth, the steppes of what is now Mongolia were divided between a number of political entities (such as the Kereid, Merkid, Tatar, Jürkin, and Tayichi'ut). In the dominant interpretation of the *Secret History of the Mongols*, these are described as tribes or clans. In fact we know very little about the internal organization of these entities. What is clear, however, is that these polities were aristocracies with common subjects, and that the commoner-nobility distinction long predated Chinggis Khan's rise to power. The term for groups defined largely (but probably not exclusively) through descent was *yasu* ("bone") and nobles were referred to as of *chaqa'an yasu*—"white bone"—this color contrasting with black—*qara* used for with commoners. Documented traditions of aristocracy and hereditary overlordship in the Mongolian region stretch back as far as the Xiongnu Empire of the second century B.C.[22]

There is plenty of evidence, if one chooses to look for it, that these ruling houses or lineages were *not* related by descent to the people they ruled. The people known as the Jürkin, for instance, were one of several named groups living in Mongolia at the time. They have been described as a tribe (Cleaves 1982: 245) or a clan (De Rachewiltz 2004: 289), and from this it would appear they formed a homogeneous kin-based unit composed of clansmen. In fact it is clear from section 139 of the *Secret History* that this political unit had originally been formed by an emperor (Qabul Qahan) and that the term 'Jürkin' more properly referred to the ruling lineage or house only. "Chinggis Qahan made such arrogant people submit (to him) and he destroyed the Jürkin *oboq* (family, line, lineage). Chinggis Qahan made their people, and the subjects (they ruled), his own subjects."[23] The conquest of other polities, such as the Tatar and Tayichi'ut, for example, are described in very similar terms with the name of the polity attached most specifically to the nobility who were clearly distinguished from their subjects.[24]

Instead of a map of a segmentary or conical clan kinship system, then, the *Secret History of the Mongols* describes sets of ruling lineages or houses with a large number of subjects.[25] The standard translation of terms, however, gives the impression that it describes a prestate society of clans and tribes.

There is no single term that corresponds to the way that the word "tribe" has been inserted in the translations of the *Secret History*. Instead a series of different words—*irgun* (people, subjects); *ulus* (polity, realm, patrimony, apanage); and *aimag* (division, group)—have been translated as "tribe" in places in the text where the unit concerned is believed to be tribal. Similarly, there are two terms *oboq* (family, lineage, line) and *yasu* (bone, descent, lineage) commonly translated as "clan" depending on the context, and often the term clan has simply been inserted next to any group noun that the translator believes to be a clan.[26]

Ratchnevsky has a similar tendency. Knowing that the *Secret History* describes a clearly stratified society he pushes the mythic nomadic kin-based society back to the turmoil before Chinggis is born. He writes, "the kinship group lost its homogeneous character" (1991: 12). This is a strange comment to make as Ratchnevsky uses Persian sources to show that both the predecessors of Chinggis Khan (Qutula Khan and Ambagai Qahan) ruled steppe empires, but presumably he conceives of these empires as consisting of homogeneous kin groups, much as Krader conceived of Chinggis's early empire.

The insertion of kinship has been accompanied by the deletion of stratification; the importance of aristocratic power and heritage has been consistently downplayed.[27] At some points in the text, for example, the term *ulus* is usually translated as "nation," which is the current meaning of the term (see Onon 1990: 11 and Cleaves 1982: 11). Elsewhere translators have habitually rendered it as "people"—e.g., when the Khan of the Kereid tells Chinggis that he will help him reunite his scattered *ulus* (Pelliot 1949: 25; Onon 1990: 28; Cleaves 1982: 33; and De Rachewiltz 2004: 30), and this helped support the impression of egalitarian tribalism. A more accurate translation for the term in this period would actually be "patrimony," as Morgan (1986: 95) notes, and in Chinggisid states such as the Yüan and Ilkhanate, it is consistently used for the apanages assigned to nobles. But it has been assumed that this usage was a state-induced distortion of an original, more "tribal" concept. The more probably accurate translation of the Kereid Khan's offer—"I will reunite for you your divided patrimony"—appeared rather too feudal, so most translators chose to render this as, "I shall unite for you your scattered people."

Colonial and Imperial Notions of the Tribe in Inner Asia

In the colonial period Europeans encountered a Chinese literature that had itself a long history of representing societies beyond the boundaries of the state in certain ways. Literary traditions for the description of "barbarians"—peoples known by terms such as Yi, Rong, Di, Man, and so on—stretch at least as far back as the Han dynasty. As Hostetler puts it, "the politics of representation encapsulated in the idea of 'orientalism' is not simply a feature of Western modernity, but of the colonial encounter itself, wherever colonial relations are played out. This capacity or inclination to 'orientalize' is not unique to the Western world" (2001: 99). Chinese representations of "barbarian" outsiders are susceptible to similar analysis. "The central issue is . . . how centers of power with a monopoly on the production and dissemination of knowledge define peripheral groups and attempt in one way or another to dominate them. The struggle for control is not only a product of 'Western' hegemony" (Hostetler 2001: 96). European scholars of the colonial period found a workable correspondence between their own categories and those of the Imperial Qing state when describing peoples on the peripheries or beyond the boundaries of their states, whose societies and elites were described as of a lower political order than their own.

The widespread use of the term "tribe" to describe the societies on China's Inner Asian frontier was partly a result of translation. The conventional translation of the Chinese term *buluo* was "tribe" in English. The first term *bu* means "a class, division, section, or sort." It can also mean "public board." It was combined with *luo* to mean an aboriginal or native "tribe," but could be more precisely translated as "indigenous division." For colonialist discourse, however, the translation fitted well enough— both terms reflected the notion of a political division of the uncivilized.

The Mongol term *aimag* was conventionally translated into Chinese as *buluo*. In modern Mongolian *aimag* means a section or administrative division—such as province; in historical documents it is commonly translated as "tribe" (e.g., Bawden 1997: 10). However, as Atwood (2004:5) notes, as long ago as the thirteenth century Yüan dynasty, the term *aimag* was used in Mongolian documents for provinces of China, and it would be more consistent to assume that the term meant "administrative division" even at that time. None of the conceptual baggage that was attached to the term tribe is actually contained in the terms themselves, so their translations in early documents is a matter of convention based on particular models of steppe society at that time.[28]

There has been a good deal of persistent unease with the use of the term "tribe" by more critical scholars of Inner Asia. Lattimore sometimes placed the term in inverted commas to show the provisionality of its use and remarks, "a tribe is not so 'real' a thing as the genealogy of a princely family" (1934: 76). He was also very conscious that the English word stood for the Mongol administrative terms *aimag* and *chuulgan*—units of regional government that formed part of the Qing state. When describing the Manchurian Tungus-speaking group Oronchon, for example, Lattimore describes it as having become "sufficiently 'tribal' to be organized in the modern Mongol style on a tribal-territorial basis" (1934: 165). The "modern administration" Lattimore is referring to involved the "tribal" system of local offices and incorporation into *chuulgan* princely assemblies that characterized Qing indirect rule of the Mongol territories.

Specialists have also questioned the interpretation of historical materials through the prism of kin-society theory in the Middle East. One example is the exchange between two historians Helfgott and Reid in the journal *Iranian Studies*. Tapper writes that Helfgott

> characterizes Iranian tribes as pastoral nomadic kinship-based chiefdoms that form closed economic systems; . . . Unfortunately he produces little evidence for his argument, overstresses the role of pastoral nomadism, kinship and chiefship. . . . he is accused of theoretism by Reid, whose own version of tribal organization, to which he is led mainly by data on administration and the perspective of the state, is that its essence in Iran was the highly complex centralized *oymaq* system that flourished under the Safavids; oymaqs were neither simply pastoral nor based on kinship (1983: 7–8).

The word *oymaq* is in fact the Mongolian word *aimag*, introduced by the Chinggisids in the Ilkhanate period. Although historians agree that these were clearly administrative divisions and not based on kinship in the Safavid period (1501–1722), scholars have been loath to conclude that it is likely to have been just that in its original Mongolian setting, and assumed again that the term was transformed as a result of contact with sedentary states.

Contemporary specialists such as Peter Golden are often cautious about the term "tribe," treating it as a matter of convention rather than a good description (2001: 20).[29] Nicola Di Cosmo has to modify the term to be able to use it with a clear conscience. He takes "tribe" to mean "a large group of people recognizable by one single ethnonym and *possibly* united by kin ties and kin relations" (1999: 18, emphasis added). In Inner Asian history, he says, this was "preeminently a political formation" replete with made to order genealogies, but united in "a common political project."[30] Such specialists have largely abandoned the content of the term so that it really simply indicates a political formation of some kind. However, the "technical" meaning of a term cannot be separated from its connotations and the contexts of its habitual application. The term "tribe" retains subtle echoes of its earlier meanings and its popular application to societies thought of as "primitive." Never having been explicitly exorcized, the wider model of tribal society continues to haunt the scholarship on the region. Soucek, for example, describes Mongolia up to the advent of communist control in the 1920s and 1930s as "a confederation of tribal groups governed by a two-pronged aristocracy of lay tribal and Buddhist church leaders" (2000: 298).

Nomadic Tribes in the Colonial Imagination

In the late colonial period popular representations of nomads portrayed them as simple people, fierce and free. Some of the best known travel writing on Inner Asia in English was the work of Mildred Cable and Francesca French, two intrepid missionaries who traveled in the region in the late 1920s. "In nomad land the spaces belong to the tribes, and the Mongol rides over them singing and shouting, free as the air he breathes, tied to no building and confined by no walls of city or of home. He belongs to the desert and the desert belongs to him" (Cable and French 1950: 267).

In fact, such accounts are extremely misleading. From the seventeenth century, if not before, the territory of Mongolia was divided into administrative divisions (*hoshuu*), each ruled by a nobleman (*zasag noyon*) (Natsagdorj 1967). Later, after the Mongol nobles had sworn fealty to the Manchu emperor, some administrative districts were governed by Buddhist monasteries or Qing officials with similar powers. The default rank for noblemen was the title of *taij* ("prince"), and there were eight classes of aristocratic title, from the greatest lords down to the generic title of *taij* without a *hoshuu* to govern.[31] Each *hoshuu* prince had his own administrative staff, treasury, and offices, as well as personal serfs and numerous herds of livestock. His subjects were divided among subunits—the *sumun* of a notional hundred and fifty households, made up of *bag* of around fifty households, which were divided into *arban* units of a nominal ten. Pastureland was under the jurisdiction of the ruling lord or monastery who managed pastoral movement in their districts. There were vast inequalities in wealth with rich aristocrats and monasteries owning tens of thousands of livestock, and the poorest herders having none at all but working for others to make a living. Members of the Mongolian aristocracy had intermarried with the Manchu nobility since the seventeenth century, and were frequently appointed to high Imperial office, particularly in the military. They were generally highly literate, often multilingual, and coordinated policy through regional assembles (*chuulgan*) chaired by a rotating head.

One would hardly suspect any of this from the picture painted by Cable and French, who were writing at a time when, in the wake of the collapse of the Qing, the Mongolian nobility led by Princes such as Gungsangnorbu and Demchugdongrob were negotiating an uneasy course between Chinese Warlords, the Guomindang nationalist government, and expanding Japanese and Soviet influence.[32] Their account evokes visions of an ancient tribal life: they frequently describe the Prince as a Chief or Chieftain while hinting at a sort of exotic, barbaric lawlessness.

> We went to Etzingol. . . . we learnt that the old Prince, at whose invitation we came, had recently died, and that the new head was a usurper who seized the Chieftainship, with all the tents and all the riches of the old Prince. Next morning we sat in the tent of this bold supplanter, and with the help of his Chinese

interpreter we talked to him of many things. . . . The Chieftain's simple mind was bewildered by two irreconcilable assertions that simultaneously claimed his attention, and both of which were new and foreign to his thought. One concerned the Mongolian New Testament which we had sent ahead and of which he turned the pages as we talked. The first great proposition which faced him was the call from God to repentance: "God commandeth men everywhere to repent." The other word was a denial of the existence of God, and a declaration by the strange lama [who had just returned from a journey into Soviet territory] that religion was the weapon of imperialism and the dope of the people. . . . That day, in the audience-tent, the destiny of the Etzingol tribes seemed to be outlined before our eyes. . . . Young boys would be claimed for school-life and their outlook cleverly biased, amplifiers carrying the voice of a Moscow broadcast might speak in the tent of Chieftains, and the conversion of fearless herdsmen into dashing cavalry could be easily effected. This might well be the future of the Etzingol nomads (Cable and French 1950: 270–1).

Cable and French must have met the Prince of Ejine gol *hoshuu*, who around 1930 would have been embroiled in the administrative consequences of the inclusion of his principality into the newly formed Ningxia province in 1928, within territory controlled by the Soviet-leaning Chinese warlord Marshal Feng.[33] Their description of him as a usurper is very puzzling, as succession was entirely governed by law, but the resulting hint of barbaric daring succeeds in making the account more exciting.

Lattimore notes that this tendency among travelers to portray Mongolian nomads in romantic terms dated back to the previous century:

Western travellers in the second half of the nineteenth century were attracted by the free spaces of the open steppe, the hospitality and noble manners of the aristocracy. . . . Abundant herds gave the impression of great wealth. Only the sharper observers noted that the common herdsman consumed very little of the mutton and beef and milk that walked about the pastures under their charge, and that the poorer people were bitterly poor. . . . few travellers were interested in deducing from the comparison between poor people and rich herds that the "free" life of the nomad was restricted even in freedom of movement and that ownership [of property] had passed from the herdsman to princes and ecclesiastical dignitaries (1951: 96).

Lattimore, however, remained sufficiently uncritical of longstanding European notions of the egalitarian nomad to displace the existence of nomadic freedom and equality into the pre–Qing and pre–Chinggisid period, for which there were almost no historical records describing steppe society.[34] Stratified political structures were explained away as "distortions" of the original kin-based nomadic society, caused by contact with sedentary states.

In another of his entirely inaccurate flights of fancy, Krader uses the notion of kinship society to try and explain away the starkly obvious importance of aristocracy in pre–Soviet era Mongolia. "Nevertheless, this uniform kinship structure was divided into unequal estates, the nobility and the commoners. Both were estates related by descent from the clan founder; but in practice they were divided by differences in birth, wealth, accident, migrations, wars. Descent lines were not equal; the line of the firstborn was more highly placed than any other, having the right of seniority. . . . Leadership was a status that was not assigned by rote—it had to be achieved, and achievement was based on social recognition of leadership qualities" (Krader 1968: 87).

Krader is, again, wrong in almost every respect. There was no established right of primogeniture in the Imperial period.[35] A ruler could generally choose any of his sons to succeed to his domain, and this selection is presumably what Krader misleadingly describes as the "achievement" of leadership positions, unless he is referring to the process by which the Prince selected his subordinate officials. In the Qing period the major status categories of *albat* ("commoner"—literally "with duties") and *noyan* ("noble") were entirely hereditary. Throughout most of Mongolia only the Borjigin aristocracy kept genealogical records and these show no shared descent with commoners, let alone a neat ranking of different "lines" within a conical clan structure. The *hoshuu* districts were administrative units, not clans, and in most *hoshuu* the majority of commoners used no clan names. The areas in which such named descent groups and genealogical records were usual for commoners were those under direct Manchu or Tsarist Russian administration, and were almost certainly the result of administrative imposition by these states.[36]

Descent Groups as State Policy

Rather than one of the "earliest acts of human intelligence" as Morgan supposed,[37] the organization of people into named descent groups was an act of state administration in much of Inner Asia. Comprehensive kinship organization was a product of the state, not a precursor to it.

In most of Mongolia there are no clans, lineages, or extensive genealogies apart from those of the Borjigin aristocracy (the descendants of Chinggis Khan). However, in some areas, notably eastern Inner Mongolia, named descent groups are common, and these have been taken as surviving remnants of a once-general organizational form and evidence of the general applicability of the segmentary kinship model. But any sort of critical examination of the history of these institutions reveals no evidence for this whatsoever.

In the seventeenth century Mongolia became part of the Manchu empire, largely by diplomatic means. Inner Mongolian Mongol nobles were relatively early supporters of the Manchu ruler Nurhachi and his son Hong Taiji, who founded the Qing dynasty in 1636. The Manchu attempted to impose a system of lineages upon their Inner Mongolian subjects, using any convenient terms that could be made to stand as clan names. This was not carried out fully in the larger and more distant Outer Mongolian region, but Inner Mongolian groups such as the Daur and Horchin had been incorporated into the Manchu state in the seventeenth century, and were organized into descent groups in a similar way to Manchu subjects. Szynkiewicz notes:

> Nurhachi (the founder of the Manchu state) based his organization on kinship groups. . . . Following established practice, the Manchu began with registering the kinship groups in the conquered areas. They succeeded in putting on record 233 groups of the *obug [oboq]* type in southern Mongolia (Lebedeva 1958), a very modest number in comparison with the potential number of lineages in the entire society. . . . Quite a few of them were presumably somewhat artificial constructs put on the list—as argued by Mergen Gegen (1977: 32).

Mergen Gegen was a leading Mongolian ecclesiastical intellectual of the eighteenth century, and was in an excellent position to have witnessed this process.[38]

In fact, the Manchu "clan" itself does not appear to have been a preexisting descent group either, but was an administrative device used by the early Manchu state. The Qing organized its Manchu subjects into *mukun*—groups that became known as clans, but in the early period were probably not descent groups at all, and were "constantly formed and reformed by economic and environmental circumstances" (Crossley 1997: 29). But in the new seventeenth century Qing state administration, it became important to know to which of these various administrative units people belonged, and so these units became descent groups, resembling clans. The Manchu nobility came to administer a huge empire, which included China, and their Manchu subjects had particular military and administrative obligations and entitlements. Membership lists were kept, the heads of descent groups had control over their members, and an enormous bureaucracy developed to keep track of genealogies, eligibilities, and rewards.

To find something resembling conical clan society, then, one must look further back historically to the medieval period; but, again, first impressions can be misleading. One of the largest steppe powers that preceded the Chinggisid Mongol state was the Kitan polity, for example. Based in what is now Manchuria, the Kitans founded the Liao dynasty that ruled northern China from the tenth to the twelfth centuries. At first glance the pastoral Kitans seem to conform to the conical clan model of Inner Asian tribes—a set of kin-groups united by common descent from ancestors. Historical sources refer to an ancestral pair whose eight sons became the founders of the eight original Kitan tribes (Franke in Sinor 1990: 406). However, yet again, on closer inspection this turns out to be nothing like the clan-society model, but rather a description of aristocratic houses or lineages. Not only were nobles unrelated by descent to their subjects, but the commoners seem to have had no clans at all. Franke writes, "originally there existed no clan groups within the tribes. . . . The Chinese exogamous clan-system was adopted under the Liao only for the ruling Yeh-lü clan and the Hsiao clan of the imperial consorts; as a consequence the Kitan commoners and tribesmen had no family names" (1990: 403–5). This pattern seems to predate the Kitan period. The predecessor power in Manchuria was the Bohai state of the eighth to the 10th centuries. Crossley notes that the Bohai class system was rigid (1997: 19). Elites tended to be affiliated with large families and had surnames, but there is no evidence that commoners did.

In fact, the earliest descriptions of Inner Asian steppe society have noted the importance of aristocratic power. The second century B.C. historian Sima Qian who described the steppe empire of the Xiongnu writes of an aristocracy composed of three families. The Xiongnu emperor commanded a number of high officials, whose positions were hereditary. Of these leaders "the more important ones commanded ten thousand horsemen and the lesser ones several thousand, numbering twenty-four leaders in all, although all are known by the title of "ten thousand horsemen" (*Shih chi,* cited in Barfield 1981: 48). The units of a thousand and ten thousand described for the Xiongnu appear in descriptions of one steppe polity after another from that period on. Fourteen centuries later the *Secret History of the Mongols* mentions the position of *tümen-ü noyan* "Lord of Ten Thousand" in conversations that predate the Chinggisid state (Pelliot 1949: 31). The accounts of this decimal organization of thousand (*mingqan*) and ten thousand units is so clear in the more abundant sources on the Chinggisid empire, and so unlike the "tribal model," that conventional work (such as Barfield 1989: 195–7) has been to treat it as a purely military form of organization. But in fact it is very clear that these were administrative units from which a military force of one or ten thousand horsemen could be raised (Bold 2001: 177; De Rachewiltz 2004: 762–3).[39]

Rethinking State and Tribe

The trope of the egalitarian tribal nomad owed much to the theories of kinship and tribal society that dichotomized kin and class, tribe and state, tradition and modernity. If we suspend our commitment to these distinctions, we see various continuities and similarities in power structures within a single analytical frame. The success of aristocratic houses or lineages over very long periods reveals descent and kinship as techniques of power and aspects of stratification, rather than its antithesis.

There is clear evidence of powerful indigenous aristocratic orders since the Xiongnu, and they form the basis of each steppe polity for which we have significant historical records.[40] The continuities are striking—the root metaphor for commoner status in modern Mongolian—black or *har* (*qara*)—for example, stretches back at least as far as the Orhon Türk state of the sixth century, in which *kara bodun* was the term for commoners (Sinor 1990: 310). Throughout recorded history, states and empires were established in different regions of the steppe, or beyond it, and brought parts of the steppe nobility into their political orbit as vassals. Much of the Chinggisid nobility who ruled fiefdoms throughout Mongolia, for example, were largely autonomous of their nominal overlord Ligdan Khan by the early seventeenth century, and most of the eastern and southern aristocracy changed their allegiance and swore fealty to the increasingly powerful Manchu monarch Nurhachi.

Whenever there is evidence that describes them, it is clear that these aristocratic orders gave ruling nobles control of both production and destruction on the steppe, all the local powers needed for the grander imperial states. Subjects were divided into administrative units that would produce a nominal number of horsemen for military service under their lord. Otherwise they were bound to remain in their allotted seasonal pastures and render the lord corvée labor or military service if required to. In addition they were liable for various levies of produce. Since the twelfth century at the very latest, nobles exercised proprietorial authority over their personal servant families (*Khamjilga*) and sometimes also had slaves (*bool*). Groups of their subjects could be sent as dowry with a noble bride to another aristocrat's domain (*inj*), and in general the position of commoner subjects resembled serfdom in a number of important ways. The local power relations of aristocracy had all that was required to operate both the local political and economic formations in the Quing period *hoshuu* districts, and the wider Manchu imperial state into which they fitted. When the Qing state collapsed in 1911, the *hoshuu* continued to operate, unless reorganized by Chinese Warlord or Japanese administration, until the advent of communist control in 1947.

Although in his early work Lattimore was still sufficiently convinced of the tribal model to reject the notion of nomadic feudalism, in his later work he became convinced of the opposite view (1940: 381). He writes, "there are those who hesitate to call the Mongolian social order 'feudal,' but I do not see how the term can be avoided: aristocratic rank was hereditary and identified with territorial fiefs, and serfdom was also hereditary and territorially identified" (Lattimore 1976: 3). His approach conforms to that of Mongolian historians such as Natsagdorj (1967) and Sanjdorj (1980) who find the term entirely applicable.

This marked stratification clearly long predated the Mongolian incorporation into the Manchu empire. The observant Franciscan Friar Giovanni
Da Pian Del Carpini, who travelled to the court of Güyük Khan (Chinggis
Khan's grandson) in 1246, left the first eyewitness account by a European
of the Mongol polity. He noted:

> The dukes have like dominion over their men in all matters, for all Tartars [Mon-
> gols] are divided into groups under dukes. . . . The dukes as well as the others are
> obliged to give mares to the Emperor as rent . . . and the men under the dukes
> are bound to do the same for their lords, for not a man of them is free. In short,
> whatever the emperor and the dukes desire, and however much they desire, they
> receive from their subjects' property (Beazley 1903: 59; Dawson 1955: 28).

The translation of terms is, again, highly revealing. Carpini used the Latin
word "dux" for senior Mongol and European nobles alike, and early translators such as Hakluyt (1598) translated these as "duke" (as I have done in
the passage above).[41] However, nineteenth and twentieth century translators such as Rockhill (1900) and Dawson (1955) introduced an astonish-
ing dual system whereby when "dux" referred to a European noble, such
as the Russian noble Vassilko, it was translated as "duke," but where it
applied to a Mongol it was translated as "chief," thus confirming the tribal
model of Mongolian society.[42]

Without the theory of an essentialized pastoral nomadic type, toward
which steppe society was bound to gravitate, we have no reason to dis-
believe the evidence of a long history of stratification, and its continuity between the eras of powerfully centralized imperial power such as the
Chinggisid and Qing states.

In the seventeenth century, for example, when the authority of the
Chinggisid imperial house had decayed, Ligdan Khan, the nominal inheritor of the Yüan throne, had his remaining power base in the southeast
and exercised weak authority over much of the northern and central part
of Mongolia. When he died in 1634 no clear successor emerged. In the
west the growing power of the Oirat Empire was drawing western parts of
Mongolia into its orbit. Agreements made between the Oirat and remaining Chinggisid Mongol nobles (both of whom are described as "tribal" by
Soucek 2000: 167–170)[43] are documented in the *Mongol-Oirat Regulations
of 1640*, and these make clear the mutual interests both aristocracies had
in controlling their subjects and preventing commoners defecting to the
jurisdictions of other nobles: "Those (people) who go to another *hoshuu*
and those who move between them shall be gathered and seized. If they
have no *otog* [pasture and commoners belonging to a noble] they shall
belong to an *otog*, if they have no *aimag* [administrative division] they
shall belong to an *aimag*." The regulations detail the punishments in the

case of subjects leaving their allotted *nutag* [pastoral area] (Altangerel 1998: 70).[44] It is clear from this and other documents that the basic power relations between nobility and their subjects predates Manchu administration, which only really became established in most of Mongolia in the eighteenth century. Nobles were giving commoners to senior Buddhist figures in the seventeenth century.[45] Indeed the Manchus had to prohibit the Mongol nobility's habit of selling and giving away *hamjlaga* and *albat* subjects (Bold 2001: 123).

Having abandoned the notion that the assumed characteristics of putative "tribal" society would reassert themselves in the interregnum, there is no reason to suppose that these aristocratic orders were transformed between the Chinggisid and pre–Qing periods in which they resemble each other so closely. Power was largely distributed among the aristocracy, and the extent to which they were integrated into larger imperial polities varied with the historical fortunes of the various Chinggisid, Tumet, Manchu, and Oirat imperial projects of this period. The much-remarked tendency for steppe polities to fragment as constituent parts were allocated to the rulers' sons was real enough. But what has been commonly cast in terms of the struggle between "tribalism" and "the state," is much better seen as processes that produced more or less centralized and imperial versions of an existing aristocratic order.

Cultures of Aristocracy

The aristocratic character of Mongolian society before its incorporation into the "modern" communist-run states of Mongolia and China is well documented. The prerevolutionary political discourse did not construct the polity with reference to a general "people." Subjects came in discrete categories: nobles, commoners, and the members of the Buddhist monastic establishments. Political statements were constructed with respect to these different constituencies, and it was usual to make separate statements or edicts for these different classes of subject.[46] Nobles were part of the political project of rulership, even if they held no administrative posts. They were free of the tax and corvée labor duties owed by commoners to their lord, and were entitled to a personal retinue of servants. The legal punishments for nobles were quite different from commoners and generally confined to fines of livestock, while commoners faced flogging, enslavement, or death, should they break the law.

The broad status of commoner was divided into four categories: (a) personal servants of nobles and officials (*hamjlaga* or *har'yat*); (b) the imperial subjects owing legal obligations to their lord (*albat*, or *sumyn ard*)

(c) monastic servants and subjects (*shav'nar*—described by Bawden [1968: 106] as "church serfs"); and (d) slaves who could be owned by nobles or commoners (*bool* or *hüvüüd*). This latter stratum appears to have been quite small, but in theory both nobles and commoners might own slaves, provided they had the wealth to buy and support them. Legal documents from the eighteenth century bear testimony to both the suffering of slaves and a certain, if very limited, concern for them by the Qing authorities.[47] The *sumyn ard*, were in a position analogous to serfs in a feudal society. They were tied to their *hoshhuu* district and its lord, and were liable for taxation and corvée duties, such as serving the officials as messengers, clerks, or laborers. In the seventeenth century the Manchu formalized the number of *hamjlaga* or personal servants that the different grades of aristocracy were permitted, ranging from four to twelve families for the humblest nobles without *hoshuus*, to up to sixty families for senior nobles (Bold 2001: 120). Treated as part of a noble's retinue, these families were theoretically exempt from tax and corvée duties.[48] These "personal serfs" could be punished by their masters, but not killed out of hand. Legal documents from 1822, for example, describe a case in which a nobleman punished a son of one of his *hamjlagas* for being slow to learn his lessons by leaving him tied up naked outside on a winter's night. Of course the boy froze to death. The noble was fined "two nines"—eighteen head of cattle (Bawden 1968: 141). Commoners could, occasionally, be elevated—not to the nobility, but to the status of *darhan*, comparable perhaps to the medieval European "freemen" and nominally free of the obligation of corvée service.[49]

The bulk of written historical sources, as one would expect, were written by or for the elite strata, and it is difficult to discern a distinctive commoner voice before the twentieth century. Commoners figure rather little in the *Secret History* and when they do they reinforce aristocratic values. There is the lament of Chilger, for example, who is racked with guilt for living with a captured noblewoman (Temujin's wife). "I, Chilger, . . . touched the Lady, the qatun, . . . Ignoble and bad Chilger, his own black [i.e., common] head will receive [a blow]."[50] Two commoner horse herds, who overhear a plot against Chinggis Khan and report it to him, are rewarded by being elevated to the status of "freemen" (*darhan*) (*Secret History* §187; De Rachewiltz 2004: 108).[51]

The Tale of the Two Dapple-Greys, a poem thought to date from the fourteenth century Chinggisid period, for example, is a parable with the moral that one should be loyal to one's lord. It tells the story of two fine horses who rebel against their lord and escape to live in freedom, only to return as they realize the value of loyalty (Bawden 2003: 73–88). Epics, such that of Geser Khan, are largely tales of princes, lamas, monsters, and emperors. There is a strong tradition of Buddhist-inspired histories that date from the seventeenth century—works like the *Altan Tobchi* and *Erdeni-yin Tobchi*—and these are largely concerned with rulership, substantiating the ancient and sacred origins of the Mongol Borjigin Khans, for example. There is also a body of "traditional" Mongolian folktales published in the communist period in both the Mongolian Peoples Republic and Inner Mongolia, and many of these tales include motifs of resistance in the face overbearing nobles. There are Robin Hood-like social bandits such as "Tiger Black" and trickster figures such as Balansangge (Bawden 2003: 327–556). But, published as they were in states that had recently waged revolutionary struggle and their own versions of class war, we must suspect claims that they represent a long tradition of commoner social critique. Aristocratic values are readily recognizable—a concern with military victory, wealth, position, title, marriage alliance, horseflesh, and hunting all figure prominently; later piety and patronage of Buddhism. There was also a high value placed on justice and a fatherly concern for one's subordinates.

Notions of order and authority underpinned both household organization and the aristocratic order. Both the polity and the household required a "master"—*ejen*. The Qing emperor was the Ejen Khan, the head of a household the *geriin ejen*. The propriatorial authority of the *ezen* over his (or occasionally her) subjects was a central value, one that applied to a series of social scales—from the Imperial to the domestic. The duties and obligations that subjects owed their lords and, ultimately, the emperor were modeled metaphorically on those of the household.[52] In a Foucaultian sense the relations of power contained in the notion of the *ejen* could be seen as "the concrete, changing soil in which the sovereign's power is grounded, the conditions that make it possible to function" (Foucault 1980: 187).

One of the highest-ranking Buddhist dignitaries to escape from Inner Mongolia before the communist victory was the Kanjurwa *Hutagt*. In his writings he represents relations with subordinates in a characteristically paternalistic way, describing rulers as looking on their subjects as "our children and grandchildren," and stressing that superiors and subordinates "served each other in many ways" (Hyer and Jagchid 1983: 62). In his analysis of precommunist Chahar society, Aberl notes similar attitudes: "The *amban* (ruling *hoshuu* official) was a 'father' to his people" (1962: 53).

Propriatorial authority was so central to the notion of social order that to be masterless was to be wild or chaotic. The term *ezengüi baidal* (literally—a situation without an *ejen*) means "anarchy." This logic also applied to the spiritual world. The *gajaryn ejed*—literally "*ejens* of the land"—are local deities propitiated at the annual ceremonies held at an *oboo* (ritual cairn) and reflect the central role that notions of jurisdiction play in conceptualizing the environment.

Something of the norms and values available to commoners can be deduced from the texts of such rites. Probably the earliest known Mongolian sutra describing *oboo* ritual was written between 1649 and 1691. This text (*obugan-u egüdku jang üile selte orusiba*—"customs and so on for the foundation of an *oboo*") describes three different types of *oboo* to be placed in different locations—the royal *oboos* for the highest mountains, the noble *oboos* to be placed on highland terraces, and the *oboos* for commoners to be placed on mountain saddles. The list of benefits gained by worshippers include, protection from illnesses and ghosts, the increase of children and grandchildren, and the multiplication of livestock and produce, understandable enough aspirations for commoners and aristocrats alike. The list ends with the following line: "By pleasing the stern authorities, great lords of the land, [one will] find rebirth in a great noble lineage." Written as it was in the age of noble patronage of Buddhism, one cannot read this as an expression of commoner aspiration to noble rebirth, but it gives some indication at least of the public transcript of ceremony. Ritual sites were to be divided in the same way as they were for political subjects, between royal, noble, and commoner.[53] Stratification appears as central once again.

Conclusion: The Headless State

Twentieth century social science represented political centralization as a key feature of "the state," and the notion of acephalous society represented its antithesis. Evolutionist social theory advanced the notion of kinship as the organizing principle for nonstate society, most famously illustrated in the structural functionalist model of segmentary kinship proposed in *The Nuer*, and this Morganian tradition was also highly influential in Soviet ethnography of Inner Asia. As Kuper notes: "The idea of primitive society served imperialists and nationalists, anarchists and Marxists" (1988: 239–240). Models of tribal, nomadic, and kin-organized society were applied to the indigenous societies of Inner Asia, and these constructions have led to the consistent misinterpretation of historical and ethnographic materials to give the impression of tribal societies organized by principles of kinship. This has tended to obscure the continuities between the state and decentralized aristocratic power in Inner Asia. A critical reevaluation of the material shows that the dichotomies of tribe and state, tradition and modernity, kinship and class, have been projected onto material that cannot be usefully analyzed in these terms.

Classical social theory sought a clear distinction between territorial-ized, stratified, state societies, and nomadic, egalitarian nonstate societies, and the understanding of Inner Asian mobile pastoral society was condi-tioned by these narratives. Deleuze and Guattari represent an influential strand in Euro-American social sciences, which essentializes "the State" as a single, timeless form, closely identified with its titular "head." In Deleuze and Guattari's case this is also characterized by the dual nature of this head (magician-king and jurist-priest), and state order being interiorized.

The trope of the free, egalitarian nomad provided an irresistible coun-terpoint to the notion of the interiorized, disciplinary state. But steppe society was stratified for much, probably all, of its history, and these aristo-cratic orders demonstrate the implausibility of the dichotomized distinction between state and nonstate societies. In actual polities power is evidently distributed between myriad sites, practices, and persons. Given the aristo-cratic values apparent in the historical literature, the key distinction between noble and common status has as much reason to be thought of as interiorized as the governmentality posited for state subjects. The political relations of aristocrats determined the size, scale, and degree of centralization of politi-cal power, and these varied in historical time. This history shows no clear dichotomy between highly centralized, stratified "state" society and egalitar-ian, kin-based "tribal" society; but rather principles of descent deployed as technologies of power in a range of more or less centralized polities, ruling subjects engaged in various kinds of productive practices.

Without Deleuze and Guattari's *a priori* separation of social forms by their presumed essences, we can see state and state-conditioned processes distributed throughout the life worlds of those subject to all manner of political authorities. This is quite as true of the industrial "governmental" state as it was of aristocratic orders. Power relations are inescapably present, certain configurations—such as domestic and aristocratic orders—have been reproduced and acted as the substrata of power in a series of historical polities that have resembled the central-ized, bureaucratized "state" to a greater or lesser degree depending on historical contingency.

The broader picture that emerges is of power structures, more or less centralized, interacting in various modes of articulation, competition, and superimposition as part of contingent, path-dependent historical processes. An examination of the substrata of power that underpins these processes reveals aristocratic orders that include many of the power technologies associated with states—stratification, forms of territorialization, taxation, corvée, and military service. The local power relations that, since ancient times, have operationalized the Inner Asian state were reproduced with or without an overarching ruler or central "head." Although more and less centralized *polities* may be clearly recognized, the distinction between state-organized and stateless *societies* becomes meaningless here. This political environment, in which almost all of the operations of state power exist at the local level virtually independent of central bureaucratic authority, I term the "headless state." Foucaultian treatments of governmentality have stressed the distributed, rhizomatic nature of power in liberal democracies, and I see no reason to apply completely different methods or terminologies when examining techniques of power in other political environments. The aristocratic orders of Inner Asia were based upon decentralized power and exhibited aspects of both the governmentality and sovereignty models. It is not that these aristocratic orders simply stand somewhere between the state and "nonstate" forms, but rather that many of the forms of power thought to be characteristic of states actually existed independently of the degree of overarching political centralization. The centralized "state" then, appears as one variant of aristocracy.

Notes

1. This chapter includes extracts from *The Headless State*, by David Sneath. Copyright © 2007 David Sneath. Reprinted with permission of Columbia University Press.

2. *Tribu* appears in Middle English in the mid thirteenth century and had itself replaced the Greek *phylon* in Biblical texts. The "tribes of Israel" were thought of as descendants of a common ancestor, although neither *tribus*, *phyla*, [Greek plural form for *phylon*] nor the Hebrew terms they indicated (*matteh*, *shebet*, or *shevet*) were necessarily groups defined essentially by descent. The *phylon* in classical Athens was an administrative division whose origins are a matter of speculation (see Osborne 1996), and *tribus* itself was used to describe the constituents of the trifold division of the people of Rome into Latins, Sabines, and Etruscans, political categories which may or may not have been defined by descent (Fried 1975: 3–5).

3. For the Soviet view see Kozlov 1974: 77–78.

4. Sahlins 1968: 5–6 is at pains to retain this theory despite the abundant evidence to the contrary. "The state differentiates civilization from tribal society. . . . A contrast with tribalism is not usefully made by reference to one or a few simple features. It has proved futile to search for some decisive invention standing at the evolutionary divide . . . 'kinship to territory'—supposing primitive society to be 'based on' kinship, civilization on territory—better expresses the evolutionary transformation. But it is overly compressed, and thereby vulnerable to naïve criticism. The rankest anthropological novice can point out that many primitive peoples occupy and defend discrete territories. . . . The critical development was not the establishment of territoriality in society, but the establishment of society *as a* territory."

5. Mair 1977: 134–9.

6. There is not space here to properly review the anthropological discussion surrounding the definition of the State, but it is worth noting that on close inspection most of the rationales advanced by the structural-functionalists for the distinction between State and nonstate societies are, to say the least, highly debatable. (Meyer and Koppers, for example, argued that the State was universal to all societies, and Lowie accepted this up to a point, but placed in an evolutionary scheme of increasingly stable and permanent.) The compound definition of the State was rather vague and circular, depending a good deal on its not being tribal.

7. It was clear, however, that, superficially, chiefdoms seemed very much like European aristocracies and monarchies. "When [vassalage] systems become institutionalized as the power bureaucracies of hereditary chiefdoms, they resemble in certain important respects the hereditary aristocracies of late or postfeudal times in Europe. But none of these chiefdoms combine those features with the complicated land tenure systems and devolution in political unity of European feudalism closely enough to be classified with it" (Service 1975: 82–83).

8. "We are compelled to say that there has always been a State, quite perfect, quite complete . . . the State itself has always been in relation with an outside. . . . The law of the State is not the law of All or Nothing (State-societies *or* counter-State societies), but that of interior and exterior. The State is sovereignty. But sovereignty only reigns over what it is capable of internalizing, of appropriating locally" (Deleuze and Guattari 1986: 15–16, original emphasis).

9. "Attempts have been made to apply a properly military category to the war machine (that of 'military democracy'), and a properly sedentary category to nomadism (that of 'feudalism'). But these two hypotheses presuppose a territorial principle: either that an imperial State appropriates the war machine, distributing land to warriors as a benefit of their position (*cleroi* and false fiefs); or that property, once it has become private, in itself posits relations of dependence among the property owners constituting the army (true fiefs and vassalage). In both cases, the number is subordinated to an 'immobile' fiscal organization, in order to establish which land can be or has been ceded as well as to fix the taxes owed by the beneficiaries themselves" (Deleuze and Guattari 1986: 73–74).

10. I might add that the division of the population into numerically defined administrative groups appears to be as old in "sedentary" polities as steppe ones. The Chinese *jun-xian* system in which "county" districts (*xian*) are defined as having a notional 500 hearths is at least as old as the Qing dynasty (third century B.C.) and dates from the same period in which we have the first evidence of a steppe empire using a decimal system of administrative units based on notional numbers of subjects.

11. Mobility appears so exotic that nomads are even cast outside historic time. They remark, for example, with an almost zoological turn of phrase: "It is true that the nomads have no history; they only have a geography" (Deleuze and Guattari 1986: 73). Chinggis Khan's decimal organization that they find so remarkable was a combined civil and military administrative form that stretches back to the Xiongnu empire of the third century B.C.

12. In their account the imperial "barbarian" state is created when the despot (described as the "great paranoiac") harnesses the existing "autochthonous rural communities" with their "primitive" regime, just as in the Marxist account of the Asiatic Mode of Production (Deleuze and Guattari 2004: 213). Elsewhere they remark that, "In the Orient, the components [of the State] are much more disconnected, disjointed [than in the West], necessitating a great immutable Form to hold them together: 'despotic formations,' Asian or African, are rocked by incessant revolts" (Deleuze and Guattari 2004: 58).

13. There was a good deal of criticism of this approach at the time. Asad (1979) had rejected the notion of the pastoral nomadism as an ideal type and Beck (1983) follows

Asad in pointing out that as all "pastoral nomadic" societies interact with "state-organised" societies the "internal dynamics" of the former cannot be seen apart from relations with the latter.

14. Hager describes Pashtun tribal structure in segmentary terms as one of "progressively more inclusive groupings of lineage and faction" (1983: 94). But Glatzer writes that "Pashtun nomads . . . are organized socially not on the basis of a segmentary lineage or clan system, but on other bases" (1983: 221). It is not descent but locality, interest, and political and economic structures that are the bases for social organization in Pashtun areas.

15. Hager, for example, writes, "with the gradual growth of government and the urban classes, and with the penetration into rural areas of modernizing technology, from roads and radios to tractors, tribes and tribal organization have undoubtedly weakened" (1983: 107).

16. Elsewhere Krader writes, "The nomadic village as a corporate body has the same structure as a clan in miniature" (1963: 335); and he also generalizes that, "The village of the ordinary nomads contains about ten families" (1963: 337). He is quite wrong in both respects. Mongolian pastoral encampments are fluid, changing residential forms, very frequently include nonagnates and nonkin, and rarely include more than eight households (see Sneath 2000: 212–215; Humphrey and Sneath 1999: 139–178).

17. The work of Simukov, who conducted a survey of 100 encampments in a district of Outer Mongolia in the 1920s, revealed nothing resembling Krader's kin village, but a process of encampments continually changing their composition. Agnatic relations between household heads accounted for only 41 percent of encampments, compared to 56 percent with other sorts of links (1933: 24–29). Vreeland notes that among the Chahar (Inner Mongolia) at that time, "the *törel* ('kindred') was not a residential group, and persons who were of the same *törel* might be widely scattered" (1962: 155).

18. Thoroughly indoctrinated by the writings of Krader and company, when I began fieldwork in Inner Mongolia in the late 1980s, I was at first perplexed to find nothing that corresponded to his picture of kinship organization, but I assumed it must have been based on Outer Mongolian research. However, fieldwork in Outer Mongolia in the 1990s convinced me of what the more detailed historical studies already clearly indicated—that Krader's model really was entirely wrong.

19. Szynkewicz notes that, "towards the end of the Yuan dynasty . . . the lineage organization, composed of a network of maximal lineages going back to the forefather of the clan and subdivided into segments, can be assumed to have ceased to exist. The few surviving maximal lineages may have comprised the aristocracy" (1977: 31). Szynkewicz still implies, however, that a segmentary kinship system had *once* existed, and that it included most Mongolians, not just the aristocracy.

20. This document has been read as a sort of "mythic charter" of a simple tribal people. So, for example, it is often translated as showing Chinggis Khan's original ancestors to have been two fantastical animals—a blue-grey wolf and a fallow doe—whereas Onon (1990) suggests these are much more likely to actually represent the names of nobles.

21. Most of the named groups that are mentioned were thought to be descended from a number of brothers, thus providing little of the classical structure of segmentary kinship (see Onon 1990:174–176).

22. For example, to battle with the forces of a relative (Jamuqa) whose army included forces led by a named group closely related to him (the Tayyichi'ut), Chinggis Khan allied himself with the Khan of the Kereid who, like most of the other important

named polities of the region, (the Tatar, Merkid, and Naiman) had no genealogical connection with the Borjigid at all. A generation earlier, the Khan of the Kereid had recruited the military support of Chinggis Khan's father against his own family (see Onon 1990: 65). In both cases the politically expedient relationship of *anda* ("sworn brotherhood") was used without reference to genealogical distance.

23. See Barfield 1981. The Xianbe, who replaced the Xiongnu around 100 A.D., were also ruled by an aristocracy. The *Secret History* describes Chinggis Khan's ancestry in such a way as to include many with titles (often derived from both the Liao dynasty and the Orkhon-Turkish empire): even some of the most distant matrilateral ancestors are said to be lords of large territories (Cleaves 1982: 2; Onon 1990: 3–11).

24. Onon 1990: 56; Cleaves 1982: 66–67.

25. See the *Secret History*: "Then Chinggis Qahan plundered the Tayichi'ut. The people of Tayichi'ut bones (lineages/houses)—A'uchu-ba'atur, Qoton-orcheng, Qudu'udar, and others of the Tayichi'ut, from their seed to their seed—he killed. . . . The people of their *ulus* (nation/people) he brought (with him)." Clearly the people of the Tayichi'ut *ulus* were not members of the Tayichi'ut bones (Onon 1990: 63; Cleaves 1982: 76).

26. Two military units of ten thousand were raised from the Kereid, for example (see Pelliot 1949: 26).

27. De Rachewiltz provides a typical example in a passage describing a meeting of two men on the steppe: "Dobun Mergen asked him, 'To which clan do you belong?' The man said 'I am a man of the Ma'aliq Baya'ut, and I am in desperate straits'" (2004: 3). However, the reconstructed Mongol text actually reads, "ya'un gü'ün chi kä'än?"; the answer "bï Malig Baya'udäi" (Pelliot 1949: 6). Cleaves translated this as "What [manner of] person art thou?" (1982: 3); but literally this means "of-what you (addressed familiar/junior) where?" and this could as well mean, "what work-unit are you a member of" as anything else. The reply is "I with/of Malig Baya'ut." No actual kin term is used at all.

28. Indeed one of the very earliest ancestors mentioned, Batachi, seems to have the title of Khan (*qan*), but such was the impulse to downplay aristocracy that Cleaves (1982: 1) and De Rachewiltz (2004: 1) made the title part of the name—*Batachiqan*. In the actual text the term "qan" appears, however, in the same way as it does for those who clearly *were* Khans, such as Ong Khan (see Pelliot 1949: 5, 49). Onon (1990) notes Chinese records of Batarci Khan and dates him as living around 790 A.D.

29. Similarly, the term *obogton*, which means "family" or "line" in modern Mongolian, has been taken to mean "clan" or "tribe" in the older texts.

30. He notes that the term "tribe" is commonly understood to mean "a group descended from a common ancestor, divided into clans, possessing a territory, common language, culture and shared identity, and often economic pursuits" (Golden 2001: 20).

31. See Golden 2001: 21, note 87.

32. There were four grades of *taij*, the first being for those governing *hoshuus*, and the second to fourth, for those without *hoshuus*.

33. See Jagchid 1999: 36–43.

34. See Atwood 2002: 949.

35. Ratchnevsky, who makes much use of Persian sources, has a similar tendency. Knowing that the *Secret History* describes a clearly stratified society, he pushes the mythic nomadic kin-based society back to the turmoil before Chinggis is born. He writes, "the kinship group lost its homogeneous character" (1991: 12). This is a strange comment to make as Ratchnevsky uses Persian sources to show that both Kutula and Ambagai ruled steppe empires, but presumably he conceives of these empires as consisting of homogeneous kin groups, much as Bacon must have conceived of Chinggis's early empire.

36. There was a tradition by which the youngest son inherited the core possessions of the parental couple while older siblings received a portion on marriage, and this seems to have applied to apanages in the Mongol imperial period (Lattimore 1951: 292).

37. These were limited to parts of Inner Mongolia and Buryatia (Sneath 2000: 196–215).

38. Morgan wrote: "The family relationships are as ancient as the *family*. . . . A system of consanguinity which is founded upon a community of blood, is but the formal expression and recognition of these relationships. . . . A formal arrangement of the more immediate blood kindred into lines of descent, with the adoption of some method to distinguish one relative from another and to express the value of the relationship, would be one of the earliest acts of human intelligence" (1871: 10 cited in Schneider 1975: 257–8).

39. For example, the Daur Mongol descent groups (for which they used the Manchu name *hala*) seem to have been newly created at the time of their incorporation into the Manchu administration. When the Dagur moved from the Amur to the Nonni River in the seventeenth century, the groups that later became *hala* were named after rivers, and were almost certainly territorial groupings at that time, rather than preexisting kinship groups (C. Humphrey, personal communication 1990).

40. De Rachewiltz follows received wisdom that Chinggis Khan imposed the *mingqan* units on earlier tribal groupings, but there is no convincing evidence for this at all. Quite the reverse, the thousand and ten thousand units as military formations clearly predate Chinggis Khan's enthronement in 1206, and no distinction is made in the term used for the civil units that Chinggis lists in such a way in his 1206 declaration as to give the impression that these are preexisting units.

41. To name but a few of these: Sima Qian describes the aristocracy of the Xiongnu of the third century B.C. to the first century A.D.; the Orkhon inscriptions refer to nobility in the early Türk empire of the sixth to eighth centuries A.D. (Sinor 1990: 297); the *Liao-shih* describes the Khitan aristocracy of the ninth to twelfth centuries (Franke 1990: 405); and the *Secret History of the Mongols* details the aristocratic political landscape of the twelfth century.

42. See Beazley 1903: 121 and 59.

43. Carpini writes of a *dux* by the name of Correnza (Beazley 1903: 94), for example, but Rockhill (1900: 6) in his translation calls him a "chief," while Carpini's Dux Wasilco (Beazley 1903: 92) is translated (along with all the other European nobles) as a Duke (Rockhill 1900: 3).

44. Soucek has thoroughly absorbed the tribe–chief terminology. Tümen-Sasakhtu, for example, is described as "chief of the Chakhar tribes" (2000: 168)—an extraordinary description for a Chinggisid prince who had inherited the rich apanage of the late Yüan empire.

45. This is my translation of this passage. For alternative wordings in Russian and English see Dylykova (1981: 53, 117) and Bold (2001: 117).

46. Bawden (1968: 106).

47. As late as 1934, when a politically active senior lama sought to address the Mongolians of Inner Mongolia, he issued four separate pamphlets addressed to the *nobles*, the lamas, the youth, and the commoners respectively. (See Yang and Bulag 2003: 88–89.)

48. In 1789, for example, a 32-year-old slave woman named Dashjid tried to kill herself and her children, one of whom was killed before help arrived. She was the daughter of a *hamjlaga* named Nomon, who was so poor that he had sold her as a child to a noble

before himself dying of starvation. Unhappy with each of a succession of masters the girl repeatedly ran home to her mother only to be sold to someone else. Eventually, in despair and pregnant for a fourth time, she had tried to kill herself and her children. The Qing authorities punished almost everyone connected with the case except Dashjid (Bawden 1968: 139–140).

49. In fact they often became liable for such obligations in practice (see Bawden 1968: 150).

50. This status is not to be confused with the Darhad ethnic group of Northern Mongolia. See Jagchid and Hyer (1979: 287–288) for a discussion of the rights and status of the Darhad.

51. (Onon, 1990: 40; Cleaves 1983: 46.) Chilger appears actually to have been of the Merkid nobility himself, but the idiom of common status was used to indicate lord-subject relations, so in the wake of Chinggis Khan's defeat and subjugation of the Merkid polity Chilger's humble lament indicates that with respect to the new royal family he is but a lowly commoner.

52. Indeed they are granted the right to wear quivers, which appears to have been forbidden to commoners. They were also given the whole of Ong Khan's palace tent and its rich contents, but could not be made nobles (see De Rachewiltz 2004: 108).

53. The norms associated with the position of *ezen* entail some obligations as well as rights; indeed, in a number of contexts the meaning of the term resembles that of the English word "patron." It can also be taken to mean "host," and this indicates that the householder has an obligation to act in an appropriate way. The position of *ejen* entails a responsibility for one's subordinates—the phrase, *ejen boloh* (to become an *ejen*) means to vouch for something or someone, or to take responsibility for them. This is the usage in which it most resembles our term patron—as someone who supports a junior. The Mongolian term *ezengüi hüüihed* (a child without an *ejen*), means an illegitimate child.

54. Later, with the increasing influence of the Buddhist monastic establishment, *oboo* ritual became more inclusive, but better embodied the administrative hierarchy of the Qing state. Officials responsible for the political divisions of administrative districts oversaw the *oboo* ceremonies for their own unit and attended those for the larger districts as representatives. The administrative architecture of the state was reproduced in rituals of this sort (Sneath 2000: 235–250).

References

Aberle, David F. 1962. *Chahar and Dagor Mongol Bureaucratic Administration: 1912–1945*. New Haven: Human Relations Area Files.

Altangerel, T. 1998. *Mongol Oiradyn Ih Tsaaz*. Ulaanbatar: Tuuünii Sudalgaa.

Asad, Talad 1979. "Equality in Nomadic Social Systems? Notes Towards the Dissolution of an Anthropological Category." In *Pastoral Production and Society: Production Pastorale et Société*, ed. L'Equipe Ecologie et Anthropologie des Sociétés Pastorales. Cambridge: Cambridge University Press.

Atwood, Christopher P. 2002. *Young Mongols and Vigilantes in Inner Mongolia's Interregnum Decades, 1911–1931*. Leiden, Boston, Köln: Brill.

———. 2004. *Encyclopedia of Mongolian and the Mongol Empire*, New York: Facts on File.

Bawden, Charles 1997. *Mongolian-English Dictionary*. London and New York: Kegan Paul International.

Barfield, Thomas J. 1981. "The Hsiung-nu Imperial Confederacy: Organisation and Foreign Policy." *The Journal of Asian Studies* 41: 45–61.

———.1989. *The Perilous Frontier: Nomadic Empires and China*, Cambridge: MA and Oxford, U.K.: Basil Blackwell.

———. 1993. *The Nomadic alternative*. Englewood Cliffs, N.J.: Prentice Hall.

Beck, L. 1983. "Iran and the Qashqai Tribal Confederacy." In *The Conflict of Tribe and State in Iran and Afghanistan*, ed. R. Tapper. London, Canberra: Croom Helm; New York: St Martin's.

Beidelman, T.O. 1971. "Nuer Priests and Prophets: Charisma, Authority and Power Among the Nuer." In *The Translation of Culture: Essays to E.E. Evans-Pritchard*, ed. T. Beidelman. London: Tavistock.

Bold, Bat-Ochir. 2001. *Mongolian Nomadic Society: A Reconstruction of The 'Medieval' History of Mongolia*. Curzon: Richmond, Surrey.

Burnham, P. 1979. "Spatial Mobility and Political Centralisation in Pastoral Societies." In *Pastoral Production and Society: Production Pastorale et Société*, ed. L'Equipe Ecologie et Anthropologie des Sociétés Pastorales. Cambridge: Cambridge University Press.

Cable M., with French F. 1950 [1942]. *The Gobi Desert*. London: Readers Union & Hodder and Stoughton.

Carneiro, Robert L. 1981. "The Chiefdom: Precursor of the State." In *The Transition to Statehood in the New World*, ed. G. D. Jones and P. R. Krautz. Cambridge: Cambridge University Press.

Cleaves, Francis W. 1982. *The Secret History of the Mongols*. Cambridge, MA: Harvard University Press.

Crossley, Pamela K. 1997. *The Manchus*. Cambridge, MA and Oxford, U.K.: Blackwell.

Dawson, Christopher. 1955. *The Mongol Mission: Narratives and Letters of the Franciscan missionaries in Mongolia and China in the Thirteenth and Fourteenth Centuries*. Trans. a nun of Stanbrook Abbey. London and New York: Sheed & Ward.

Dahl, Gudrun. 1979. "Ecology and Equality: The Boran Case." In *Pastoral Production and Society: Production Pastorale et Société*, ed. L' Equipe Ecologie at Anthropologie des Sociétés Pastorales. Cambridge: Cambridge University Press.

Deleuze, Gilles and Felix Guattari. 1986. *Nomadology: The War Machine*. New York: Semiotext(e).

———. 2004. *Anti-Oedipus: Capitalism and Schizophrenia*. Minneapolis: University of Minnesota Press.

De Rachewiltz, Igor. 2004. *The Secret History of the Mongols*, vols. I & II. Leiden, Boston: Brill.

Di Cosmo, Nicola. 1999. "State Formation and Periodization in Inner Asian History." *Journal of World History* 10 (1): 1–40.

Durkheim Emile. 1893. *De la Division du Travail Social: Etude sur l'Organisation des Sociétés Superieures*. Paris: Felix Alcan.

Dylykova, S.D., ed. 1981. *Ih Tsaaz "Velikoe Ulojenie [the great code], Pamyatnik Mongoliskogo Feodalinogo Prava XVII v.* Moscow: Nauka.

Evans-Pritchard, E.E. 1940. *The Nuer: A Description of the Modes of Livelihood and Political Institutions of a Nilotic people*. Oxford: Clarendon Press.

Ferguson, R. B. 1997. "Tribes." In *The Dictionary of Anthropology*, ed. T. J. Barfield. Oxford: Blackwell, 475–476.

Franke, Herbert. 1990. "The Forest Peoples of Manchuria: Kitans and Jurchens." In *Cambridge History of Early Inner Asia*, ed. D. Sinor. Cambridge: Cambridge University Press, 400–423.

Fried, Morton. 1975. *The Notion of Tribe*. Menlo Park, CA: Cummings.

Glatzer, Bernt. 1983. "Political Organisation of Pashtun Nomads and the State." In *The Conflict of Tribe and State in Iran and Afghanistan*, ed. R. Tapper. London, Canberra: Croom Helm; New York: St Martin's.

Gellner, Ernst. 1983. "The Tribal Society and its Enemies." In *The Conflict of Tribe and State in Iran and Afghanistan*, ed. R. Tapper. London, Canberra: Croom Helm; New York: St Martin's.

———. 1994. *Conditions of Liberty: Civil Society and its Rivals*. London: Hamish Hamilton.

Gledhill, John. 1994. *Power and its Disguises: Anthropological Perspectives on Politics*. London and Boulder: Pluto Press.

Golden, Peter B. 2001. "Ethnicity and State Formation in Pe-Chinggisid Turkic Eurasia." *Central Eurasian Studies Lectures* No. 1, Department of Central Eurasian Studies. Bloomington: Indiana University.

Gough, Kathleen. 1971. "Nuer Kinship: A Re-Examination." In *The Translation of Culture: Essays to E.E. Evans-Pritchard*, ed. T. Beidelman. London: Tavistock.

Hager, R. 1983. "State, Tribe and Empire in Afghan Inter-Polity Relations." In *The Conflict of Tribe and State in Iran and Afghanistan*, ed. R. Tapper. London, Canberra: Croom Helm; New York: St Martin's.

Humphrey, Caroline and David Sneath. 1999. *The End of Nomadism? Society, State and the Environment in Inner Asia*. Durham: Duke University Press.

Irons, William. 1979. "Political Stratification among Pastoral Nomads." In *Pastoral Production and Society: Production Pastorale et Société*, ed. L' Equipe Ecologie at Anthropologie des Sociétés Pastorales, Cambridge: Cambridge University Press.

Jagchid, Sechin and Paul Hyer. 1979. *Mongolia's Culture and Society*. Boulder: Westview Press.

Khazanov, Anatoly M. 1983. *Nomads and the Outside World*. Trans. Julia Crookenden, foreword by Ernest Gellner. Cambridge Studies of Social Anthropology 44. Cambridge: Cambridge University Press.

Kirchhoff. Paul. 1955. "The Principles of Clanship in Human Society." *Davidson Journal of Anthropology* 1, 1–11.

Kozlov, V.I. 1974. "On the Concept of Ethnic Community." In *Soviet Ethnology and Anthropology Today*, ed. Y. Bromley. The Hague: Mouton & Co.

Krader, Lawrence. 1963. *Social Organisation of the Mongol-Turkic Pastoral Nomads*. The Hague: Mouton & Co.

Kuper, Adam. 1988. *The Invention of Primitive Society: Transformations of an Illusion*. London & New York: Routledge.

———. 2004. "Lineage Theory: A Critical Retrospect." In *Kinship and Family: An Anthropological Reader*, ed. R. Parkin and L. Stone. Malden, MA, Oxford, U.K., and Carlton, Victoria: Blackwell. [Reprinted from 1982 *Annual Review of Anthropology* 1: 71–95.]

Lattimore, Owen. 1934. *The Mongols of Manchuria*. New York: The John Day Company.

———. 1940. *Inner Asian Frontiers of China*. American Geographical Society, Research Series No. 21. London and New York: Oxford University Press.

———. 1980. "Inner Mongolian Nationalism and the Pan-Mongolian idea: Recollections and Reflections.' 5n *Journal of the Anglo-Mongolian Society* 6 (1): 1–24.

Maine, Henry S. 1861. *Ancient Law*. London: Dent.

Morgan, David. 1986. *The Mongols*. Oxford: Blackwell.

Morgan, Lewis H. 1877. *Ancient Society: Researches in the Lines of Human Progress from Savagery through Barbarism to Civilisation*. New York: Holt.

Mair, Lucy. 1977. *African Kingdoms*, Oxford: Oxford University Press.

———. 1972. *An Introduction to Social Anthropology*, 2nd. ed. Oxford: Oxford University Press.

Murray, James, ed. 1933. *The Oxford English Dictionary*. A corrected re-issue with an introduction, supplement, and bibliography of *A new English dictionary on historical principles*, ed. Murray, James, et al. Oxford: Clarendon Press.

Nadel, Sigfried F. 1942. *A Black Byzantium*. London: Oxford University Press.

Natsagdorj, S.H. 1967. "The Economic Basis of Feudalism in Mongolia." In *Modern Asian Studies* 1 (3): 265–281.

Onon, Urgunge. 1990. *The History and the Life of Chinggis Khan: The Secret History of the Mongols*. Leiden: Brill.

Osborne, Robin. 1996. *Greece in the Making, 1200–479* B.C. London: Routledge.

Patterson, T. C. 1991. *The Inca Empire: the Formation and Disintegration of a Pre-Capitalist State*. Oxford: Berg Publishers.

Pelliot, Paul. 1949. *Histoire Secret des Mongols: Restitution du texte Mongol et traduction Francaise des chapitres I a VI*. Paris: Adrien Maisonneuve.

Ratchnevsky, Paul. 1991. *Genghis Khan: His Life and his Legacy*. Trans. T. N. Haining. Oxford: Blackwell.

Rattray, Robert S. 1929. *Ashanti Law and Constitution*. London: Oxford University Press.

Richards, Audrey. 1970. "The Political System of the Bemba Tribe—North-Eastern Rhodesia." In *African Political Systems*, ed. M. Fortes and E. Evans-Pritchard. London: Oxford University Press.

Sahlins, Marshall. 1968. *Tribesmen*. Englewood Cliffs, NJ: Prentice-Hall.

Sanjdorj, M. 1980. *Manchu Chinese Colonial Rule in Northern Mongolia*. Trans. Urgunge Onon. London: C. Hurst and Co.

Schneider, David M. 2004. [1972]. "What Is Kinship All About?" In *Kinship and Family: An Anthropological Reader*, ed. R. Parkin and L. Stone. Malden, MA: Blackwell.

Simukov, A.D. 1933. "Hotoni" [Hotons]. In *Sovrennaya Mongoliya* [Contemporary Mongolia], Number 3: 19–32.

Sneath, David. 2000. *Changing Inner Mongolia: Pastoral Mongolian Society and the Chinese State*. Oxford: Oxford University Press.

———. 2003. "Ritual Idioms and Spatial Orders: Comparing the Rites for Mongolian and Tibetan 'Local Deities.'" In *Proceedings of the International Association of Tibetan Studies*, Oxford University.

Strathern, Andrew. 1983. "Tribe and State: Some Concluding Remarks." In *The Conflict of Tribe and State in Iran and Afghanistan*, ed. R. Tapper. London, Canberra: Croom Helm; New York: St Martin's.

Szynkiewicz, S. 1977. "Kinship Groups in Modern Mongolia." *Ethnologia Polona* 3: 31–45.

Vail, Leroy, ed. 1989. *The Creation of Tribalism in Southern Africa*. London: James Currey.

Vladimirtsov, Boris I. 1948. *Le Regime Social des Mongols: Le Feodalisme Nomade*. Paris: A. Maisonneuve.

Vreeland, Herbert H. 1962 [1954]. *Mongol Community and Kinship Structure*. New Haven: Human Relations Area Files.

Yapp, M.E. 1983. "Tribes and States in the Khyber 1838–42." In *The Conflict of Tribe and State in Iran and Afghanistan*, ed. R. Tapper. London, Canberra: Croom Helm; New York: St Martin's.

CHAPTER 6

The Perfect Sovereign

The Sacralized Power of the Ottoman Sultan

Kjetil Fosshagen

The question I discuss in this essay is what we can learn about hierarchy from the comparative study of the structure of power of the Ottoman Empire. The essay is thus in continuity with Dumont's program of analyzing hierarchy comparatively in terms of differing relations between political power and religious status. Against the portrayals of Dumont as an intellectualist by empiricists (see Berreman 1971), an orientalist (Dirks 1987) or an ahistorical structuralist (Appadurai 1986), he should be considered an important political anthropologist. At the core of his discussion of hierarchy is the question of the historical and cultural constitution of power. Dumont's great achievement was to insist on a comparative historical perspective on structural and cultural differences, against the reductionist approach of functionalist models, old and new. This essay however argues that the structure of Ottoman society poses a challenge to Dumont's assumption of a single basic principle underlying all forms of society.

As is well known, Dumont saw premodern societies as holistic or totalizing, in the sense that the whole is ordered by a dominant holistic value, while modern European societies are ordered by an individualist ideology. It is this individualist ideology that has produced the Western model of hierarchy as rank of command or power, he argues.[1] In contrast to this, the Indian model clearly demonstrates the structure of "pure hierarchy"—where hierarchy is not mixed with power. As pointed out by Parry (1998: 159), there is an underlying assumption in Dumont that human history evolves through the increasing differentiation of the domains of religion and politics, starting from the undifferentiated figure of the priest-king. The Indian relationship between status and power (as analyzed in *Homo Hierarchicus*) represents a transitory stage between an originally undifferentiated structure (Polynesia

---

Notes to this section begin on page 206.

and ancient India), and the modern Western separation of religion and politics.[2] In India, princely power is distinguished from, but is still dependent on and subordinated to, the Brahman's religious authority. Political sovereignty is thus *encompassed* by the religiously defined totality.

The Indian model brings out the *principle* of hierarchy that Dumont sees as basic and universal, but it is not a pure form; he sees it as a transitory development of the ancient Indian and Polynesian form. Dumont thus sees all forms of power as evolving out of one basic form, in which religious authority encompasses political power. Political power in traditional societies is thus not a separate and autonomous domain, but dependent on the religious structure (Parry 1998: 156). The European medieval model of sovereignty parallels this Indian model in its religious ordering of the whole and the hierarchical complementarity of kings and priests (Dumont 1986: 46).[3] The political power of the king was subordinated to the status of the bishops on the superior level of religion, which defined the totality. The bishops had the authority of being God's highest servants on earth through the sacramental functions of ordination and anointment of kings (Duby 1980). The subsequent European development showed, however, the gradual encompassment of the religious by political power. In the modern West the political domain achieves full autonomy along with the emergent economic domain.

Dumont's first main argument is thus that there are two basic structures of power (as the Indian case is a subtype of the Polynesian form). Power can either be encompassed by religion, as in the Polynesian, Roman, and Indian structure of hierarchy; *or* power can exist in unity with religion or dominate it, as in the medieval and modern stages of the European development. The modern European form thus represents the exceptional evolution from the basic underlying principle. While the Indian model explicitly demonstrates this basic hierarchical principle, the European model hides it. Dumont's second main argument is that pure hierarchy constitutes the basic underlying principle of all societies, and *not* egalitarianism, which is a modern European ideology.[4] Society is by nature hierarchical.

The Islamic world and the Ottoman Empire were largely left out of Dumont's comparative discussion of power and status. In a note Dumont states briefly that, "Islam does not give autonomy to the political domain, although 'the word of God is addressed directly to the individual'" (1980: 444). This essay argues that Dumont overlooked the distinctive relation between political power and religious status in Islam, and that the Ottoman Empire represents a structure which defies his basic assumption that all premodern forms of political power are encompassed by religious authority. The Ottoman Empire represents a third form which does not fit into Dumont's dual scheme of power. Religious authority stands in a deep tension with political power, both personalized powers. Emerging from this argument is a second and more fundamental point, namely a challenge to Dumont's basic assumption that society is universally based on the principle of hierarchy.

The Emergence of an Ottoman State

The Ottomans were a Turkic tribe originating in Central Asia and probably arriving in Anatolia in the twelfth to thirteenth centuries, and named after the successful thirteenth century leader (*beğ*) Osman. In its early centuries (thirteenth to the early fifteenth), the Ottoman polity was a frontier principality, expanding through conquests and alliances in "the political wilderness" of Western Anatolia (Kafadar 1995).

Among historians of the Ottoman Empire there has been a long debate about the structural dynamics of the early Ottoman polity and about the transition to a centralized state. The debate centers on the question of whether the dynamics of the early Ottoman polity were structured by an Islamic *gaza*-ethos, or by a Turkish tribal structure. For our comparative discussion of the nomadic origin and the later structure of sultanic power, it is necessary to go into this debate.

Since the 1930s the dominant position has been the so-called "*gazi-thesis*" of Paul Wittek, which presents the early Ottomans as tribal confederations driven by an Islamic *gaza* ethos, and thus fighting for the expansion of Islam (Kafadar 1995).[5] His main opponent Lindner (1982, 1997) argues that the Ottoman *gazis* formed *inclusive* tribal or corporate coalitions, in line with the tribal organization known from recent anthropological literature. The Ottoman coalitions were composed of Muslim and non-Muslim warriors who shared the booty from raids into new territories, and who were motivated by the desire for booty alone. The inclusive tribal dynamics are what structured the process of expansion and warfare. He thus replaces Wittek's ideational model with a structural model. Lindner however posits a contradiction between the inclusive principle of tribal organization and what he assumes to be the "exclusive or adversary ideology" (1997: 1) of the *gazis* (an alleged Islamic ethos or mentality of war against the infidels),[6] and therefore dismisses the idea of any religious component altogether.

Recent contributions by Kafadar (1995) and Lowry (2003) are mainly in line with Lindner's refutation of an Islamic ethos as the driving force, although they consider his contradiction between *gaza* and tribal organization as false. They both argue for the necessity of understanding the *gaza* concept within the particular historical context, and not applying a modern and canon-dominated understanding of religion, as Lindner and others do. In the frontier environment of the early Ottomans, there was no necessary contradiction between the raiding of the *gazis* and the inclusive structure of the polity. Such a contradiction is based on a modern, text-centered model of what religion is. Kafadar emphasizes how the *"gaza"* concept originally referred simply to a predatory raid into foreign territories—a codification of rules from the fourteenth century includes rules of the distribution of booty to "infidels" participating in raids (1995: 80). *Gaza* could even involve warfare against coreligionists. Kafadar argues against Lindner, however, that among the various social groups constituting the Ottoman forces, there actually was an important social group of warriors who saw themselves as *gazis* fighting for what they perceived to be true Islam. That their conceptions of Islam rested on syncretist or "unorthodox" conceptions of Islam does not alter the fact that they were an important faction among the frontier warriors, he holds. They were a particular social group, with a distinct code of honor and conduct, similar to the "quasi-corporate male organizations in medieval Islamic history" (Kafadar 1995: 56).[7] The group of *gazi* frontier warriors were eventually left out of the state elite in the process of centralization.

In Kafadar's model, the early Ottoman polity was an inclusive mixture of frontier warriors and lords, recently arrived nomadic tribes, mercenaries, converts, as well as dervishes and religious mystics of various backgrounds. They were united in the activity of frontier raiding, and this raiding was conceptualized through a discourse of *gaza* and faith.

Lowry also holds that the *gaza* concept primarily referred to the activity of raiding. The raids were conducted by a "predatory confederacy" which was open also to Christian warriors (2003: 57). Lowry supports this claim by referring to rules prescribing the share of infidels in the booty and the synonymous use of the terms *gazi* and *akıncı* (raider) in the fourteenth century, and dismisses Lindner's idea of an exclusive Islamic ideology of the *gazis* (2003: 132). He goes further however and also dismisses the "tribal origins" of the early Ottomans as an explanation of their dynamics, since converted Christians clearly provided a major source of manpower. Here however he mistakenly identifies a "true" consanguine genealogical structure with tribal structural dynamics per se. Lowry's dismissal of a tribal model—because the Ottomans clearly recruited Christian noblemen—does not disprove the importance of the tribal structural dynamics, I argue. As contested by Lindner, and as evident from anthropological literature, tribal genealogies are flexible and incorporative, and often more post facto charters of political alignments than accounts of consanguine relations.[8]

Despite their disagreements, I choose to synthesize Lindner, Lowry, and Kafadar, and view the early Ottoman polity as an inclusive structure of a tribal type, with some continuities from Central Asian traditions as they appear in the literature.[9] In the Ottoman frontier setting, the inclusive and flexible tribal organization provided a highly effective structural dynamics for expansion across borders. The concept of *gaza* and the figure of the *gazi* were furthermore a product of a frontier setting, and appear to have referred more to a social practice and certain types of heroic acts and figures than to a religious doctrine. As such it fitted well into the structural dynamics of the frontiers.

It still remains however to look at the structural dynamics of the nomadic tribes and their transition to imperial structures. I should emphasize here that I do not consider all kinship or genealogical models of social organization, such as that of segmentary opposition or tribal structure, as having been falsified (see Salzman 1978, 1999). I think it has been convincingly argued that these are models of social structure and do not determine or explain all social phenomena on the ground. Neither do I consider the concept of "tribe" as necessarily implying a romantic and evolutionist model of political development.[10] I use the term "tribe" as a shorthand for a social structure that is based on a genealogical principle, but which is flexible and inclusive to incorporate non-kin, as in the case of Nuer and Dinka. I consider kinship as a structural principle preceding empire, and thus do not agree with Lindner and others that the kinship-basis of tribes is the creation of contact with states (Lindholm 1986: 339).

Shaw describes the early Ottoman leaders—the *beğs* (lords)—as first among equals within their own tribes, and as equal to the other leaders within the tribal councils (1976: 22). The authority of the *beğ* was limited to those functions involved in his role as a military leader, and his followers' loyalty seems to have been situational. His followers would leave him if the promises of booty were not fulfilled, or for other reasons (Shaw 1976: 22). Furthermore, there were no rituals delimiting the access to the leader or secluding him, and no permanent capital or court. This picture of tribal political structure—which resembles Lindner's model—as a purely egalitarian type may however be somewhat simplified. The concept of "tribal structure" needs an elaboration for our later discussion of hierarchy.

Lindholm (1986) and Barfield (Khoury and Kostiner 1990) have argued convincingly that the Central Asian tribes were organized in a more ranked pattern than the indigenous Middle Eastern tribes. The former had a kinship system of the Omaha type, with "conical clans,"[11] as in Polynesia. The distinctive feature of the conical clan structure is that it combines segmentation and rank along genealogical lines. Lineage structure was based on generational distance from a common ancestor and on birth order, resulting in a collateral ranking of senior and junior descent lines according to the birth order of their founders (Lindholm 1986: 341). The same principle of ranking went through the entire system: seniority of birth and generational distance produced a type of ranking which was very complex. The eldest son of the eldest son of the first generation preceded the second eldest son of the first generation (Hage and Harary 1996). In this system "no one has his exact equal; everyone finds his place in a system of collaterally ranked lines of descent from a common ancestor" (Krader 1963 cited in Lindholm 1986: 341). Service noted that "every individual is his own class" (cited in Hage and Harary 1996: 114).

Lévi-Strauss classified the marriage system as a "hybrid system," which mixed the two "elementary structures" of generalized and restricted exchange (Lindholm 1986: 337). Between the exogamous clans there was generalized exchange of women, and the clans were united in large tribal confederations led by chiefs and councils of elders. Above these egalitarian clans there emerged a nobility of families with hereditary claims to leadership. The Mongol and Turkic empires were led by leaders drawn from dynastic families. The administration of the state and the armies were organized according to tribal and kinship structures (Krader 1963). New alliances were struck with groups outside the exchange circles, and external groups were incorporated into the genealogical structure (Lindner 1982) or integrated through adoptive relationships (Parkes 2003). Trade in luxury and prestige goods also created networks of importance, as in Polynesia.[12] Political processes were cast in terms of kinship, and the principle of ranking (genealogical seniority) was the same throughout the entire body of society. The leaders and the nobility were thus not set apart from society by a set of particular principles or by their relations to divinity, which was decentralized.

Although lineage ranking reportedly was important in leadership succession (Krader 1968; Lindholm 1986: 337), that succession clearly also depended on ability (Lindholm 1986: 341). "Leadership was a status that was not assigned by rote—it had to be achieved, and achievement was based on social recognition of leadership qualities" (Krader; 87).[13] Lindner (1982) sees ability alone as deciding the matter. The weight given to social recognition is interesting, because it points to an egalitarian element in the structuring of leadership: the leader still had to prove that he was first among equals in a sense. In the Central Asian tradition inheritance was split between brothers, and it was actually an innovation of the early Ottomans to institutionalize unigeniture (and later even codifying fratricide), according to Kafadar (1995: 137).

Lindholm argues that the Central Asian ranked kinship system implies an acceptance of inequality and hierarchy that "inevitably" leads to political structures of the state type. A further feature that he sees as pushing in the same direction, is a fundamental internal contradiction in the generalized exchange system that leads to "feudal ranking and the diminution of clanship" (Lindholm 1986: 342). This contradiction is that "the system assumes the basic equality of all the groups" while it simultaneously leads to "hierarchy," as one group seeks to accumulate more women or surplus to pay for bridewealth.

Friedman, writing about the conical clan structure within prestige-good networks in Polynesia, also argues for an internal contradiction within the generalized exchange system that leads to the emergence of ranking and differentiation through accumulation of surplus and debt (Friedman 1998). However he argues against the absolutist distinction between non-state and state structures shared by neo-evolutionists and primitivists (like Clastres [1996]) alike, which presents the state as a clean historical break with nonstate society.

Leach's (1964) analysis of the Kachin political systems boils down to the same question of the relation between the egalitarian and the hierarchical (*gumsa* and *gumlao*). His answer, like those of Barfield (1990) and Lindner in the Central Asian context, is that hierarchical structures in tribal societies can only arise as a response to contact with external states.

In comparative perspective, the nomadic tribal organization was "based on an original premise of equality" as admitted by Lindholm (1986: 342). I acknowledge however the tribal structure's potential for ranking and differentiation and thus do not consider it a pure type of nonstate society, but as containing also state-type dynamics as potentials (Deleuze and Guattari 1987). It appears that the great states and empires with divisions between ruling nobility and ruled commoners can be considered as "indigenous developments of the state mechanism" (Krader 1963). In terms of its structural dynamics, tribal society worked through lateral networks of kinship and alliance, and central to our discussion of Dumont's concept of hierarchy, leadership did not support itself on the religious structure.

To return to our look at the early Ottoman state, we should thus conclude that it represented a conjuncture of the Central Asian inclusive tribal structures and bureaucratic techniques from the Byzantines and early Islamic states (Kafadar 1995). The outcome of that historical conjuncture was fashioned by the particular frontier environment it occurred in. This environment created a special sociopolitical order, which at first was highly inclusive and later on implied a particular form of centralization process: there emerged a reluctance to recognize aristocracy and a freezing of inheritable distinction in specific lineages, even after settling down, according to Kafadar (1995: 141). The Ottomans developed a tradition of unigeniture, which set them apart from other frontier principalities and which facilitated a centralization of the state. The gradual elimination or incorporation into the state functionary elite of the nobility was also an innovation. Kafadar sees the *devşirme* system of slave bureaucracy (outlined below) as being "conceivable only in a state born of those frontier conditions" (1995: 141).[14]

Ottoman organization was influenced by surrounding bureaucratic state formations, such as the Abbasid, Seljuk, and Ilhanid states. Murad I was the first Ottoman leader to take the title of "sultan" in the latter half of the fourteenth century. This title was originally developed by the Seljuk Turks who drew upon the traditions of the Turkic and Mongol empires of Central Asia, where the Khan had been the secular regulator and compiler of existing traditional law.[15] The Seljuks "developed the institution of the sultan as the secular ruler in Islam, standing beside the caliph, who retained authority only in religious and personal matters" (Shaw 1976: 62).[16] The title of "sultan" was a sign of an emerging distancing of the sultan from the egalitarian tribal structures, but still the function of the sultan was mainly that of a military leader. During Murad I's reign, two new offices of "military judge" and "frontier lord" were created, and this represented a significant step in the "delineation of boundaries around the ruling class vis-à-vis the people," and also vis-à-vis the sultan himself, as Kafadar observes (1995: 142). It was "an announcement of the fact that the military-political elite were no longer a band of more or less equal warriors" (Kafadar 1995: 143).

The early Ottoman tribal leaders had in an important sense been firsts among equals. They were warrior leaders, not sovereigns, and they had no sacerdotal functions or leadership. As in other tribal contexts, their leadership was limited, and decisions were often taken by tribal councils. Even after the Ottoman *beğs* adopted the title of *sultan* and gradually gained more authority, they still operated through kinship and alliances, and used marriage alliances to incorporate Christian noble families and their territories into their networks. They had no claim to divinity, and no religious class serving them with sacrificial services.

By the fourteenth century the Ottoman leader was still a frontier lord, and until that century Islamic law was not incorporated into the workings of the Ottoman tribal organization (Shaw 1976: 22), which continued to operate through tribal customs and laws that varied from tribe to tribe. From the fourteenth century, however, Islamic law began to become incorporated into the organization of the polity.

In order to understand the relation between the political power and religious authority in the Ottoman Empire, we must look at the structure of Islam. The Ottoman Empire represents a conjuncture of Islamic-Middle Eastern and Turkic political and cultural structures.

The Social and Cultural Structure of Sunni Islam

In the Indian and medieval European cases, the Brahmans and the bishops were, respectively, responsible for the sacerdotal functions. The Indian kings were dependent on the Brahmans' carrying out sacrifices for them. In Christian Europe the distribution of sacraments was a priestly monopoly, and the bishops were, in this sense, religious sovereigns. They stood at the apex of a bureaucratic structure that regulated both the doctrine and the social structure and function of the sacred, monopolizing the symbolic interaction with God. The medieval Christian Church inherited the Roman theory of the absolute and universal jurisdiction of the supreme authority and developed it into the doctrine of the *plenitude potestas* of the Pope, who was the supreme dispenser of law and the sole legitimate earthly source of power (Figgis 1960, in Dumont 1986: 67). If we look at India and medieval Europe, we thus see a religiously defined totality within which the sacerdotal power of the clergy was not subordinated to the *potestas* of the king. The European medieval ideological model came out of the integration of the church into the Eastern Roman Empire from the fourth century onwards, and of the inheritance of the Roman theory of the absolute and universal jurisdiction of the supreme authority. The Church became transformed into a bureaucratic state structure through its integration into the Roman Empire (Dumont 1986: 45). The Church was furthermore not just *a* state; after the collapse of the Roman Empire it became *the* state in the European Middle Ages (Figgis 1960, in Dumont 1986: 67), in the sense that it was the sole totalizing structure embracing all particular institutions of society. It also meant that, in contrast to the Indian case, the Church assumed the political powers in its spiritual hierarchy (Figgis 1960, in Dumont 1986: 67).[17]

Sunni Islam, on the other hand, was and is very differently organized, as there has been no priestly class acting as intermediaries between man and God. There are no sacerdotal functions in Islam that can be monopolized. The function of the *imam* is simply to lead the prayer, and whoever is locally approved as fitting can be an *imam* without any formal requirements. In their interaction with God, humans are thus more equal than in medieval Christianity or Brahmanic India. There was no centralized control or appointment of *imams* in Islam—and there was furthermore no central agency deciding on doctrine. Furthermore, the Koran itself does not contain a system of doctrines. Islamic belief and practice was not centralized and systematized as they were in the Christian church, where doctrine became bureaucratically regulated and the basis for unity.

In Anatolia, different paths of Sufism constituted the common form of Islam on the popular level and well into the elites too.[18] Sufi Islam was organized in different orders: *tarikats* centered on lodges, which were centers led by a sheikh or a guide (*murshid*) providing spiritual guidance, religious education, and social welfare for the common population. The graves and shrines of such Muslim saints or martyrs were important places of sacrifices and offerings in popular Islam. Sheiks, "saints," and *ulema* were all religious specialists and parts of the organization of Islam. Although *ulema* have often perceived the personalized and miraculous powers of Sufi orders as a threat, the distinction is not inherent, and the two groups of specialists have often overlapped in many regions in the past centuries.[19]

The structure of *saintship* illustrates the crucial difference from the organization of the Christian church. Throughout the Islamic world there have always been widespread cults of saints or holy persons, such as sheikhs, mystics, and martyrs, who have been the object of popular veneration.[20] The grave of a saint often functions as a shrine, serving as "a center of concentration of his power and the blessing he bestowed during life" (Gilsenan 1973: 44). There is thus a category of human beings, living or dead, who are considered by Muslims to stand in a special relation to God, and therefore able to mediate between men and Allah. In Christianity, sainthood is decided through a bureaucratic and juridical process of canonization, which can only take place after the candidate is deceased. There has also been a tendency for monastic personnel and theologians—thus for personnel from the bureaucratic organization itself—to achieve canonization (Turner 1974). In Islam, by contrast, "saintship"[21] has been achieved by persons gaining local recognition as such during their lifetime. Eickelman describes from North Africa how "saints" are considered to be filled with *barakat*—blessing or grace. Gilsenan also analyzes how possession of "grace"—manifested in miracles and extraordinary abilities—is a central constitutive element of sainthood in modern Egypt (1973). Gilsenan warns against the danger of viewing blessing only as a property of saints (1973: 33). The grace or blessing that a saint can transmit through various acts and objects represents benevolent forces that may help and protect people living in a cultural universe that is a complex of forces, malevolent as well as benevolent.

Turner cites a contemporary description of how a married woman in Tetuan apparently had intimate physical contact with such a saintly figure in the street and was "felicitated on her good fortune" by her companions, and how her husband "received complimentary visits on this occasion" (1974: 68). A similar phenomenon, involving what is presented as "a wandering dervish," is described from eighteenth century Cyprus by a contemporary traveller (Mariti 1971: 35).[22] Blessing was a contagious quality diffused in individuals and collectivities (through descent), and not a scarce resource controlled and used by a bureaucratic organization to strengthen itself. Religious authority was thus a personal and embodied force.

The organizational and cosmological structure of Islam reflects the particular cultural and political context within which it emerged. In contrast to Christianity, which emerged from within a flourishing empire, Islam was born between the gradually collapsing Sassanid and Byzantine empires, in a period of drastic social upheaval and change, and among an egalitarian tribal people who were accustomed to a low degree of state presence. The early community of believers—the *umma*—was structurally actually a tribal confederacy or a "replacement tribe" (Lapidus 1991: 35).[23]

An Islamic empire, the caliphate, was then founded by the Arab tribes, unified by the Prophet Muhammed. Arabia had no tradition for strong kingship,[24] but was predominantly pastoral and politically fragmented (Lapidus 1991: 11), and the *caliph*, the ruler, was not a sacred king, but merely the successor of Muhammed's political functions. The caliph was the *Khalifat rasul Allah*—the successor of God's Prophet, and not the representative of Allah on Earth (Vikør 2003: 78). Crone and Hinds (1986) argue that the Umayyad caliphs actively claimed to be sacred monarchs and interpreters of divine law. While it seems to be an established fact that the title *Khalifat Allah* was in use at that time, their claim that the caliphs sought religious authority is however more disputed (Vikør 2003: 78). These claims to be *Khalifat Allah* were rejected by the religious scholars, and never had any practical consequences. Sunnism in its developed form, from the Abbasids onwards, regarded the caliph neither as a prophet nor as an infallible interpreter of the faith. The caliph never developed into a divine ruler nor into a pope. The caliphate continued to be a political office, and religious authority was never centralized. Neither was Islam in its Sunni form ever subordinated to any political power.

In a sense, the ruler and his legal system stood outside the Islamic legal structure, which regulated many aspects of daily life of society.[25] The early caliphs had "no say at all in the definition of the law by which [their] subjects have chosen to live ... Rulers were obeyed as outsiders to the community" (Crone and Hinds 1986: 109). Even in the classical Islamic, caliphate states, the *shari'a* law "had little influence on the activities of the actual ruler" (Gerber 1994: 60). The Abbasid caliphs were absolute military rulers dependent on a personal bureaucracy, and they delegated authority to their own officials such as the police force, rather than to religious scholars. These rulers did not remain outside of law, however, but established alternative court systems. Under the Abbasids or probably earlier, alternative *Mazalim* courts were established, not depending on Islamic law but presided over by the ruler himself, acting according to his own will (Gerber 1994: 60). Furthermore, already under the Umayyads, there was also the institution of the police *(shurta)*, which acted as public prosecutor, courts, and prison. They originated as elite military divisions to protect the ruler. The two juridical state institutions above were established by the caliphs to protect the state and regulate the relation between the military elite and the common population.

Shari'a courts and judges thus had no judicial monopoly, and were not even supposed to be endowed with this according to the ideology of the religious scholars themselves (Gerber 1994: 60). Islamic law was not seen as a legal political document, but "as a basis for arranging the relations between man and God" (Gerber 1994: 60). In the eleventh century the Abbasid caliph was reduced to a figure with authority only in religious and personal matters by the Seljuk Turks who conquered the caliphate (Shaw 1976: 62). As we see, even in the classical Islamic states, the rulers and the rulers' legal systems were external to Islam.

The structure of the *shari'a* legal system was different from the Roman tradition. Islamic law was not a fixed, immutable code like Roman law, but rather the result of a great deal of study and rationalist discussion between legal experts over the centuries" (Shaw 1976: 137). The religious scholars were rational interpreters of the holy texts, the examples of the prophet, the juridical traditions of the various schools and customary law. Whereas the Roman tradition presented the sovereign as the sole source of jurisdiction on earth (see Dumont 1986), Sunni Islamic law did not see any human sovereign as the source of jurisdiction. The legal process was thus less hierarchical and centralized than in the Roman tradition.[26] Judges *(kadis)* were appointed by the Ottoman government, but *any* member of the *ulema* could in principle act as a *mufti* (student and interpreter of law, jurist) if qualified and *recognized as such* by the person wanting and paying for a *fetwa*—a legal interpretation.[27] *Fetwas* were widely ordered and used by the involved parties and judges in *shari'a* court cases, and as such were important in the legal process. They were legal theoretical interpretations that were not binding for the judges, but were drawn in as guidance for verdicts or as support of claims by the legal parties (Gerber 1994).[28]

Sunni Islam, as a system of ritual practice and belief, was thus not encompassed by the Ottoman state. Neither was it transformed into a bureaucratic state structure by its interaction with the Ottoman Empire. By this I mean that there did not emerge a centralized organization that was hierarchical in theological or sacerdotal issues. The educated religious class in the Ottoman Empire, the *ulema*, were judges, jurists, and theologians, and had no religious sovereign like the pope at their apex. The Ottomans did actually centralize the *ulema* by establishing the state office of Şeyhülislam or Chief *Mufti* in 1453, but this was a state office and not a religious one. Furthermore, he had no executive powers in the state system, and was not a member of the Imperial Council (Imber 2002: 241). His main responsibility was to appoint religious officeholders in the empire. His religious authority was, however, theologically equal to that of the other *muftis* (Gerber 1994: 81). The Ottoman bureaucracy was dependent on the king, and not on God, as in Europe.

To sum up, due to the particular historical formation and cultural structure of Islam, the sacred functions were not monopolized by a religious class, and religious practice and religious doctrine were not centralized. Furthermore, law was not such a centralized and codified process as in the Roman tradition, and there was no religious sovereign figure who was considered to be the single source of jurisdiction. Islam, as a system of ritual practice and belief, was not transformed into a bureaucratic state structure by its relations with the empires of the region. It was still a decentralized religious structure, where local recognition and not centralized bureaucratic regulation structured ritual practice and belief and the distribution of "blessing." Religious authority was personalized, in the figures of the prophet and the saint. Islam has therefore always stood in a tense relation with political power. The only encompassing of the political by the religious in Islam is in the life of the Prophet and in the Koran. As we shall see below, the political power of the sultan was also personalized.

The "Classical" Ottoman State Structure

The Ottoman state can be characterized as a redistributive economic structure, where the sultan was the accumulative center. The development from a frontier tribal structure to a world empire implied an expansion of this accumulative center, but still partly within the structure characteristic of the redistributive nomadic economy. Halil Inalcik cites an example of ancient nomadic Turkish advice to the prince: "Open your treasury and distribute your wealth. Make your subjects rejoice. When you have many followers, make Holy War and fill your treasury" (Inalcik 1973: 67). The same views are repeated in eighth century *Gök Türk* inscriptions. The nomadic leaders hosted large outdoor communal meals, and shared the war booty according to set rules. This Turkic nomadic structure, where the sultan was the first among equals, entered into a conjuncture with the bureaucratic structures of the Near Eastern state traditions. The Ottoman Empire therefore represents a particular conjuncture of "the personal" and the bureaucratic.

After the conquest of Constantinople in 1453, the Ottoman sultans ascended to what the Europeans saw as a position of impressive and awe-striking sovereign power. The Ottoman rulers had moved from being frontier lords and tribal leaders in the fourteenth century to becoming sovereigns, a concentration of power unique among the historic Turkish empires (Shaw 1976: 24). Sultan Mehmet II (the conqueror) enacted new state regulations, which "decisively transformed his state system into an imperial system" (Meeker 2002: 128). The sultans had long since started to disentangle themselves from the tribal and kinship structures in which they were enmeshed. They had also mostly eradicated the Ottoman notable families or turned them into provincial officials rather than princes. They carried out large-scale confiscations of the properties and land fiefs of Ottoman noble families and of rebellious commanders who had received land fiefs. A new state structure with a large body of state officials was emerging. This new system was a highly centralized and bureaucratic state where the sultan was the formal owner of all wealth-producing property in the empire. The principle of hereditary positions or property was almost completely denied in this new system. There was a meritocratic recruitment system of bureaucrats, a rule-governed and impersonal bureaucracy and a strict rotation system for provincial officials (Barkey 1994; Gerber 1994).

During the fifteenth century the Sultans Bayezid and Murat II instituted and developed the *devşirme* bureaucratic system of recruitment, whereby non-Muslim boys periodically were "collected" and brought to the palace to be converted to Islam and trained into elite bureaucrats and soldiers (Shaw 1976: 46).[29] This practice originated in the right of the early war leaders to a portion (*pencik*) of the war booty in the form of young slaves who were used in the army, in the household, or in the administration. After the conquest of Constantinople, most of the important offices of the empire became reserved for the slaves of the sultan, the boys collected from Christian subject families. Whereas the pre-Ottoman Islamic states had used slaves mainly in the army and used the religious class in the administrative system, the Ottoman sultans started to award administrative positions mainly to slaves (Inalcik 1973: 77). The *kapıkulu* (slaves of the palace) became a major class in the Ottoman Empire, filling the important positions in the new army, the central bureaucracy, and the provincial administration. It was this group which filled the highest positions in the bureaucratic hierarchy, and not the religious scholars. This "slave elite" had no bonds of loyalty or kinship to local interest groups, and thus were bound to the sultan and the state. They were converted and educated in the palace, and not in the religious schools, so the bureaucracy was not, as it were, dependent on God. They filled up the ranks of the administration and the elite army force of the *Jannisaries*. Entrance into the army was barred for the Muslim population. The other group upholding the social order, the provincial administrators and judges, were constantly rotated, in order to prevent the development of loyalty ties to local groups.

The classical Ottoman social order became a dyadic structure of the "military" (*askeri*) class and the "people" (*re'aya*). This division was not based on any Islamic tenet, but derived partly from customary state practices from the pre-Islamic Near East, modified by Turco-Mongol traditions (Inalcik 1973: 66) of secular tribal rulers who enacted justice according to customary derived laws. The difference from the dyadic order of the pre-Islamic Near Eastern states was that their administrations were based on religious personnel, and that the rulers were priest-kings or divine kings, while the Ottoman sultan was a secular ruler. The military class of the Ottoman social order included both military and civilian officials, while the second class included all tax-paying producers, regardless of faith. The function of the Ottoman officials was warfare and tax collection, thus to control the periphery and to extract revenue from the subjects. Above these two classes stood the sultan. Although some scholars, like Karpat (1973), place the sultan within the military class, it seems more correct to regard him as standing outside or "beyond" the social order.

Max Weber rightly recognized the personalized structure of the sultan's power. He took the Ottoman state system as his model for "sultanism," a strong version of "patrimonialism," wherein state administration and society are totally subordinated to the ruler's commands and random will (Weber 1978). It seems clear that Weber exaggerated the randomness of the bureaucratic operations, and that the Ottoman bureaucracy was in fact much closer to his ideal-type of bureaucracy with rule-governed and jural/impersonal operation, also within the legal system (Barkey 1994; Gerber 1994). An important part of the bureaucratic state apparatus was the personnel of the *shari'a* legal system to which the state gave a judicial monopoly and made its official system. This operated according to strict rules and in predictable ways after it was codified by the sultans (Gerber 1994). The sultan nevertheless remained a personalized power—outside the structures of law and alongside the bureaucratic structure—who could at any moment interfere in the legal and bureaucratic process. The Ottoman Empire therefore seems to represent a particular conjuncture of personalized power and bureaucracy. As religion was not bureaucratized, the bureaucracy did not depend on God, as in the Christian case, but solely on the king.

The Ottoman state had adopted Islamic Law as its legal system from the fourteenth century onward. Between the fifteenth and seventeenth centuries, after the conquest of the imperial city Constantinople, the sultans started to issue and codify law, and the *shari'a* courts and the *kadis* were given a judicial monopoly over contesting systems such as the secular state courts of the Abbasids (Gerber 1994: 60–69). The sultans issued secular *kanun* laws by decree, enforcing them without any approval by the *Şeyhülislam*. These *kanun* laws covered the areas of criminal law, land tenure, and taxation, and were codified into a system by the sultans. The rule of the sultan was based on the "divine right of the king," as Karpat (1973: 6) states, but this right was not based in Islam, and there were "no requirements such as the necessity of securing religious approval for legislation. These new state laws mostly followed the *shari'a* closely, constituting a parallel set of law codes. The entire body of what we might call the *shari'a* penal code, for instance, found its way into the *kanun* criminal law" (Gerber 1994: 62). Some of the laws however were open violations of the *shari'a* laws, as for instance in the cases of implicitly accepting the charging of interest by setting a legal limit, and by allowing torture (Gerber 1994: 63). The *kanun* code also made murder a state violation, "thereby turning the entire concept of *huquq Allah* (the laws of Allah, regulating the gravest offences) on its head" (Gerber 1994: 63), by transferring it to the moral sphere of "the laws of man." At the same time, murder was in practice treated as a violation of private law, as a case of retaliation or blood money to be decided on by the next of kin. It is evident from the records that the *kadis* of the *shari'a* courts actually implemented secular *kanun* laws alongside the *shari'a* law in their practice (Gerber 1994). Beginning as a dual system of law, where the *kanun* criminal code offered the additional punishment in the form of fines, the evolving pattern was a gradual welding together of *shari'a* and state law into a symbiotic or compromising structure through the actual practice of the judges in the *shari'a* courts (Gerber 1994: 72). The bureaucratization of the judges and *muftis* made the working of the *shari'a* courts much more predictable and rule-governed than it had been before (Gerber 1994: 72). Judges were rotated constantly, and *muftis* were as a rule appointed by the *şeyhülislam* according to qualifications. The *muftis* issued legal opinions in general legal terms, devoid of any particular details of the court cases in question. In this way, Islamic law practice became permeated by universalistic principles and governed by rules, according to Gerber. Because the judges were rotated and the *muftis* issued only abstract interpretations, the courts functioned according to juridical principles and rules, and therefore worked to counter abuse of positions by officials.

To sum up, the sultans "appropriated" the *shari'a* courts as their court system, while issuing their *kanun* laws, which most often were parallel to existing Islamic laws. The sultan as a legislator was therefore mostly a "compiler" of existing Islamic law and customary law practices. He could not rise to the position of the divine source of law. He was bound to accommodate his legal system to the religious legal system which already regulated most social relations. "The Ottomans had a serious problem of legitimation in terms of Islamic political theory, and the *kanun* may have been their answer" (Gerber 1994: 63). The significant point is that by enacting the *kanun*, the Ottoman sultans partly emerged as the constitutors of law, order, and justice, even if most of the state laws were almost completely a copying of the preexisting *shari'a* laws. The *kanun* laws were implemented by the *shari'a* courts alongside the Holy Law, thereby drawing the secular law code into the realm of society. According to Gerber, the enacting of *kanun* law was obviously not motivated by the need to "fill in gaps" in the existing *shari'a* laws. It should thus not be seen as the answer to the Hobbesian "problem of order." One must rather see the issuing and codification—the constituting—of law as a critical issue for the establishment of the sultans' sovereignty. The sultans tried to appropriate the constituting power of the Holy Law by using the *shari'a* courts as their vehicle. By turning the personnel of the Islamic law system into state officials, and by issuing *kanun* laws that were almost parallel to the Islamic laws, the sultans tried to write political power into society. At the same time they were still "legally outside the law."

The very social order that divided society into the secular classes of *askeri* and *re'ayah*—the officials and the taxpayers—was, as mentioned above, not derived from Islamic law. The *kanun* law code issued by sultanic decrees established the rule of the sultan and the role of the state, and regulated the relation between government and people (Barkey 1994: 29). Its basis was the distinction between the taxpaying subjects (*re'aya*) and the officials (*askeri*) who "received a salary either from a fiefhold or directly from the Treasury" (Imber 2002: 244). This dyadic social order was a feature of the pre-Islamic Near Eastern bureaucratic states with divine kings or priest-kings. The functions of the sultan's officials were basically expansion by war for the soldiers and tax collection for the bureaucrats. The Islamic legal system was turned into a fitting bureaucratic mechanism that regulated the social relations between the ruled, and between them and the administrators.

The bureaucratic machinery became a buffer between the sultan and society. The bureaucratic order performed two functions: It collected taxes and controlled the periphery, seeking to expand the state. The Ottoman state thus became a "container state," containing a diversity of communities within its borders. By removing the aristocratic tendencies and with them the hereditary rights to property, a system with a certain degree of social mobility was created, both within the religious establishment (for Muslims) and within the secular bureaucracy (for converts only). We can see this process of bureaucratization as a withdrawal or ascendance of the sultan from the social order he was enmeshed in: the tribal and the Islamic social and cosmological structure. The sultan emerged, by his foundation of the large bureaucratic machinery and his role as lawgiver, as the founder of a new social order. At the same time he was beyond the laws and regulations.

The point I wish to make is that the sultans never became, nor could become, divine kings of the "primitive" Polynesian type nor of the Egyptian type. In the Turkic tribal structures there was no room for a sacred sovereign within the cosmology. Nor did the structure of Sunni Islam install the sultan with priestly authority or divinity. The route to sovereignty implied a withdrawal from society and social bonds. In a sort of reversal of the mythological structure of sovereignty described by Dumézil (1988) from ancient Indo-European cultures and by Sahlins (1985) for Polynesia, where the stranger king is eventually domesticated by the native people, the Ottoman sultan became a sovereign by gradually estranging himself from the social bonds he was entangled in.

The Sultan's Sovereignty: Sacralized Power

How are we then to perceive the sultan's power? As I have outlined above, the Ottoman leader emerged from the position as a frontier war leader in a tribal association directed at expansion, to become a sovereign sultan by the fifteenth century. The conventional way of understanding the power of the Ottoman ruler is as deeply embedded in the structure of Islam. This is the view of Lewis (1968), Shaw (1976), Berkes—who even describes the sultan as a "theocratic ruler" (1964: 13)—and Meeker (2002) who presents the sultan as the center of a unified structure of Islamic values and symbolism.

Michael Meeker (2002) argues in a Geertzian analysis (cf. Geertz 1980) that the sultan's power was divinized because it was constituted by a representational structure that paralleled the structure of divinity in Islam. The empire rested upon "a normative model of interpersonal association" based on Islamic ethics, he argues. In spite of its emergence in warrior associations, the symbol structure of the empire was based on an Islamic ethics.

The sultan was in a sense similar to the Hawaiian "stranger king," but there was no divinity beyond his person. He had no sacerdotal functions and no place within the religious structure. The sultan had no authority to interfere in religious matters, and stood outside the religious organization. The claim to the title of "Caliph" made by sultans was a move that sought to legitimate his political leadership by genealogy in the eighteenth century.[30] The Caliphate was, as outlined above, never a religious authority, but a continuation of Muhammed's *political* leadership. The Caliphs of the classical Islamic states were political leaders without any privileged "priestly" authority and, as outlined above, the legal systems of these states were not based on the *shari'a* (Vikør 2003). The Ottoman sultan was not sacralized by the services of the religious experts, as they had no sacerdotal powers. So what sort of hierarchy might we have here, in Dumontian terms? The sultan was clearly not a priest-king, and he was not dependent on the authority of a priestly class. The question is rather if the sultan's power in some sense was subordinated to the religious system, or if he was installed into the cosmology of Islam. I would answer "no" to these questions, too.

Contrary to this, I suggest that the sovereignty of the Ottoman sultan represents a radically different form. He is similar to the divine Polynesian stranger kings, but without any divinity beyond him. He represents the absolute sacralization of power. The power of the sultan was *personalized*, as Turkic and Islamic cosmology had no place for a transcendental sovereign. His power was in principle unlimited, because his function was not inscribed by the religious structure, and the new dyadic structure of the social order was not based on Islamic principles. The sultans' legislation and codification actions can be seen as attempts to inscribe themselves into the social order as its founders or constitutors. Islamic law was fully formed by the fourteenth century and regulated most daily affairs by the fifteenth century (Imber 2002). The sultan's appropriation of Islamic law and court system as the state legal system may be seen as the only possibility in that cosmology. This was the outcome of the context of a cosmology without human divinity. At the same time, the incorporation of the religious class as state officials made possible the sultan's withdrawal from social reciprocity with society, to a position above and beyond the social order. That the sultan achieved a semi-transcendent position as a sacred figure was produced not by his attachment to Islam, but by something inherent in his sovereign power.

Let us look at the figure of the sultan in the fifteenth century, after the conquest of Constantinople. There were no formal regulations of royal succession, and no religious rites of anointment or ordination. Succession was determined by the *de facto* ascendance to the throne by the candidate who had won the fratricidal war of succession. Pure force and not primogeniture or consecration thus defined the accession to sovereignty. An act of violence outside the morality of society thus founded the sovereign power. This was not, however, a mythical foundational act, as in the Indo-European and Polynesian cases, but a concrete act which repeated itself in the installation of each new sultan. There was no elaborated succession ceremony to consecrate him. Furthermore, the entire empire and all property in it were considered his personal property. There was no elaborate funeral ceremony like the ceremonies of the pagan imperial Roman or the medieval Christian kings (Agamben 1998; Kantorowitz 1997) to divinize the kings. The sultan's body had no magical or divine qualities like those of the European kings; he was fully human. When a sultan died, he simply ceased to exist socially (Berkes 1964: 13). When a sultan died, furthermore, all appointments and legal regulations were "considered null and void until the new sultan confirmed them" (Inalcik 1973: 61). Although the sultan himself was formally unconstrained in his executive role, he increasingly emerged as the pseudo-founder of social order through his role of legislator. This implied a retreat from sociality. He was not entangled in a network of nobility, as he had eradicated or outmaneuvered the notable families by turning them into dependent state functionaries.[31]

The sultan's palace was very different from a European royal court. After Mehmet II had conquered Constantinople and set the state on an imperial track, he began to withdraw from society and from the state officials. The palace can be read as a physical embodiment of that principle, as Necipoğlu (1991) argues. In contrast to the splendor and exhibitionism of the French kings, the Ottoman sultans were secluded and invisible. Foreign visitors reacted to the lack of grandeur, and many likened the palace to a tent camp. The palace was monumental only when seen from afar. Inside the buildings were single storied, with temporary furnishings like tent curtains and awnings, and monumentality was expressed through the "sprawling horizontal spaces" rather than through "dominating verticality" (Necipoğlu 1991: 243).[32] The buildings inside the palace were organized non-axially, and there was an "asymmetry of compositional schemes." In its horizontal emphasis and noncentralized layout, the palace structure was also akin to the sultan's military tent camps and thus to the nomadic origins of the empire (242). The palace was a physical construct that emphasized the seclusion and inaccessibility of the sultan, and the fundamental division between the state elite and the common population. The structure of the new palace "set the sultan well apart from other men" (250). The royal quarters at the power center of the world empire were invisible and inaccessible. It was a "diagram of absolutist rule" (250), but in a culturally particular manner.

Michael Meeker discusses in detail how the sovereign of the new empire had become "seeing but unseen, hearing but unheard," and how he was now "unfit to engage in any form of reciprocity" (Meeker 2002: 128, 133). He became virtually invisible to the general populace and to the members of the state elite, by retreating into the inner, closed quarters of the third courtyard, where only his slaves and officials could enter. His personal servants were individuals with physical disabilities such as eunuchs, mutes, and dwarfs, persons cut off from normal social interaction. Mutes were freely allowed into the palace, and around two hundred eunuchs were employed there, according to the sixteenth century traveller (Bon 1996). The palace hosted some hundred *devşirme* recruits: young boys who had been gathered and cut off from their origins, living in the palace for training. The largest category of inhabitants was women, around 1200 of them, according to Bon. These were servants, old women, and the sultan's concubines in the harem, as Meeker puts it: "Mothers who could not be wives, wives who could not be mothers" (2002: 133). Thus the palace was a place full of persons with physical and "status debilitations." It was not the feudal knights or property-holding lords who frequented the court, but the state elite of slaves who were totally dependent on the sultan for their income and their fate.

The palace was a silent place. Communal ceremonies were carried out in dead and grave silence according to contemporary descriptions, and the soldiers and officials would stand still like statues for several hours on end (Meeker 2002: 133). Within the third court the servants were not allowed to speak or to reveal themselves, but "communicated in signs and hid behind columns," and visitors to the sultan were normally not reciprocated socially in any way (Meeker 2002: 133). Invisibility was also central to the operations of the servants. For visitors, the entering of the palace was a gradual revelation of the low and confusing structure through gates and courtyards toward its immensely powerful center (Necipoğlu 1991).

The sultan was not a social person one could engage with in horizontal interaction. The exception from the rule of silence were the loud declarations of the officials' loyalty made at the end of the silent banquets. Foreign visitors were amazed by the order and obedience of the vast crowds of soldiers and servants who did not appear as crowds at all, but rather as a unitary body, by their silence and "the gravity of their movements" (Meeker 2002: 131). The ceremonies of the new palace "stressed the unbridgeable gap between master and slave; they were not for hereditary nobles but for household slaves and dependent *ulema* appointed to fixed offices by the sultan" (Meeker 2002: 256).

The few occurring palace ceremonies also underline the withdrawal of the sultan. There was a tradition of communal banquets, stretching back to Osman, the founder of the dynasty, and also to Turcoman and Mongol traditions (Inalcik 1973), in which the leader had hosted and shared communal meals with his officials and troops. This tradition had continued within the palace, and was altered by Sultan Mehmed II. The high officials and troops started to gather in the middle court to show their loyalty to the sultan, without the latter appearing before them. He now overlooked the ceremony from a latticed window in the Tower of Justice, where he could not be seen. It was impossible to see if he was actually watching from behind the lattice. The egalitarian redistributive ritual of nomadic origin thus continued, while the sultan withdrew from direct social exchange. He withdrew from society and from all horizontal social relations. In a sense he thereby became external to the social order, by withdrawing his person from communication and sight, and by emerging as the foundation of society through sultanic legislation and codification. The sultans performed a reversal of the mythical career of the stranger king who is eventually encompassed by society.

The palace was also the location of the empire's impressive treasury, an enormous collection of booty from the conquered lands. The treasury and the harem with its hundreds of women both signify the sultan's "endlessly" regenerative potency. The palace was thus the accumulative center of a vast redistributive economy, and in this respect similar to the Polynesian system (Valeri 1985; Sahlins 1981, 1985), where the kings appropriated the regenerative powers of the Gods. The difference is of course that the sovereign at the center was not divine, as were the Polynesian kings. The sultan's power was not installed in him by any position within Islam or by his relation to religious experts. The organization and order of the Ottoman palace, the ritual gatherings, and the silent, grave, and unanimous behavior of the sultan's slave soldiers and dependent servants in the presence of the sultan should be considered as the development of a political form into something resembling a religious form. Although the sultan became sovereign, he had no divine "backup" and was therefore still entangled within the first-among-equals structure of tribal origin, although this was hidden by the imperial structure.

The sultan had no religious function. His mosque in the third court was only used for private prayer, and there were no religious ceremonials inside the palace. Michael Meeker emphasizes the weekly royal excursions to the imperial mosques as central to the structure of the imperial symbolic structure, and thus to sultanic rule. He regards the palace as a culturally particular imperial machine which functioned to install and reproduce an Islamic ethics of interpersonal relations. In contrast to Meeker's assertion that the sultan stood at the center of a unified system of Islamic values and symbols, and that he ruled *qua* his placement within the value structure of Islam, I argue that it was not Islam that gave the sultan a divine aura but his *pure power in itself*. The Ottoman sovereign was thus clearly not a divine king—like the Polynesian, ancient Indian, or Indo-European ones—since there was no divinity beyond him. On the contrary, his power became its own divinity.

Conclusion

The theoretical issue in this chapter has been to discuss Dumont's claim that the relation between political power and religious status has two possible basic forms, demonstrated through the Indian and the modern European examples.

I have outlined how the Ottoman polity emerged as a warrior association of a tribal and nomadic type, in a historically particular frontier environment. The Ottoman polity was initially oriented toward expansion by war. The early sultans were warrior leaders who were first among equals. This egalitarian structure then developed through a structural conjuncture with Islam and the bureaucratic state traditions of the pre-Islamic and classical Islamic Near East, as well as with the Byzantine Empire. The leader then gradually became a sovereign, and expanded his bureaucracy of slaves while eradicating the notable Ottoman families. Especially after the conquest of Constantinople in 1453, the process of bureaucratization was accelerated and expanded, and the sultan increasingly withdrew from society and his loyal slave officials. His large bureaucracy depended fully on him and not "on God," as in the West. This transformative process from war leader to sovereign implied the expansion of an accumulative center of a redistributive economy.

In place of the Dumontian totalizing and modernist analysis of values, I have attempted an analysis of the relation between political power and religious status. My first argument is that the Ottoman Empire represents a radically different form that cannot be fitted into Dumont's dichotomy of the premodern, holistic structure versus the modern European one. It was not religious values that produced the fundamental ranking of the state elite over the common populace of producers, but political power. Islam did not encompass political power, except in the Koran and the life of the Prophet Muhammed. In the Ottoman Empire and the Islamic world the political and the religious stood in a relation of unresolved tension. The personalized power of the ruler stood in a structural relation of deep tension with the personalized authority of the religious leaders. The sultan had to accommodate his rule to Islamic law by turning the *shari'a* courts into the state courts, and by erecting a political law code which ran parallel to the Islamic laws, but he could not appropriate the role of lawgiver within Islam.

The Ottoman Empire represents a particular conjuncture of personalized power and the bureaucratic state. The sultan remained a first among equals in the sense that he did not become divine or a priest-king, but this was concealed by his withdrawal from sociality. He was the perfectly human potent center of a redistributive system. This redistributive system was similar to the Polynesian system, but the center was very differently constituted. The power of the sultan was not based on a divinity beyond himself, and in this sense he was the opposite of a divine king. The sultan was not a divine figure, but his power became its own divinity. The Ottoman sultan represents the absolute sacralization of power. In this sense he became the perfect sovereign, almost perfectly external to the social order. This illustrates Agamben's argument that the sacred of sovereignty is founded "before or beyond the religious" (Agamben 1998: 9). Agamben argues that sovereign power, by its exception from sociality and by its absolute power over life and death actually constitutes both nature and the political, and thus in itself produces a structure of sacrality that is the hidden foundation of Western democracies. This partially echoes Sahlins's discussion of sovereignty, where he argues that both "power and nature are alike as what is beyond and apart form the norms of ordinary culture" (Sahlins 1985: 76). One could likewise read the Indian structure as being determined by its extremes—the Brahman and the untouchable—who are both outside the social order, rather than by the commitment to ultimate values.

My discussion has also opened a second argument that I cannot pursue here in length, namely that the Ottoman and Islamic structure challenges Dumont's assumption that social life is by nature hierarchical. Even though the state-employed religious scholars were ranked within the bureaucracy, this ranking was based on political principles. The Islamic view of the totality did not produce a ranking of groups in terms of value, and religious authority was not centralized in religious terms. As explained above, the religious whole did not encompass the political. Dumont sees sovereign power as founded within the religiously defined totality, whereas I am suggesting that the power of the sultan depended on his externalizing himself from society.

Notes

1. The development process whereby individualism emerged as the ideological image of society goes back to the early Christian church fathers, in Dumont's analysis (Dumont 1986).

2. Dumézil's analysis (1988) supports Dumont's assertion that India and Rome both originally had unified sovereign figures: the priest-kings *rex-flamen* and the *raj-brahman*. Dumézil shows how a dual model of sovereignty was the ancient pattern in all Indo-European religions. In the mythologies of these societies, sovereign power emerges in the figure of a stranger king: a warrior God or king who founds the state in a violent feat. Sahlins describes from Polynesia how the stranger king in the mythology eventually is "encompassed by the indigenous people" (Sahlins 1985:78). Sovereign power was seen as based on a founding act of violence or brutality, which simultaneously constituted a new social order. Dumézil (1988) argues that the same structure of sovereignty is found also *outside* the Indo-European area: in Polynesia, in the precolonization Americas, and in ancient Ireland.

3. The difference was of course that the Church claimed political power, while the Brahmans did not.

4. By saying this, I mean that Dumont sees social nature as hierarchical in the sense that human action is always crucially informed by an ideology of the totality, which is always structured around a dominant value. Human action is always oriented toward value in relation to the social whole, and social groups will be internally ranked in relation to this value.

5. I should also mention here Köprülü's influential thesis, which came before Wittek's. The former held that the Ottomans' was a lineage-based nomadic tribe clearly defined by consanguinity, and that very few Christian converts were involved as warriors or bureaucrats (Kadafar 1995; Lowry 2003).

6. The concept of *gaza* is not synonymous with *jihad*, and although the latter can only refer to war against non-Muslims, it should not be understood as a duty of incessant warfare against non-Muslims (Kafadar 1995: 79). Muslim states have generally been accomodationist in their relations with non-Muslim subjects.

7. Similar concepts and groups (*Akritas*) appear to have existed on the Byzantine side of the frontier (Kafadar 1995: 81).

8. See among others Evans-Pritchard (1940) and Krader (1968) for the inclusive and flexible nature of tribal genealogies.

9. One of the main exceptions was the consequent Ottoman practice of unigeniture, as opposed to the Central Asian tradition of splitting the realm between the male heirs (Kafadar 1995: 120).

10. See Sneath (this volume) for a critical discussion of genealogical models and the "tribal" concept. See also Salzman's and others' discussion of inequality and egalitarianism in nomadic societies (Salzman 1999).

11. See Kirchhoff (in Fried 1968) for the first formulation of the term, and Hage and Harary (1996) for an overview of the subsequent development of the model.

12. See Krader (1968) on trade and tribute relations between Mongols and China.

13. See also Salzman (2000) for a discussion of hierarchy and egalitarianism in leadership among the Middle Eastern Basseri nomads.

14. Slave bureaucracy was also practiced by the Seljuks before the Ottomans, but they were also a Turkic nomadic people.

15. Ghengis Khan's law *(yasa)* compiled various tribal traditional laws into one body. It was thus an "overcoding" or synthesis of preexisting customary laws.

16. The caliph was however also a secular ruler, as I outline below.

17. In the eighth century this hierarchical relation between church and state began to change. From that century the popes started to claim political power by installing and ordaining the Frankish kings, and thus claimed spiritual supremacy on the temporal level. Dumont sees the modern state as a "transformed church, in discontinuity with other political forms, because it is not made up of different functions or orders, but rather of individuals" (Dumont 1986: 51).

18. The Bektaşi order was closely connected with the Jannisaries, while the Mevlevi order often were closely connected to other state elites.

19. See Gilsenan (1973: 12).

20. Such holy persons were often miracle-working, and the rituals connected with their tombs were (and still are) sacrificial offerings directed to the "saint" as an intermediary to God.

21. Saints are known as *wali* in Arabic, *evliya* or *asiz* in Turkish, and *Marbut* in North Africa.

22. From both these descriptions it is hard to determine the nature of the contact between the women and these holy figures. The witnesses describe them as sexual encounters, but according to Knut Vikør (personal communication), an expert on Islamic history and Sufism, this is unlikely.

23. Knut Vikør (personal communication).

24. The exception was Yemen (Turner 1974).
25. See Ira Lapidus (1992, 1996) for an outline of the relation of political power and religious authority in the Middle East.
26. The legal system also did not favor the ruling classes, as the European system did (Gerber 1994: 57).
27. After the creation of the state office of the *Seyhülislam*, most *muftis* became state appointed. The state appointed *muftis* to the major towns and cities of the empire. The point I wish to make is that private *muftis* still practiced, and their legal authority was not inferior to that of the state *muftis* (Imber 2002).
28. Bernard Lewis argues that the *muftis* and the *Seyhülislam* became like bishops because they had territorial authority and stood at the apex of a religious hierarchy (Lewis 1996: 208). This may in a sense be correct, but Lewis overlooks the fact that the *muftis*, including the *Seyhülislam*, only issued legal interprations, and had no right of interference in the workings of the courts. Nor did the *Seyhülislam* have higher religious or theological authority than the other *muftis* (Gerber 1994: 81). They had no doctrinal or juridical power within the religious organization.
29. The practice of slave recruitment had a precedent in the Seljuk Mamluk armies, and was also found among the Abbasids. The Ottomans however extended the system to the administrative sector (Shaw 1976).
30. Knut Vikør (personal communication).
31. I should stress that I am not arguing that the sultans acted intentionally, with a consciousness of the course and future outcome of the development, but rather that it was an observable, empirical process, and that it was the outcome of the conjuncture of the nomadic tribal structures, the religious structure of Islam, and the bureaucratic structure of the Near Eastern states.
32. This feature may also have been inspired by the Byzantine royal palace, which occupied the site until the Ottoman conquest (Necipoğlu 1991: 244).

References

Agamben, Giorgio. 1998. *Homo Sacer: Sovereign Power and Bare Life*. Stanford: Stanford University Press.

Appadurai, Arjun. 1986. "Is Homo Hierarchicus?" *American Ethnologist* 13 (4): 745–761.

Barfield, Thomas F. 1990. "Tribe and State Relations: The Inner Asian Perspective." In *Tribes and State Formation in the Middle East*, ed. P. S. Khoury and J. Kostiner. Berkeley: University of California Press.

Barkey, Karen. 1994. *Bandits and Bureaucrats: The Ottoman Route to State Centralization*. Ithaca and London: Cornell University Press.

Berkes, Niyazi. 1964. *The Development of Secularism in Turkey*. Montreal: McGill University Press.

Berreman, Gerald. 1971. "The Brahmanical View of Caste." *Contributions to Indian Sociology* n.s. 5: 16–23.

Bon, Ottaviano. 1996. *The Sultan's Seraglio: An Intimate Portrait of Life at the Ottoman Court*. London: Saqi Books.

Crone, Patricia and Martin Hinds, ed. 1986. *God's Caliph: Religious Authority in the First Centuries of Islam*. Cambridge and London: Cambridge University Press.

Dirks, Nicholas. 1987. *The Hollow Crown*. Cambridge: Cambridge University Press.

Deleuze, Gilles and Felix Guattari. 1987. *A Thousand Plateaus: Capitalism & Schizophrenia*. London: Athlone Press.

Duby, Georges. 1980. *The Three Orders: Feudal Society Imagined*. Chicago and London: The University of Chicago Press.

Dumézil, Georges. 1988. *Mitra-Varuna: An Essay on Two Indo-European Representations of Sovereignty*. New York: Zone Books.

Dumont, Louis. 1980. *Homo Hierarchicus: The Caste System and its Implications*. Trans. M. Sainsbury, L. Dumont, and B. Gulati. Chicago and London: The University of Chicago Press.

———. 1986. *Essays on Individualism: Modern Ideology in Anthropological Perspective*. Chicago and London: The University of Chicago Press.

Evans-Pritchard, Edward Evan. 1940. *The Nuer: A Description of the Modes of Livelihood and Political Institutions of a Nilotic People*. Oxford: Clarendon Press.

Fried, Morton H. 1968. *Readings in Anthropology*. New York: Crowell.

Friedman, Jonathan. 1998. *System, Structure and Contridiction: The Evolution of "Asiatic" Social Formations*. Walnut Creek, Calif.: Alta Mire Press.

Geertz, Clifford. 1980. *Negara: The Theatre State in Nineteenth-Century Bali*. Princeton, NJ: Princeton University Press.

Gerber, Haim. 1994. *State, Society, and Law in Islam: Ottoman Law in Comparative Perspective*. Albany: State University of New York Press.

Gilsenan, Michael. 1973. *Saint and Sufi in Modern Egypt: An Essay in the Sociology of Religion*. Oxford: Oxford University Press.

Glassé, Cyril. 1991. *The Concise Encyclopedia of Islam*. San Francisco: Harper San Francisco.

Hage, Per and Frank Harary. 1996. *Island Networks*. Cambridge: Cambridge University Press.

Hourani, Albert. 1991. *A History of the Arab Peoples*. London: Faber and Faber.

Imber, Colin. 2002. *The Ottoman Empire: The Structure of Power*. Hampshire and New York: Palgrave Macmillan.

Inalcik, Halil. 1973. *The Ottoman Empire: The Classical Age 1300–1600*. London: Phoenix.

Kafadar, Cemal. 1995. *Between Two Worlds: The Construction of the Ottoman State*. Berkeley: University of California Press.

Karpat, Kemal. 1973. *An Inquiry into the Social Foundations of Nationalism in the Ottoman State: From Social Estates to Classes, From Millets to Nations*. Princeton University: Center of International Affairs, Research Monograph no. 39.

Khoury, Philip S. and Joseph Kostiner. 1990. *Tribes and State Formation in the Middle East*. Berkeley: University of California Press.

Krader, Lawrence. 1963. *Social Organization of the Mongol-Turkic Pastoral Nomads*. The Hague: Mouton.

———. 1968. *Formation of the State*. Englewood Cliffs, NJ: Prentice–Hall.

Lapidus, Ira Marvin. 1991. *A history of Islamic Societies*. Cambridge: Cambridge University Press.

———. 1992. "The Golden Age: The Political Concepts of Islam." *The Annals of the American Academy of Political and Social Science*, vol. 524: 13–25.

———. 1996. "State and Religion in Islamic Societies." *Past and Present*, issue 151: 3–27.

Leach, Edmund. 1964. *Political Systems of Highland Burma*. London: The Athlone Press.

Lewis, Bernard. 1968. *The Emergence of Modern Turkey*. London, Oxford, New York: Oxford University Press.

————. 1996. "The Ottoman Legacy to Contemporary Political Arabic." In *Imperial Legacy: The Ottoman Imprint on the Balkans and the Middle East*, ed. L. C. Brown. New York: Columbia University Press.

Lindholm, Charles. 1986. "Kinship Structure and Political Authority—the Middle-East and Central-Asia." *Comparative Studies in Society and History* 28 (2): 334–355.

Lindner, Rudi Paul. 1982. "What Was a Nomadic Tribe?" *Comparative Studies in Society and History* 24 (4): 689–711.

————. 1997 [1983]. *Nomads and Ottomans in Medieval Anatolia*. Uralic and Altaic Series 144. London: Curzon Press.

Lowry, Heath. 2003. *The Nature of the Early Ottoman State*. Albany: State University of New York Press.

Mariti, Giovanni. 1971 [1908]. *Travels in the Island of Cyprus*. London: Zeno Booksellers & Publishers.

Meeker, Michael. 2002. *A Nation of Empire: The Ottoman Legacy of Ottoman Modernity*. Berkeley, Los Angeles, London: University of California Press.

Necipoğlu, Gülru. 1991. *Architecture, Ceremonial, and Power: The Topkapi Palace in the Fifteenth and Sixteenth Centuries*. New York, Cambridge, MA, London: The Architectural History Foundation and The MIT Press.

Parkes, Peter. 2003. "Fostering Fealty: A Comparative Analysis of Tributary Allegiances of Adoptive Kinship." *Comparative Studies in Society and History* 45 (4): 741–782.

Parry, Jonathan P. 1998. "Mauss, Dumont, and the Distinction between Status and Power." In *Marcel Mauss: A Centenary Tribute*, ed. W. James and N.J. Allen. New York and Oxford: Berghahn Books.

Sahlins, Marshall. 1981. *Islands of History*. Chicago and London: The University of Chicago Press.

————. 1985. *Historical Metaphors and Mythical Realities: Structure in the Early History of the Sandwich Islands Kingdom*. Ann Arbor: The University of Michigan Press.

Salzman, Philip Carl. 1978. "Does Complementary Opposition Exist?" *American Anthropologist*, 80 (1): 53–70.

————. 1999. "Is Inequality Universal?" *Current Anthropology* 40 (1): 31–61.

Shaw, Stanford. 1976. *History of the Ottoman Empire and Modern Turkey, 1280–1808, vol. 1*. Cambridge: Cambridge University Press.

Turner, Bryan. 1974. *Weber and Islam: A Critical Study*. London: Routledge & Kegan Paul.

Valeri, Valerio. 1985. *Kingship and Sacrifice: Ritual and Society in Ancient Hawaii*. Chicago and London: The University of Chicago Press.

Vikør, Knut S. 2003. *Mellom Gud og stat: Ei historie om islamsk lov og rettsvesen*. Oslo: Spartacus Forlag. [Published in 2005 in English as: *Between God and the Sultan: A History of Islamic Law*. Hurst and New York: Oxford University Press.]

Weber, Max. 1978. *Economy and Society: An Outline of Interpretive Sociology, vol. 2*, ed. Guenther Roth and Claus Wittich. Berkeley and London: University of California Press.

CHAPTER 7

Marriage, Rank, and Politics in Hawaii

Valerio Valeri

R ecent discussion of Oceanic systems, and particularly Polynesian
ones, has shown the theoretical poverty of ethnological thinking
concerning the societies that anthropologists call "complex," which are
generally approached with the categories elaborated for societies called
"simple." Their structure and function are forced to fit the constraints of
categories such as "descent," "residence," and "private property" in land
(Goodenough 1955; Frake 1956). The old warhorses of ethnological theory, "alliance" and "descent" are imposed on these rebellious phenomena.
It hardly matters that these theories can only be used to define the systems
in regard to, rather than in accord with, the categories that they postulate.
The methodological attitude stays the same: It does not recognize the
complex character of these societies, but defines them with the models
created for simpler ones, or stops with the affirmation that, as Lévi-Strauss
has said, they present a "vast zone where the elementary layers of kinship
have collapsed" (1969: 535). This collapse should put into question the
very notion of kinship elaborated on research that is restricted to simple
systems. The future of kinship theory must begin with a confrontation
of these complex systems, to provide a general definition of the role and
significance of these phenomena in prestate societies.

Let us first note that, although Hawaii is often cited for its system of
terminology, there has never been a complete analysis of its political system or its kinship system. The monograph by Handy and Pukui (1958)
does not provide this, since it is limited to an analysis of the internal relations of a segment of the kindred: the *ohana*. This absence is not, in my
opinion, an accident. In effect, Hawaiian society gives lie to the idea that
underpins almost all earlier definitions, which have derived their analytical categories from the study of "simple societies," that is, from the
homogeneity of the system. Whether the structure is "real" or "ideological,"

Notes to this section begin on page 239.

it would be found everywhere: for the empiricists, as a real structure; for some structuralists, as a "system of systems." A fundamental homogeneity of society is postulated, either at the visible level, or as an unconscious structure as a supposed "system of systems," which would assure the coherence of all its contradictions.

Anthropology has fallen prey to the ideology of a particular class of societies: those which try to cleanse the social body of its contradictions and discontinuities, instead of incorporating them into its very structure. But it is exactly this difference in the treatment of discontinuity which should provide the key to understanding a major opposition, which is not that between "simple" and "complex" societies but between those societies which see discontinuity as external *and* insurmountable and those which see it as internal *and* surmountable. This will allow us to show that we are not dealing in Oceania with a major opposition between a real and a pseudo-kinship (an "ideological" kinship and one which has "collapsed"), but instead between two opposed types of uses of the idea of kinship. Polynesian systems demand, before any other kind of analysis, an adequate and specific definition of the kind of kinship that they use.

All human societies must confront the *natural* discontinuity of groups, determined by ecological, geographic, productive, and demographic factors. To control these factors, a cultural discontinuity has to be substituted for the natural one. If we analyze the natural conditions in Hawaii, we realize that they could have produced a discontinuity similar to the one that characterizes Melanesian societies. The Hawaiians were perfectly conscious of this: they have left behind traditions about the origins of the chieftainship that speak of the passage from "natural groups" to political ones (cf. Kamakau 1964: 3). Melanesian societies have in effect kept this natural discontinuity as the dominant characteristic of their political and kinship systems. The leadership that characterizes Melanesia can only surmount the discontinuities and warfare in a provisional and transitory way. I argue that there is a close connection between the political conditions and kinship notions at work in these societies.

Categories, Terminologies, and Etymologies

The documents concerning the relation between kinship organization and political organization, and especially territorial organization in Hawaiian society, are insufficient. The oldest documents, traditions, and ethnography, written by the Hawaiians themselves (Malo 1951; Kamakau 1961, 1964; Papa Ii 1959, 1963), concern mainly the relations between chiefs.

Archival documents (especially those concerning the land reform, the *Mahele*, from 1846–1854), which have been studied by M. Sahlins and D. Barrère, might allow us to improve our knowledge of kinship organization among the commoners and their relations with the chiefs (cf. Sahlins 1973; Kirch and Sahlins 1992; Barrère 1994). The first results of this research confirm the mistakenness of the traditional Hawaiian organization that Handy, especially, has superimposed on the facts (cf. Handy and Pukui 1958; Handy 1972). The affirmations of Handy and Pukui (1958) concerning the *'ohana* are contradictory. In some cases, they consider the *'ohana* as a ramage or a ranked lineage system. In others, they identify it as very widespread and a "horizontal" notion of kindred (cf. Handy and Pukui 1958: 5).

In a later work, Handy perpetuates the confusion by defining the *'ohana* as "kith and kin" (1972: 289), that is "relatives by blood, marriage, and adoption" (287), but also as "family or clan" (352). In their 1958 monograph and even more in their 1935 work, Handy and Pukui seem to use the term *'ohana* in another sense as well: that of the localized genealogical segment and holder of land rights. In 1972, Handy continued to consider the *'ohana* as a genealogical segment inside a unified territory or *ahupua'a*, occupying a territorial segment or *'ili 'aina* (288). Handy was no doubt impressed by the etymology of the word *'ohana*, which can in effect suggest an ancient lineage connotation. *'Oha* is the term for taro which grows in an old tubercle, and especially for the stem, which is called *kalo*. Metaphorically, it means the "offshoot," "branch," and also "the young ones." The idea of ramification from a single ancestor thus seems associated with the term *'ohana*. But the etymology should make us suspicious of an abusive extension of the notion of descent implied by the term: *'oha* or *mu'u* designates the second generation of taro, after the parental generation, which is called *kalo* (cf. Pukui and Elbert 1957: 115). The depth of commoner genealogies is not more than two generations, according to archival documents (Sahlins 1973: 8).

'Ohana means simply "kin," member of a kindred, and one which is relatively narrowly extended because of the strong endogamy of commoners (cf. Sahlins's analysis of marriage registers from 1833 to 1860, at Waimea and Koloha). It is thus not a group, and it would be hard to allow it to include "the totality of dead and living members," as Handy and Pukui would like us to believe, using a typical lineage ideology.

In fact, Hawaiians seem much more preoccupied by relative and horizontal distances in kinship, which can be modified much more easily, than by absolute hierarchical distinctions, like those implied by a lineage system strictly ordered by a principle of seniority. We will see the refinements that the *ali'i* ("chiefs" of various rank, as opposed to "commoners") bring to this horizontal hierarchization. But even among the commoners, differentiation and cohesion depend on horizontal relations much more than on a widespread genealogical structure.

The term *pili koko* ("blood tie") seems for example to suggest a lack of differentiation. In fact, the expression *he iwi, he 'i'o, he koko* ("bone," "flesh," "blood") to indicate the kindred seems to presuppose distinctions familiar from the ethnography of Southeast Asia (Lévi-Strauss 1949) and Melanesia (Valeri 2001). The different forms of kinship are not equivalent. Besides, *pili koko*, the tie of consanguinity, is opposed to *pili kamau*, which indicates a relation which is "added." *Pili*, which means "relative" but also "limit," "touch," and "unite," is a term that is used in many Hawaiian expressions concerning personal relations, and the meaning of which is refracted across a multitude of categories, which are frequently not genealogical ones (Pukui and Elbert 1957: 303).

As for the kin category *kuleana*, it shows that relations of affinity are important because they can be transformed into relations of consanguinity. In effect, if one man *x* marries a woman *y*, she will be the *"kuleana"* ("link for reclaiming"), which will allow the relatives of *x* to trace a relationship with the relatives of *y*, and especially the children of members of her generation, who can also be considered *kuleana* (Handy and Pukui 1958: 70). It must be underlined that the relationship traced here is a relationship of consanguinity, not alliance, because it uses the *kuleana* to find genealogical links to living people and important ancestors. In this way, transformed into relations of consanguinity, relations of affinity are a fundamental means to approach persons of high rank and affirm a kinship link with them. From this follows the importance of marriage in modifying personal rank.

Two questions which arise are: if there was no lineage system, what was the relationship between kin ties, political ties, and territorial ties? And what was the role of marriage and its usefulness in establishing relations of privileged filiation? We will limit ourselves in the following to answering the first question, which is a necessary stepping stone toward the resolution of the second question.

The Death of a Chief and the Strategies of Marriage

In 1782, Chief Kalaniopu died, having named as his successors his son Kiwalao and his nephew Kamehameha (see Figure 1). Kiwalao became the *ali'i nui* or "supreme chief." Kamehameha became the guardian of the state god Ku-Ka-'ili-moko. The conflict between the two chiefs for supremacy—symbolized by the right to do human sacrifices—was sparked immediately when, after a rebellion, it was necessary to sacrifice the chief.

Kiwalao claimed that he had this right, but Kamehameha denied this, saying that he had inherited it a short time ago and had ceded provisionally to his uncle Kalaniopu (cf. Papa Ii 1963: 4). Kamehameha took the initiative and performed the sacrifice. War broke out and finished with the victory of Kamehameha (cf. Papa Ii 1963; Kamakau 1961). Despite this precedent, Kamehameha, at the moment when he named his successor, repeated the decision of Kalaniopu: his son Liholiho would be the *ali'i nui*, his nephew Ke-Kua-o-ka-lani the guardian of the state god. There again, the cosuccession was probably a way of anticipating and provoking the inevitable conflict between two descent lines too close in rank. Kalanimoku, the first minister, and Keopuolani, the wife of Kamehameha and mother of Liholiho, assured the preeminence of her son by abolishing the system of taboos, and so with them the religious authority of his rival. A war followed, and Liholiho won. The rank system (founded on the taboo system) was definitively abolished, doubtless to avoid a repetition of these conflicts between the pretenders to very close ranks.

Davenport (1969), Webb (1965), Levin (1968), and Fisher (1970) have given other reasons, equally valuable, to explain this decision. I believe nonetheless that it does not make sense unless we analyze the genealogical situation that existed in Hawaii at the end of the eighteenth century. The progressive concentration of power in the hands of a few chiefly descent lines, and their multiple and repeated alliances had equalized their ranks and sharpened conflicts which concerned not only the possession of certain districts, but all of the island of Hawaii and, later, the whole archipelago. In addition, the line which succeeded in unifying the island under a single power was not the most noble one. The only way it could affirm its supremacy was by military conquest and the destruction of competing descent lines. What is more, it had to destroy the very bases of the traditional legality of power: under the influences of European advisors (Vancouver had already encouraged Kamehameha along this path), and receiving the support of commoners (Davenport 1969), the chieftainship was transformed into a hereditary constitutional monarchy.

A glance at the genealogy shows how the differentiation of rank was at the same time useless and impossible to obtain by consanguineal marriage. We note first of all that both cases of cosuccession helped to regulate problems created by the marriage of Kamaka'imoku with three chiefs: 1) Ka'-I-i-mamao, whose descendants were Kalaniopu and his son Kiwalao; 2) Kalanike'eoumoko, whose descendants were Keoua and his son Kamehameha; 3) Alapa-'I-nui, whose descendant was Keliimaikai, the "younger brother" of Kamehameha and one of his most faithful allies in the struggle for power (Fornander 1878–1885, II: 328, 336).[1] The first cosuccession, which appointed Kamehameha and Kiwalao, expressed the equal rights of two descendants of the same woman. It was settled by a conflict that allowed Kamehameha to get rid of his "brother" (a brother by a common grandmother). This situation provides a concrete illustration of the importance of the grandmother, which is particularly visible in myths. The second cosuccession associated two other descendants of the same woman: Liholiho, son of Kamehameha, and Ke-Kua-o-ka-lani, son of Kelimaikai. The equivalence of their rights created a new conflict, which allowed the descent line of Kamehameha and Liholiho to defeat a second rival from the descent line, born from an alliance with their own ancestress.

This all shows the importance of kinship through women, accentuated by the fact that it was a woman, Kaekealaniwahine (Papa Ii 1963: 4) who inherited the right to make human sacrifices that Kamehameha and Kiwalao quarreled over. From a genealogical point of view, it was the link that Kamehameha had with this woman, which validated her claims to power. But these claims could not be validated without difficulties, because Kaekealaniwahine was the mother of Kaulele, whose alliances with almost all the important chiefs of the island provoked the rivalry of the many descent lines that she gave birth to. The generation of Kaulele (and those that preceded it, to a lesser extent) was characterized by a very great dispersion of alliances between the dominant descent line in Hawaii and those of most of the other islands. It is because Kaulele was

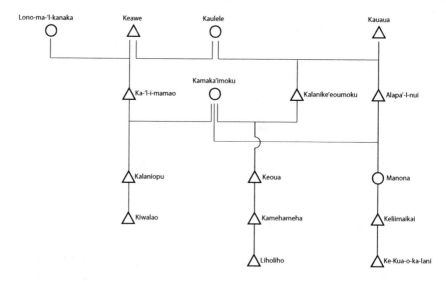

Figure 1. Genealogical chart of chiefly origins.

so "excessive" that the basis of the genealogical unification of the islands was laid.[2]

Her husband Keawe was no less accomplished, since as Beckwith says, he "has the name of having mingled his strain with that of every family in the realm, chief or commoner" (1951: 30). The dispersion of alliances was almost always accomplished by another matrimonial strategy: the creation, by consanguineal marriage, of a successor of very high rank. But this dispersion put this "concentration" at risk, because it gave to the affines a way to trace cognatic relation (preferred over agnatic relations), which tied them to the designated successor and equalized their relative rank. If alliance equalizes and allows for the challenges of cognates, it is nevertheless necessary and, at the time of Keawe, to be desired: alliance makes it possible to forge new coalitions with rivals and reclaim their lands.

Because of the many alliances of Kaulele, the chiefs of Kona (Hawaii), Kohala (Hawaii), Kau (Hawaii), Kauai, and Maui were very close in rank, and could also lay claims to succeed Keawe. This also came from the fact that Keawe himself had formed an alliance with a woman whose rank was higher than his own. His successor in terms of patrilineal descent was not sufficiently differentiated from the other children of his wife Kaulele, who descended from a line that was senior to that of her main husband. The situation became worse because the designated successor was the first born son of Keawe, but by Lono-ma-'I-kanaka and not by Kaulele. It was perhaps with a view toward the future challenges that the *Kumulipo* genealogy was composed for this child, to prove that he was the highest-ranking person in his generation, and that 'I, the grandfather of Lono-ma-'I-kanaka, was the most noble of the 'I line (cf. reports on the *Kumulipo* in Beckwith 1951: 8). The genealogical challenge to this assertion came without delay: representatives of the elder branch of Oahu, cut off from alliances with the chiefs of Hawaii, and less noble than him only in terms of descent, quickly composed a chant asserting the purely human character of the genealogies of Keawe, in contrast to the celestial character of those of Kuali'i (the chief of Oahu), who was one of a series of reincarnations of Ku (cf. Fornander 1916–1919: 394–395).[3] But this challenge, expressed in lineage terms, came down to an affirmation of the supremacy formulated by chiefs who were not in direct competition for power over Hawaii. More dangerous was the challenge expressed in terms of rank. It was Alapa-'I-nui, son of Kaulele and Kauaua-a-Mahi, chief of Kohala (Hawaii) who took power away from Ka-'I-i-mamao.

The expulsion of Ka-'I-i-mamao was presented as a response to his efforts to differentiate himself from his rival: the statement that introduces the *Kumulipo* tells us that his subjects threw him out "because of his evil acts, since he slept with his own daughter, Kaolaniali'i" (Beckwith 1951: 8). The unseated chief had to flee to Kauai, where he "went into the rain forest of Kahihiholo, went crazy and wandered in the mountains" (Beckwith 1951: 8). According to other traditions, he was forced to work as a *maka'ainana* ("commoner") and lost his chiefly status and his genealogies.

Since the text dates from the "European" period of Hawaii, one might object that the conception of incest as a sin seems very Christian. That is certainly true, but I think that we are seeing a transformation, in Christian terms, of a political accusation expressed a short time previously against Ka-'I-i-mamao. It could not have been invented later—at the time of Kalakaua, who was the one who had the *Kumulipo* written down—because Kalakaua would have no interest, as a good Christian, in inventing an incestuous ancestor. On the other hand, it was very much in his interest to remind others that he came from a particularly "noble" union: he would thus legitimate his own selection to royalty as the successor to the line of Kamehameha, a line that was junior to his own. Kalakaua's assumption of power represents, in effect, the final victory of the "legitimate" line against the usurping junior lines. These events prove that the Hawaiians, even in 1874, although they were already Christians, used their traditional political ideology.

Interestingly, Kamehameha and his line tried to devalue unions between parents and children. The proof lies in the fact that Malo does not mention this type of union, while Fornander claims that it is the origin of the *naha* rank, which is inferior to the rank obtained by the marriage of real or classificatory brothers and sisters. These claims, which contradict what we know through genealogies and legends (notably those of the famous ancestor of the Hawaiians, Wakea, who married his daughter to give birth to the senior lineage of Hawaiian society), doubtless represent an ideological reelaboration to justify the fact that Kamehameha's line had usurped power to the detriment of Ka-'I-i-mamao's line. Malo was in effect the student of Auwae, Kamehameha's favorite genealogist and a figure of the court until 1820 (cf. N. B. Emerson, in Malo 1951).

My argument can be summarized in these terms: Ka-'I-i-mamao, threatened by several chiefs who had the same or a similar rank to his own, tried to make himself stand out by marrying his own daughter. But this only precipitated conflict, and one of his rivals profited from this by taking power himself. These events prove what the myth of Wakea (to which I shall refer intermittently) reminded Hawaiian chiefs: consanguineal alliance is a dangerous means and not recommended because it isolates the supreme chief and provokes a coalition of the other lines against him. Besides, it was in the time of Malo that the existence of the marriage of Wakea and his daughter Hoohokulani was denied, and it was claimed—contradicting most genealogies—that although Hoohokulani was the wife of Wakea, she was the daughter of the main *priest* Komoawa and Popokolonuha. Or else, as in the genealogy collected by Fornander, it was said that the daughter of Wakea married a certain Manauluae, and not her father, thus creating a secondary line (*PR* I: 205).

Marriage with the daughter sets before us two contradictory traditions, one of which became preponderant at the time of Kamehameha and his children. Both traditions use Wakea, the ancestor of the Hawaiians, to express opposed points of view: either the chief must define his rank by marrying his daughter, or else he must not do it; and if he does it, he is punished by his allies. In the second version, in effect, Wakea suffers the revenge of his first wife Papa (who represents "exogamous" alliance because she descends from a different line than Wakea) and must make war with his brother Lihaula. He manages to defeat him, but weakened by his "isolation" he then loses the war against a stranger, Kaneia-Kumuhonua, who seizes his power and his territory (Fornander *PR* I: 162, 205).

The genealogy of the 'I line shows that consanguineal marriage does not always work to demarcate rank. When different lines have intermarried for several generations, the half brothers are no longer of a single line, closed in on itself, but kinsmen who are very closely related in terms of kinship but not in terms of politics, because they belong to the dominant lines of different and opposed chieftainships. Consanguineal alliance, especially between lines which belong to different chieftainships, must be nonrepetitive in order to demarcate rank. If not, it results in the opposite of the desired goal: it equalizes rival lines instead of hierarchizing them. The politics of repeated alliances can be used by a chief who is strong enough to exploit the fact that a large number of chieftainships end up dominated by a group of close kin, by one single cognatic line, which he could hope to direct. But, on the one hand, lines which are bound by alliances try to distinguish themselves in unilinear terms, because the transmission of power to the most senior person of each line tends to create lines of an unfamiliar continuity in a purely cognatic system. On the other hand, up until the end of the eighteenth century—that is to say, until the introduction of firearms—the technical and economic conditions that would allow one line to definitively modify the equilibrium between itself and the others did not yet exist.

Two strategies are thus possible. From the eighteenth century onwards, either certain chiefs have deliberately carried out a politics of repetitive external alliances, or else, like Kamehameha, they have profited from a favorable military situation and, instead of renouncing kinship relations after a certain number of generations as they usually did, they have exploited them politically.

Hawaiian ideology gives us an exemplary history of the political uses of alliances. This is the history of Chief Umi, who found himself in a situation similar to that of the successors of Kalianiopu, because he tried to reconquer all the districts of Hawaii, which had been unified by his predecessor but had become independent again after his death. His story demonstrates that it is best to marry kin who are well placed in the rank system when one wants to become powerful, but, on the other hand, once already installed, the best way to dominate other chiefdoms and, at the same time, to distinguish one's line is to refuse consanguineal marriage. Umi's advisor told him, in effect: "Umi must not marry a woman of his own blood, because he already owns the whole of Hawaii. He should take as a wife the daughter of Piilani of Maui, Piikea by name, so that Maui would be united to Hawaii by ties of blood which would assure a lasting peace with that island" (Fornander *Coll.* IV: 214). Besides, Umi seems to have specialized in the politics of "demarcation" by extreme exogamy. In the version of his story given by Kamakau, it is claimed: "He had many wives, among whom were the daughters of the common people; so that he became an ancestor both of the chiefs and the common people" (1961: 228). The type of chief incarnated by Umi is the inverse of the stereotype of the Hawaiian chief. If he marries his half-sister and refuses to "give" the daughter of his predecessor, Hakau, he defines his rank and assures his power through exogamy. He tries to make alliances with rival chieftainships and reinforces his kin relations with the people, in order to oppose those "strangers" to his close kin. We might even wonder if his systematic consanguineal alliances are not a sign of weakness and a dependency of the chief on his collaterals rather than a proof of strength, because the only alliances that would really demarcate him from his collaterals would be those very rare ones, with the "real" sister or daughter.

If the chief does not manage to avoid repeated alliances with immediate collateral lines, the only demarcation that his consanguineal unions succeed in producing is that of an endogamous group of the *ali'i*[4] (where rank tends to become equalized, resulting in a sort of entropy which prevents all discontinuity) in relation to the group of *maka'ainana*. It is not surprising that a skilful and powerful chief, like Umi, tried to avoid this situation by forging alliances with other *ali'i nui* and with the people, nor that Keawe tried to multiply his alliances with everyone around, even the *maka'ainana*. When Liholiho abolished the system of rank and taboos, with the assistance of the people, he achieved the same thing: far from losing his own power, he reestablished it in a less sacred but more concrete form, and he removed it forever from his collaterals and particularly the priests.

Hawaiian alliances, and the rank that stems from them, can only be understood by deciding which kinship unity can be defined in terms of consanguinity and which can be apprehended as "affines." Endogamy and exogamy, as we have known since Lévi-Strauss, are not defined in absolute terms. As we have stated many times, in Hawaiian society the opposition between affines and consanguines is not very strong and one can often choose to consider a group or an individual as an affine or as a consanguine. Hawaiian oral traditions are full of stories of chiefs who "discover" that they are consanguines. It was always possible for an upstart chief to "discover" these relations to justify his seizing of power *a posteriori*. This strategy must have been very widespread and legalized, since the Hawaiians had a special term for this type of chief: *ali'i ho'opilipili*, "a chief who grafts himself onto the chiefly genealogy" (Kamakau 1964: 4). These traditions, besides, also illustrate steps in the opposite direction: those of consanguines who are considered strangers or affines (Fornander *Coll.* IV: 122).

In any case, it is the chief who decides, according to the political problems with which he is faced, between "real" endogamy or making himself—in opening, through an exogamous alliance, a new series of marriages with an external line—the origin of an exogamous group opposed to the one which is given to him "naturally" by the kinship system.

The preceding pages have tried to "situate" Hawaiian rank in its concrete context and functions, as a prelude to the exposition of its ideology, and to show that the principle of "endogamy" on which it is founded should not be taken too literally. I also wanted to show that this ideology does not derive, as it has been believed, from a distinction of one "class" in relation to another, but from the struggle of descent lines for power, and from their respective efforts to appropriate rank and to hierarchize themselves.

Acquiring Rank

Thus it is marriage that is the principal operator of rank, and that regulates even those genealogical attributions that allow rank to be expressed in vertical terms. Genealogy does not refer to a group, then, but is instead attached to a definitive status, for each individual, by his or her own rank title. Rank titles are terms of address which designate the relative status of chiefs not through seniority (which would imply the use of a kinship terminology and a notion of consanguinity) but according to their own logic.

The highest rank (*pi'o*) formally excludes the use of the terms of consanguinity, even for the half brothers or half sisters of the *pi'o* (Kamakau 1954: 5). Each title is obtained, as we shall see, through the alliances that have produced a particular person. The most fundamental alliance is that of the parents, but those of more distant ancestors are taken into consideration because they determine the relative status of the descendants of each generation. There is thus both increase and loss of rank in genealogical time: this leads to the construction of genealogies where, in each generation, it is the alliance contracted which must be taken into consideration. We are thus far from a simple "ambilateral" genealogy, which would not explain the care exercised in recording the marriage of each ancestor, a care that we can see in the genealogy of Akahi.[5]

In spite of that, we note that it is often the female line that is followed. The earliest authors were all struck by this particularity (Jarves 1845: 36; Alexander 1891: 32; Rivers 1914, I: 373–387; Fornander *Coll.* VI: 308) without, however, being able to explain it adequately.

We are thus confronted with two problems: 1) Why, within the limits of six to ten generations that are considered pertinent for "ambilateral" genealogies, do the Hawaiians take such care to indicate the marriages of their ancestors and eventually the type of union and the title of rank that it produced? 2) Why, for so many chiefs, were feminine links preferred to masculine ones? Only a detailed analysis of rank titles can allow us to answer these questions.

We distinguish between the "sacred" (*kapu*) ranks, like *pi'o*, *ni aupi'o*, and *naha*, from the nonsacred ranks (cf. for example Davenport 1969: 3). The distinction is in fact arbitrary, because if the highest ranks are associated with extremely strong *kapu*, the sources make clear that each rank and status position is made evident by ritual prescriptions and reciprocal behaviors, which are all called *kapu*. Rank is made visible not only through a title, which is absolute, but also through behaviors, which are relative, and by prerogatives, which are displayed (cf. especially E. W. Liliokalani in Beckwith (ed.) 1932: 195–198).

Sources concerning rank titles (*kapu*) are often very contradictory. This should not astonish us, since it concerns a delicate subject, and each person is trying to present an image of the system that seems favorable to him. In addition, profound changes occurred in the nineteenth century: the abolition of the *kapu* system by Liholiho had its repercussions on the ranks, which could not continue to exist without the associated ritual behaviors. The transformation of the Hawaiian chieftainship into a hereditary monarchy, Christianization, and the division of society into classes, have all weakened the foundations of the rank system. The earliest sources (Malo, for example), and the first European witnesses who knew the chiefs well, insisted that rank depended on marriage and thus on its variability (cf. for example, Stewart 1828: 124, 129–130). The last representatives of the monarchy have tried, on the contrary, to show that rank was hereditary in a descent line, independent of marriage. The notes written by Queen Emma on 25 August 1883 (in the possession of K. Pukui) are an example of this. According to her, all the lineal descendants of Kamehameha have the rank *ni'aupi'o, wohi,* and so on. It is clear that, in spite of a certain persistence of the earlier ideology, the adoption of the European theory of royalty and the dynastic principle led inevitably to the privileging of notions of lineage and heredity.

It is possible however that for certain ranks titles, such as the *wohi,* the principle of inheritance was introduced much earlier. According to Papa Ii, the *wohi* title comes, in effect, from the woman chief Kaulele, who transmitted it to all her children (1909: 52–53). Given the great number of her children, this hypothesis can only be accepted with caution (see below). It is not impossible that it was used to justify the possession of this title by an upstart chief like Kamehameha. The *lo* rank was also hereditary, but, as we have seen, it could only be maintained by a certain kind of marriage.

The theory that automatically makes all the reigning chiefs into *ni'aupi'o* by right of inheritance from the mythical ancestors Wakea and Papa is in any case clearly false. Kepelino, who supports it (Beckwith 1932: 130) is even forced to admit that these chiefs had different *kapu,* which contradicts his theory, because all the *ni'aupi'o* enjoyed the prerogatives of prostration *(kapu moe).*

Contradictions in the sources force us to consider, for each rank title, the principal definitions in the sources, and to gauge their reliability. We will go from the highest ranks to the lowest ones.

Kapu pi'o

According to Malo, this is the term for marriage between a brother and sister born of the same father and mother. The parents must be of high rank, but of which rank is not specified. The child born of this union would receive the title *ni'aupi'o. Pi'o* means "a bow, a loop, a thing bent on itself" (Malo 1951: 54). *Ni'aupi'o* is "a coconut midrib, i.e., of the same stalk" (Pukui and Elbert 1957: 245). The child had the highest possible rank; he was "so sacred that all those who came into his presence must prostrate themselves *(kapu moe).* He was called divine, *akua.* He could go out only at night, because if he went out in open day everyone would be required to fall to the ground in an attitude of worship, and all work would be impossible."

According to Kamakau, the marriage of a brother and sister born of two chiefs had the title *ni'aupi'o,* and "their wondrous marriage *(ho'ao)* was called a *ho'ao pi'o* or "a marriage in the form of an arc," or sacred marriage, a *ho'au waliweli,* a revered marriage, a *ho'au kapu ali'i,* a marriage of chiefly *kapu*" (1964: 4). He adds that they have no *kapu* in relation to each other, and that they are above all laws: "No divine law (*kanawi akua*) would arise between them (Kamakau 1964: 4). According to him, the child born of these two would be called with the same name as the union itself, *pi'o*. This marriage was called a "return" (*ho'i*) of the sister to the brother.

According to Liliokalani, everything was exactly as Kamakau said. The *pi'o* marriage was said to be "terrifying," the *pi'o* were "gods," a "fire," "heat," and "raging blazes." They could talk "to people" only after nightfall. Liliokalani gives an excellent example that shows that the principle of seniority does not have any role in the attribution of this title. The three children (Kapueookalani, Kaneoneo, Lanipipio) born from the marriage between Kamehameha (male) and Lonokahikina (female) were all considered *pi'o* (Beckwith 1932: 195).

According to Fornander, the children of the brother and sister whose parents are *ni'aupi'o*, or the two half-siblings whose parents were *ni'aupi'o*, have the right to the title of *pi'o* (*Coll.* VI: 308).

According to Rivers, it was as Malo says. He translates *ni'aupi'o* as "branch of the *pi'o*" (1914, I: 380).

In genealogies, *pi'o* unions are extremely rare. They are the exception, not the rule. If we take, for example, the genealogy of the descendants of chief Liloa, from whom came Kamehameha and his rivals, we find only two *pi'o* unions over about thirteen generations. They were contracted in periods very close to each other. We can doubtless explain them by the rivalry between the descendants of Keliiokaloa and Keawenui, sons themselves of an upstart chief, Umi. Like their father, the two brothers multiplied their alliances with high ranking chiefs from different chieftainships. Several generations after their ascension, obtained by anisogamic marriages, their descent lines were challenged: each of them contracted a *pi'o* union, and they thus faced off with each other for the position of highest rank. But it was finally the line born from Keliiokaloa that got the upper hand, because Keliiokaloa's descendant Iwikauikaua, after having contracted a *pi'o* union with Kapuhini, married the daughter of a *pi'o*, born of a union between brother and sister in rival lineages, who could not keep this rank for herself. From this marriage was born Keakealaniwahine (female), who, according to Papa Ii (1963: 52), inherited the *kapu moe* of her mother and transmitted it to the chiefs of Hawaii.

The extreme rarity of *pi'o* marriage seems compensated, in fact, by the possibility of transmitting the principal *kapu* that it creates. This explains why this *kapu* is associated with at least some of the chiefs of inferior rank to the *pi'o*—the *ni'aupi'o*. The meaning of this title "of the same branch" seems to suggest a transmission and not simply the turning back on oneself in marriage, which is indicated by the title *pi'o*. Once it is created by an extremely rare kind of marriage, this *kapu* then becomes a transmissible prerogative, but one that can only be acquired and used in the conditions that will be explained.

Kapu ni 'aupi'o

Our discussion has already shown how hard it is to interpret rank. According to Malo, the title *ni'aupi'o* is reserved for children born of *pi'o* unions. Also considered *ni'aupi'o* are the children born of half-siblings (*naha*) and those of children born of uncle and niece (*ho'i*). In the first case, the *ni'aupi'o* do not, however, have the *kapu moe* but only the *kapu nohu* (obligation to sit in their presence, which is done for chiefs of inferior rank). The *ni'aupi'o* born of a *ho'i* receives, on the other hand, the *kapu moe*. This shows the equivalence between the sister and the niece. These two women, to the extent that they are kept and one refuses to give them up, allow for a return back to one's self (*pi'o*) or a return (*ho'i* means in effect "return") (Malo 1951: 55). All the unions that produce *ni'aupi'o* (*pi'o, naha, ho'i*) concern the bearing of the *hiapo*, the firstborn. The things which are forbidden, as for the *pi'o*, have been discussed by earlier authors.

According to Kamakau, the *ni'aupi'o* is not defined in terms of consanguinity. For him, a *ni'aupi'o* is produced by the marriage of two *ni'aupi'o*, who can be very far apart genealogically or even not related. *Ni'aupi'o* is thus a title that is not necessarily produced by a consanguineal marriage. It is possible to marry a *ni'aupi'o* woman who belongs to another chieftainship and to conceive a *ni'aupi'o* child. So the acquisition of an elevated title or its conservation can be obtained just as well through exogamy as through endogamy. No one is tied to the servitudes of marriage with her or his own consanguines, but can choose instead an exogamous marriage with a high ranking woman, of the same rank as his consanguines. Kamakau makes no mention of the *ho'i* union, as Malo defines it.

Liliokalani's definition is the same as Kamakau's. Kamakau adds that two *ni'aupi'o* chiefs should have the same rank, and especially that they should not have the *kapu* (bark cloth) that would oblige one of them to take off his *kapa* in the presence of the other or that would oblige one of them to touch the *kapa* of the other (because this would indicate a relation of an inferior to a superior).

According to Fornander, the *ni'aupi'o* is a much wider and more fluid category: "By *ni'aupi'o* we understand the very highest case, not only by descent, but also by power, such as the sovereigns of the islands, the *moi*, their children—if their mother were of sufficient rank—and the *aimoku*, or district chiefs" (*Coll.* VI: 308). He recognizes that a *pi'o* chief is superior in rank to a *ni'aupi'o* or a *naha*, but he claims that all these titles provide the right to a *kapu moe*, and that they do not perform it to each other. For him it concerns a "social" distinction, not a "political" one.

According to Rivers (Poe Poe), Malo's account holds. He does not talk at all about *ho'i* unions, but says that the sexual union of a father and daughter was possible. This is assimilated, in tradition, to marriage with a blood sister.

It is fairly difficult to understand rank, because the ways it is represented in the sources are very different. One source (Malo) helps us to understand its origins, but ends up considering three different types of rank as *ni'aupi'o*. *Ni'aupi'o* would then mean only "the chiefs of the highest rank" who practice consanguineal marriage and refuse to give up their women. The other, that of Kamakau, differentiated consanguineal unions (*pi'o*) from unions that are not necessarily consanguineal between chiefs of high rank.

Both representations, nevertheless, presuppose the rank of *ni'aupi'o* more than they explain it. In effect, they presuppose that the *ni'aupi'o* already exists, that it is an absolute reference point, in relation to which the other ranks, as we will see, acquire their own significance. But how does one become a *ni'aupi'o?*

It is not enough to marry your niece to have *ni'aupi'o* children. It is only between chiefs who are already *ni'aupi'o* that these marriages can give birth to new *ni'aupi'o*. In this sense, Kamakau seems to make more sense than Malo, because he presupposes the existence of this rank as an *a priori*, so that it can be used to explain others, and especially the *pi'o* and *naha*. At the same time it is necessary to presuppose two other things:

1) either this title is given automatically to those who are at the top of the chieftainship and their consanguines (as Fornander seems to affirm)
2) or else this title is hereditary only for those who keep it through consanguineal marriage.

The first presupposition is false, because Kamakau confirms that the highest rank does not always coincide with the highest chief (*mo'i*) and that the rank obtained at birth cannot be modified and especially not increased (Kamakau 1964: 9). But, on the other hand, the chief who has political power could, by a hypogamic union, appropriate, for his children, at least some of the rank of legitimate *ali'i*, his hierarchical superiors. The second presupposition seems more likely, if we expand it: rank is hereditary to a certain extent, but the "endogamic" condition to conserve it operates only negatively. Endogamy becomes significant in opposition to an exogamic practice that would lead to the diminution or loss of rank.

The crucial role that women play can explain when rank remains attached to a group, and when it becomes lost. It is no accident that the *kapu moe* was originally created by a female ancestress and transmitted by her daughter. On the other hand, for the *ni'aupi'o* to become transmissible along with its *kapu*, there had to be an original incest. This presupposes what it produces and should explain, but that is precisely because it is a myth. For the same reason, hierarchy and its mechanisms are finally founded on a vicious circle: the rules should explain how marriage engenders hierarchy, but the system of differentiated marriages presupposes a hierarchy of titles, which it cannot engender. The myth of Wakea outlines an explanation, though a transition from marriage with the matrilineal cross-cousin is a situation of complementarity between endogamous marriage and the hypogamous marriage. In effect, Wakea marries his own daughter and creates the absolutely highest rank. Papa marries a fallen man, a *kauwa*, and perpetuates in this way the absolutely lowest rank. In the last analysis, the dichotomy at the origin makes it possible to justify, through unions that are "mixed" from the standpoint of rank, the whole set of titles. The transformation in the significance of marriage asymmetry justifies—at a mythical level—the passage from an elementary structure to a hierarchical one. "Before," the asymmetry was horizontal, linked to reciprocity; "after," it became vertical, implying, as we will see better later on, that there is no symmetry between the giving and taking of wives, the giving and keeping of a sister.

The direction of exchange is replaced by the direction of the possibility of transmitting rank through women: the fact that women are given and taken in all different directions does not produce reciprocity but hierarchy.

Kapu naha

According to Malo: see notes on the *ni'aupi'o*.

According to Kamakau, a chief of the *naha* rank was conceived in the following way: two *ni'aupi'o* men married, in *punalua* fashion, a *ni'aupi'o* woman.[6] One of the marriages produced a boy, the other a girl. If they married, they would have a *naha* union. There is no apparent difference with Malo here. In fact, Kamakau would only accept the union between uterine half-siblings. In addition, he writes that this union is a "return" (*ho'i*) "when these two returned and married each other (*ho'i hou a'e launa noho ho'au*), this is a *naha* union" (Kamakau 1964: 5). So, Kamakau considered the union between two uterine siblings a *ho'i*, while Malo uses the term for the union between an uncle and a niece. We find here the same idea of "return" as soon as the chiefs concerned represent more than one line of filiation. It is a matter of recuperating a woman who could leave the closed circle of marriages and rank. If, according to Malo, a *naha* union produces *ni'aupi'o* chiefs, according to Kamakau, always faithful to the rule of the correspondence between the name of the union that produced a person and the rank he or she is, this would produce the rank of *naha*.

The *kapu* of the *naha* chiefs was inferior to the *pi'o* chiefs. Even if they had the same mother, the *naha* chief could not call his *pi'o* half-sibling *hoahanau* ("sibling" or "cousin") because the *pi'o* chief was "like a god" (Kamakau 1964: 5).

Liliokalani's description is identical to that of Kamakau.

According to Fornander, *naha* is what Malo calls *ho'i;* the union of an uncle with his niece, and, he adds, of a father with his daughter as long as they are both *ni'aupi'o* (*Coll*. VI: 308).

Rivers's description is the same as Kamakau's.

If it is relatively easy to define the *pi'o* rank, we have seen the difficulty in defining the *ni'aupi'o* and especially in differentiating the *naha* from the *ni'aupi'o*. It is interesting to note that for Emma (ms. cited 1883: 5), the *naha* rank is not old and is inferior to the others. It simply allows a person to belong to the class of the *kapu* chiefs. In effect, *naha* rank only gives rights to *kapu noho*. But it is still hard to see why the *naha* rank would be considered inferior to other *kapu* ranks.

If we take the definition of Malo, we could believe at first glance that this inferiority depends on the fact that those who contract *naha* unions are only half-siblings. But why would they be less *close*, in terms of consanguinity, than uncle and niece? The theory that the rank of offspring depends upon the degree of consanguinity between the parents cannot be held if we accept at the same time the definition of *naha* given by Kamakau and a narrow definition of *ho'i* as marriage with the agnatic niece. In addition, it would be necessary to suppose a patrilineal theory of consanguinity. Thus, the agnatic niece would be closer than the uterine half-sister. But these hypotheses are in flagrant contradiction of the definition of *naha* and *ho'i* and with the Hawaiian notion of consanguinity.

On the other hand, two children who contract a *pi'o* union can only be born to *ni'aupi'o*. If these *ni'aupi'o* are half-siblings, then their union could only be a *naha*, and the *pi'o* union would not be between two *naha* spouses. If we accept Malo's definitions, either it is not true that *naha* is an inferior rank to the *ni'aupi'o* (otherwise we would have the paradox of a *pi'o* born to a *naha* and thus to two chiefs who are not of the highest rank) or else the *pi'o* are produced only by the marriages of two siblings born to a *ho'i* union or the marriage of two siblings born to another *pi'o* union.

In the genealogy of the descendants of Liloa already mentioned, we find only two *pi'o* unions. One of them was realized by the marriage of two siblings who came from a *ho'i* union, but the other is produced by the union of two siblings who came from a marriage that was certainly not a *ho'i*.

Ho'i unions are, besides, more common than *po'i* unions and much less common than *naha* unions. Must we conclude that in effect the *ho'i* union is hierarchically superior to the *naha* union? It is possible, all the more so since the niece, uterine as well as agnatic, is considered the equivalent of a sister who should not be given away. But this privileging of the *ho'i* relationship is only found in Malo. Fornander, who remembers it, only gives it the status of *naha*. And Malo was very tied to the genealogist of Kamehameha, who gave him some of his information. The rank of the children of Kamehameha, and of Liholiho in particular, depends precisely on a *ho'i* union, which not everyone was prepared to recognize as hierarchically superior. It is possible then, as we have tried to show elsewhere (Valeri 1972: 51–52), that Malo chose the version most favorable to Kamehameha, even if it was not perfectly coherent.

It is certain, in any case, for all the authors, that the *naha* rank, although it is *kapu*, only gives rights to a *kapu noho*, and it is thus inferior to the rank of *ni'aupi'o* and *pi'o*.

I think that, in fact, the real opposition is between *pi'o* and *naha*, because the *ni'aupi'o* who are not born from a *pi'o* marriage (and, according to Malo, a *ho'i* marriage) cannot become more than a *naha*. The *ni'aupi'o* must in fact be a common name for *pi'o* and *naha* chiefs or, if we follow Kamakau, there is a certain preference for agnatic relations, which is seen among the highest chiefs. In effect, the definition of *naha* given by Kamakau, Liliokalani, and Poe Poe (in Rivers) also presupposes, through its silences, a definition of *ni'aupi'o*: that is to say that the marriage of two agnatic half-siblings, in opposition to that of two uterine half-siblings, produces true *ni'aupi'o* and not simple *naha*. We could thus distinguish three categories of rank, and understand why *pi'o* and *ni'aupi'o* are opposed together, by their association with *kapu moe*, to the rank of *naha*.

In this way, we could prove what I have tried to show several times: that the highest chiefs, by their consanguineal marriages, tried to create, in a society dominated by bilaterality, a line with a patrilineal tendency, where agnatic relations are opposed to dangerous relations through women. This depends on a political necessity: the marriage of the highest chief with two different women cannot have the same meaning as the marriage of a woman with two different chiefs. While he contracts many alliances, the chief is motivated not to disperse his descendants among others, but to bring them back into his own line, by encouraging consanguineal unions. On the other hand, the sister of the chief, if she has several *punalua* husbands or gives her daughter to her brother (in a *ho'i* union), can only hope that her children will have the same importance as the main children of her brother.

This all seems implied by the abstract rule that opposes *ni'apui'o* to the *naha*. In all cases this rule has no sense unless the chief really manages to have his son succeed him, and if, finally, a veritable patriline is constituted by a constant succession in the paternal line. That has not been the case in Hawaiian history, especially since Liloa. Thus, the rule has no veritable application, and as a consequence, the genealogies do not show much inequality between ni'aupi'o and naha. On the contrary, it is often true that the naha, or the children of the "sister" of inferior rank, are the ones who come out on top of the heirs in the agnatic line.

There is still a time lag between hierarchy and power, which explains why children born to these women are required to regularize the hierarchical situation of their children by alliance with the line of those who have been dethroned.

This rule makes it possible to explain, in the last analysis, why the further we go back in the genealogical past the more "patrilineal" royal genealogies appear. The chief has a practical interest in following a certain agnation. So a position often obtained by feminine ties and by force implies the acquisition of genealogies that appear, after a certain number of generations, in a much more patrilineal form.

I must leave out here an analysis of the lower ranks—which would show a radical reversal of the relative value of paternal and maternal ties—and instead reconfirm several facts that define the set of the three highest ranks, which are called "sacred."

I cite a passage of Kamakau, which shows two things:

1) Consanguineal marriage is reserved for the highest chiefs, for whom it is not what it would be for anyone else: a shame.
2) It does not even have to be a real marriage, that is, one that is ritually marked, nor a relatively durable union.

The mating to sister or near relative (pi'o or naha union), which was not permitted to lesser chiefs or to the relatives of chiefs (the 'ohaha ali'i or kakau ali'i) was considered desirable between very high chiefs in order to produce children of divine rank who carried the sacred fire (ahi) taboo. Such a mating was for the purpose of bearing children, but the two need not become man and wife. Thus the chiefs multiplied, thrived, and spread out over the islands (Kamakau 1961: 238).

Kapu wohi

This is also hard to interpret, because the explanations that exist are very divergent. Here again we find the problem that we met earlier: the relation between the inheritance of a title and its acquisition by the alliance, which brought about the birth.

Malo (1951: 57) mentions this kapu without explaining it. In a note, Emerson cites an explanation that he himself considers pure fantasy (62).

According to Kamakau, a *wohi* chief was born to a *ni'aupi'o, pi'o,* or *naha* father and a mother who had a *pili hoahanau* (classificatory sibling/cousin) relation with the father. The parents of the mother were in effect the younger consanguines of the parents of the father *(kaikaina hoahanau na na makua)*. If, on the other hand, it was the mother who was *ni'aupi'o, pi'o,* or *naha,* the *wohi* rank was obtained for the child when the father had a *mau ali'i kuhaulua* relation. *Kuhaulua* indicates a relation across two generations (Pukui and Elbert 1957: 159). The relation, if expressed in terms of consanguinity, had to be through a common ancestor two generations distant. The *wohi* chief did not even have the status of a *naha* chief, but he had a privilege *(kanawai)* that permitted him not to observe the *kapu* that was usually due to the *ni'aupi'o* and *naha* chiefs when their genealogies were being chanted. But if, on the other hand, the *wohi* transgressed the *kapu* that surrounded the *pi'o* chief, or the gods, he would have to be sacrificed and burned in fire.

According to Liliokalani, if the father had one of the three highest ranks and the mother came from a "family of rank" and was the father's cousin or the younger cousin of the father's parents, the children would be *wohi.* And vice versa, if it was the mother who had the superior rank.

Liliokalani's definition seems to follow in part that of Kamakau. But for Kamakau, there is a difference in the relations of a husband and wife according to which one of them had the higher rank. Unfortunately Beckwith (1932) does not give the Hawaiian text of Liliokalani, and it is hard to understand which kinship terms are translated by "cousin" or "younger cousin of the parents" (it seems that that could mean instead the "younger cousin by the parents").

According to Fornander, the *wohi* is not a title of rank but a political charge. It first existed in Oahu and Kauai, and then was imported to Maui and Hawaii. The *wohi* was not required to follow the *kapu moe* in the presence of the highest chief, but he marched in front of the sovereign to force all those present to prostrate themselves. The charge tended to pass from father to son, if the chieftainship also passed from father to son. In effect, the son of the *wohi* chosen by a sovereign often became a *wohi* himself; but when the dynasty changed, the charge was also transferred.

Fornander confuses, in fact, the rank that would qualify someone for certain political charges and the charges themselves, which he classifies as *wohi.* His account, coming later, is negated by most of the other sources. For him, besides, the only titles of rank are the first three.

According to Rivers, the union of a *naha* man and a *ni'aupi'o* woman is called *wohi,* as are the children born to it (Rivers 1941, I: 380).

Leaving aside the false definitions of Fornander and Rivers, we have only one definition that is clear about the conception of a child of *wohi* rank by a certain kind of alliance, and it is that of Kamakau. It still has its problems. Before attacking them, I will analyze a concrete case taken from a genealogy.

We know with certainty that Kamehameha had the rank of *wohi* (Kamakau 1964: 5). Since we are familiar with his genealogy, we can see if the creation of his rank corresponds to the rule given by Kamakau. According to the rule given by Kamakau, a *ni'aupi'o* woman who marries a *kuhaulua* man would have a *wohi* child.

Daughter of Kaulele, Kekelaokalani had the *ni'aupi'o* rank. She married Haae, who was at most a *kahaulua* in relation to her, since we have been unable to find any genealogical relations with Kekelaokalani within two generations. Haae was a descendant of Kauaua-a-Mahi, who was considered by Papa Ii (1959: 19) to come from the same stock as Kaulele and her husband Keawe (Figure 1). Their daughter, Kekuiapoiwa II, was in effect *wohi*. With the marriage between Kekuiapoiwa II and her matrilateral cousin Keoua, we have a reversal of the rank of the husband and wife. According to the definition given by Kamakau, here the relationship is much closer than that of the preceding generation. However, Kamehameha, the child born from their alliance, would always have the rank of *wohi*. The mother of Kekuiapoiwa was the younger sister of the father of Keoua. As for the father of Kekuiapoiwa II, he could only be considered the younger classificatory brother of the father of Keoua. The relations between husband and wife were in any case much closer in the second marriage, where it was the husband who was the *ni'aupi'o*, and less close in the first, where it was the wife who had that rank.

We see therefore that, at least at this level, women of high rank are able to transmit to their children much more rank than their brothers of equivalent rank. Thus we see the importance of matrilateral relations for the juniors of intermediate rank. We also see that patrilateral marriage can be used to root the father's sister's daughter in the rank of her mother's line. But this also results in elevating the rank of cadet lines so that it is sufficiently close to that of the senior lines as to be dangerous for their *ni'aupi'o* and *naha* cousins. Besides, there is one *wohi*, Kamehameha, who had the upper hand over his rival *ni'aupi'o* for the chieftainship, Kiwalao, showing that the lowering status was not enough to bring him down in the political domain, even if it was successful in the hierarchical domain and the system of proximities regulated by taboos.

The acquisition of the *wohi* rank by Kamehameha is presented by John Papa Ii in a way that seems completely different. According to him, the title came from Oahu, and was transmitted to Kamehameha by inheritance. We have already seen that the *kapu moe* was associated with Keakealaniwahine, of the family of Hawaii. This woman had a union with the chief of Oahu, Kaneikauaiwilani, according to Papa Ii (1963: 52) the inheritor of the *kapu wohi*. The two *kapus* were thus united by this alliance.

But how is this transmitted among their descendants, who could claim it both from the line of chiefs of Hawaii as from those of Oahu? Their daughter, Kalanikauleleleiawi (whom we call "Kaulele" [see Figure 1]), was the one who first inherited the two *kapus*. This woman was very important in the genealogies, because she seems to have had sexual unions with almost all the important chiefs of Hawaii. Her descendants of first rank find themselves with a great many collaterals and rivals, all issuing from this woman, who plays a role in historical reality that is comparable to that of Hinaikapa'ikua in the myths.

Kaulele had a union with a powerful chief, Keawe i Kekahialiiekamoku, who was also her uterine half-brother. Curiously, Keawe asked Kaulele for one of the *kapus* she had inherited. The *kapu* was not for the children Kaulele had borne him, but for his "firstborn" son, Lonomaikanaka, whose mother was another woman. Keawe received this *kapu* by virtue of the alliance and gave it to his oldest son, Kalaninuiiamamao, who was not, however, born from this alliance. Keawe could not himself claim the title from Keakeaklaniwahine, his mother and the mother of Kaulele, because his father was of insufficient rank. Kaulele's father, however, was high ranking. In capturing the *kapu* for his firstborn son, Keawe kept Kaulele from bestowing the title on her own children. In effect, he reversed the political order of his children and the children that his uterine half-sister Kaulele had by other men, by virtue of the relative rank of their respective fathers, by marrying her himself and securing the *kapu* for his son by another woman. Keawe had political power, and that is why he was able to acquire the title of his sister, simultaneously denying it to her children by other men. The transmission was thus from paternal aunt—the father's uterine half-sister (who was also the *punalua* or "secondary" wife of his father)—to her nephew.

We have here an example of the importance of the sister and of the father's sister–brother's son relationship, which reminds us of eastern Polynesia. The *kapu moe* is thus transmitted to the *ni'aupi'o* who descends from Keawe, including chief Kiwalao, the rival of Kamehameha. But the acquisition of *kapu moe* still provoked protests from the competitors of Kalaninuiiamamao, the son of Keawe, and they cost him his power. It was in fact Kalaninuiiamamao's patrilateral cross-cousin Alapa'-I-nui, who was the son of Kaulele by a man other than Keawe, who kicked him out and took his place. Keawe had forced Kaulele to renounce her *kapu moe*, inherited from her mother, and to keep for her own children only the *kapu wohi*, inherited from her father (Papa Ii 1963: 52). It was thus one of the children who had the inferior title of *wohi* who took over the wife of Kalaninuiiamamao.

But what John Papa Ii is interested in doing is explaining how the title came to the chief who installed himself definitively in the chieftainship: Kamehameha. He does this by a genealogy that shows that

Kamehameha is the son of Kaulele (Papa Ii 1963: 53). We could thus believe that the transmission was achieved solely on the criterion of descent. But in fact the genealogy given by Papa Ii contains much more than the transmission of the title by descent would require: all the marriages are given, and it is not specified from which line—masculine or feminine—that Kamehameha received the *kapu wohi*. Keeping quiet about the rank of the spouses concerned, Papa Ii gives all the marriages, showing thus that it is these marriages more than the simple criterion of descent that determine this transmission (cf. Papa Ii 1963: 53). The contradiction between the representation of this transmission by inheritance and that which explains it by alliance is illusory, since if the *kapu* is transmitted by inheritance, it can only be given to those children who qualify for it by the rank they have acquired from the alliance to which they were born. Pure and simple descent, the fact of being born to Kaulele, does not qualify them for anything. Besides, it was an alliance more than a relation of descent that allowed Keawe to acquire the *kapu moe* for his own son.

Whether we consider this title as an inheritance or a category of alliance, acquired by descent or by marriage, the result is identical, as soon as this inheritance belongs only to the children of those who have contracted alliances of the type defined as *wohi* by Kamakau. If there is a "line" associated with the inheritance of *kapu moe* and a "line" associated with the inheritance of *kapu wohi*, this depends only on the differential value of Kaulele's alliances, from which come not so much two lines as two categories of chiefs with a different hierarchical value. These two lines have competed for power for three generations. These categories have been reproduced by the constant value of their alliances and not by simple descent. Thanks to a marriage that he would not have been able to make without his victory over the hierarchically superior chief Kiwalao, Kamehameha managed to modify the rank of his children to make them pass into a category higher than his own. He was then required to treat his own children "like gods," showing that the *kapu moe* is not the property of a lineage but the property of a hierarchical category (Kamakau 1961: 208).

One more time, we see that the model of alliance is more powerful in explaining these facts than the "vertical" model of descent. It is important in mythical traditions, and we find it again in historical reality. An explanation in terms of pure and simple descent lines is finally contradictory, because each time the rank of the mother and the father is considered, it becomes impossible to have a real lineage, especially in a regime of endogamy. In this system, we would instead define the position of each individual in a rank category. If "inheritance" is there, this would not contradict the hierarchical possibilities of transmission.

But the definition of *wohi* by alliance does not come without difficulties of its own. It seemed to me earlier (Valeri 1972) that there was an asymmetry in the definition of the rank of *wohi* given by Kamakau: the distance in degree of consanguinity (or even of rank) between spouses would vary as a function of sex in the person who had the higher rank.

Kamakau distinguishes, in effect, the case where the father is the one with the higher rank and where it is the mother who has it. This care to distinguish the two, which is not at all justified if the pertinent criterion were only the degree of consanguinity between the spouses, is something that we have already found in the definition of *ni'aupi'o* given by Kamakau.

We must always recognize that, for the rank of *wohi*, it is initially very hard to attribute any precise content to the opposition made between the two possibilities. In effect, if the case where the wife has the higher rank than her husband is defined by Kamakau in genealogically precise terms, in the inverse case, he only invokes a genealogically vague and "classificatory" relation between the two spouses. How can we explain that?

The hypothesis that allows a narrower relation of consanguinity between spouses when the man has the higher rank would seem to be confirmed by the genealogy of Kamehameha (see Figure 1) and the origin of his *wohi* title. We still need to explain why this asymmetry does not necessarily exist in terms of consanguinity if we follow the definition of Kamakau: the *kuhaulua* man is separated by two degrees of consanguinity from his *pi'o*, *ni'aupi'o*, or *naha* wife. In the case where one of these three ranks is held by the husband, we say that the wife is the daughter of a father and a mother who are a younger brother and sister of the husband's parents. The relationship would be closer than the preceding one if the father and the mother of the wife were siblings or half-siblings of the father and the mother of her husband. We have seen in effect that the maternal grandmother and the paternal grandfather of Kamehameha were siblings (Figure 1).[7] But the rule to create the *wohi* rank from a couple where the husband has the superior rank speaks of a relation of classificatory consanguinity (*hoahanau*) between the parents of the spouses whose child is a *wohi*. Kamakau adds that the father and the mother of the spouses should be "close" kin (Kamakau 1964: 5), without giving any more details. On the other hand, in the case where it is a woman who has the higher rank, he adds that the father and mother of the spouse must be agnatic half-siblings.

We must look more closely at the opposition between the genealogical precision that characterizes the definition of the hypogamic *wohi* union and the imprecision that characterizes the hypergamic *wohi* union. As we will see, the imprecision in the second case corresponds to the possibility of a choice, exercised by the father (of high rank) in the attribution of rank to children of his *wohi* unions. In effect, the inferior rank of *lokea* can be attributed to them.[8] The care to specify the genealogical relations between spouses in the hypogamic case shows that these relationships are much more important for inferiors than those that are produced by hypergamic unions. This explains why inferiors have to trace the borders more precisely in everything that concerns relations through women.

The Paradox of Marriage and the Value in Hierarchy

There are several reasons for that, and for reasons of space I cannot go into them here, but I think that they are founded on a principle of general application, which narrowly associates hierarchy to a dialectic between the giving up of, and the refusal to give up, women. The fact of receiving a woman from a chief of high rank implies the recognition of his superiority, but at the same time it offers the possibility—for a descent line—to accede to the position of this chief, through ties produced by marriage and prolonged by descent.

We find ourselves here in front of a paradoxical relationship between endogamy and exogamy. For the superior rank of some to be concretely recognized by others, it is necessary for those of superior rank to give away, at least from time to time, a woman others recognize as superior in rank, but whom still others can then use to climb the hierarchical ladder. To avoid that, chiefs of high rank might simply try to keep themselves from perpetuating alliance relations with inferiors. Hypogamy presupposes that it is alternated with consanguineal marriage.

I must stress the fact that consanguineal marriage would not have any sense if sisters did not become valuable precisely because they were subtracted from an alliance with "others," who would remain inferior by this very fact. It is thus the alliance refused to "others," to those "excluded," that determines the value, for the chief of high rank, of his consanguines. Exogamy depends, at its base, on the hierarchical signification of endogamy. The "value" attributed to the chief's sister could not exist if the removal of this sister from circulation did not imply the inverse—that is, the giving of this sister, from time to time. To take her out of the exchange system, she must have been in it before. For the person who is removed to have value for the person who removes her, there must be another choice that could have been made, periodically or potentially.

The gift and the exchange are to be found, then, always at the base of hierarchy. Through an alternating movement of satisfaction and frustration, of giving and holding back, women acquire their value and hierarchy articulates the relations between men both by opposing them and welding them together through the values incarnated in the women that they all recognize. Without the women "who eat in front and behind," as

Tahitians say (Henry 1928: 402–3), hierarchy and the possibility of going up or down the scale of rank would not exist. The mythic prototype of these women, whose role we have seen in Hawaiian genealogies and legends is the wife of Kane himself: La'ila'i or "the woman who sits by the side" as the *Kumulipo* defines her metaphorically (Beckwith 1951: 173).

Hierarchy does not only imply refusing to close cycles of reciprocity; it also affects the permanence of relations of alliance. The more developed it becomes, while still staying attached to marriage, the more marked becomes the refusal to maintain a structural or temporal continuity in the asymmetric prestation of women. We saw in the first part of this study that a myth illustrated the passage to hierarchy as a passage from generalized exchange, in its elementary form, to a system of endogamy and exogamy (in its anisogamic form) alternating irregularly. The "crossed" relation does not lose its importance for all that; it is only an optimal possibility that can be realized through the relationship of brother and sister, which is itself the pivot of the system.

Conclusion

The principle that makes rank depend on the marriage of one's parents makes it possible to modify hierarchical positions. So, as we have seen, these positions depend especially on those women whom men have been able to wrest from their rivals. If, in a system without hierarchy, we could say that men exchange women according to a principle of reciprocity, in a hierarchical system like that of Hawaii, we could say that men are in competition to monopolize women who, consanguine or not, are the symbols of rank because they are the means and the measure of status positions. From being "signs of exchanges" women become "signs of rank," inequality, and nonreciprocity. Such is the profound sense of asymmetry between the sexes in the transmission of rank. If it appears more clearly in anisogamatic marriage, this asymmetry is also presupposed by "endogamous" marriage, which tries to neutralize, but which, in recreating the "absolute" rank, only reconstitutes periodically the possibility of producing it.

As we have seen, it is by a subtle game of holding back and giving out, of "endogamy" and "exogamy," that women become the symbol of rank and its principal agent. Those things that are both given up and refused are the lines of cognition, and with them the ancestors, genealogies, and the possibility for others to appropriate them and make them into a cult.

Thus, *affinity is in Hawaii a horizontal line that is projected always onto vertical, genealogical relations.* This is the sense of the correspondence between two "languages," those of marriage and descent, the "horizontal" and the "vertical," corresponding to what we have seen as well at the mythical level and at the level of social practice. This correspondence is made possible by two aspects of Polynesian systems, aspects that are particularly accentuated in Hawaii:

1) Relations of affinity are not reciprocal and have a hierarchical meaning.
2) The principle of reciprocity is found instead in the relations between brother and sister.

The Hawaiian system of rank is produced by the conjunction of these two aspects. From the moment when the marriage of sisters produces lines that are considered as affines and consanguines at the same time, the relation of (relative) equality between brother and sister becomes a competitive relation among their descendants. The system of rank titles, by bringing together the alliance relations of siblings and their relations of consanguinity, regulates this competition and introduces the crossed relationship. Crossed relations are important not only as a continuation of the consanguinity between brother and sister, but also as the encompassment of relations of affinity produced by their marriage. They are distinctive because they cannot be reduced to either alliances alone (as in the elementary structures) or to consanguinity alone.

If, in Hawaii, the crossed relationship has an operational existence at certain levels of hierarchy, it is due to the fact that Hawaiian society is located at a transition point between a structure founded on alliance and an undifferentiated structure. More exactly, its hierarchical system is located at this transition point, which explains why at the zero level of the hierarchy we find an undifferentiated kinship system, also found in the real society, and the marriage of cross-cousins, and the "origins" postulated in myths.

In conclusion, hierarchy springs paradoxically from the very reciprocity of the brother/sister relationship. The equality of rank between the brother and the sister implies a matrimonial competition to get the sisters of high-ranking men and determines the importance of affinity. Affinity, in any case, has no meaning by itself, but can only project its meaning onto those descendants, who, through "the gift of the sister," will also become the descendants of the chief. Rank is diffused in this way, to different degrees, throughout society. Inversely, discontinuity is recreated by the refusal to give away the sister, at least for a principal marriage—a refusal that, in this system, must have a matrimonial content, because it only becomes meaningful in relation to children and their descendants.

The optimal relation between brother and sister is realized only at the level of marriage. The reciprocity and equality of the sibling relationship produces hierarchy by the two complementary procedures of endogamy and exogamy, which engender, justify, and encompass this relationship.

Alliance is thus not subordinate to consanguinity in any general sense, but it is subordinate to the brother/sister relationship and its precursors.

From here, as well, we derive the fundamental role of women in the transmission of rank, a role that would not have any meaning in a system founded only on alliance or in a system founded on an undifferentiated notion of consanguinity.

* * *

A more extended study of Hawaiian rank titles would take us further than we can go here. It would put the "immense structural phenomenon" (Lévi-Strauss 1967: 279) of hypergamy into play and also the related relations of agnation and cognation. More generally, it would concern the problem of treating alliance relations in systems of "asymmetric marriage," and thus the fundamental question of the relation between "elementary systems" and "complex systems," as well as the possibility, formulated many times by Lévi-Strauss, of reducing these systems to the language of degrees of consanguinity. It is enough here to affirm that, in my opinion, if we consider that many of these hypergamic systems are founded in turn on a system—more or less explicit—of rank titles, then an extremely vast problem opens itself up, especially for the comparative study of systems of generalized exchange and systems like the one we have studied in Hawaii (which seems much more widespread in Austronesia than one might believe at first glance). In effect, bride price rules in numerous Southeast Asian societies characterized by generalized exchange (like the Kachin, Lakher, Batak, and Nias) seem to correspond to the principle pf privileging cognatic relations and using these relations as agnatic ones (according to the definition of Lévi-Strauss 1967: 279). This is the same principle expressed, in other ways, by the Hawaiian rank system.[9]

Translated by Aletta Biersack and Janet Hoskins

Notes

1. *Polynesian Race*, which will henceforth be cited as *PR*.
2. [Editors' note: Valeri's discussion of Kaulele's "excesses" in what follows can be compared usefully with the section "Royal Sacrifice and Royal Incest" in *Kingship and Sacrifice* (Valeri 1985: 161–168).]
3. *Collection of Hawaiian Antiquities*, henceforth cited as *Coll.*
4. The *ail'i* is composed, naturally, of the firstborns of each union.

5. The genealogy of 'Akahi, mother of Umi, who came from a commoner background, shows us a middle way between the genealogy of a court functionary, like John Papa Ii, and that of an *ali'i nui*. Genealogists had to look for all the important relations that this woman had to increase as much as possible for the status of her son Umi, who became an important chief but who had a low rank. The father of Umi was the great chief Liloa, but Umi was the issue of a brief liaison with a commoner woman. It was only through force and cunning that Umi managed to displace the legitimate heir of Liloa, who did not even consider him as his brother (Kamakau 1961: 8). According to tradition, the mother of Umi was nevertheless the offspring of chiefs who had completely lost their rank through marriages with commoners. The genealogist tried to show this ascendance.

    The genealogy of the mother of Umi given by Kamakau (1961) follows one side of each generation, patrilateral or matrilateral, but does not forget to mention the consanguines of the particular forebear chosen for each generation who had some importance. The analysis of this genealogy is difficult because the sex of the forbear is rarely indicated and, when it is not revealed by name, we cannot know which line of filiation has been chosen. The choice of which forbear to trace descent from is not always governed by the importance of the parent himself or herself, or by the importance of the chosen parent's consanguineal connections. Rather, either name, the father's or the mother's, serves as a metonym for the marriage itself. The simple memory of an alliance can be enough to raise someone's status. In this way a genealogy appears as a sequence of unequal and impermanent ranks that depend upon the marriages contracted in each generation. It is nevertheless certain that in this case, the ascent is placed at the head of the genealogy: in this way the mother of Umi, an upstart with no rank but the founder of a powerful dynasty, was a descendant of Kanipahu and Hualani, two important chiefs.

6. It would seem that the *hiapo* (firstborn) is assured of his succession to the chieftainship, and no one else could take his place. However, the "license" of his parents and his kin can create rivals who often have a rank close to his own. Many apparently "secondary" unions are made with high-ranking *ali'i*. The diffuse rank anxiety that is thus created around the heir engenders rivalries, and coalitions may keep him from holding onto power without sharing it or may make him lose it. Since, even if the *hiapo* has obtained a rank that no one (or almost no one) can question, he has not been assured of the power (at the same time political and "supernatural") which should accompany this rank.

    Secondary unions also have a contradictory role. They create around the presumed heir a large number of "brothers" who could be used to constitute a faction, which the chief will need to assert his rank concretely and to keep himself at the head of the chieftainship. But these "brothers" can also threaten the heir. The contradiction is in fact that between the principle of hierarchy and the principle of political power: rank constrains the *hiapo* to observe such *strong* taboos that he is often excluded from all concrete political activity, which is placed in the hands of his "younger brothers," the sons of the "secondary" or *punalua* unions of his parents. Hierarchy and power should in principle be interdependent. The exercise of power requires certain freedom from taboos, which only the younger brothers can be allowed. On the other hand, the chief of high rank is required to observe these taboos to conserve his hierarchal position. Yet the temptation to create a hierarchical line equal or superior to that of the chief, by marrying the sister of the highest ranking chief, and then to remove him from office, was always strong for the younger brothers. Hawaiian history is rich in successful attempts to make real power correspond to the highest possible rank (cf. Kamakau 1961: *passim*).

    This explains the fundamental role played by the "secondary" or *punalua* unions. They represent, at the level of marriage, the "political" complement of the ho'omau keiki marriage, which has a hierarchical function. This "political" aspect should be underlined, because *punalua* unions become important only when it is decided not to kill the children produced by these unions. The choice between infanticide and "adoption" is most often a strategic decision (Handy and Pukui 1958: 79–80).

As genealogies show, *punalua* unions were often not at all secondary. For some chiefs, it is impossible to tell which was the secondary union. These unions were often contracted to create relations with the other chieftainships, which could be exploited politically (Beckwith 1951: 30), and especially, as I argued earlier, to create a group of clients and "functionaries" around the heir whose hierarchical relations were set out, thanks to the *punalua* unions, by true and classificatory relatives of the future chief. Malo clearly shows how complementary *ho'omau keiki* marriage and *punalua* unions were when he writes:

> When the couple had begotten children of their own, if the man wished to take another woman or the woman another man, even though the second partner were not of such choice "blood" as the first, it was permitted them to do so. And if children were thus begotten they were called *kaikaina*, or younger brothers or sisters of the great chief, and would become the backbone (*iwi-kua-moo*), the executive officers (*ilamuku*) of the chief, the ministers (*kuhina*) of his government (Malo 1951: 55).

We must nevertheless stress the fact that, because of *punalua* unions, the opposition between the "absolute eldest" (*hiapo*) and his younger brothers is only relative. The term *punalua* is mainly a kinship term designating two husbands who share a wife or two wives who share a husband. Polyandry and polygamy can be combined (cf. Pukui and Elbert 1957: 327; Handy and Pukui 1958: 56–57; Forster 1960: 96–97). The entanglement of these unions can cause a certain confusion concerning the relative rank of the children, and can even neutralize, in some cases, the opposition between firstborn and subsequent children. In effect, if after the "principal" union, which made it possible to conceive a *hiapo*, a successive union was contracted with a partner of greater rank than the first, then this union became the principal union, and the child produced by this union could dethrone the *hiapo* born of the earlier union (cf. Handy and Pukui 1958: 58).

Thus, the rule that makes the rank of the child depend on that of his or her parents is in conflict with the opposition between a "principal" marriage and a "secondary" one (which is useful only in relative terms) and with the ranking determined by birth order. These last criteria of rank are thus subordinated to the first, which is the most important criterion.

But the relative status of the *hiapo* depends not only on his father and his group but also on his mother and her group. If, for instance, a man married two unrelated women, the firstborn would be the *hiapo* of his father and his group, but the firstborn of each of these two women would be respectively her *hiapo* and the *hiapo* of her origin group, if this group were hierarchically inferior to her husband's group (cf. Handy and Pukui 1958: 58). So one of these *hiapo* was both the *hiapo* of his father and his father's group and of his mother and her group, while the other *hiapo* was junior in relation to his father and his group but the senior offspring of his mother and her group. If two wives had the same rank, birth order was supposed to establish the relative position of the two *hiapo*. But it is clear that children considered "senior" by their maternal family sought the support of their maternal kin in the inevitable conflict between the firstborns of the other wives of the father. It is certain that this is yet another reason to accord fundamental importance to maternal relations for certain individuals. The principle of seniority loses a lot of its operational value at the global level, because Hawaii does not have a lineage organization or "ramage."

7. [Editors' note: Valeri probably refers to "Figure 1" in *Kingship and Sacrifice* (see Valeri 1985: 162.]

8. In effect, a hypergamic *wohi* union can produce a child of *wohi* rank, but it seems that it more often results, instead, in an inferior rank, *lokea*. These two ranks are produced by the same type of union (cf. Kamakau 1964: 5; Liliokalani in Beckwith 1932: 156). In the hypergamic case, the father has to choose between attributing a lower or higher rank. This choice does not seem to exist in the case of a *wohi* union contracted by a woman who has one of the three highest ranks. In addition, if the relationship between this woman and her husband is more distant (in terms of consanguinity) than in the normal *wohi* case, their marriage would produce a child who would have the rank of *papa*, that is to say, one rank higher than *lokea*.

   This confirms that there is an asymmetry between sexes in the possibility of transmitting rank, and thus between hypergamy and hypogamy, since hypogamy—even if the distance between spouses is great—produces children a rank higher than that given by a hypergamous union in which the distance between spouses is lesser.

9. Let us remember here that bride price among the Lakher or Batak, for instance, is calculated according to the rank of the bride, that is to say the rank she can transmit and the relations that can later be traced through her. This rank is calculated not only through the patrilineage of her father but also by considering the rank of the lineages with which the father, the father of the father, and the father of the father of the father had contracted alliances. The woman's bride price and her rank thus reflect the price paid for her mother and for all of the wives of the ancestors of her patrilineage (Leach 1961: 116sq.). The Batak seem to go even further when they say that the price of a woman depends on what has been paid for her mother and her grandmother (Loeb 1935: 58). The bride price is thus the sign of rank calculated in relation to the value of the alliances which have produced this woman: it is also—as such—the expression on a tendency to consider alliance relations like cognatic relations, *used genealogically to define rank*. The ties traced through women give men their rank and make it possible for them to modify this rank (cf. Vergouwen 1964: 28–50, 157, etc.) In "buying" women, they "buy" rank.

References

Alexander, William DeWitt. 1891. *A Brief History of the Hawaiian People*. New York: American Book Company.

Barrère, Dorothy. 1961. "Cosmogonic Genealogies of Hawaii." *Journal of the Polynesian Society* 70: 419–428.

———. 1994. *The King's Mahele: The Awardees and Their Lands*. Hawaii: D. B. Barrère.

Bastian, Adolf. 1881. *Die heilige Sage der Polynesier: Kosmogonie und Theogonie*. Leipzig: F.A. Brockhaus.

Beckwith, Mary W. 1951. *The Kumulipo: A Hawaiian Creation Chant*. Chicago: The University of Chicago Press. http://www.sacred-texts.com/pac/ku/

Beckwith, Mary W., ed. and trans. 1932. "Kepelino's Traditions of Hawaii." *Bernice P. Bishop Museum Bulletin* 95, Honolulu.

Bryan, Edwin H. 1965. "Astronomy and the Calendar." In *Ancient Hawaiian Civilization*, ed. E. S. C. Handy et al., rev. ed. Rutland, VT and Tokyo: Charles E. Tuttle.

Davenport, William H. 1969. "The 'Hawaiian Cultural Revolution': Some Political and Economic Considerations." *American Anthropologist* 71: 1–20.

Fisher, John L. 1970. "Political Factors in the Overthrow of the Hawaiian Taboo System." *Acta Ethnoghraphica Academiae Scientiarium Hungaricae* 19: 161–167.

Fornander, Abraham. 1878–1885. *An Account of the Polynesian Race*, vols. I, II, III. London: Trübner (cited: *PR*).

———. 1916–1919. *Collection of Hawaiian Antiquities and Folklore*, vols. IV, V, VI. Honolulu: Bernice P. Bishop Museum (cited: *Coll.*).

Frake, Charles O. 1956. "Malayo-Polynesian Land Tenure." *American Anthropologist* 58: 170–172.

Goodenough, Ward. H. 1955. "A Problem in Malayo-Polynesian Social Organization." *American Anthropologist* 57: 71–83.

Handy, Edward S. C. et al., ed. 1965. *Ancient Hawaiian Civilization*, rev. ed. Rutland, VT and Tokyo: Charles E. Tuttle.

Handy, Edward S. C. and Mary K. Pukui. 1958. *The Polynesian Family System in Ka'u, Hawaii*. Wellington: Polynesian Society.

Ii, John Papa. 1963 [1959]. *Fragments of Hawaiian History*, 2nd ed. Trans. Mary Pukui, ed. Dorothy Barrère. Honolulu: Bishop Museum Press.

Jarves, James Jackson. 1845. *History of the Hawaiian Islands*. Boston: Tappan and Benner.

Kamakau, Samuel M. 1961. *The Ruling Chiefs of Hawaii*. Honolulu: Kamehameha Schools Press.

———. 1964. *Ka Po'e Kahiko*. Honolulu: Bishop Museum Press.

Kirch, Patrick Vinton and Marshall Sahlins. 1992. *Anahulu: The Anthropology of History in the Kingdom of Hawaii*, 2 vols. Vol. 1. Historical Ethnography by Marshall Sahlins with the Assistance of Dorothy B. Barrère. Chicago: The University of Chicago Press.

Leach, Edmund R. 1961. *Rethinking Anthropology*. Monographs of Social Anthropology 22. London: University of London, The Athlone Press.

Levin, Stephanie Seto. 1968. "The Overthrow of the Kapu System in Hawaii." *Journal of the Polynesian Society* 77: 402–430.

Lévi-Strauss, Claude. 1948. *Les structures élémentaires de la parenté*. Paris and La Haye: Mouton (1st ed. Paris: Presses Universitaires France).

———. 1969. *The Elementary Structures of Kinship*. Trans. James Harle Bell, John Richard von Sturmer, and Rodney Needham, ed. Rev. ed. Boston: Beacon Press.

Loeb, Edwin M. 1935. *Sumatra, Its History and People*. Wiener Beiträge zur Kulturgeschichte und Linguistik 3. (1972 ed. with an additional chapter by Robert Heine-Geldern, Kuala Lumpur: Oxford University Press.)

Malo, David. 1951 [1903]. *Hawaiian Antiquities (Mooolelo Hawaii)*. Trans. E. B. Emerson. Bernice Pauahi Bishop Museum Special Publication 2, 2nd ed. Honolulu: Bishop Museum Press.

Pukui, Mary K. 1949. "Songs of Old Ka'u." *Journal of American Folklore* 62: 247–258.

Pukui, Mary K. and Samuel H. Elbert. 1957. *Hawaiian Dictionary*. Honolulu: University of Hawaii Press.

Rivers, William H. R. 1914. *The History of Melanesian Society*. 2 vols. New York: Cambridge University Press.

Sahlins, Marshall. 1958. *Social Stratification in Polynesia*. Seattle: University of Washington Press.

———. 1973. *Stone Age Economics*. Chicago: Aldine-Atherton.

Stewart, Charles S. 1828. *Private Journal of a Voyage to the Pacific Ocean, and Residence at the Sandwich Islands in the Years 1822, 1823, 1824 and 1825*. 2nd ed. New York: J. P. Haven.

Valeri, Valerio. 1972. "Le Fonctionnement du Système des Rangs à Hawaii." *L'Homme* 12: 29–66.

———. 1985. *Kingship and Sacrifice: Ritual and Society in Ancient Hawaii*. Trans. Paula Wissing. Chicago: The University of Chicago Press.

————. 2001. *Fragments from Forests and Libraries: A Collection of Essays.* Edited by Janet Hoskins. Durham: Carolina Academic Press.

Vergouwen, Jacob Cornelis. 1964. *The Social Organization and Customary Laws of the Toba Batak of Northern Sumatra.* The Hague: M. Nijhoff.

Webb, Malcolm C. 1965. "The Abolition of the Taboo System in Hawaii." *Journal of the Polynesian Society* 74: 21–39.

CHAPTER 8

Polynesian Conceptions of Sociality

A Dynamic Field of Hierarchical Encompassment

Ingjerd Hoëm

I n the following I shall explore a sociocultural dynamic that many have argued is central to Austronesian-speaking societies, past and present (Fox 1995; Hoëm 2004; Hoëm and Roalkvam 2003; Smedal in press).[1] I present my argument in order to illustrate how, in certain respects, our classical understanding of social organization and patterns of sociality in Polynesian societies phrased in terms of analytical concepts such as social stratification, hierarchy, and egalitarianism, is at best insufficient, and at worst misleading. This strand of analysis is perhaps most commonly known to the larger anthropological audience from the works of Marshall Sahlins, in particular *Social Stratification in Polynesia* (1959) and "Poor man, rich man, big man, chief: Political types in Melanesia and Polynesia" (1963). Irving Goldman's encyclopedic *Ancient Polynesian Society* (1970) also exemplifies this trend. Whereas these and similar works have provided us with insights into the variation in political systems and forms of ecological adaptation throughout the region, the legacy of stereotypical images of Polynesian chiefdoms accompanied by a focus firmly set on the precontact past has also served to obscure the dynamic and enduring character of social formations in the contemporary Pacific.

In terms of the Polynesian society that I draw my main empirical examples from in this chapter—that of Tokelau—the application of the traditional perspective of social stratification, and its associated interpretations of the concepts of egalitarianism and hierarchy, would lead us to assume, for example, that historically we have witnessed a transformation from a "hierarchical" conquest state (cf. Goldman 1970); to an egalitarian intermediate period (Hooper and Huntsman 1996); and into the present, where the beginnings of a modern class and individualist society emerge (Hooper 1982).

Notes to this section begin on page 265.

Against this perspective I argue that it is possible to find evidence of the same form of sociality informed by largely identical, identifiable underlying mechanisms throughout the known history and also into the present. In other words, I believe that the seeming fluctuation in social organization between "hierarchy" and "egalitarianism" is more a function of the analytical perspective, than of the principles informing the social organization described. However, note that I do not argue against Hooper's empirical observation of an incipient monetary economy in contemporary Tokelau, but against trends that allow enduring social formations to be obscured in our descriptions of processes of modernization.

Throughout this chapter, I discuss the analytical consequences for our conceptualization of social change that we can draw from the discovery of such enduring empirical continuities in terms of social formations. Furthermore I explore the underlying mechanisms that allow for such enduring social formations by also drawing inspiration from the perspectives developed by Dumont and others, mainly though their theoretization of values (see, for example, de Coppet et al. 1995, and Tcherkézoff in this volume).

My approach to what I describe as enduring social formations is greatly indebted to the work of James J. Fox. He has drawn attention to the key role played by notions of origin in local representations of specific forms of social differentiation (here used in the traditional sense of the term). He argues that for Austronesian-speaking populations, the notion of multiple origins has consistently served as a prime means of social differentiation. He adds, "such a notion may operate at many levels within a society" (Fox 1995: 217).

In his analysis of Pan-Austronesian conceptions of leadership structures, Fox draws upon Sahlins's analysis of the role played by the so-called stranger king. Fox describes how the concept of a ruler with another origin than the population who identify themselves through local ties—a "stranger, a guest, a person of the sea as opposed to a person of the land"—is contained in classic origin narratives found throughout the region. He further explains that:

> [I]n many Austronesian societies, origins are conceptualized as a form of growth: derivation from a "source," "root," "base," or "trunk." In this structure, which may be graphically described as a tree, vine, or climbing plant, growth is either upward or outward toward a "tip" or apical point (Fox 1995: 218).

He makes the important observation that, "where this metaphor is used to describe specific groups," it is "more appropriate to refer to these groups as "ascent groups" rather than "descent groups," as for these groups, "social reckoning is from a base upwards, rather than from some apex downwards" (Fox 1995: 219). He then contrasts this form of growth through a process of social ascendancy with the practice of claiming descent from the outside, for example through heavenly origins or through descent from a group of strangers, such as is the case of the precontact rulers of Fiji described by Sahlins.

In Austronesian-speaking societies, historical as well as contemporary, knowledge of the kind associated with narratives of origin has one thing in common, namely the fact that it is not socially neutral. Genealogical knowledge, in the sense of knowledge of the paths (*ala, auala*) that links contemporary persons with the ancestral past and associates them—such as with particular land areas, fishing, and other occupational rights—is a social resource and a political asset. Such conceptualizations of paths are thus intimately connected to local authority structures on the one hand, and to the specificities in historical process on the other.

Tokelau, as is common in other Polynesian societies as well, has developed what I in earlier works have described as a "sense of place" (Hoëm 1995b, 1999, 2004). By this I refer to a constant awareness of the social composition of a social situation, caused by a concern with social life in terms of relative status positions (*tulaga, nofoaga*, see also Tcherkézoff in this volume). The system of kinship is cognatic. The significant social groups—such as extended families (*kaiga*), the villages (*nuku*), and the atolls—all have their own gatherings or meeting fora, the *fono*. In such gatherings, the place to be seated (*nofoaga*) is determined by status position (*tulaga*), and the congregated group most commonly sit in a circle along the posts (*pou*) that uphold the roofs of the open-walled houses. Whoever is eligible for possible occupation of a position, depends on the nature of the congregation. In the village councils, only older men and family heads are eligible participants. In a family gathering, other principles are followed.

I shall describe these mechanisms of inclusion and exclusion in more detail below. Here I have included this brief description in order to provide an illustration of how the villages are ordered: on the one hand in terms of concepts of interlocking groups that ideally exist as a harmonious and well-functioning (*teu, maopoopo*) whole; while, on the other hand, the actual processes of composing groups in terms of matching persons and positions are most commonly characterized by fierce competition. I shall describe this aspect of interaction later in terms of Fox's concept of ascendancy, which I label competitive identification.

The male elders in the villages and the senior men and women in the extended families have the privilege of deciding how the lives of their dependants should be ordered. The elders can, for example, place a restriction (*lafu*) on the plantation areas on the outer islets across the lagoon, owned by the extended families, thereby pronouncing them off-limits for a period of time. They may also ban individuals or families from the villages for improper behavior. The moral universe is heavily influenced by Christianity, but the regulation and assessment of actual behavior is also and ultimately carried out in terms of such notions as *noa* (free, unbound, improper) and *tapu*, or more commonly *ha* (or *sa*) (off limits, restricted, forbidden, or sacred) (cf. Hoëm 2004; Tcherkézoff in this volume; Valeri in this volume).

Values and Social Relationships: Parts and Wholes

Through illustrations taken from various points in Tokelau history and into the present, I explore a sociocultural dynamic that is central to Austronesian societies, past and present (cf. Hoëm 2004; Tcherkézoff in this volume; Valeri in this volume). This sociocultural dynamic allows patterns of exchange in Tokelau society to exhibit hierarchical characteristics under certain conditions, but at other times the patterns of exchange emerge showing markedly egalitarian traits. This variation can also be observed in a synchronic, comparative perspective, and it is my contention that the classification of societies as one or the other (hierarchical or egalitarian) misses the actual fluctuation between these two poles, historically and throughout the region.

In other words, I see these patterns of exchange, and the "hierarchical" and "egalitarian" social formations, as evidence of enduring empirical continuities in terms of underlying mechanisms. The glimpses that I show to argue this cover a period of approximately 150 years, that is, the known history of the Tokelau atoll communities.

Tokelau is a marginal society in terms of subsistence, comprising three atolls situated north of Samoa, in a landscape that may afford livelihood for approximately 1500 inhabitants altogether. Geographically, the atolls are strategically placed at the crossroads between Micronesian Kiribati and Polynesian Samoa, Tuvalu, Pukuapuka and the more remote northern Cook Islands.

In local representations, throughout Tokelau history, the proliferation of groups that characterize village life—such as extended families, village councils, men's and women's organizations and so on—are all subsumed within an encompassing framework. What this encompassing framework consists of however—which dimension, group, or position is selected as emblematic of the larger collective—varies according to social context and external historical circumstances.[2]

I have described elsewhere how hierarchy, in the traditional sense as denoting material and political stratification, seems to vary and alternate with egalitarianism (denoting an absence of such material and political stratification) according to context (Hoëm 2003: 137–52). In the following I shall take this analysis one step further, by entering into a discussion of the underlying values that inform conceptions of relationships between parts (the subsumed) and wholes (the encompassing).

The first glimpse from Tokelau history shows how patterns of exchange take the form of tribute. Tribute is presented by the vanquished Nukunonu atoll to their Fakaofo overlords, and the offering of tribute takes place within a context of what Goldman describes as typical traditional leadership (1970).

The second glimpse shows patterns of exchange in a form called the *inati*. *Inati* is a polysemous term that denotes "(a) share," "share-groups," "(the) system of sharing," and also the acts and practices of sharing. In this period, the practice of external tribute has been discontinued, and a distribution pattern of generalized reciprocity within each atoll is dominant. In this historical phase, from 1915 to the mid 1960s, the *inati* system is described in local ideology as a kind of welfare system, intended to secure material and social equality.

The third glimpse shows the *inati* or "share-system" within a historically more recent context of emergent nationhood, and this time *inati* is used in a metaphorical sense. The basic meaning of "distribution of equal shares" is in this particular case adopted by policymakers, in order to develop a model to help regulate external political relationships between the three atolls. This attempt to create an acceptance of sharing also as a "sharing of political power" is, however, as deeply contested as the conquest state of the earlier historical period referred to above. I use "contested" here related to the dynamics of competitive identification described below. As most claims to positions are backed up with accounts of genealogical paths and narratives of origin, the versions presented are frequently challenged or counterclaims are made.[3]

Common to these three illustrations are the sociocultural dynamics involved. I propose that they can best be seen as relations of competitive identification, within an encompassing, and thus inherently hierarchical, conceptual framework. Note that this use of the term hierarchical is qualitatively different from the traditional definition referred to above. I shall conclude with a discussion of the cultural issues that are at stake, related to the values that inform the patterns of sociality that I describe, in order to throw light on what aspects of social formations this alternative definition of hierarchy bring to the fore.

However, as the concept of competitive identification will be central to my discussion throughout, it must be given content at present.

In Tokelau today, Tokelau narratives of origin and other "tales of the past" serve as a storehouse that people draw upon to legitimize current social positions (*tulaga, nofoaga*). In other words, this kind of knowledge is of contemporary political significance. It serves to inform and define relations between groups of people in the present in spite of the historical demise of the chiefdom represented by Fakaofoan rule.

In such a system, it is simply not possible to make unequivocal claims to ascendancy through reference to principles of ascription, except perhaps if the legitimating source of authority is from the outside.

Due to the "thoroughly cognatic" (Huntsman 1971) nature of Tokelau kinship, it is difficult to base any claim to ascendancy on kinship alone. So in this sense, claims to positions of authority are at best precarious. A position of authority will always be challenged, either from other claimants with competing, but frequently equally valid, genealogical "paths," *ala*, or from the point of view of other groups in the local atoll communities. This pattern of interaction then is what I refer to when I use the term "competitive identification," or what in Fox's terms would be "fighting for ascendancy."

The First Glimpse: War, Conquest, and Tribute

The Tokelau atolls of Fakaofo, Nukunonu, Atafu, and Olohega (the latter currently counted as U.S. territory by the United States) are outposts compared with their closest neighbors, the larger Polynesian island nations such as Samoa, Tuvalu, and Micronesian Kiribati. Fakaofo, Nukunonu, and Atafu were periodically inhabited prior to discovery by Americans and Europeans, and there are reports of earlier inhabitants of Atafu being driven off by a war party from Fakaofo.

The first written reports from Tokelau describe the islet of Fale on Fakaofo as containing a *malae*, a circular, open air ceremonial ground, situated in the middle of the village. On this ceremonial ground stood a large, oval shaped, open walled meetinghouse. The house had a thatched sloping roof and close to it stood two upright megalithic slabs. The stone statues were wrapped in fine mats. The larger stone is described as the seat of Tui Tokelau and the smaller stone the seat of Hemoana. The god Tui Tokelau controls fecundity, life, and death, and the ethnologist MacGregor refers an account of the god's power, describing how people who wanted to die would approach the stone statue and stay there until they expired (Macgregor 1937: 59, from Lister 1892). The god Hemoana's powers were related to the ocean (Macgregor 1937: 60, from Lister 1892).

The first known historic period among the three atolls has been analyzed and described in great detail by Huntsman and Hooper (see, for example, 1985, 1996). Of relevance for our argument is the fact that Fakaofo was home of the chiefly (*aliki*) line, it was *te fenua aliki*, "the land of the chiefs" (Huntsman and Hooper 1996: 138). Furthermore, Fakaofo had, after some unsuccessful attempts, conquered Nukunonu and extracted women from that atoll, and set up a new regime in Atafu, after having driven away the original inhabitants.

Goldman describes the social organization of this period as a "conquest state" (1970: 340). He refers to Macgregor's work, and recounts the chiefly genealogies following the first conqueror chief on Fakaofo, Kava Vahe Fenua, "Kava Definer of Boundaries." The pattern of seniority and the sanctity of the chiefly male line is clearly established by this stage: From Kava's son Tevaka comes the *aliki* or chiefly line. The other son, Pio, who was born to a woman, Nau, from Nukunonu, is excluded, from the Fakaofoan point of view, in that his children are not counted in the *aliki* genealogy (Huntsman and Hooper 1996: 156).

From the above it may be argued that relations between the atolls involve ranking. Huntsman and Hooper further analyze the relation between Nukunonu and Fakaofo as that between wife giver and wife taker, based on Fakaofo's appropriation of chiefly women from Nukunonu. The Nukunonu account of this event agrees that the union was established, but state that the woman was not taken by force but given voluntarily. The important disagreement lies in how the genealogical lines are to be valued after the union. Fakaofo count only their male line as *aliki*. Nukunonu also counts the offspring through their female line as of *aliki* status.

The relationship between Fakaofo and Atafu, Hooper and Huntsman describe as that between older brother and younger brother, based on the genealogical, generational precedence of Fakaofo. This is in agreement with the Fakaofo view described above. Atafu count their genealogies from the point of origin on Atafu, and thus seem to consider the relationship to the founder, Tonuia, to Fakaofo to be of no importance in terms of ranking.

The relationship between Nukunonu and Atafu, Hooper and Huntsman describe as that between mother's brother and sister's son (*tuatina* and *ilamutu*). A sister's son's most significant relationship with a male relative is to his mother's brother. In war he is to act as a human shield (*mate*) for his mother's brother. In peacetime the mother's brother is responsible for his nephew's well being. I have never heard or seen evidence that this kind of relationship exists in any concrete or metaphorical way between Nukunonu and Atafu. Consequently, I have never seen it challenged either.

In other words, and important to our discussion, is the fact that, as Hooper and Huntsman note parenthetically, each of the atolls represents these relationships differently (1985: 140). Thus, true to what in Goldman's terms would be described as traditional status rivalry, the ranked order of social relationships that Hooper and Huntsman describe, is contested by the involved parties except by Fakaofo, whose claims to overlordship this interpretation seems to support.

Once every year, during the "Tokelau month of *uluaki hilinga* or April/May," with the "dawn rising of the 'precursor of the Pleiades'" (Huntsman & Hooper 1996: 155), the people of Atafu and Nukunonu brought their "offerings of mats and pearl shell" (Lister 1892: 50) to the celebration of Tui Tokelau held on Fakaofo. The literature discusses whether these offerings should be seen as tribute, or as ceremonial goods produced for that particular religious occasion. Seeing that the flow of goods, of ceremonial objects, and of women goes one way, from Nukunonu to Fakaofo, and political control the other way, from Fakaofo to Nukunonu, and later also to Atafu, the answer may vary according to the respective atoll's perspective.

The chiefly line is in Tokelau terms called *latupou* ("standing branch") and the commoner lines are *lafalala* ("leaning branches"). As I have described elsewhere (Hoëm 1995, 2004), the public presentation of groups or genealogical lines as the one (chiefly, senior, dominant) or the other (commoner, younger, subject) is still even today likely to stir up powerful emotions and to cause concern. As genealogical relationships are presented and interpreted differently according to atoll affiliation, claims to ascendancy (on any level) are usually contested. Fakaofo's position as, in Goldman's terms, a conquest state, met with resistance from Nukunonu until the *aliki* (chief or overlord) position was abolished by the British colonial power in 1915 on an appeal from Nukunonu.

The Second Glimpse: Peacetime, Seniority, and the *Inati* "Share System"

There was sporadic contact between people living on the atolls and various visitors on seafaring vessels during the late eighteenth and early nineteenth centuries. Missionary activity, both Catholic and Protestant, commenced in the early 1860s. This activity coincided with the most tragic incident in the known history of Tokelau: in 1863 slavers engaged in the Peruvian slave trade raided the three atolls. More than 45 percent of the population, mainly adult males, was lost in this raid (Maude 1968). After this incident, the establishment of the missions met with little resistance (Hooper and Huntsman 1972). In 1889 Tokelau was declared a protectorate of Great Britain. In 1910 it was incorporated into the Gilbert and Ellice Island Protectorate, which in 1916 became the Gilbert and

Ellice Islands colony. Deannexed in 1924, the islands came under the New Zealand Administration of Western Samoa in 1925. As a consequence of the dramatic decimation of the population (by the slave raiders and due to a dysentery epidemic occurring at the period of first extensive contact with people from the world outside the Pacific), the precontact system of chiefly *(aliki)* lines and of fights for ascendancy (Fox 1995)—in the form it had when it was first described, at least—was disrupted. As mentioned above, Fakaofo's overlordship was formally ended by colonial decree in 1915, and with this the chiefly form of leadership was transformed and retained in a new shape in all three atolls in the institutions of Village Councils *(Fono o Taupulega)*, in which since then the elders *(toeaina*, men from approximately their mid sixties and above) and *matai* (male family heads) rule (Hooper and Huntsman 1985). In the literature this form of leadership is described as a gerontocracy.

Until the 1950s, contact with New Zealand was in the form of short-term visits by officials. The churches had representatives staying for longer periods, but these were selected from other parts of the Pacific, in the main from Samoa (Huntsman 1980). Apart from this, Tokelau was largely left to itself (Hooper 1982). Western Samoa (from 1997 named only Samoa) became independent in 1962, and in 1964 Tokelau was given the choice of becoming affiliated with either Western Samoa or the Cook Islands. In response to this Tokelau asked to be allowed to continue its association with New Zealand. In terms of UN classification, Tokelau is today still a "non self-governing territory"; but it is currently assuming more responsibility for its own government and administration.

All villagers either have rights to land on their island of birth or else are married to someone who does have rights to land on their island of residence. Land is inalienable in the sense that it is forbidden by law to sell it. The village councils mentioned above *(fono o taupulega)*, still consist of male elders *(toeaina)* on Fakaofo and Nukunonu; on Atafu they also elect *matai* (titled male family heads) to sit in the councils. The village councils hold weekly meetings where they decide on the "timing of all major activities of the population, the days for village work, for communal fishing enterprises, village-wide games, etc." (Hooper 1982: 17).

In other words, the village councils have the right to order people to do jobs for the village, such as when the women are told to weave hats, mats, and fans as gifts for guests to the village, or to prepare a feast for them, or as when the men are ordered to clear the reef channel of stones or to help construct a house. The Village Councils also adjudicate in village disputes, such as those concerning land rights. They have the power to settle conflicts, and decide on family internal affairs such as cases of extramarital pregnancies. In recent years, the councils work in closer cooperation with the Tokelau Public Service, and they elect representatives to partake in the inter-atoll assembly: the General Fono.

Describing the position of the Village Councils and the dominant leadership structure from the late 1960s to the 70s, Hooper comments that, at the time, "this centralized direction is one of the keystones of Tokelau community structure, and it is not called into question by any notion of 'individual rights'" (1982: 19).

The economy of the village's subsistence sphere is run through the institution of *inati*, that is, a system which dictates an equal share distribution of any major catch of fish, or of any other major collective food resource, to all members of the villages, and in the main regardless of age and social status. (See Huntsman and Hooper 1995: 76–83 for a thorough description.) One man working as distributor (*tauvaega*) of *inati* shares is appointed by the village council. Interestingly, Huntsman and Hooper note that the men who hold this office are chosen on genealogical criteria, and from among the lines who have held this office earlier (1995: 78). When there is a major distribution, the *tauvaega* collects the goods to be divided out to the villagers, and he calls out the names of the share groups. The share groups, commonly represented by a child, come and receive their share and take it to their *kaiga* homestead to be distributed among its members. Young children in general serve as errand boys and girls, and go as messengers between adults in different households.

The goods prototypically distributed in an *inati* are the *ika ha*, sacred fish. This category includes such species as turtles, swordfish, and shark, and is an interesting category, in that by definition it is a kind of fish that must be shared with all (but which is taboo for some families). It is explicitly forbidden to keep such a catch within the family group. This restriction on consumption also applies to any large catch of fish (for example if the catch counts over twenty skipjack it must also be shared with the village). Other goods are also distributed to the village in this manner: it may be the case that the surplus from the village cooperative store is divided out, or the remaining excess funds from some public project.

So, to address the question of the apparent transformation between the social formation of the "conquest state" that we saw in the first glimpse and what we encounter here in this second glimpse: what is the empirical evidence for the development of an egalitarian (nonstratified) society? Or is it more fruitful to view also this manifestation of social organization as hierarchical in the sense employed by S. Tcherkézoff in his discussion based on empirical evidence from Samoa (this volume), as an encompassing system of belonging?

As a starting point for this discussion, in a very fundamental sense—according to its system of redistribution of subsistence goods, that is, and due to its relative absence of materially visible signs of social stratification—Tokelau of this period is commonly described as an egalitarian society (cf. Sahlins 1958; Hooper 1969). Describing atoll societies in general, Sahlins writes:

> Instead of the development of stratified hierarchies for regulating surplus distribution, one would expect a trend towards egalitarianism. When surpluses are relatively small and deficiencies liable to arise in different localities, a premium is put on direct or reciprocal types of distribution, not types that travel up and down hierarchies. Kinship organization on an egalitarian basis would be of selective advantage (1958: 236).

Commenting specifically on social organization of Tokelau, based on Lister's (1892) and Macgregor's ethnographic descriptions, Sahlins adds: "All of the evidence shows at least 'underlying' ramification, coupled perhaps with an egalitarian emphasis on age" (1958: 225). In conclusion he writes: "The stratification structure was extremely simple. Two nonegalitarian status levels can be distinguished: an upper level consisting of the village chief and presumably, in earlier times, the village priest: and the remainder of the population in a lower level" (1958: 226).

After conducting fieldwork in the late 1960s, Hooper is able to fill in missing ethnographic information, and he then lends support to Sahlins's description. Hooper reaches the conclusion that the exchange system is structurally complex in the sense predicted by Sahlins's model for atoll societies, and that distribution (the *inati*) "copes with both shortage and plenty, and could not be other than egalitarian in principle" (1969: 240).

It is important to note, however, that these descriptions are cast within a theoretical framework of ecological adaptation, and accordingly analytical terms such as "stratification" and "egalitarian" are used in the traditional sense, to refer to concrete, material accumulation of surplus goods and concomitant evolution of ranked statuses.

If we choose to retain a characterization of atoll societies as egalitarian, it must be so in contrast to other, more markedly stratified Pacific societies, such as that of Samoa, where distribution of subsistence goods at all periods at the same time serves a marker of social differentiation. In particular, food distributions at *feasts* epitomize allocation of difference (Keating 2000). In Tokelau this is also the case to a certain degree, in that prominent elders, village leaders, the pastor, and other visiting dignitaries frequently receive a better share in feast situations. In this sense then, it is probably more correct to say that the social order is characterized by a marking of social difference in all known historical periods.

However, in the phase described in the second glimpse, the "neo-traditional" social order, to use Hooper's terms, the common distributions of subsistence goods are explicitly geared toward leveling social differences and ensuring that everybody receives an equal share. This mechanism is stressed and strongly valued in Tokelau. If we are to accept the terms employed by Sahlins, and supported by Hooper, the exchange system of Tokelau, as it has been described here in this second glimpse may be described as egalitarian. However, even in this period, we see that social difference is marked locally in the distribution of better (if not larger) shares to high status positions, such as the village priest or a visiting dignitary.

In terms of local ideology in this period, the collective orientation and the egalitarian ethos are predominant. Furthermore, this "cult" of the collective points to its function as an encompassing whole. That the villagers are still under strict control by the village councils, the *taupulega*, and the elders, the *toeaina*, demonstrates the elders' superior position of power of definition and practical command over the lives of their villagers. And as noted above, this state of affairs is not openly contested in this period. The competing for ascendancy constitutes the dynamics of political life, both internally in the village councils and externally in the inter-atoll assembly, the General Fono. It can also be argued (Hoëm 2004) that competitive acts of identification characterize much everyday interaction as well.

In conclusion it seems then that Tcherkézoff's definition of hierarchy as an encompassing system of belonging provides us so far with a more fitting perspective in terms of describing enduring patterns and conceptions of sociality, than what we get from assessing social change solely in terms of systems of exchange.

A Glimpse from the Present: the Vision of Power Sharing

Since the mid 1960s, Tokelauans have migrated to Samoa, Australia, the United States, and in the largest numbers to New Zealand, where they hold rights of citizenship. There is a constant movement back and forth between Tokelau and New Zealand, as people visit the atolls to look after family interests, to have a vacation, to get work, and in the case of the generations born in New Zealand, to see the place for the first time. People move to New Zealand if finances allow it more or less for the same reasons: to be reunited with family members and seek new opportunities. Many of the early migrants to New Zealand went as scholarship students. Some in this group tend to return to Tokelau for shorter or longer periods to work in the Tokelau Public Service, that is, the bureaucracy, which has been established as a step toward becoming a nation state. The processes of putting into place the infrastructure deemed necessary to allow for an Act of Self-Determination have been followed by a marked increase in inter-atoll interaction, for political negotiations, but also for sports or other cultural events. Families or individuals also increasingly move between the atolls for departmental positions.

To move between social spaces (in terms of authority and leadership, but also in terms of gender) is not always easy: in particular because to exercise authority over any kind of local resource—that is, through genealogical ties to land *(fenua)* and positions *(tulaga)*—first of all demands presence. We have here at least two different, and occasionally conflicting, frames of reference informing acts of identification: One is within the competitive striving for honor and ascendancy between the atolls (cf. the *latupou/lafalala* relationships), which demand primary allegiances to geographical place. The other is the framework provided by the so-called "Pan-Pacific Movement," by the demands of international politics; and in association with this, the demands of the institutions associated with the emerging nation state (cf. Hoëm 1999).

The existence of a national assembly can be dated back to 1964. Historically, one has to go back to precolonial times, to "the days of war," that is, to the time of Fakaofo's dominance over the other two atolls, to find the existence of something akin to a nation-like tie between the three atolls. In the Tokelau *tala anamua*, accounts of the past, and in many songs with historical themes, we find accounts of rivalry and wars between the atolls. As mentioned above, Fakaofo's dominance lasted all the way into the beginning of the twentieth century, and was formally ended after the appeal from Nukunonu to the British Administration to lift it.

Accordingly, the existence of national sentiment is new, and as yet precarious. The most important and immediate ties of attachment and allegiance are to one's family group and atoll of birth and/or of residence, rather than to Tokelau as a whole.

An example of the tensions inherent in this situation is an incident which occurred in connection with the sensitive issue of relocation of the Tokelau Public Service from Samoa to Tokelau. During the April *General Fono* held in Nukunonu in 1992, the Fakaofo delegation alleged that they have a claim to all the administrative departments, as well as to become the *laumua* or capital of Tokelau, on the basis of their historic claims to ascendancy. Meeting resistance from the other delegations they walked out of the *Fono*, effectively demonstrating that without the cooperation of all three villages there is no *General Fono* and hence no national government. Their walkout accompanied by a heavy rainfall was interpreted (by their supporters) as a sign that their action was blessed from above.

In concession to the principle that the new national infrastructure should be based on Tokelau culture, a solution was sought to what was called in foreign affairs language the "problem of rivalry." The major obstacle to implement the new infrastructure was the issue of the location of the head office for the Tokelau Administration. This presented a particular difficulty because to choose a permanent location would effectively be to single out one of the atolls as the capital, thus placing the chosen island in a position of permanent ascendancy. This solution proved impossible, as no unanimous agreement could be reached among the three atolls. The only possible choice left, then, was to rotate the head office among the three atolls. The *inati*, in the sense of "an equal share to all" was explicitly used as the guiding metaphor in the political discussions leading up to this solution.

However, and ironically in the light of the intention of seeking a solution based on Tokelau culture, the model chosen contains a principle of fixed "equality." This principle is a clear contradiction of the underlying social dynamic that gives life to Tokelau political practice, that is, the competing for honor and ascendancy. However, regardless of the institutional framework chosen by the political leadership in cooperation with external advisors, the local conceptualization of the relationship between parts (any interest group, the subsumed) and wholes (always the larger collective, the encompassing) works its power as always before.

Dominant Values as Seen though a Tale with a Twist

Finally, I shall embark on a brief exposition of the values that give shape to the sociocultural dynamic I have described so far. My approach is akin to the one Tcherkézoff employs for Samoa in this volume, but as will become apparent, the Tokelau universe contains its own logic, which differs from the Samoan in certain significant aspects.

In order to make my illustration more "experience-near," I shall use a Tokelau tale that in a typical fashion makes vital statements about the nature of male and female domains of life, and how the relationship between these spheres is conceived in terms of the distinction between *tapu* (restricted) and *noa* (unbound) states. Ultimately, the tale is about legitimate and not so legitimate forms of leadership, authority, and agency.

Below is an extract from a Tokelau speech that quotes a cognate of a Tikopian sacred tale or *kai tapu*. This small, enigmatic piece is considered to be powerful. Furthermore, it is very popular, as is shown by its frequent occurrence in contemporary Tokelau speeches and songs.

At the conclusion of one of many United Nations visiting missions to Tokelau, Tokelau's political leader for external affairs (or *Ulu o Tokelau*) gave a speech to the visitors and the community leaders. The speech addressed the issue of Tokelau's future political status and its relationship to New Zealand. After a formal discussion of various topics, particularly matters having to do with finance, which are critical when it comes to the question of Tokelau's independence, the *Ulu* or "Head" concluded his speech in the following way:

> [I]t is said that when the legendary Tokelau brothers, Kalehi and Tafaki, were asked to record the wealth of their father to the gathering of the people, they then counted out the wealth of their mother—the woman, the *Matua-ha* or "the sacred one," the distributor of wealth, the *Fatupaepae*, or literally "the white stone"—she who must go through pain in order for others to survive.

When the two brothers stood up, this is what they told the people:

> "Strike, strike the post. Crash, crash.
> Loosen the structure.
> Strike, strike. The post splintered, splintered, splintered.
> Loosen the attachments.
> Hey skipjack, may you frolic in your sea.
> Frolic wildly, frolic on the surface, frolic belly up;
> Creating ripples, standing to prey.
> Because the tail of Kalehi and Tafaki have struck.
> Hey kingfish, may you frolic in your sea.
> Swarm in tens, in twenties, in thirties.
> Swarm madly, swarm to port, swarm to starboard.
> Because the tail of Kalehi and Tafaki have struck."

Accounts of the elders tell us that the boys then left the people. They walked. They walked on until they reached the sea never to be seen again. But the people of Tokelau continued to live by the endowment of their mother.

The Tokelau folk tale, the *kakai o Hatipuga*, from which this quotation is drawn, has been recorded in four versions by Huntsman. She notes how the tale has "more or less closely related cognates . . . known throughout Polynesia" (Huntsman 1980: 115). The English version of this speech was recorded in the document "Report of the United Nations Visiting Mission to Tokelau, 1994" (paragraph 43: 35–6).[4]

The cognate *kai tapu* is a tale which, according to Park's analysis, contains the following information: "The sacred tale includes all social relationships between individuals, it refers to the cosmological identity of these individuals, and, finally, it refers to the location of the action contained in the tale in geographical (vertical and horizontal) space" (1973: 157).

The Tokelau tale concerns, as most Tokelau tales do, social relationships and cosmological identity. It also locates the actions in the factual atoll landscape, in a manner that allows potential listeners to identify and situate the action. The tale of the man Hatipuga tells of his marriage to a sacred "sky-being," from which union sprang the culture heroes, the two brothers Kalehi and Tafaki. Subsequently the man Hatipuga married again, this time to an ordinary female, named Puga. This union resulted in ten children, all male, who all have the prefix *niu* (coconut palm) in their names (that is, *niu*-one and so on).

The ten boys wanted to woo a virginal village maiden or *taupou* (that is, *tapu*, "restricted"), but the two brothers from the first marriage were in mourning for their mother and refused to join the procession until after the proscribed ten days of mourning were completed. The ten brothers all went and called them, one night after the other, but it was not until the period of mourning was over that the two brothers agreed to join them in wooing the maiden. As the procession walked through the village islet, the group of brothers quarreled among themselves as to where in the procession Kalehi and Tafaki were to walk. Initially they were placed at the very back, subsequently they were moved to the middle, and when the procession arrived at its destination, they had been placed in front. Kalehi and Tafaki then told the ten to go ahead with the wooing, and they went off to a pool where the girl was bathing. She was struck by their beauty and agreed to mate with them. At the house, the ten brothers counted out the wealth of their father. Finally, the turn came to the two brothers who had already had the maiden, and who then chose to count out the wealth of their mother. They delivered the speech with their attack on "the post" (*pou*), and then went to the sea with the maiden, "never to be seen again."

It is common to use this kind of imagery in speeches: taken from songs, legends, and folktales, from the sphere of kinship and not least from specialist knowledge of open ocean fishing. It is also common that a large proportion of the audience do not fully understand the esoteric references made by the orators.

Not making claims to an exhaustive interpretation of this passage, I would like to use it in order to further elucidate dominant values that inform social relationships, communication, and patterns of interaction in Tokelau.

As the brothers Kalehi and Tafaki are "the same" (*tutuha*) they may be substitutes for one another (*hui*) in their capacity as representatives of their side of the kin-group. In this context, theirs is an equal relationship, and they function together as a team (or group, *vaega*). This unity is further underlined by the fact that their names are commonly used to refer to pairs of butterfly fish, which are always seen feeding together. On this matter, the Tokelau version differs in a significant manner from the Tikopian version. In the Tikopian *kai tapu*, only the eldest brother has sexual intercourse with the woman. This can be seen to reflect the consistently patrilineal dominance, and thus the overriding importance of the principle of seniority in that society. However, it is also unusual in some (particularly in the sphere of sexual relations), if not in all other, social contexts for a pair of brothers to be interchangeable in Tokelau. Clearly, the actions of the two are something out of the ordinary.

I interpret the post (*pou*) that they lash out against as a symbol of the authority structures of the village. As such, they may in principle be the posts of any Tokelau style house, generally symbolizing the "backbone of the kin-group," represented by the family homestead. Given that the setting for this action is a "gathering of the people," however, this passage most likely refers to the structure of the meeting house and, more specifically, to the communal aspect of kinship apparent in the internal ranking of the male family heads (*pule*) of the kin groups (*kau kaiga*), according to "main stems or posts (*latupou*)" and "side or leaning branches (*lafalala*)." This is reflected in the ranking of seating arrangements along the posts that support the roof of the meeting house, from the "highest" to the "lowest" positions.

This building is the most dignified (*mamalu*) structure in the villages (in addition to the Church). It is the center where all major communal gatherings are held, also hosting the weekly meetings of the political leadership of the villages, the Council of Elders. Thus, according to the way in which the atoll areas are symbolically ranked as center and periphery (or front and back), the brothers are attacking the male power structures associated with the village center.

Firth comments on the symbolic aspects of "posts," *pou*, in Tikopia. He writes:

> [O]ne must realize that a major house post in Tikopia is more than a structural support to the building. It is a conventional back-rest for seated men, especially men of rank; and in the traditional society it was often a material symbol and putative abiding place of an ancestor or god, and a site for libation and offering for household welfare. So a post (*pou*) was and still is associated with respect and power (1985: 38).

He describes that, to Tikopia, posts

involve bundles of rather imprecise criteria: solidarity, stoutness, uprightness . . . , supportive function, status, focus of social interest and respect, power of somewhat indeterminate kind (1985: 38).

There is also a determinate association with maleness, he comments, but not primarily in its sexual aspect, and ritually, a house post may represent female deities as well.

But then comes the Tokelauan twist to the tale: intriguingly and counter to everyday conceptions of the nature of kinship-relations, this story seems to communicate the message that the "male side" (or *tamatane*, that is, offspring, both male and female, counted on the side of the man of a founding couple) of kin groups is ephemeral. (Remember that the Tokelau kinship system is cognatic.)

In the story, the wealth of the "male side" is not even considered worthy of mention by Kalehi and Tafaki. Its most permanent structures, represented by the posts of the house, may be violently attacked and destroyed. On the contrary, the "female side" (*tamafafine*, or offspring, also of both sexes counted on the side of the woman of the original couple), can distribute the wealth from the sea, thus continuing to benefit "the people of Tokelau" even after the two brothers have disappeared.

This is an attack on what in everyday perceptions of kinship relationships would be seen as the dominant, in the sense of commanding (*pule*) or "male" side. Further, the attack is made by a couple of youngsters, as yet without any legitimate say or standing in the community. Contrary to the consequences of such an action in everyday life, here it is said to bring fortunate results, an abundance of highly valued fish.

Huntsman (1983) refers to the folktale from which this image is taken, and points out that the father's wealth in this case is land, access to which is restricted; whereas the mother's wealth is "from the sea," and therefore available to "anyone with skill." She adds that this story is about rivalry, that is, what I describe as competitive identification. According to her, the moral of the story is that the underdog wins, a point consistent with what I have interpreted as the main point of this part of the speech. The brothers of the first marriage are senior to the ten brothers of the subsequent marriage, and it is therefore fitting that they should walk first in the procession and that they should "marry" first.

Sacred Beings: War, Legitimate Authority, . . . and Fertility

But there is a more significant moral to be learned from this story. That an action which in this case would be deemed subversive "in the normal order of things" is linked to natural fecundity, and reproductive fertility marks it as blessed, as socially legitimate. Besnier (1996: 7) has made a similar observation of what he calls a "constitutive association of authority and fecundity" in Nukulaelae, Tuvalu. He writes: "The community prospers when food and labor are plentiful, when the sea is fecund, and when *filemu* 'peace' and *fealofani* 'mutual empathy, harmony' reign amongst all members of the community." He notes that the association between authority and fecundity is most evident when people talk about the "golden days" of the past, when, people say that the community prospered because it was ruled "with an iron fist," "when a command was issued and people would cheerfully comply." He comments that people contrast the image drawn in "nostalgic discourse, with the sad conditions of today, where people grumble and negotiate the community decisions." Recently T. Ryan (personal communication) has pointed to a similar connection in the Niue of the late 1970s, where he observed a clear continuity between sacred rituals associated with the sea and previously used to ensure luck in war, and those employed in connection with contemporary competitions.

This bears a close resemblance to conceptions held in Tokelau. It is still common that people in Tokelau associate unsolved conflicts and secrecy with periods of drought, scarcity, and eventually famine (*oge*), and great care is taken to ensure that such cases are brought out in the open so that harmony and abundance may reign once more.

To illustrate a similar connection between sacred rituals and contemporary phenomena in Tokelau: during one of my periods of fieldwork, there was a long spell of sunny days. After a while, there was much talk in the village about a girl whom people accused of being pregnant. The problem was not so much that she was thought to be pregnant, but that she had not told anybody. This, people said, was what had caused the rain to stay away, and everybody who talked about this agreed that her pregnancy had to be made public (by her) so as to put an end to the drought. A lack of tobacco, for example, which happens regularly when people run out of cigarettes before the next boat is due to arrive, is also frequently attributed to unresolved conflicts. Ability to win a game in a similar fashion is attributed to harmonious relationships within the team. Accordingly, I have observed people being forced to make their grievances known and to resolve their differences before a game, lest they jeopardize the winning chances of their side.

So, according to this way of thinking, if an abundance of a limited good, such as fish or rain, results from an action, that action bears the sign of being blessed. In other words, human fertility and nature's fecundity serve to lend legitimacy to an action, and, thus, fecundity serves to constitute authority. Likewise, the primary responsibility of someone in a position of authority is to control, that is, to bring about and regulate fecundity and fertility. The practice of *tapu*ing, of placing more or less temporary restrictions upon (and the opening of) land-areas, marine resources, and various activities, may be seen as expressive of this concern with regulating production and reproduction.

The female counterpart of the male exercise of legitimate power is that exercised by the *matua ha*, referred to in the speech presented above as "the sacred one." Another term designating legitimate exercise of female power is *manu ha* or "sacred being." As sisters, women hold life giving or life threatening powers. By cursing, they are believed to be able to afflict the reproductive capacity of their brothers' wives (Hooper and Huntsman 1975). They are also expected to intervene in situations of social (and physical) conflict, and their presence, occasionally accompanied by a few words, will in the normal order of things be sufficient to stop the fighting. This quality is referred to in the speech in the lines that say of the "sacred one" that she is the one who "must go through pain in order for others to survive."

During "the days of war" referred to in the first glimpse presented above, the Fakaofoan invasion of Nukunonu is said to have come to a halt, when the conquering war party came to a place where a woman's leaf shirt or *titi* hung on a branch. This made passing beyond this point *tapu*, and the physical conquest of the village islet of Nukunonu was therefore never completed.

Men are considered to be strong, *malohi*, and in control of their powers. Women are seen as weak, *vaivai*, and liable to become vessels for dangerous forces emanating from spirits: *aitu*, associated with the bush; *vao*, or backside; *tua*, of the villages. The dark side of female sexuality and reproductive capacity lies on the one hand in its connection with death and destruction. On the other hand, this force can also be used effectively in order to stop war and social conflict.

This double quality of power, beneficial and destructive, wild and controlled, is a prevalent theme throughout the region. As reflected in the many debates on the relation between *tapu* and *noa*, between social restriction and unboundedness, social action in general is geared toward the regulation of these forces in order to produce a life space for humans in the larger universe (see in particular Gell 1993 on this point). This concern leads to a pattern in which, in any given sequence of interaction, one person sets the pace and the others follow. Relatively speaking, one is high and the others are low. This can be further illustrated by the Tokelau designation of "speech out of place," *hopotu-laga* (literally, "to rise above [one's] place or position"), which means to speak as if one had authority, to speak or do something which is outside one's area of control or authority *(pule)*. This dynamic then is what I describe as producing a "sense of place" (Hoëm 1995b, 1999, 2004), and which Tcherkézoff in this volume describes as a hierarchical or encompassing whole informed by the value of belonging.

Conclusion

My final interpretation of the story of Talehi and Kafaki is that it presents and concerns the limits between established, "restricted" and "restricting" authority structures in the villages, represented by the posts of the meeting house, and their relation to the nonrestricted, uncontained forces originating from outside the social world: in this case emanating from the sacred sphere of the heavens and returning to the sea.

This Tokelau narrative discusses the most basic elements from which an ordered society is produced. And as we have seen through the glimpses from various points in Tokelau history and up to the present, despite challenges and disruptive actions from within and without, through encounters with stranger-kings and differently ordered patterns of sociality, enduring social formations can still be found if we shift our focus also to include the conceptions of the inner workings of society held by those who participate in them.

Notes

1. I would like to thank the editors, Knut M. Rio and Olaf H. Smedal, for valuable comments to an earlier version of this chapter.
2. What symbolizes the larger whole can be an institution, such as the *fonos*, the meeting fora vested with exercising customary law. It can be a genealogical founder, such as Kava Vahe Fenua, or Kava Definer of Boundaries, mentioned below. It can be the ancestral couple of a *kau kaiga*, an extended family group in its temporal aspect. It can be the elders, the *taupulega*, who constitute the village political leadership (see the second illustration presented below). It can even be the *fatupaepae*, literally, "cornerstone," the senior female kin, who reside in the extended family's (*kaiga*) homestead and whose responsibility it is to hold the family group together.
3. For a discussion of the possible qualitative difference between "competition"—in terms of a (common) value and "contestation"—where alternative values are proposed, see Smedal forthcoming. In what I describe here, the "contestation" or challenge definitely takes place within a universe of shared values.
4. A Tokelau version is to be found in Huntsman (1980: 82–90).

References

Besnier, Niko. 1996. "Authority and Egalitarianism: Discourses on Leadership on Nuku-laelae Atoll." Presented at the Conference on Leadership and Change in the Western Pacific: For Sir Raymond Firth on the Occasion of his 90th Birthday. London School of Economics.
De Coppet, Daniel and André Iteanu, ed. 1995. *Cosmos and Society in Oceania.* Oxford: Berg.
Firth, Raymond. 1985. "Degrees of Intelligibility." In *Reason and Morality,* ed. F. Overing. ASA Monographs 24. London and New York: Tavistock Publications.
Fox, James J. 1995. "Austronesian Societies and their Transformations." In *The Austrone-sians: Historical and Comparative Perspectives,* ed. P. Bellwood, J. J. Fox, and D. Tryon. Canberra: Australian National University Press.
Gell, Alfred. 1993. *Wrapping in Images: Tattooing in Polynesia.* Oxford: Oxford University Press.
Goldman, Irving. 1970. *Ancient Polynesian Society.* Chicago and London: The University of Chicago Press.
Hoëm, Ingjerd. 1993. "Space and Morality in Tokelau." *Pragmatics* 3 (2): 137–153.
———. 1995a. *A Way With Words.* Bangkok: White Orchid Press. (Joint Publication with the Institute of Comparative Research in Human Culture, Oslo.)
———. 1995b. *A Sense of Place. The Politics of Identity and Representation.* (Ph.D. diss., University of Oslo).
———. 1999. "Processes of Identification and the Incipient National Level." *Social Anthropology* 17 (3): 279–95.
———. 2004. *Theatre and Political Process: Staging Identities in Tokelau and New Zealand.* Oxford and New York: Berghahn Books.
Hoëm, Ingjerd and Sidsel Roalkvam, ed. 2003. *Oceanic Socialities and Cultural Forms: Ethnographies of Experience,* Oxford: Berghahn Books.
Hooper, Anthony. 1968. "Socio-Economic Organisation of the Tokelau Islands." In *Proceedings of the Eighth Congress of Anthropological and Ethnological Sciences.* Tokyo.
———. 1982. *Aid and Dependency in a Small Pacific Territory.* Working Paper 62, Department of Anthropology: University of Auckland.
Hooper, Anthony and Judith Huntsman. 1972. "The Tokelau Islands Migration Study: Behavioural Studies." In *Migration and Related Social and Health Problems in New Zealand and the Pacific,* ed. J. Stanhope and J. S. Dodge. Wellington: Epidemiology Unit, Wellington Hospital.
———. 1975. "Male and Female in Tokelau Culture." *Journal of the Polynesian Society* 84: 415–30.
———. 1985. "Structures of Tokelau History." In *Transformations of Polynesian Culture,* ed. A. Hooper and J. Huntsman. Auckland: Polynesian Society Memoir 45.
Huntsman, Judith. 1971. "Concepts of kinship and categories of kinsmen in the Tokelau Islands." *Journal of Polynesian Society* 80: 317–54.
———. 1980. *Tokelau Tales Told by Manuele Palehau.* Working Paper 58, Department of Anthropology, University of Auckland.
Huntsman, Judith and Anthony Hooper. 1996. *Tokelau. A Historical Ethnography.* Auckland: University of Auckland Press.
Keating, Elisabeth. 2000. "Moments of Hierarchy: Constructing Social Stratification by Means of Language, Food, Space, and the Body in Pohnpei, Micronesia." *American Anthropologist* 102 (2): 303–20.
Kirch, Patrick. V. 2000. *On the Road of the Winds: An Archaeological History of the Pacific islands before European Contact.* Berkeley and Los Angeles: University of California Press.

Lister, J. J. 1892. "Notes on the Natives of Fakaofu. (Bowditch Island). Union group." *Journal of the Anthropological Institute of Great Britain and Ireland* 21: 43–63.

Macgregor, Gordon. 1937 (1971). *Ethnology of Tokelau Islands*. Bernice P. Bishop Museum Bulletin 146. Honolulu.

Park, Julie. 1973. "A Consideration of the Tikopian 'Sacred Tale'." *Journal of the Polynesian Society* 82: 154–175.

Sahlins, Marshall. 1958. *Social Stratification in Polynesia*. Chicago: Chicago University Press.

———. 1963. "Poor Man, Rich Man, Big Man, Chief: Political Types in Melanesia and Polynesia." *Comparative Studies in Society and History* 5 (3): 285–303.

Smedal, Olaf H. (In press). "Hierarchy, Precedence, and Values: Scopes for Social Action in Ngadhaland, Central Flores." In *Precedence and Social Differentiation in the Austronesian World*, ed. Michael. P. Vischer and James J. Fox. Canberra: ANU E Press.

CHAPTER 9

On the Value of the Beast
or the Limit of Money

Notes on the Meaning of Marriage Prestations
among the Ngadha, Central Flores (Indonesia)

Olaf H. Smedal

How are we to conceive of "the persistence of social formations" to which this volume is devoted? As vestiges of previous configurations that have just happened to linger on? Or rather as consciously protected niches of social activity without which central values of self and collective would be critically diminished?

Perhaps there is no general answer to this question: it begs further questions about (political, cultural, economic) self reflexivity and the nature of the historically highly variable relationship between any one society and other societies, and especially other (greater) powers, secular or celestial: it becomes immediately apparent that vexing problems of delimitation (containment) and border transgression (flow) are already integral to the problematic. But what if the investigation is restricted to those persisting social formations that are hierarchical?

It is easy to argue that "the modern world" is not one that celebrates hierarchy: "It is appropriate to keep in mind our aversion to hierarchy," as Louis Dumont warns us (1980: 239). But to understand what is at issue here, it is important to heed Dumont's quite precise statements about what hierarchy is not and what it is:

> I believe that hierarchy is not, essentially, a chain of super-imposed commands, nor even a chain of beings of decreasing dignity, nor yet a taxonomic tree, but a relation that can succinctly be called "the encompassing of the contrary" (Dumont 1980: 239).

And how is this hierarchical encompassment envisaged?

Notes to this section begin on page 290.

This hierarchical relation is, very generally, that between a whole (or a set) and an element of that whole (or set): the element belongs to the set and is in this sense consubstantial or identical with it; at the same time, the element is distinct from the set or stands in opposition to it. This is what I mean by the expression "the encompassing of the contrary" (Dumont 1980: 240).

The reason moderns are averse to hierarchy is that we tend to posit or assume that any opposition is "level"—that the paradigmatic and legitimate form of any opposition is binary—expressing either complementarity or contradiction. "As moderns, we tend to put everything on the same plane" (Dumont 1980: 244). That one of the elements in the opposition *contains* its opposite while simultaneously maintaining its position *qua* opposite is, to us (such is Dumont's claim), logically scandalous because we cannot think of two elements being identical to each other, that is to say united (at a superior level) and separate from each other (at an inferior level) at the same time.

Now, by way of interrogating empirical material on marriage exchanges among the Ngadha of Flores, eastern Indonesia, I hope to be able to demonstrate how certain practices uphold precisely this "double vision." The overall theme is "value" (thus I aim to stay close to the Dumontian thematic according to which a hierarchy is a hierarchy of facts and values)—both in rather tangible meanings such as "use value" and "exchange value," and in a more general sense ("symbolic value," "superior value").

These instances of "value" may appear to force too many meanings into one and the same word. But these meanings are intrinsic to the main object of analysis here—bridewealth items in the form of livestock—not only in that the animals in question are treasured in the practical and pecuniary senses and thus constitute a crucial form of economic capital, but also in that the Ngadha understand some of them to embody a highly complex set of cosmological notions fundamental to Ngadha social and cultural existence, being precious also for this reason. At any rate, I shall also attempt to show that in the final analysis the Dumontian argument of simultaneous identity and opposition of elements should be abandoned for a perspective in which the very distinction between identity and opposition dissolves.

Since the following discussion concerns the persistence of a singular traditional practice that involves the circulation of valuables (of which State money is one, but restricted, medium), it is useful for a moment first to consider in theoretical terms the role money might play.

Money, Money, and Money

In an intriguing attempt to determine how value circulation and ecological sustainability are related under differing social conditions (premodern,

modern, and postmodern—terms used as analytical not historical categories), Alf Hornborg (1999) suggests that the more fundamental question to ask is how value is signified more generally. Without committing myself either way to Hornborg's overall argument, I think his mobilization of Peircean semiotics is fruitful. Briefly, Hornborg proposes that under premodern conditions value is generally represented indexically. These conditions are moreover characterized by a certain epistemological naïveté, where signs appear "as straightforward indices of essential identities" and where power relations, for example, appear to be "opaque to critical scrutiny" (Hornborg 1999: 147). In contrast, the modern condition "is one of *reflexive scrutiny*" (original emphasis) where signs of value have become symbols, open to interpretation; "where the wearer of the crown may be an impostor and Scripture may be mistaken." The accelerated traffic in all manner of signs typical of the postmodern condition has resulted in a situation "where the exhausting attitude of radical scepticism tends to give way to a structurally enforced, *feigned gullibility* (Hornborg 1999: 148, original emphasis). Here, signs are once more "perceived as indices of identity, but now simply by virtue of positing themselves as such, rather than through assumed correspondences with essences" as is the case under premodern conditions.

Having followed Hornborg so far, it is not difficult to see how the money sign would be transformed correspondingly. It will be recalled that according to Peirce, there are fundamentally three ways or modes in which we can apprehend signs—ways he simply designated "firstness," "secondness," and "thirdness":

> The first is that whose being is simply in itself, not referring to anything nor lying behind anything. The second is that which is what it is by force of something to which it is second. The third is that which is what it is owing to things between which it mediates and which it brings into relation to each other (Peirce 1931–1958, quoted in Hornborg 1999: 151)

Now gold occupies a prototypical if not unique place in the history of money, in that its value was an essential attribute of the very substance itself. Semiotically, therefore, gold is its own index—its value having the quality of firstness. It symbolizes nothing; it simply is itself. Paper money represents the next step: Here the variously denominated sheets of paper (that together with variously denominated coins constitute the total of "a currency") symbolize a minute fraction of the gold presumably stored in the vaults of the National Bank; paper money instantiating secondness. Nowadays, the gold standard having been abandoned since 1971 (Hornborg 1999: 150), electronic money signifies paper money but no longer the gold that the paper once signified. With the credit card and online banking we have reached thirdness, according to Hornborg.

In the following, I shall deal little with thirdness in the postmodern; the material at my disposal concerns primarily the first two sets of parallels. And I should note at once that even if the Ngadha in the past sometimes exchanged items of gold, the preeminent object of value under consideration here is the water buffalo. But before I continue one caveat is in order: Even if Hornborg's application of Peircean semiotics to money is accepted, its relevance to what I shall call "buffalo value" is another matter entirely. As I hope to show, the water buffalo embodies the entire gamut of Hornborg's value triad: not only the intrinsic, immediate, obvious, brute value of firstness, but also a wide range of symbolic valuations of great importance (i.e., secondness) and, arguably, even—in its status as an object of immense, socially constitutive speculation of totality—the imaginary instantiation of thirdness. In short, the water buffalo would seem to qualify as a Maussian "total social fact" or "privileged phenomenon" in that it condenses within itself the entire range of potential economic, social, and cultural aspirations (or, alternatively, that these aspirations emanate from it). But I am leaping ahead of myself: first now to the essentials of ethnographic context.

Setting

The perhaps 60, 000 speakers of the Ngadha language—virtually all of whom are now Catholic (missionaries began evangelizing in the late 1920s)—are bordered by the Manggarai to the west, to the north by the people in So'a and, further north, the peoples in the Riung district, often collectively referred to as Rembong.[1] To the east are the Nagé and Kéo peoples. Depending on elevation, Ngadha cultivate potatoes, carrots, coconuts, cassava, and other tubers, bananas, maize, coffee, cocoa, vanilla, candlenuts, various pulses, and rice—rice now also being grown in irrigated plots—and they keep dogs, pigs, poultry, and water buffalo.

As is common in eastern Indonesia the Ngadha evince a pervasive concern with scalar, stepped classification. Houses are placed in ranked classes, tracts of land are divided into ordered categories, and persons are ascribed to social strata. Central to Ngadha social organization are first of all the categories *sa'o* ("House") and *woé* ("House coalition network") into which every Ngadha person is born. Thus every person is referred to as the "child" (*ana*) of such and such House and *woé*.[2] Second is a principle of social stratification. Ngadha are divided into three strata: nobles or aristocrats, commoners, and (former) slaves, between which marriage is strictly regulated.

With respect to Houses and lands the graded classification is most abstractly to do with what one could label seniority, or authority; "an ordering on a gradient of stepped differences from low to high," as Adams (1974: 328) puts it with regard to Sumba intellectual order—or simply "precedence," as E. D. Lewis (1988) has used it. And the primary idiom employed, implicitly or explicitly, in this discourse of gradient order or degrees of precedence is that of "origin." The closer the classified entity (House, land) is to its origin (its conception, inception, source)—of which it is in a sense merely a later version, pale copy, or weak reflection—the grander, loftier, mightier, more important, and more valued it is held to be.—I should stress that the following analysis does not concern this "chain of beings of decreasing dignity" or "taxonomic tree" (Dumont 1980: 239). As just noted such "chains" and "trees" fall outside the purview of hierarchy in the (Dumontian) definition of the term on which this article is premised.

Ngadha Houses are placed in villages, and each *woé* (House coalition network) in a village has placed two conceptually gendered emblems or ritual foci at the center of the village plaza. Known as *ngadhu* and *bhaga*, they can provisionally be described as a "male" sacrificial pole and a "female" ceremonial house respectively—and villagers think of them as being husband and wife.

Ngadha Houses, like houses in a great number of eastern Indonesian societies, are simultaneously dwellings, corporate estates, ancestral abodes, ritual centers, and repositories of heirloom sacra. They are also frequently partners in exchanges of prestations predicated on marriage. In short, Ngadha Houses are—if any such thing exists—prototypical Houses in the Lévi-Straussian (1982) definition of that term (Smedal 2000).

It is precisely in their capacity as partners in marriage that the Houses loom large in the background for the following discussion: It is not that my informants or I ascribe actor status to *buildings* but that Houses (*sa'o*) in Ngadhaland are the principal social unit; they are "jural persons" and the Ngadhaland counterpart to the classic if contested "African lineage" (anyone's sample of relevant works—spanning some fifty years of debate and rethinking—would include minimally Evans-Pritchard 1940; Fortes 1953; Barnes 1962; Keesing 1970; Holy 1979; Verdon 1982; Southall 1986; and Kuper 1988).

The former differ from the latter in two important respects: There is in Ngadhaland neither a principle nor an ideology of unilineal descent, and House-endogamous marriages are not frowned upon.[3] For reasons of space I must leave out the ethnographic evidence on which these two claims rest and turn immediately to the implications they have for matrimonial exchanges: If two affiliates ("children"/"members") of one and the same

House decide to marry, the question of bridewealth may be laid to rest immediately. But when the prospective marriage partners belong to separate Houses, then the bridewealth issue is raised as a matter of routine.

I must ask that yet a third claim be accepted—one that is likely to surprise anyone familiar with studies on social organization in eastern Indonesia, namely that the distinction between wife givers and wife takers are meaningless to the Ngadha (Smedal 2002). But despite the absence in Ngadha matrimonial discourse of this set of complementary categories, the bride's group (House) expect and are entitled to receive certain culturally prescribed prestations from the groom's group (House)—the bridewealth— and *vice versa*. More accurately, what bridewealth negotiations concern is the size or value and nature of (especially the initial) transfer(s). And in Ngadhaland, these transfers consist of a—locally determined—number of horses and water buffaloes. In one region (Wéré) there is a long-standing tradition to exchange some twenty animals in return for a few pieces of fine cloth and certain other valuables (such return gifts being vastly more lavish elsewhere in Flores). In other regions (Jérébu'u, for example, where the major part of my own fieldwork took place), the requisite number of animals is minimally two, maximally three per set (one set for the bride's mother's House, the other for her father's House)—depending on whether the groom is a local member or belongs to a more distant village. The counter prestations consist of a medium-sized pig and large scale feasting only. Not surprisingly, in the former region postmarital residence is virilocal, in the latter uxorilocal.[4]

The relevant parameters when determining the value of animals are their size, sex, health, general excellence, and above all—in the case of buffaloes—the length of their horns; an index of their age and, by implication, the labor invested in them (all livestock need tending).[5] And the value thus assigned determines into which of the named categories any particular animal may be placed.

One indication of the importance of marriage transactions in Ngadhaland is the existence of bridewealth specialists. These are men who keep tabs on pledges, payments made, and payments deferred, and who know precisely how former transactions took place; who recall in what order payments were made and to what degree the quality of the animals then transferred deviated from the ideal (if a buffalo's nose was torn, for example); who remember if certain animals presented were rejected but perhaps never replaced, and who can recount how social contexts and skilful negotiations might have altered the paradigmatic norm of bridewealth proceedings—who have committed to memory detailed data on the past composition of the relevant social units (especially genealogies, including the results of polygynous unions). Such knowledge is highly valued because claims on specific items of bridewealth cannot be exposed as illegitimate unless the histories of past transactions are known in detail. This is all the more necessary in communities, such as Ngadha ones, where women (in Wéré) and men (elsewhere) do not circulate in any prescribed (or even "preferred") manner but may marry along "new pathways" all the time; where marriage may be House endogamous in one case and woé or even village exogamous in the next. The role of a bridewealth specialist can therefore be likened to that of a corporate accountant without whose expertise the financial situation of the corporation would become chaotic—this holds especially for Wéré, where the sheer number of bridewealth categories transacted over many years ensure complex exchange conditions in constant flux. It is perhaps all the more remarkable that all this information is memorized by men who do not know how to read and write.[6]

As is the case in marriage transactions in other parts of Flores, and further afield as well, traditional items in Ngadha marriage prestations are sometimes substituted for with money. But asking when a money substitute is acceptable to the bride's group, and when it is not, revealed that, for bridewealth items nominally designated "horse," its equivalent in money is easily accepted. When the item is designated "water buffalo," however, recipients insist that what must be presented is a buffalo in the flesh. Hence my topic: what I wish to explore is the value content of Ngadha marriage prestations.[7]

Marriage Payments and Spheres

In his Introduction to The Meaning of Marriage Payments, John L. Comaroff asks, "is it valid to reduce [marriage payments] to a single analytical class?" (1980: 2). After having considered contributions from the structural-functionalist, Marxist, and structuralist camps, his answer is largely negative. Inspired partly by the subversive epistemological critique by Leach, Needham, and Rivière—referring to Needham's (1975) important notion of polythetic classification—Comaroff still wishes to consider "how a comparative discourse on the meaning of marriage payments may be constituted without either creating a conceptual artifice or dissolving the category entirely" (1980: 3).

One outcome of Comaroff's discussion is that "marriage is merely an element in an encompassing exchange system and, therefore, is a moment (or cycle) within the embracing and interrelated processes indicated by that system" (1980: 30). On this view, marriage payments cannot be singled out for separate analytical treatment since the social units between which marriage payments flow would also be exchange partners—often allies—in a host of other contexts. If so, the question "What do marriage payments mean?" can only be answered by comparing whole societies: by way of a Maussian "total" analysis—anything less would amount to a decontextualized analysis. But this of course raises a whole new set of problems. If the decontextualized, label-prone, scientistic strategies of the structural functionalists went a long way down the positivist track, the "total" analyst clearly stands in danger of drowning under the truly immense amount of empirical data that would have to be amassed for the purpose of providing the full, relevant context.

Opting here, pragmatically, for a solution that allows for an analysis of "marriage payments" separate from other exchange forms, but noting how the items are embedded in encompassing social and cosmological notions, I hope to show that far from just being "payments" in the narrow, pecuniary sense—with obvious economic and sociological effects—marriage prestations are also, and more importantly, vital in the attempt to secure the continued existence of the social units that engage in them.

Since the analysis I offer bears some resemblance to that of the Tiv economy by Bohannan (1959), it might be helpful if I indicate briefly how the two cases differ. Bohannan, it will be remembered, was interested in the effects of the introduction of general-purpose money into a traditional economy with various media of exchange. Certain sets of goods were exchanged (routinely) only for certain other sets of goods, and the "spheres," as Bohannan termed these circumscribed activities (of which he identified three) *within* which goods were "conveyed," were insulated (but imperfectly so) from each other in ways that "conversion" *between* them was made difficult and risky—by moral injunctions. The present-day rural economy of the Ngadha, in contrast, is fully integrated in the world economy. The Ngadha are peasants (Chayanov 1919) who produce much for their own subsistence—rarely engaging in wage labor (exceptions include teachers and those who have temporarily or semipermanently migrated out)—but who grow cash crops as well, and who have been handling (colonial and postcolonial) currencies for generations.

But even if theirs is no "sphere economy" proper, on a number of occasions when goods are exchanged, it is precisely goods not cash that Ngadha require. More often than not these occasions are ritual: occasions when kin (sometimes joined by affines and allies) rally to celebrate House or *woé* affairs. In their already classic Introduction to *Money and the Morality of Exchange* (1989), Bloch and Parry accentuate the vast difference between "a cycle of short-term exchange which is the legitimate domain of individual—often acquisitive—activity, and a cycle of long-term exchange concerned with the reproduction of the social and cosmic order" (Bloch and Parry 1989: 2). While there is neither space nor need to provide comprehensive evidence of the former—the crucial, socially integrative potentials of which Piot (1991) subsequently explored—I wish to demonstrate the existence and nature of the latter. The point here is the very simple one that when Ngadha men and women require certain items (as opposed to their monetary equivalent) to be presented, it is a safe indication not only that the occasion is a ritual one but that it speaks directly to cardinal, social principles deriving from a pre–Christian cosmology.

With these remarks I turn to an examination of animal value appraisal in Ngadhaland.

Animal Values

The value of a horse correlates directly with its size, health, and strength—in other words with qualities expressing its use value in practical terms. Donors relinquish a coveted beast of burden (horses loaded with produce led to and from markets are a frequent sight along the steep paths in Ngadhaland) and a highly useful means of transportation in a mountainous terrain with few vehicular roads. Those who own no horse often rent one, if they can afford it, when they wish to bring cash crops to buyers at the coast or in town. Men assess the qualities of horses owned by friends and relatives, sometimes ponder buying one of them, and discuss which one they would choose were money no object.

In contrast, the value of the buffalo seems considerably less to do with its practical use value. Where irrigation rice is a major crop, the buffalo is of course important, if not indispensable, for ploughing and softening the soil. But very little wet rice is grown in Ngadhaland, in many villages none at all.[8] Because in the early 1990s the State launched a massive campaign for the planting of crop-producing trees (partly in an effort to limit erosion), and because there are large scale irrigation schemes under way elsewhere on central Flores (for example, in the Mbai region to the northeast), which the authorities encourage people from regions disadvantaged in terms of soil or climate to join (this is known as "internal transmigration"), the areas under irrigation are not likely to increase in the immediate future. However, where a buffalo is used in agriculture it is crucial, and the animal is frequently leased, on a short-term basis, to others who need one but possess none. It is hardly ever exchanged for cash. Furthermore, buffaloes and horses both require grazing grounds, and over the last decades, pasture has become scarce. This is partly due to demographic growth whereby agriculture has literally supplanted animal husbandry. But because the population to land ratio varies greatly from one village domain to the next, this explanation does not apply overall. The hand of the authorities can be seen in this, too, in that another State policy is to discourage, and curtail as far as possible, the "pointless extravagance" of former livestock carnage. While the policy has had no direct bearing on bridewealth transactions, since they involve live rather than dead buffalo, it has contributed to a decreased interest in livestock production generally, and in buffalo rearing particularly, which is now nostalgically associated with the past. One practical measure the State has taken, apart from admonishing villagers through its various nation-building institutions to invest in cash crop plants and trees rather than in livestock, is to introduce a levy on slaughtering. All domestic animals except fowl, cats, and dogs are registered by village level officials, and a levy must be paid for each animal (sheep, goat, pig, horse, and buffalo) slaughtered. While the levy may seem small compared with the market value of a buffalo, it is quite considerable to people who are primarily engaged in subsistence production and whose cash flow is modest—in any case the levy comes on top of the theoretical "loss" of slaughtering the animal instead of selling it, or transferring it in the form of bridewealth.[9] These are the principal reasons why buffalo herds proper are no longer seen.[10] They also explain why the large scale buffalo killings reported as integral to certain Ngadha rituals (cf. Daeng 1988 for a published account of one) are events of the past: older informants willingly related to me how in the 1930s and 40s large scale buffalo carnage was integral to any major village ritual and feast of merit.[11]

But other grounds can be adduced also. Herds of buffalo could once roam relatively freely over what was then largely underpopulated grassland—as they still do in the low, deforested hills in northern central Flores between So'a and Riung—with occasional commotion and subsequent litigation when stray animals demolished crops. But the few persisting beasts must now be individually tethered and moved twice a day within the confines of the meadows remaining here and there between cultivated fields, and guarded much more closely. Perhaps more importantly, in the dry season the buffaloes need to spend considerable time in water, or at least splash about in wet mud, lest they overheat. And while in the past young sons and nephews of livestock owners (and also, I speculate, slaves) shepherded the herds and led the buffaloes to streams or mud pools (poma) and hand-fed them salt to subdue them, boys are nowadays at school until mid afternoon (and former slaves, now cultivating their own leased plots, are no longer dependants in the old sense). Hence it would fall largely upon the owners of the animals themselves to tether and tend to them—often on pastures far from their agricultural fields—and this, according to my Ngadha friends, is nothing to cherish.

These, I think, are the factors that have combined to effect an increase in the monetary value of buffaloes in Ngadhaland over the last decades. Since the animals, as just noted, have become so scarce that they are hardly ever put up for sale any more, an owner is unlikely to part with his buffalo unless the bidder is prepared to offer a high price, and the owner is desperate for cash. This is well known by potential buyers, who, when they require an animal, roam the parts of the sparsely populated savannah tracts of central Flores beyond Ngadhaland—sometimes for days on end—where the buffalo is still a common sight.

Animal Death

The occasions when a buffalo in the flesh, rather than its monetary equivalent, needs to be procured and presented include: on the one hand, those where sacrifice is essential to the event—when a village is relocated, when a *ngadhu* and/or *bhaga* is erected, moved, or repaired, when a House is rebuilt, when (in the past) feasts of merit were celebrated, when mortuary ceremonies are conducted, and when instances of "bad death" are rectified (Smedal 1996; Schröter 1998), none of which can be discussed here;[12] and on the other, those where certain human relationships of great significance are positively or negatively sanctioned, such as when specific transgressions (often sexual ones) and murders are compensated, and when marriages are contracted or dissolved. Importantly, Ngadha never subject the horse to ritual killing; this is done only to fowls, pigs, and buffaloes, all of which must, on these occasions, be consecrated (*maté*) before they are killed in the variously prescribed manners befitting a consecrated animal:[13] A fowl is killed by way of a knife forced between the two halves of its beak, thereby splitting its head horizontally (*kajé*). The pig is killed by splitting its head lengthwise and "vertically" (*wela*). The buffalo, after its ringed nose has been pulled upwards with the help of a rope, is killed by slashing its throat in an upwards movement, an action referred to as *wéla*, or *toa*.[14] The standard bush knife is the instrument in all three cases (although formerly buffaloes may have been *wéla* with a sword).

The buffalo, however, is exceptional. It cannot be consecrated directly. A chicken must be consecrated on its behalf. This usually very young chicken is, in all cases I know of but one, referred to as the "buffalo chicken" (*kaba manu*). A section of a palm leaf rib is inserted through its nostrils, so that in at least one aspect it will remotely resemble a buffalo (the palm leaf rib being referred to as the chick's "horns"), and before being ritually killed, the chicken is tied to a stick inserted in the House hearth (see Smedal 1996: 47). The stick explicitly represents the *ngadhu*, the "male" ancestral sacrificial pole at which buffaloes are killed. Of the three species it is possible to consecrate for ritual killing, only the buffalo must die at the *ngadhu*—the sole place where it can be ritually killed.[15] And while one is strictly obliged to offer a small portion of the meat cooked from ritually killed animals to the ancestors *(kuwi)*, buffalo meat constitutes an exception, in that—and this imperative holds for the buffalo only—the sacrificer should place a small cut of the beast's uncooked liver under his shirt, offering the ancestors a cooked "buffalo chicken" morsel instead.

But it is not only the ritual killing of a buffalo that is referred to as *wéla*. The common term for killing someone (say, an enemy) is also *wéla*. There is no reason to believe that this is a case of homonymy. Ngadha men, when recounting to me episodes of rage, have sometimes clenched their teeth, said the equivalent of "I could have killed him!"; "grabbed" an imaginary bush knife and "slashed" it upwards into thin air in a movement mimicking the one made when a buffalo's throat is slit. Arndt in fact mentions the "two" senses of the word one after the other (Arndt 1961: 566). So we must rather conclude that buffaloes and men are killed in essentially identical fashion.

It is now possible to approach the question of what makes a buffalo especially valuable. Clearly both horses and buffaloes, when transferred as part of bridewealth, represent use value. Certainly both animals endow its owner with a measure of prestige also—perhaps even more so now when they are far more rare than in the golden past, and when money may be converted to several novel commodities (education, agricultural machinery—such as petrol driven Honda coconut graters—and motorized vehicles are three). But the buffalo seems to embody something more. I think the bottom line of this "surplus" lies in a notion that the buffalo is, to put a word on it, a noble being.

Buffaloes and Men and Women

It is necessary therefore to turn for a moment to the inception of the two ranks "noble" and "commoner."[16] They originate, according to a number of versions of a commonly known myth, in the incestuous relationship between a brother and a sister (unbeknownst to them, according to some versions), both noble, although properly speaking there were no distinctions of rank at this time (Arndt 1954: 321–25; 1955: 273–74; 1960a: 42), nobility being, as it were, the natural state. It was the brother who belatedly discovered that they were siblings and pronounced his own and his sister's punishment: The two of them were to go separate ways and never see each other again lest, according to at least one version, the Earth perish in drought. Upon this they became stars, yet kept their earthly names, and the myth therefore at one level explains why the Antares, *Wawi Toro* or *Dala Wawi* (the brother) and the Pleiades, (*Dala*) *Ko* (the sister) are never seen simultaneously.[17] In taking it upon himself to draw the consequences, the male remained noble, while the female, irrevocably disgraced, became a commoner. A close reading of the versions of the myth Arndt presents (1954: 321ff.) reveals also that in some instances the sister-wife has known all along that she is her husband's sister; or else that, when he is shocked by the realization that they are siblings and asks her what to do, she replies, "Nothing." The general idea, given narrative form in these myths, appears, therefore, to be that the woman, rather than the man, is responsible for sexual transgressions (*Ko* having trapped *Wawi*).[18] At any rate, sexual relations, and by extension marriage, between noble women and commoner men were then prohibited and have remained so ever since. Even today, as has been detailed elsewhere (Smedal *In press*), it is only the women who, on account of sexual liaisons with men of lower rank, can fall from grace, be banished, become a person of lower rank, and henceforth give birth only to persons of lower rank.[19]

The three Ngadha ranks (nobles, commoners, and [former] slaves) are distinguished from each other along several dimensions, one of which is the alleged color of their blood, the life fluid *par excellence*. The nobles have black, the commoners yellow, and the (former) slaves white blood; noble blood is also hot (Arndt 1954: 328, 336). Significantly, of all animals only the buffalo has "black" (*mité*) blood. Furthermore, nobility is also ascribed to the sun, the blood of which is hot, too (Arndt 1960a: 49). The most commonly expressed motivation for ritual killing I encountered was that certain objects periodically need to be "moistened" or "daubed" (*basa*) with the blood of an animal. And the preeminent blood—the black and, it may be inferred, hot and noble blood—is that of the most highly valued animal, the buffalo.

Moreover, while a great number of objects can be daubed with blood from sacrificed chickens and pigs, the *ngadhu* (the "male" sacrificial pillar) should be moistened with buffalo blood only. It should be noted, however, that buffalo blood may be sprinkled on other objects as well, first and foremost the "female" *bhaga* facing the *ngadhu* in the village plaza. The *ngadhu*, the unifying symbol of the *woé* in its male aspect—its "king" (*raja woé*)—and the *bhaga*, its female complement, are, say Ngadha, husband and wife. Together they signify the *woé*, the entire House coalition network. But in rituals that feature sacrifice only the buffalo is killed at the *ngadhu*, which also emanates heat—it is "hot and must remain hot" (Arndt 1958: 111) and in this sense alive—while fowl and pig are killed at the *bhaga* or at the House.

Buffalo blood constitutes the *ngadhu*'s proper food, but it is only offered this on the rare occasions when a buffalo is ritually killed in front of it. So for it, or more aptly, he,[20] to stay content, three live animals are buried under the *ngadhu* when it is put in place. A red dog, a red fowl, and, most notably, a red boar, are inserted into small holes dug next to the *ngadhu*'s three roots. This, then, is what the *ngadhu* feeds on in the long intervals between buffalo sacrifice. The red boar is especially significant for the simple reason that "red boar" = *wawi toro*, and I think it is warranted to suggest that these two "red boars" are ultimately one and the same—simultaneously mythical, forever in the firmament, *and* physical, forever at the roots of the *woé*'s paramount symbolic expression of its male principle. The "red boar" is the husband-brother who caught his sister at being his wife, and who took such honorable action as befits nobles by sentencing both of them to eternal separation and her to be demoted—from her status as *ga'é mézé*, "noble," to that of *ga'é kisa*, "commoner"—and by instituting the interrank sexual prohibition. The "red boar" also feeds the *woé*'s cardinal noble, the *ngadhu*. *Wawi Toro* is in the sky, *wawi toro* in the ground.

Let me summarize so far. Buffaloes have black blood, as do noble persons. The sun is of noble rank also, and its blood is hot. Only the buffalo can be killed at a *ngadhu*, and buffaloes and humans are killed by being *wéla*. Once a *ngadhu* has been erected in the village plaza, only buffalo blood can nourish it/him. This is how "he," the personified male progenitor and ultimate ancestor, remains active. The noble *ngadhu* feeds on the noble blood of the buffalo and, when none such is forthcoming, on the perpetually interred "red boar" under it. This interred boar (*wawi toro*) is the mundane world replica of the brother-turned-husband-turned-star *Wawi Toro*, the noble originator of the incest prohibition and himself the maker of the very distinction noble versus commoner.

The separation of the brother-husband and sister-wife and the subsequent distinction between nobles and commoners are possibly mythical elaborations succeeding an earlier representation of the origin of social classification. Arndt notes that a lunar eclipse is understood as a case of the moon, a "female" commoner, not moving out of the way—as commoners should—of the male, noble sun. This results in a temporary obliteration of the erring cold moon (*wula la'a sala; la'a sala* significantly also being the term for incest and interrank sexual offence) by the superior hot sun (Arndt 1929: 841–42; cf. Bader 1953: 96, n17). Whichever of the two versions one wishes to draw on, it would seem that virtue in these representations indisputably inheres in the hot male, while vice is a quality of the cool female.[21]

To say that the buffalo is "noble," however, is to beg the question of how nobility is construed. It is only possible to offer an answer to this by examining more closely the nature of the buffalo, intrinsically connected in Ngadha exegesis, to how the creator, *Déwa* and *déwa*—the deities, the creator's "subordinates"—are conceived.

Buffaloes and the Divine

I must rely here on Arndt and his sources. The success of Catholic missionaries and priests in modifying Ngadha thought over the last 70 years or so is perhaps most conspicuous with respect to *Déwa*, the creator (nowadays often glossed as *Tuhan*—the Indonesian word for God), and *Nitu*, the "Earth Mother," *Déwa*'s "feminine," subterranean complementary counterpart (nowadays usually glossed *Setan*—the Indonesian word for Satan). To elicit even the eldest people's associations in the 1990s at the level of reflection I am concerned with here meets with inevitable resistance on their part; connections enacted in ritual blatantly do not match what they have been instructed to believe. Aware of how amenable such hoisting into the present of statements of the past is to criticism, I nevertheless see no way around it in this case. So, then, according to one of Arndt's sources: "*Déwa* protects and cares for us, as we protect and care for a buffalo. If *Déwa* is angry with us humans, then he will kill us, exactly as we humans kill a buffalo" (Arndt 1929: 818). Another put it thus: "They [the *déwa*] celebrate their feasts and then slaughter their buffaloes; then also many humans die here on earth" (Arndt 1929: 818).[22]

It is beyond doubt, I think, that such statements attest to the profound relationships seen to exist between *Déwa* (or the *déwa*—Arndt admits the difference is not always evident; see also Molnar [1990: 121ff.] on this problem), humans, and the buffalo. From them one would also think it clear that the relationships are conceived of as analogous and hierarchical (or asymmetrical):

Déwa/déwa : humans :: humans : buffaloes

But the matter is more complicated. A third person Arndt consulted told him: "One also says that the buffalo is the *Déwa*'s soul. When humans here on earth slaughter a buffalo, *Déwa* avenges himself and fetches the soul of a human, so that [this human] dies" (Arndt 1929: 820).

From this it would appear that at one level the buffalo represents the very essence of the deity.[23] At another, the very essence of humans: "Only the buffalo has a soul resembling the human soul" (Arndt 1929: 841); sometimes a human's soul invades a buffalo and unless it is given a fright so it returns to its own body the human will die when the buffalo is slaughtered

(Arndt 1929: 836). Elsewhere Arndt informs us that a particularly old buffalo whose horns are yellow-tipped with age, a so-called "trunk male beast" (*mosa pu'u*) can easily transform itself into a human being (1963: 68), that the practice of throwing a mouthful of masticated coconut into the buffalo's pool ensures it does not so transform itself, that the buffalo is sometimes given small offerings and thus considered a deity (*déwa*), and that wives are admonished never to let anyone into the house lest a buffalo in the shape of its owner enter, deceive them, and overpower them (Arndt 1963: 70).[24]

To this must be added the idea, still prevalent among Ngadha, that very old persons, women as well as men, may grow tails that resemble buffaloes' tails. These are never seen; the antediluvians themselves would take great care to conceal them beneath their clothing when others are present. But adults know they exist (and that they are of practical use to their owners who sweep the floor slats with them) and counsel children to treat the ancients with the respect they are due. Together, the evidence suggests that deities, humans, and buffaloes have identities that, at least in part, merge.[25]

Or, perhaps more precisely, they suggest how under certain conditions buffaloes and humans assume the shape of the other. The most important condition for such transformation seems to be that of advanced age. Old buffaloes can become men, and old humans can grow tails. And only after having grown old is it possible for men and women to become one of the ancestors, themselves immeasurably old—and to sit in the nooks and crannies of the sharply ascending thatch ceiling after having been formally invited to a ritual by one's descendants, enjoying their joy and partaking of their food and palm gin.[26]

In some contexts the buffalo, rather than transgressively assuming the shape of humans reestablishes a part of their humanity—especially as far as nobles are concerned. I have already noted how rigorous are the behavioral rules applying to nobles (see note 19). One instance often quoted to me concerns the noble who, while walking across the village plaza, slips and falls into the mud. This is just the sort of thing a noble must not do and, worse, the fall is probably observed by all who happen to sit on their verandas. Now, according to Ngadha, a buffalo, insofar as it ever makes a sound, utters a nasal *hoa*.[27] What the (presumably noble) mirthful onlookers say when they see the noble falling into the mud is precisely that, "*hoa*." Or they just raise their chins, baring their throats as a buffalo is made to do at sacrifice. What everyone understands is that unless the noble immediately fetches a buffalo and kills it he is no longer considered noble.[28] It is a moot point if in such cases nobility is restored *ipso facto* through the act of sacrifice (as an intrinsically honorable act), or if it is the intangible aspect of the spilt black "life essence" of the buffalo that itself revitalizes the imperiled noble status by migrating, as it were, from the dying buffalo to the hapless human, reestablishing his superior humanity—much as the soul of humans can sometimes invade a buffalo.

I should like to adduce one last fact, and explore its implications, before concluding the analysis. Ngadha, who frequently perform various forms of augury, never examine the livers of buffaloes. One can only examine livers or entrails of consecrated animals, and only pig and fowl are consecrated. I noted above that a young chicken is consecrated in the buffalo's stead. What does this signify? I submit that, given ritual expression here is the notion that the buffalo is too exalted to be directly inspected. It is well known that in societies where the viscera of sacrificed animals are scrutinized in order to ascertain if the recipients (deities, ancestors) accept the offering, and where humans are also sacrificed, it is assumed a priori that the latter gift, on account of its sublime nature, will be accepted, and that no inspection is required. In Ngadha rituals the buffalo occupies this distinguished place of the ultimate "gift." After all, pig and fowl are slaughtered as well as ritually killed; the buffalo (if we disregard the recent possibility of collective slaughter noted above) can be killed only in ritual. Or, to put it the other way round, whenever a buffalo is killed the context is a ritual one. By definition, it seems, the buffalo is a sacrificial animal, and its essence is arguably on a par with the essence of the deity.

Support for this interpretation can be found in Andrea Molnar's unpublished thesis on the Austronesian spirit category *nitu*, where the two last chapters are devoted to a comprehensive analysis of the dual Ngadha concept *Nitu/Déwa* and its multiple expressions. On the relationship between the buffalo and the deity she writes:

> the blood of the sacrificial animal should be understood as something that is conducive to fertility, for it is in the form of the sacrificial blood of the buffalo that fertility and generative power are returned to the earth (see Forth 1989). Since the *déwa* can be regarded as an aspect of *Déwa*, the Creator, one may surmise that the blood of the water buffalo is equated with the essence of *déwa*, and thus with *Déwa*'s fertilizing potential, his semen. Hence, the sacrifice of a buffalo might be regarded as a recreation of the primeval union between *Déwa*, the Creator, and *Nitu*, the Earth Mother (Molnar 1990: 130, spelling modified, reference updated).

The idea here is that the divinely male substance "buffalo blood" saturates the divinely female medium "soil" and transmits onto or into it a generative potential. This is a tantalizing thought, and while I do not wish to distance myself from the notion outright, I think it invites one comment. While *Nitu* is undoubtedly "of the earth," it is not similarly evident how she can be seen as a deity of the village. The buffalo, as I have noted repeatedly, is not ritually killed anywhere but in the center of the village plaza, at the *ngadhu*.[29] The notion that the killed buffalo constitutes the mediating link between the *Nitu* and *Déwa* is problematical because it immediately raises the question of the nature of the simultaneous conjoining and separation of the *Nitu/Déwa*. On the one hand these are invoked together, as are *iné* and *ema* ("mother-father"), to signify the, to put it rather crudely, dual-gendered Divinity. But, on the other hand, they do in fact also exist *qua* opposites. What we need to know are the contexts when *Nitu* and *Déwa* are addressed together, and when they are invoked separately. It appears that *Nitu*, on her own, is envisaged as close, the Earth Spirit, the source of crop fecundity, the supplier of game, and a nurturer, while *Déwa*, on his own, is remote, the Sky Spirit, the Creator, the Final Judge. Also, in Molnar's explicitly Dumont-inspired analysis (see Dumont 1980), *Déwa* ultimately encompasses his female complement so that (simplified)

$$Déwa = [Nitu = (Nitu + nitu) + Déwa = (Déwa + déwa)]$$

(Molnar 1990: 131–36, esp. 134). The notion that *Nitu* (or *nitu*) is an earth-related deity has been confirmed by fieldwork; *Nitu* is explicitly addressed in invocations of agricultural rituals (again I must leave out the evidence) and, less explicitly, is alluded to throughout the ritual actions themselves. *Déwa* is rarely referred to in invocations except in the dual manner (*Nitu-Déwa* or, more commonly, *iné-ema* "mother-father"), when the signified is less obvious anyway since the expression often refers to the category "ancestors." *Déwa* (or its compound form *Nitu/Déwa*) is not mentioned in any of the agricultural invocations I recorded. And I registered neither invocatory mention of *Nitu* nor allusions to her in village contexts; when I questioned ritual specialists on the matter they confirmed that *Nitu* is absent from village rituals. Of course, if what Molnar's suggestion amounts to is that the buffalo's blood is offered to the soil in its capacity as "encompassed" *Nitu*, that is, as *Déwa = (Nitu + Déwa)*, there is little to question. That, if in other terms, is akin to the point I have tried to establish.[30]

It is, however, possible to advance another interpretation of the postulated relationship between buffalo blood, soil, (male) fecundity, and the *ngadhu*—one that does not require the problematic (in village contexts) introduction of the *Nitu*. To begin with, the phallic character of the *ngadhu* is indisputable.[31] When, after dark, it is erected in the village soil by the men, the women are obliged to stay inside. They remain behind bolted doors for the many hours it takes to get the huge pole inserted into its deep hole (of its estimated length of four and a half meters only the upper three are visible). All the while the interred women incessantly keep beating the floorboards with split-bamboo brushes (*regha*) to keep the *ngadhu* from entering the House and themselves; the *ngadhu*'s rampant sexuality is not curtailed until the pole's roots are firmly in the ground (see Arndt 1931: 361–62 for a legend "explaining" this practice). Now when the buffalo relinquishes its life, it does so at the *ngadhu*. It must die at the hands of a man, but in a characteristically double stage which distinguishes the sacrifier from the sacrificer: First, the House leader (a "brother" *[nara]* or a matrilateral "uncle" *[pamé]* of the nominal female master of the House, the *mori sa'o*) takes the House's sacred sword (*sau*) and strokes it lightly across the buffalo's throat (a practice known as *noza*). Then, taking shelter in the House (nowadays bringing the *sau* with him inside), he delegates the task of actually killing the buffalo (with a regular bush knife) to someone else, often a son or a son of one of his (classificatory) sisters (*weta*). But in principle, I was told, anyone except the House leader may do this.

The blood gushing out from the animal's severed carotid artery the first seconds after the fatal blow has been delivered is soaked up by the earth at the *ngadhu*'s base. What this observation suggests is that, insofar as blood, soil, and *ngadhu* connect meaningfully at this moment, there is a direct transmittance of the generative potential of the blood to the *ngadhu*'s roots. The earth of the village, in this interpretation, plays no other role than to let the blood filter through it, essentially a role of passive mediation. Village grounds, notably, are routinely kept meticulously free from any sort of vegetation; what a visitor on a Ngadha House veranda looks out on is a (frequently terraced) bare, sandy square. Nothing suggests "natural," vegetal growth (*Nitu*'s province); everything suggests human, social investment. At any rate, most of the blood is immediately collected by young boys who come rushing to the animal as soon as the men responsible for killing it deem it safe for them to do so: the erratic movements of a half-ton struggling buffalo represent considerable danger. The boys bring plaited trays and bamboo containers kept ready for this purpose, and as the vessels are filled they are stored until the actual butchering of the meat is finished and the cooking begins. Then the blood, too, is put to good use. As noted, some of the blood inevitably spills onto the ground. But the fundamental fact of the matter remains: the only deliberate use of the buffalo's blood—apart from in cooking—is that men of the *woé* smear it on objects, first of all the *ngadhu*, then the *bhaga*, and finally the hearth pillar of the *woé* Houses.

Conclusion . . .

I proposed at the outset that the Ngadha practices under discussion uphold a "double vision" whereby a hierarchical opposition is maintained. What is the nature of the value transacted in marriage prestations? On the one hand, of course, is (State) money—or rather money sometimes substituting for horses. On the other hand, there is the buffalo, never to be substituted by any other valuable. Why? Let me sum up.

The buffalo supplies the *ngadhu* with its/his most exalted sustenance: in the tangible form of blood the buffalo gives life to it (or him). Simultaneously the *ngadhu*—together with his wife, the *bhaga*—protects the village and its inhabitants, and helps ensure that crops, animals, and humans stay healthy and multiply. This, then, is a proper exchange: life in one form is given for life in another in return. At one level the exchange is symmetrical in that the partners in it are nominally equal; both are "noble." But whereas the buffalo must die for this exchange to have any effect, the *ngadhu* lives—as does, by extension, every entity which by definition projects from it: the *woé* in its various forms of concreteness, the Houses, in short: people. The temporally and spatially specifiable termination of one life secures perpetual existence of succeeding generations.

As an item of bridewealth the animal "works" in essentially identical fashion. Horses, transferred in great quantity in some regions (especially in Wéré), represent practical, material, and prestigious wealth but cannot do what buffaloes do. As noted above, even in regions where the total value of bridewealth items is relatively low (for example in Jérébu'u), one live buffalo, as a minimum, is still integral to the transfers. Thus, when a buffalo of a certain category (size/age/excellence) is required, but proves unprocurable, recipients will insist that while a portion of the monetary value of the requested buffalo may be presented in cash, a tangible if substandard (smaller/younger) animal must be presented in the flesh. The coming together of two Houses through the marriage of their affiliates is a union of chains of life; it is a social act crucially constitutive for the long-term maintenance of a cosmologically inspired social order (Bloch and Parry 1989). For this fusion to be legitimate and thereby recognized, it is not sufficient simply to present a sum of money. Rather, a live buffalo—the noble giver of life, impressively and indexically (Hornborg 1999), in a striking moment of firstness (Peirce), simultaneously encompassing and opposing (Dumont 1980) its own monetary value by its very embodied presence—must accompany it.

. . . and Coda

The above conclusion to the analysis is, I think, safe. The question remains whether it is profound enough; if it is possible to push it further, arriving at a more radical theoretical statement.

Recall the elements. On the one hand, Dumont's proposition, scandalous to moderns: the cognitive implausibility of positing X and Y as—simultaneously—*opposite* ("X : Y") and *identical* ("X encompassing Y") (Dumont 1980, cf. esp. 239–245). On the other hand, Pierce's notions of firstness, secondness, and thirdness. Now, insofar as the buffalo embodies an extensive set of foundational sociocultural and cosmological values, it not so much subsumes its price as transcends it. In other words, its price—its exchange value in cash terms—is but a subordinate aspect of its being. Invoking semiotic firstness to account for the buffalo's overwhelming presence is perhaps sound enough, given its undeniable and prized corporeality. But this same being, I now suggest, is so instantly awe-inspiring precisely because it incorporates and therefore instantiates its own secondness and thirdness as well. With respect to secondness, the buffalo, in bridewealth or in ritual, cannot be apprehended except as an embodiment also of its symbolic properties: the possibly human core and the possibly divine essence it evokes. With respect to thirdness, the intricacies of the mental bookkeeping evidenced by bridewealth specialists evince a capacity to operate "virtual" value equal to, if not surpassing, that which is required to understand credit cards and online banking. During such operations, buffalo values (whether monetary, phenomenological, or transcendental) are present only in their absence. But more than this: in its capacity to absorb and contain such multiple and many-levelled sociality as described above, the buffalo is also a repository of thirdness precisely in the way Peirce defined it (here I use a slightly different formulation than the one Hornborg [1999] referred to): "that which is such as it is, in bringing a second and third into relation to each other" (Peirce 1958: §328)—in other words: an object the essential characteristic of which is the social imaginary in its fullness.

Now, since the buffalo is deemed worthy of providing sustenance for the noble *ngadhu*, it would seem that the buffalo also provides a solution to the Dumontian scandal, one that even occidentals may accept. For it is possible now to sum up yet again the crucial points, with a slightly different emphasis:

The buffalo's singular position rests on its combination of animal, human, and divine aspects, and it is in this combinatorial capacity that it—and it alone—is allowed to feed the *ngadhu*. It is the blood from the dying buffalo that regenerates the *ngadhu*, and it is the energy embodied in—even radiating from—the *ngadhu* that in turn animates the entire social unit (the *woé*) for which he/it stands *qua* ultimate ancestor and unifying emblem, an emblem laboriously carved and erected by the *woé*'s ritual specialists—and celebrated by all its affiliates—during the grandest of all Ngadha rituals. Thus in the final analysis the essence of each glorious, perished buffalo fuses with the *ngadhu*, which in turn is encompassed by the human social totality it is designed to reproduce. In this perspective, any lingering bina-rism, as in Dumont's formulation of hierarchy as the encompassment of the opposite, is simply dissolved. For in this perspective, the separate exalted entities merge and in combination constitute the whole.

Notes

1. The first version of this chapter was presented as a paper at the Workshop on Human-Animal Relations organized by Center for Development and the Environment, the Department of Social Anthropology and the Department of Cultural Studies/Eth-nology, University of Oslo, 4–7 November 1999. Field research (1990–1991, 1993, 1997, 1999, 2000, 2003, 2005) totaling some twenty-five months was facilitated by fellowships and travel stipends from the (then) Norwegian Research Council for Sci-ence and the Humanities; the Institute for Comparative Research in Human Culture, Oslo; the Department of Anthropology, University of Oslo; the Faculty of Social Sci-ence and the Meltzer Fund, University of Bergen; and, most recently, by a Research Council of Norway grant to the MEISA project (Migrants and Entrepreneurs in Insu-lar Southeast Asia). It was conducted under the auspices of The Indonesian Acad-emy of Science (LIPI) and sponsored by Nusa Cendana University, Kupang, Timor, and Palang Karaya University, Central Kalimantan. I wish to thank the bodies just mentioned for their assistance and the numerous Ngadha women and men for their patient discussion of topics that to me were sometimes difficult to grasp. I am also grateful for the critical encouragement offered—some of it years ago—by Maurice Bloch, Adrian Franklin, Janet Hoskins, Bruce Kapferer, Signe Howell, Susan McKin-non, Knut Rio, and most recently by Berghahn Books' anonymous reader. Please note that certain passages in this chapter are virtually identical with passages in a paper I wrote in 1996. As this volume goes to press, I am alerted that the earlier piece is finally being published (Smedal [in press]).
2. Whereas "House" is an accurate translation of the Ngadha *sa'o*, the (provisional) gloss "House coalition network" for *woé* is mine. Arndt offers a long list of meanings of *woé*, of which several have potential relevance here: first of all "sib," "family," "clan," and *Rangstufe* (i.e., "level of social stratification" or "place in hierarchy"); but also "friend" (gender neutral), "troupe," "gathering," "people"; "to embrace," "to bind," "to draw in," "to tie together" (1954: 204; 1961: 579). Realizing that "House coalition network" hardly evokes the semantic range—nor of course the poetic potential—of the Ngadha term, I still search for a more apposite English gloss.
3. Other ethnographers (Arndt 1954; Bader 1953)—even recent ones (Molnar 2000: 89–114 and *passim*, Schröter 1998: 421, 428; 2000: 465; 2005: 322)—translate *woé* as "clan," or with other terms that misleadingly evoke "descent" as the sole principle for recruitment; Schröter even perpetuating the erroneous notion that the majority of Ngadha are organized in "matrilineal descent groups" or "lineages," when it has long been clear that they have "a cognatic system of social classification," and that House and *woé* "membership is determined solely by the system of marriage prestations" (Barnes 1980: 110, 112)—not by any principle or ideology of "descent." (See Smedal

2002 for further elaborations and Barnes [2006: 338] who responds to this and other misrepresentations on Schröter's part.)

4. To say that the Ngadha "tend to marry without bridewealth" (Molnar 2000: 62) or that "by and large" Ngadha marriages "are contracted without bridewealth" (ibid.: 116 n3) is therefore to distort the facts. Even when House succession regularly follows female links (see Smedal 2002 for details), bridewealth passes to the bride's kin (her father's House and her mother's House) as a matter of course. There are three exceptions to this general observation: (1) If the would-be recipient of bridewealth is a member of the groom's own House, no bridewealth will be transferred to that House. (2) "Sister exchange": people recognize that givers and receivers in this case receive and give identical items at the same time—they refer to this as *papa géu* ("to exchange," "to swap"), a more archaic expression being *kili moté* ("to spin the hair bun" [I: *konde*]); practical reason prevails and the question of bridewealth is shelved. (3) Among the (steadily dwindling) nobility, bridewealth requests are often dropped.

5. This point, though with regard to the Sumbanese Kodi, has been comprehensively elaborated by Hoskins (1993a, chapter 7), who also provides a succinct description of the intricacies of comparing the values of individual water buffaloes and pigs. Regrettably, I cannot for reasons of space expand on this issue as it pertains to the Ngadha.

6. Similar feats of mental bookkeeping have been noted by Barnes (1977) and Graham (1991: esp. 163ff.) on Lamaholot communities (Wailolong and neighbouring Léwotala, respectively); and by Dietrich (1998) on Larantuka—all locations in eastern Flores. And Kennedy, in his 1949–1950 field notes (also, it appears, on Wailolong's asymmetric alliance system), wrote that "nowadays, when the tusks have become rare, [people] often merely make the transfer in their heads, talking all night, and never actually transferring the real tusks from one family to another. It is a kind of clearing-house procedure. The tusks may be 'transferred' up to twenty times in their heads, and they balance out in the end. Thus there is no real cost. It is a matter of delayed payment and really works out to a system of woman exchange between families. The tusk transfer is fictional. Thus A will 'pay' tusks to B for a girl, and B will 'pay' these to C for a girl, and C will 'pay' them to A for a girl, and so on. The tusks, however, may even be non-existent in a particular case, and since they balance out in the end, no one really pays" (1955: 47). Such remarks bring to mind the epigraph to Basil Sansom's wonderful analysis of Pedi bridewealth (1976) culled from Mauss's *The Gift*: "Let us suppose a sale where the price is paid in real or imaginary cattle."

7. Hutchinson's incisive analyses of forms of Nuer bridewealth—(various and shifting conceptualizations of) cattle and money (Hutchinson 1992), and later, guns (Hutchinson 2000)—have provided inspiration for the present study, even if, as will become clear, there are few empirical parallels between the Nuer and the Ngadha.

8. Balinese convicts were brought to Ngadhaland in the 1920s in order to instruct locals in irrigated rice cultivation. The convicts remained for several years, but had little success (Arndt 1963: 40–42).

9. The cash value of a buffalo varies greatly, but in 1991 an adult animal seldom fetched less than Rp 300, 000 and only rarely more than Rp 500, 000. At that point the levy was Rp 5000, or between 1.7 percent and 1 percent of the cash value of the animal. (In 1991 USD 1 = Rp 2000.) In 1993 prices of Rp 1,000,000 were no longer uncommon, and I was then told that a large buffalo had been sold for Rp 1,200,000 (the exchange rate, meanwhile, having had risen favorably for the USD by a few per cent only). By January 2000, in the wake of the 1997 Asian financial crisis, a large buffalo would obtain at least Rp 4,000,000, the exchange rate fluctuating between 8,000 and

10,000 Rupiah per USD. By February 2003 the price for a similar buffalo had risen to Rp 5,000,000; by July 2005 to 6,000,000, the exchange rate over the six previous years having remained fairly stable.

10. To which must be added Arndt's observation that the large herds of buffalo the Ngadha owned died out "in the distant past" as a result of a "murderous epidemic" (Arndt 1963: 66).

11. Daeng's account is puzzling. His sources with respect to the Ngadha ritual *boka goé* he seeks to elucidate are (1) one of Arndt's works (1963) and (2) himself as a native Ngadha. But, to begin with, in the work Daeng cites, Arndt never mentions *boka goé* (which would explain why Daeng provides no page references). Elsewhere, however, Arndt describes *boka goé* as one of several forms of ordeal, wager, or verificatory test, a form specifically resorted to with respect to accusations of theft, conflicts over land, and, in particular, allegations of sexual offence (1929: 855, 859; 1954: 523–543, esp. 527ff.). Its paradigm form is a spear throwing contest that may—and may not—escalate to competitive killing of buffalo. Secondly, as the captions to the photographs in Arndt's work reproduced in Daeng's article make clear, they illustrate a village relocation ritual (possibly in the then new village Wogo, see Arndt 1963: 70), not an instance of *boka goé*. Thirdly, although Daeng translates *boka goé* with the expression "to slip and fall backwards," we are not told what this slipping and falling refers to, or how Daeng understands it to have come to signify "competitive feasting" (Daeng 1988: 254). For an explanation we must consult Arndt (although not the work Daeng directs us to): *boka* and *goé* both mean "to fall" and this "double expression presumably signifies the violent plunge, the great loss of wealth and reputation, suffered at this ordeal by the loser and his entire family" (Arndt 1954: 527). Finally, nowhere in the article does the author indicate that he has conducted fieldwork, i.e., made systematic empirical inquiry, in Flores.

12. See Howell (1996b) for a comprehensive volume on sacrificial practices in eastern Indonesia.

13. Unlike the Ngadha, people elsewhere in Flores sacrifice goat, dog, and horse in addition to fowl, pig, and buffalo.

14. The neighboring Hoga Sara operate with comparable, if different, distinctions (Molnar 2000: 220), as do the Lio (Howell 1996a: 92–93).

15. My constant use of the phrases "ritual killing" or "sacrifice" may appear pedantic, but a distinction must be maintained between "profane" slaughter or killing of an animal (*zabho*) for ordinary human consumption, and the "ritual killing" of a consecrated animal for purposes that transcend people's physiological needs and palatal pleasures (even if they include them). It must be borne in mind that chicken and pig can be brought to death both ways. With regard to the buffalo, matters are less clear. I never witnessed a buffalo being killed outside of ritual. Conceivably this could be because, as noted above, the animal is now so scarce that the very idea of a buffalo being slaughtered merely in order to fill people's bellies is preposterous. Yet, buffalo are sometimes killed as part of the (nowadays extremely rare) *ana koka* inauguration of new *woé* land. Also, upon my inquiry, people related how, in recent years, a buffalo was on occasion bought by some *ad hoc* collective of households (kin and friends), put to death unceremoniously, the meat being distributed per kilo according to each unit's cash input. The latter practice, especially—known in Indonesian as *lés*—is clearly a novel development. But Arndt is categorical: "Every buffalo that the Ngadha ever slaughter must perish at the *ngadhu*" (1931: 366). Bader is equally certain: "The buffalo is only slaughtered at the sacrificial pillar" (Bader 1953: 115).

16. While Ngadha speakers have a number of expressions—in addition to the purely lexical terms already mentioned—denoting people of one or another rank, it was not easy to determine if they have a word for "[social] rank." Finally a number of speakers agreed the best candidate is *tedé* (or *teda*, which is probably a dialect variant), for which Arndt offers the following relevant glosses: "layer," "ledge," "row," "section," "shelf"; "generation," "[kin] group," "[kin] line"; "to arrange," "to encircle," "to order" (Arndt 1961: 535). Arndt has recorded the use also of *tuka* "womb" to designate not only "kinship" but rank, too: *miu kenena tuka go séi* "of which family, of which rank are you" (Arndt 1961: 554).

17. *Wawi Toro* means "Red Boar," *Dala Wawi* "Boar Star." The Pleiades are named *Ko* because they resemble the kind of net trap (*ko*) in which Ngadha catch wild pigs.

18. Indeed Arndt makes the same point, if only more forcefully, in subsequent publications: "According to another myth the sister whom Wawi Toro had banished deliberately returned and married him, without Wawi Toro recognizing her" (Arndt 1958: 125); "Then said the wife: 'Have you really not recognized me? Has the *polo*, the bad spirit, kept your eyes closed?' At these words the brother repined over his sister." (Arndt 1955: 273–74).

19. Noble men can lose rank, too, but not on grounds of interrank sexual transgression. The consequence of breaking one or another of the plethora of rules (often in the form of *piré* "taboos") traditionally applying to the behavior of nobles was that the transgressor immediately lost rank. This is no longer so (nowadays, a noble man faces rank demotion if he fails to pay certain kinds of fine), but most of the rules and taboos are still known and one's behavior is frequently judged according to them. The path of the noble "is very narrow, scarcely as wide as a reed (*wako*) leaf," as Arndt puts it (Arndt 1929: 842). One important difference between men's and women's transgressions, however, is that men are often able to rectify theirs by sacrificing a buffalo: that is, by taking action. Women are not similarly blessed (Arndt 1960b: 180). Arndt (1954: 335–343; 1960b: 242–250) provides further details on the prescriptions and proscriptions on nobles' behavior.

20. "Among the Ngadha the sacrificial pillar is not only a monument for, and mind image of, the ancestors and forebear to whom it is consecrated, but it is the ancestor himself in person" (Arndt 1958: 109).

21. To extrapolate directly from these mythistorical accounts to present attitudes would be unwise. When discussing various premarital and extramarital affairs that came to my knowledge, men and women alike tended to blame men and women equally. Quite a separate matter, however, is if women can be understood to threaten the social order by exploiting, as it were, their ancient culpability—resentfully subverting a social order that possibly disadvantages them. Such subversion, often in the form of outright gender antagonism, is well known in a number of societies in New Guinea and has been reported from eastern Indonesia (the Moluccas, for example) as well (see Valeri 2000). But I can think of no evidence for gender antagonism among the Ngadha (nor of any reference to it in Flores ethnographies.). At any rate, the mythical demotion of the sister-wife did not effect a demotion of women in general; as noted above only noble women can give birth to a noble child (and thus perpetuate a noble House) but on the condition that the child's genitor is noble as well. This very fact, however, nowadays occasions resentment among some, especially younger noble women who consider it "unfair" that a woman remains noble only as long as she avoids sex with men of lower rank. Failing to do so, she, and her lover, must endure a harrowing set of rituals—the core of which is that they are symbolically killed—if she is to be accepted at her natal House and village, from which she would have

been exiled since the affair became known (and if the liaison, in the event, can be endorsed as a legitimate marriage). Political effects of this resentment are so far negligible; by the logic of the practices already outlined, demoted women are either absent, barred from entering the village, or they have endured the rituals and thus not only atoned for their mistake but, importantly, also fortified the very rules they violated. But certain demographic effects of the stipulations on interrank liaisons have long been perceptible. One thing is that a number of noble women have refrained from marrying altogether and have lived (and died) as "old maidens"—some of them in convents—without husbands or children (a common enough feature of hypergamous marriage practices); another that the number of noble women marrying below their rank is now rising, as is everyone's assessment. In combination, the number of viable noble kin groups is steadily dwindling.

22. Later in the same work Arndt points out that, according to myth, the slaughterer—and consumer—of humans in buffalo form is *Jara Masi*, the buffalo-shaped seducer of women, and *Inérié's* (the "female" volcano—"*iné*" means "mother"—looming over much of Ngadhaland) husband (Arndt 1929:823).

23. Van Baal, discussing Ngadha sacrifice, overlooked this point: "in a few myths a *déwa* appears in the shape of a buffalo. . . . From here it is only one step to the identification of the sacrificed buffalo with the deity. The point of interest is that this step is not taken, not by the Ngadha" (Baal 1975: 175).

24. It is difficult to assess precisely the present day significance of especially this last claim. I am convinced that Arndt's prudent phrase is intended to signify sexual assault, which minimally implies that the buffalo in question is a bull. Although I cannot confirm that the sexual urge of bulls is thought to be stronger than that of men (even if bulls cannot be expected to restrain it as men should), the more crucial insinuation that the admonition warns of bestiality would suffice to make women cautious. At any rate, unaccompanied women are certainly disinclined to invite men into their house.

25. In Forth's analysis of ideas concerning animal transformations among the neighboring Nage it appears that buffalo-human transformations are temporary and reversible only (1998: 275). While some of the transformations I report here are clearly temporary, it is difficult to see how the acquisition of a buffalo's tail at an advanced age, indeed indexing advanced age, could be thought of as other than permanent. The same appears to be the case in Sumba: "In Kodi, they say that very wise old people—both men and women—grow small horns on their heads—although not tails. (Still, horns are certainly at least as buffalo-like as tails!)" (Janet Hoskins, personal communication, January 2001).

26. By saying that "only after having grown old is it possible to become one of the ancestors," I am not simply stating the obvious. Ngadha are explicit that even accomplished persons who die young will soon be forgotten. Some people's memory is better than others' and their genealogical knowledge sometimes amazing, but the fact that they can spot the mistaken place an anthropologist has accorded, say, a childless MMFFZ in a diagram is beside the point here, which is that to be "an ancestor" is to be revered in ritual invocations.

27. The fact that buffalo are silent beasts except at the moment of slaughter figures prominently in the analysis Hoskins offers of Kodi (Sumba) sacrifice. In Kodi, domesticated animals' speechlessness is "explained" in myth by their acquiescence to subjugation (1993b:164), and the sacrificial buffalo bellowing in pain is seen as finally, if hopelessly and only momentarily, rebelling. While I failed to obtain myths pertaining to the origin of animals, and cannot find one in Arndt's collection (1960a) or elsewhere in his writings, it is clear that Ngadha conceive of animals primarily in subordinate

contrast to humans in that the former cannot speak, as the designations for "four-footed animal" indicate: *boro buté, boro ngongo, ngizu buté* (*boro* "mouth," "speech"; *buté* "dumb," "unrecognizable"; *ngizu* "nose"; *ngongo* "silent," "dumb," "unable to speak" (Arndt 1961: 34, 39, 389, 392)).

28. Similarly, in Sumba: "The need to sacrifice a buffalo for a nobleman who has fallen would occur in Kodi especially if he fell inside an important ancestral house, rather than out in the muddy village plaza. I did actually see this done for a former *camat* [subdistrict head, OHS] who fell in his ancestral house" (Janet Hoskins, personal communication, January 2001).

29. The exception, already noted, is when it is sacrificed at inaugural field rituals, the purpose of which is not to ensure bountiful crops but to celebrate—publicly and dramatically—the expansion of the estate.

30. Molnar, in her monograph on the neighboring Hoga Sara (on the border between Ngadha and Nagé), reports that here, unlike among the Ngadha, *nitu* is the term also for "generalized ancestors" (2000: 177, 208ff.). Thus, when the Hoga Sara install their *madhu* (*ngadhu*) in the village plaza, they recite in the ritual *soka* chant the line "roots to wind across the ancestral spirits [*nitu*]" (2000: 182–3); the roots in question being the three deeply placed roots of the *madhu*.

31. Its phallic character is indisputable, but at a subordinate level of analysis. I hope to return to the *ngadhu*'s superior, double nature in a future publication.

References

Adams, Marie Jeanne. 1974. "Symbols of the Organized Community in East Sumba, Indonesia." *Bijdragen tot de Taal-, Land- en Volkenkunde* 130: 324–347.

Arndt, Paul, S.V.D. 1929. "Die Religion der Ngada [Part I]." *Anthropos* 24: 817–861.

———. 1931. "Die Religion der Ngada [Part II]." *Anthropos* 26: 353–405, 697–739.

———. 1954. *Gesellschaftliche Verhältnisse der Ngadha*. Studia Instituti Anthropos 8. Wien-Mödling: Verlag der Missionsdruckerei St. Gabriel.

———. 1955. "Die Rangschichten in der Gesellschaft der Ngadha." In *Actes du IVe Congrès International des Sciences Anthropologiques et Ethnologiques*. Wien: Verlag Adolf Holzhausens NFG.

———. 1958. "Hinduismus der Ngadha." *Asian Folklore Studies* 17: 99–136.

———. 1960a. "Mythen der Ngadha." *Annali Lateranensi* 24: 9–137.

———. 1960b. "Opfer und Opferfeiern der Ngadha." *Folklore Studies [Asian Folklore Studies]* 19: 175–250.

———. 1961. *Wörterbuch der Ngadhasprache*. Studia Instituti Anthropos 15. Fribourg, Suisse: Pertjetakan Arnoldus, Endeh/Posieux.

———. 1963. "Die wirtschaftlichen Verhältnisse der Ngadha." *Annali del Pontificio Museo Missionario Etnologico già Lateranensi* 27: 13–189.

Bader, Hermann, S.V.D. 1953. *Die Reifefeiern bei den Ngadha (Mittelflores, Indonesien)*. (St.-Gabrieler Studien 14). Mödling bei Wien: St.-Gabriel-Verlag.

Baal, Jan van. 1975. "Offering, Sacrifice and Gift." *Numen* 23 (3): 161–178.

Barnes, John A. 1962. "African Models in the New Guinea Highlands." *Man* 62: 5–9.

Barnes, R. H. 1977. "Alliance and Categories in Wailolong, East Flores." *Sociologus* 27: 133–157.

———. 1980. "Marriage, Exchange and the Meaning of Corporations in Eastern Indonesia." In *The Meaning of Marriage Payments*, ed. J. L. Comaroff. London: Academic Press.

———. 2006. "Maurice Godelier and the Metamorphosis of Kinship, a Review Essay." *Comparative Study of Society and History* 48 (2): 326–358.

Bloch, Maurice and Jonathan Parry. 1989. "Introduction: Money and the Morality of Exchange." In *Money and the Morality of Exchange*, ed. J. Parry and M. Bloch. Cambridge: Cambridge University Press.

Bohannan, Paul. 1959. "The Impact of Money on an African Subsistence Economy." *Journal of Economic History* 19: 491–503.

Comaroff, John L. 1980. "Introduction." In *The Meaning of Marriage Payments*, ed. J. L. Comaroff. London: Academic Press.

Chayanov, Alexander. 1991 [1919]. *The Theory of Peasant Co-operatives*. London: I. B. Tauris.

Daeng, Hans J. 1988. "Ritual Feasting and Resource Competition in Flores." In *The Real and Imagined Role of Culture in Development: Case Studies from Indonesia*, ed. M. R. Dove. Honolulu: University of Hawaii Press.

Dietrich, Stefan. 1998. "'We Don't Sell our Daughters': A Report on Money and Marriage Exchange in the Township of Larantuka (Flores, E. Indonesia)." In *Kinship, Networks and Exchange*, ed. T. Schweitzer and D. R. White. Cambridge: Cambridge University Press.

Dumont, Louis. 1980. *Homo Hierarchicus: The Caste System and its Implications*. 2nd ed. Trans. M. Sainsbury, L. Dumont, and B. Gulati. Chicago: The University of Chicago Press.

Evans-Pritchard, Edward Evan. 1940. *The Nuer: A Description of the Modes of Livelihood and Political Institutions of a Nilotic People*. Oxford: Oxford University Press.

Forth, Gregory. 1989. "The Pa Sése Festival of the Nage of Bo'a Wae (Central Flores)." *Bijdragen tot de Taal-, Land- en Volkenkunde* 145: 502–519.

———. 1998. "On Deer and Dolphins: Nage Ideas Regarding Animal Transformation." *Oceania* 68: 271–293.

Fortes, Meyer. 1953. "The Structure of Unilineal Descent Groups." *American Anthropologist* 55: 17–41.

Graham, Penelope. 1991. "To Follow the Blood: The Path of Life in a Domain of Eastern Flores, Indonesia." Ph.D. diss. The Australian National University.

Holy, Ladislav, ed. 1979. *Segmentary Lineage Systems Reconsidered*. The Queen's University Papers in Social Anthropology, Belfast: The Queen's University.

Hornborg, Alf. 1999. "Money and the Semiotics of Ecosystem Dissolution." *Journal of Material Culture* 4 (2): 143–162.

Hoskins, Janet. 1993a. *The Play of Time: Kodi Perspectives on Calendars, History, and Exchange*. Berkeley: University of California Press.

———. 1993b. "Violence, Sacrifice, and Divination: Giving and Taking Life in Eastern Indonesia." *American Ethnologist* 20: 159–178.

Howell, Signe. 1996a. "A Life for 'Life': Blood and Other Life-promoting Substances in Northern Lio Moral Discourse." In *For the Sake of our Future: Sacrificing in Eastern Indonesia*, ed. S. Howell. Leiden: CNWS.

Howell, Signe, ed. 1996b. *For the Sake of our Future: Sacrificing in Eastern Indonesia*, Leiden: CNWS.

Hutchinson, Sharon E. 1992. "The Cattle of Money and the Cattle of Girls among the Nuer 1930–83." *American Ethnologist* 19 (2): 29–316.

———. 2000. "Identity and Substance: The Broadening Bases of Relatedness among the Nuer of Southern Sudan." In *Cultures of Relatedness: New Approaches to the Study of Kinship*, ed. J. Carsten. Cambridge: Cambridge University Press.

Keesing, Roger M. 1970. "Shrines, Ancestors, and Cognatic Descent: The Kwaio and Tallensi." *American Anthropologist*, 72: 755–775.

Kennedy, Raymond. 1955. *Fieldnotes on Indonesia*, ed. H. C. Conklin. New Haven: HRAF.

Kuper, Adam. 1988. *The Invention of Primitive Society: Transformations of an Illusion*. London: Routledge.

Lévi-Strauss, Claude. 1982. *The Way of the Masks*. Trans. Sylvia Modelski. Seattle: University of Washington Press.

Lewis, E. D. 1988. *People of the Source: The Social and Ceremonial Order of Tana Wai Brama on Flores*. Dordrecht, The Netherlands and Providence, RI: Foris Publications.

Molnar, Andrea Katalin. 1990. "Nitu: A Symbolic Analysis of an Austronesian Spirit Category." M.A. thesis: University of Alberta, Canada.

———. 2000. *Grandchildren of the Ga'e Ancestors: Social Organization and Cosmology among the Hoga Sara of Flores*. Leiden: KITLV Press.

Needham, Rodney. 1975. "Polythetic Classification: Convergence and Consequences." *Man* (n.s.) 10 (3): 349–369.

Parry, Jonathan and Maurice Bloch, ed. 1989. *Money and the Morality of Exchange*. Cambridge: Cambridge University Press.

Piot, Charles D. 1991. "Of Persons and Things: Some Reflections on African Spheres of Exchange." *Man* (n.s.) 26 (3): 405–424.

Sansom, Basil. 1976. "A Signal Transaction and its Currency." In *Transaction and Meaning: Directions in the Anthropology of Exchange and Symbolic Behavior*, ed. Bruce Kapferer. ASA Essays in Social Anthropology 1. Philadelphia: Institute for the Study of Human Issues.

Schröter, Susanne. 1998. "Death Rituals of the Ngada in Central Flores, Indonesia." *Anthropos* 93: 417–435.

———. 2000. "Creating Time and Society: The Annual Cycle of the People of Langa in Eastern Indonesia." *Anthropos* 95: 463–483.

———. 2005. "Red Cocks and Black Hens: Gendered Symbolism, Kinship and Social Practice in the Ngada Highlands." *Bijdragen tot de Taal-, Land- en Volkenkunde* 161 (2/3): 318–349.

Smedal, Olaf H. 1996. "Conquest and Comfort: A Ngadha 'Bad Death' Ritual." In *For the Sake of our Future: Sacrificing in Eastern Indonesia*, ed. S. Howell. Leiden: CNWS.

———. 2000. "Sociality on Display: The Aesthetics of Ngadha Houses." *RES: Anthropology and Aesthetics* 37: 106–126.

———. 2002. "Ngadha Relationship Terms in Context: Description, Analysis, and Implications." *Asian Journal of Social Science* 30: 493–524.

———. (In press) "Hierarchy, Precedence, and Values: Scopes for Social Action in Ngadhaland, Central Flores." In *Precedence: Processes of Differentiation in the Austronesian World*, ed. M. P. Vischer and J. J. Fox. Canberra: ANU E Press.

Southall, Aidan W. 1986. "The Illusion of Nath Agnation." *Ethnology* 25: 1–20.

Valeri, Valerio. 2000. *The Forest of Taboos: Morality, Hunting, and Identity among the Huaulu of the Moluccas*. Madison: The University of Wisconsin Press.

Verdon, M. 1982. "Where Have All Their Lineages Gone? Cattle and Descent among the Nuer." *American Anthropologist* 84: 566–579.

CHAPTER 10

Hierarchy Is not Inequality— in Polynesia, for Instance

Serge Tcherkézoff

U sing a few brief examples of some Polynesian social facts, I would like to suggest that the study of social hierarchies requires a "comparative" decentering, on the part of the (Western) anthropologist, between the notion of inequality with which he is familiar—let us call it *stratification*—and certain forms of inequality that we will call "sacred," for which the term *hierarchy*, in its etymological sense, is therefore appropriate.[1] Without this decentering, the anthropologist runs the risk of creating misunderstandings with his hosts.

In a society like Samoa, the anthropologist will be received with great "respect" and placed in the hierarchy because he is a visitor, and also because he is a Westerner (a *Papalagi*, a word which may have references to something far away and wonderful).[2] The sitting places he is offered are those of chiefs and sisters. However, he must be on his guard and never think that he can permit himself to do anything he wants. Certain attitudes or requests on his part (pertaining to sexuality, for instance, or if he should become physically violent, of course), might result in his placing himself in the domain of "living beings" in general (see below), and no longer in the circle of respect. He could even risk physical or verbal assault. He would find himself located uniquely in the field of those power relations obtaining *a posteriori* among like beings ("living beings"): relations of inequality in a nonhierarchical sense that I call "stratification," even in cases when the strata of inequality are temporary and not institutionalized.

While I have obviously never carried the experiment far enough to place myself in such a position, I have on several occasions felt that a slight slip of vocabulary (the use of a term to refuse something without realizing that this very term could be considered insulting, a slip that was readily pardoned by my hosts because of my faulty grasp of their language), suddenly opened a space for a possible confrontation. In Samoan society one can easily see how an insulting word or a light blow can suddenly spill over into violence, whereas, a moment earlier, relations were taking place in the most "polite," formal, and "respectful" climate.

Indeed, there is no halfway point between hierarchy and stratification: if one leaves the former, one immediately enters the space of power relations. One must not make the error of believing that, when leaving hierarchy, one enters the field of equality, in our sense of the word. Peaceful relations of equality are located within the hierarchy, understood as a space organized by belonging to the same whole: within that space, there is room for equality at each level. To put it briefly, in this space, the only equality possible is equality among persons of the same rank. The opposite of Samoan hierarchy is the inequality of power relations, one could say that the opposite of hierarchy is inequality in general, the *a priori* definition of the individuals precisely as individuals—with the exception that the Samoan universalist-individualist horizon is "the living being" and not the "humanity" of seventeenth and eighteenth century European humanism—that opens spaces of confrontation in Samoan society among individuals according to sex, age, physical strength; just as Samoans imagine the existence of constant confrontation in the animal world (their word *mea ola*, "living beings," applies precisely to the whole realm of living creatures).

Samoa even provides an example of a debate on this misunderstanding. A fatal fight took place in the 1970s in a village where an American anthropologist was doing his research. The anthropologist, Bradd Shore, wanted to reconstruct a hypothetical history about rivalry (over land, chiefly titles, and so on), which put two families at odds for years, and which would "explain" the fatal fight of that day. Once, during a game of cards, when the two players were fairly drunk, one accused the other of cheating. The accused left to fetch his gun and shot his adversary dead without warning (Shore 1982). This card game sparked a disproportionate reaction, because, according to Shore's analysis, it took place in the context of a long-standing rivalry. Shore did not see that this disproportionate reaction could be explained differently: one of the players flew into a rage because of an "insulting" accusation that had suddenly opened up a space of confrontation of "force" between two persons who, in this game, were just two opponents; even if, in other contexts, they were both family chiefs in the same village, sitting within the hierarchized "sacred circle" of the titles of the village (and they were even friends).

It so happens that the murderer, a schoolteacher, chanced to read the works of the anthropologist, when he was released from prison ten years later. In an academic publication he wrote how deeply scandalized he was by the error and insult the anthropologist had committed toward him and, through him, toward his country (Tuitolova'a 1984). His whole argument boiled down to the assertion that violence can never be the result of social structure (the *faamatai*, the organization of titles) in the "Samoan culture" (*aganuu faaSamoa*, etymologically: "the Samoan way of the essence of a community").

Clearly the anthropologist is not obliged to agree, but here he has one more proof of the other observation that, from the Samoan point of view, there is an absolute boundary between the worlds of "hierarchy" (which contains all of the relations entailed in "social structure," in the English sense accepted by the anthropologist in question) and the violence of power relations. Certain Samoan intellectuals or authorities (in terms of rank) have confided to me that they would always hold it against an anthropologist who could believe that violence can be engendered by hierarchy.[3]

In a way, the rejection by these same persons of Margaret Mead's even older analysis (1926) of the purportedly cultural choice of Samoa concerning "sexual freedom" follows the same reasoning. We all know how this American author created a publishing shock when she reported that, according to her "observations," adolescent Samoan girls could "gently" gain experience with "numerous lovers" as they grew up, until it came time to take on adult responsibilities. The result, according to Mead, is a society in which no woman is at risk of "any neurotic trouble" whatsoever or other psychological disorders. Certain Samoans were extremely shocked for the following reason: According to them, sexuality, free or not, belongs to the world of relations between "males and females" (that we will discuss using the example of *gender* as it is represented in Samoa). Sexuality is thus relegated to the realm of "living beings," which is located, in short, outside of "culture" in the Samoan sense. Thus sexuality cannot be the result of a "cultural" choice, since Samoans understand by this English term "culture" what they see as their "custom," their "tradition," literally "the nature of the fact of living in a human group" (*aganu'u*).

Their various discourses on their notion of *aganu'u* (see Tcherkézoff 2003a passim) say in a way that this "custom" was constructed in contrast to the domain of "force or power" (*malosi, fiamalosi*), which is the only source of difference between "living beings" (inequality in the sense I use in this paper), and that it was constructed in this way so as to create a zone of sociability where humans, this time, are fundamentally distinct from animals—and once again we find the hierarchical system of belonging, constituted by the relationship whole/part (chiefs/nonchiefs, sisters/brothers: see examples below). Thus a number of Samoan intellectuals were shocked when they read into Mead's analysis the idea that their *culture* had constructed a space where sexuality had no rules, a space their culture had created to enable the "natural" form of desire characteristic of all males and females (in reference to the kingdom of "living beings") to be expressed within this culture.[4]

Mead thought she was doing the right thing in glorifying (what she interpreted as) the cultural choice of "Polynesian" societies, which, according to her reading, had chosen to give adolescents the opportunity to fulfill themselves by exercising their freedom of desire. She wanted, by means of this example, to teach the American society of the 1930s a good lesson, even if it meant exaggerating the content of her actual ethnographic notes, by destroying the prevailing idea of a natural determination—against which one could do nothing—that defined masculine and feminine roles in society, as well as the "adolescence crisis." Bradd Shore, who tried to explain a fatal fight as a structurally predictable murder, also thought he was doing the right thing in describing an underlying logic of the rivalry engendered by the social stratifications in Polynesian societies. In both cases, however, a trench of incomprehension was dug between the anthropologist and some of her/his Samoan hosts.

To avoid such misunderstandings, one has to do more than juxtapose points of view and then say: this is the explanation given by some Samoans, and this is the anthropological explication! One must go on and ask oneself if the misunderstanding might not stem from a different vision of the localization of the social contexts that are the "value providers," as Louis Dumont said (see below), from the vision each person could have of what creates or does not create a sense of belonging to a society, and thus (because a system of belonging generates a shared notion of hierarchical totality) of the forms of "hierarchy" in which individuals lead their lives.

Thus, the underlying problem is the notion of "value," which engenders the feeling of belonging to the same group, when this group is represented by each member as a "totality." In this case, when the group forms a "society,"[5] the system of belonging is always a hierarchy, while the representation of belonging through equality, instead of through hierarchy, leads to the notion of the "infinite" group: "Humanity," "Human Rights," the Western invention of the universal human being. (As a value, hierarchy creates a social belonging, whereas equality creates a belonging to humanity. The Western notion of inequality, however, which differs from these two notions, is unable to define the idea of "belonging" to a society because this notion has been understood by the social sciences as an empirical and nonideological fact, a statement of a fact, and is not represented as a value in itself.)

Often the anthropologist neglects to investigate what it is that forms the value of belonging. Paying attention to the different levels that organize social relations, he gathers facts that appear to illustrate situations of inequality between persons. Spontaneously he will use the opposition "equality/inequality," with which he has been provided by the Western political tradition. Present in his mind is every possible social inequality: from "slave-owning societies" or, in a different order, the "apartheid" societies, all characterized by a fundamental system of separation, to the various systems of social classes in the industrial societies, as well as by all the "chiefdoms" which set up a status pyramid. The anthropologist will pay equal attention to the oppositions stemming from the difference between the sexes, talking about "male domination." His careful research will result in diagrams, all of which are generated by this basic idea of an inequality between two terms: A > B. Before or after his study, he will claim to have tried to observe, or that his observations have led him to describe, an inequality "of" some kind: political, economic, gendered, and so on. Faced with a greater or lesser range of such facts, he will describe the society under study as more or less "nonegalitarian," thus suggesting that certain societies might be, on the contrary, "egalitarian."

Unconsciously, he has used a method that first identifies—and therefore defines—comparable elements, and then measures their interrelation. First he determines the nature of related elements, and then he measures their relation to one another in order to find out if it is one of equality or inequality. To describe two persons, A and B, as "the younger/the elder" in order to measure the rights pertaining to age in a particular society, as "rich/poor" to assess the power of money, as "white/black" to measure racial inequality and prejudice in a racist ideology, or even to qualify them as "man/woman" in order to measure the domination of one sex over the other, in any context, is to claim that one already knows who A and B are, and then to add on the observation of the differentiations. Thus, considered *a priori*, the notion of "gender" locks the analysis into a binary logic that then makes it necessary, to mention a few other categories, to talk about "gender liminality," "transgender," "gender crossing," and so on. Even with the best of intentions not to "marginalize" these other categories, the very thrust of this analysis has already made them into "others."

The result of this approach is that one always considers A and B as two members of the human race, and therefore first and foremost two "sames." The analysis of inequality thus remains within the universalist-individualist ideology whose horizon is the human species made up of like individuals, as well as within the ideology of a certain culture zone and a certain period of history, that is, that of the modern Western world.

This method thus turns a blind eye to situations where what we call inequality becomes, from the local point of view, that which makes the very essence of the elements—even though we see this essence as a social fact and not a fact of nature. Let us take, for instance, the distinction "divine/human" in a cultural discourse in which the human being is a divine creation, one among the other things on earth. We easily accept that: (1) one pole takes on meaning only through the other, and (2) although the two poles are thus inseparable, nevertheless, one includes the other as part of itself, while the second cannot do so vis-à-vis the first. It so happens that a certain number of social differentiation systems are of this type (this obviously does not mean that, empirically, the whole society in question knows only this kind of differentiation). Let us assume this, then. Let us also say that the logic of religious belief is of this kind. But what about the rest? We must add the possibility that the logic of certain social hierarchies among individuals is also of this type.

We need to make a distinction here. This distinction, unusual in the field of social sciences, which opposes inequality to another bloc consisting of, at the same time, hierarchy and equality, was first proposed by Louis Dumont in his work on India (Dumont 1966). In the initial paragraphs above and in the following section, I shall discuss the manner in which this distinction presented itself to me "in the field," when working in the Samoan society, and then I will explain the way in which Dumont asked us to take this distinction into consideration.

More Examples from Polynesia: The Notion of "Chief"

The Polynesian characters that Europeans dubbed "chiefs" belong (or rather belonged at the time of the "first contacts") to the category of combined hierarchy and equality. One could illustrate this case by noting, as Marshall Sahlins does, the value of sunlight and the sun's radiance in ancient Hawaii. The Hawaiian chief was often called "the celestial one," *ka lani*. More broadly, Sahlins writes: "The specific quality of aristocratic beauty is a brilliance and luminosity that Hawaiians do not fail to connect, in myth, rite, and chant, with the sun. Such beauty is properly called divine, for like the gods themselves, it causes things to be seen" (Sahlins 1985: 18).

Sahlins also mentions the importance of the gaze in ancient Hawaiian ritual. The expression for "to desire" or "to respect" someone is "to cast one's eyes on." To "see" also means "to understand" (the same applies to other Polynesian languages, like Samoan). In the case of human sacrifice, the victim was usually a man found guilty of some transgression, and his eyes were the first thing to be dealt with (once they were put out, the victim's left eye was immediately "fed" to the deity). Indeed, by his transgression, the victim became "he whose eyes were burned-cooked," *makawela*.[6] Following the same logic, one must never look at a chief. That would violate a taboo.[7]

Sahlins does not generalize, but we have here, with the notion of source of light and visibility, the best possible illustration of the way the Polynesian hierarchy worked, in the east (Tahiti, Hawaii, and so on) as well as in the west (Samoa, Tonga, and so on). This logic of hierarchy between chiefs and dependants explains the continuity between gods and humans.

In Polynesia, before the introduction of trade with the West, the superior/inferior relationship was always statutory and was not a quantitative division with a substantive and independent reference (richer/less rich, and so on). The hierarchical relationship implies two aspects that are not incompatible despite appearances: mutuality and unilaterality. The relationship is one of interdependence, and this interdependence is unidirectional. The relationship is interdependent because either pole is meaningless without the other. But the movement is hierarchical *because one of the terms is everything to the other*—and the converse is never the case.

When the reference value is something like "light" instead of, for instance, the production of metal tools, the value implies interdependence. What is a light source if this source has nothing to illuminate? (What is a god without a world he is believed to have created?) We would not even know that light existed. Light can be seen only if it falls on a human being or an object. In the same way, a Polynesian chief without dependants has no existence. But the relationship is unidirectional: one is the *source* of light, and the other becomes visible because he is *illuminated*. The dependant can participate in life (the world of Polynesian cosmogonal "light") through his relationship to the chief: in this case he is illuminated. To him, the chief is a source of life. The same holds for the chief vis-à-vis the gods. In West Polynesia (Samoa, Tonga), this relationship still exists today (in the 1980s, the time of my fieldwork), even though, in the nineteenth century, the referential divinity became the God of the Bible.

In these cases, social differentiation is perceived as a local replica of a divine/human relationship. Thus, any human who is superior to me is a god/ancestor. This does not imply any mysticism, nor any precise theory of a superhuman substance in the body of the chiefs, even though it is said that the "name" of the first ancestor who cleared the soil and built the ceremonial house "is in the body of" or "lives in" the person who is, in every generation, established as "chief" of the extended family. This is a very down-to-earth logic, having more to do with the physics of light than with the mysticism of the soul. In this logic, the gods are god-ancestors: the first ancestors are always "children" of the gods, and they acquire the powers of the gods; the chiefs personify these gods and these ancestors; in other words, they "embody" the gods. At the same time the gods are already human, and they possess by definition human character weaknesses (therefore they can be softened by offerings).

The logic of "having," however, is quite different. With a principle of superiority based on the possession of metal tools, anybody can set up his own production (of products cut by means of these tools) and compete on the market with other producers of similar goods. Indeed, after contact with the Europeans, this logic of stratification, which is a differentiation based on "having," was added to the logic of hierarchy (or its domain of application has greatly enlarged). This new logic quickly took root and sometimes eliminated the traditional rival. The new political powers as well as the new markets that grew up in Polynesia in the nineteenth century illustrate this transformation. Today in Hawaii one cannot even imagine this history without knowing these sources. Elsewhere, in Samoa for instance, this transformation is almost completed at this very moment (early 1990s), and the observer of this process will find a wealth of lessons for the entire history of Polynesia (see Tcherkézoff 2005).

The example of land, a crucial issue in modern day Samoa (Tcherkézoff 2003a) offers another clear illustration. As long as the land is not an individual possession that can be bought or sold, as long as the land is "customary" (a possession whose one and only owner is its founding ancestor), clan rivalries are expressed in terms of the founding dates of the respective territories. The importance of seniority is made visible by the sitting positions assigned in the ceremonial "circle," characteristic of the meetings of the chiefs representing every family of the village. This rivalry supposes a minimum of agreement as to the rules governing belonging to this "circle." Such is still the situation in 80 percent of the Samoan territories. On the Hawaiian island of Oahu, however, where we find the capital Honolulu, the battles are waged on the currency exchange, between the dollar and the yen, because the bulk of the land (or rather the high rise buildings and construction sites) belongs to Japanese firms. No common belonging to the same form of relation needs to be reaffirmed at every meeting. Belonging is no longer dependent on local owners, but rather on a global notion: the foreign exchange.

The "Chiefs' Language"

When discussing the Polynesian notion of "chief," one must constantly ask oneself in what differential logic this "chief" is situated: stratification or hierarchy? A wrong answer can lead to misunderstandings. Thus, most Western observers were thoroughly mistaken about what they considered to be "the chiefs' language" in Samoa, or the "aristocratic" regime of the Samoan state.[8]

The question of a chief's language reveals the source of the misunderstanding: namely a failure to understand the logic of the taboo. Hierarchy, in the sense used here, consists of a scale of prohibitions, while stratification is a scale of possession.[9] The more sacred a thing or person is, the more prohibitions there are that characterize the social position in question. In India, the higher the caste, the more things and people the members of this caste must avoid (because these things and people are considered "unclean" or impure). In Polynesia, the higher the rank, the more "taboo" the person is, and therefore the greater the number of persons who must "avoid contact" with the taboo person. The Polynesian term *tapu* or *kapu* gave the English word "taboo" at the time of Captain Cook; the perfect model is Hawaii, where the notion of rank is termed *kapu* (see Valeri 1972, 1976, 1986). The more "taboo" the chief is, the greater the number of people who have this relation with him; at the same time, the number of rules the chief must obey is also greater, or their application more strict. In the sacred kingdoms of Africa, the kings were literally smothered in prohibitions. They were forbidden to spit, to urinate on the ground, and no drop of blood, no nail clipping was supposed to fall to earth (Tcherkézoff 1987, 1989). This logic is very different from the scale of possession, where the more you "have," the more you can "do."

This difference can be easily seen in the fact that the distinction reveals a directionality, which is logical because it pertains to taboos. As for the "having" mode, there is symmetry between an ascending and a descending order: in sum, the difference is not directional. The difference between A and B is the same whether you compare A with B or B with A. On the contrary, in the scale of prohibitions, the differences are directional. In the India of castes, one protects oneself in one direction only: from below. Each caste can divide the world of the other castes into those from whom one does not accept certain things, for instance water, and those with whom contact is not forbidden. (These divisions change composition according to the object to be avoided, hence the absence of any unique, simple, and linear order.) (See Dumont 1966, chapters 3, 4, and 6.) In Polynesia, one protects oneself in only one direction, too, but this time it is from above. European observers were quite surprised by the way people expressed the greatest fear at the idea of touching a chief or anything the chief had already touched. One of the first European observations was that of people accompanying a chief on board a ship. These persons would under no circumstances touch an object that the chief had already touched on board, or eat the leftovers from the chief's meal offered by the Captain, in spite of the fact that they manifested a keen interest in the same objects or in the same food when it had not been touched by their chief. This kind of fact takes us back a couple of centuries. But other contemporary, everyday facts say the same thing.

In Samoa and elsewhere in Polynesia, an inferior must use a special language when addressing a superior—in formal salutations, of course, but also in everyday conversation, for instance when one wishes to know if he has "slept or eaten" well, and when one must say: "enter my home!" or "do sit down!" These words are learned at a certain age and are regarded as specialized knowledge. They are learned well after acquisition of the vocabulary used between equals, which we are therefore justified in considering the basic or everyday vocabulary. However, when a superior replies to an inferior, he uses this everyday language. In effect, he is talking to someone who is *noa* (who may be touched or contacted without restrictions; the question of being "free" *[noa]* or "forbidden to contact" *[tapu]* also applies to verbal contact). If an inferior addresses someone who is *tapu* (who is tabooed), he must avoid using a certain number of everyday words. He therefore uses a special vocabulary.[10]

Here we have the perfect illustration of the difference with stratification. If we were operating within this second logic, the "chiefs" would form a stratum and would use their own vocabulary among themselves, which would set them apart from commoners (and they might even use the same words when addressing commoners). But the Polynesian system of *tapu/noa* is not based on stratification, and it is the inferior who must use special words. This is only logical, after all: the inferior is addressing someone "he is not allowed to touch" and *therefore ordinary words are taboo, prohibited for him.* He must therefore use other words: the language the European visitors called the "chiefs' vocabulary." This means that the speaker is under a unidirectional prohibition to use a "free" vocabulary (freedom, *noa*—the possibility of contact without prohibitions). Stratification was the logic at work when the upper classes in the Old World used to say to workers: "We don't speak the same language as you"; they were trying to distinguish themselves. "Slang" was born in a similar manner among the popular classes or in the outlaw underworld, each milieu forbidding access to the other. In Polynesia, on the contrary, a person who uses "respectful" language when speaking to a superior or to someone whom he wants to address politely as a superior would never ask one of his equals to use the same language when speaking of him or his family. When they heard nonchiefs addressing their chiefs with special words to say things like: "Do come in. Do sit down. How is your wife? How big is your house?"—using words they would never use to say the same things when speaking to their equals—the first European observers concluded that there existed a "chiefs' language," used for them and *by them*. Which was not surprising, they said, because these were "aristocratic" societies. But in reality, as a few nineteenth-century observers had already noted (Tcherkézoff 2003a: 203–4), and as we can see from contemporary studies, these words were not used when the chiefs spoke about themselves.

Another striking example is the way that Samoans conceive of the rules of sitting in a public transport (buses for long trips). While they import within the vehicle the hierarchical rules of sitting in their village ceremonial gatherings (lower ranks must "respect" higher ranks and allow them to sit in the front part, and so on), they are strongly against any importation of the Western class system which gives two (or more) strata of comfort according to the price paid (Tcherkézoff 2003a: 177–201).

The Electoral System

The question of aristocracy/democracy is itself significant when it comes to national politics. Samoan social organization is based on the "village," which is comprised of extended families. The village council is made up of the family chiefs. In each family, the chief is chosen by discussion and the consensus of all the adults when the previous chief dies or is (declared by the majority of the family members to be) unable to carry out his duties.[11]

One can therefore easily understand that when the time came to prepare for the independence of the country in the 1950s—after fifteen years of German colonization and then thirty-five years of New Zealand "mandate,"—the Samoans demanded (by referendum) the right to organize their Parliament in the following manner: the country was divided into districts and, for every parliamentary seat, it was decided that only the (family) chiefs should have (1) the right to stand for election and (2) the right to vote. In the minds of numerous Samoan members of the Constituent Assembly, this proposition was self-evident. Only a person who is already the representative of a small community can have enough status (and also experience) to take on a new and even larger representation: the representation of a district. However, the members of the United Nation Commission charged with the independence process were deeply shocked: here was a country that wanted to keep the "aristocratic" tradition, under the rule of "nobles," and so on. The commissioners did not have any other standard for comparison than a vision of European feudalism or the *Ancien Régime*: dominant/dominated, nobility/serfs. They were unable to understand that the unidirectional interdependence (see the previous example of the "language of respect" among Samoans) linking the Samoan chiefs and commoners could never allow the creation of an autonomous political oligarchy. If a Member of Parliament were to yield to such a temptation, he would rapidly be deposed from his position of chief by the extended family and thus cease to be eligible. (Today, a certain political oligarchy does exist, and was built up during the late 1980s through "Party politics"—where belonging works precisely with the stratum logic of a closed group—and through the linkage between politics and business, opening the door to stratification through "having" [being able to handle large amounts of money]).

These misunderstandings were to have vast consequences in the long run. The United Nations put pressure on the drafters of the national constitution to leave the possibility of a rapid move toward universal suffrage. It was unthinkable to allow these people, whom the Western world would help to become independent, to remain in this scandalous state of inequality, with this all too obvious taste for stratification between nobility and commoners. Thirty years later, in 1990, these loopholes in the text of the constitution in fact permitted the passage to a system of universal suffrage by a simple act of Parliament that did not require the two-thirds majority usually necessary for a constitutional amendment, while reserving eligibility for the chiefs. The chiefs have become "popular" candidates, and have discovered the technique of campaigning for election; some have even become masters of the art of promising all and nothing to the voters. The fact that the candidate can now count on the votes of the whole population has made him less attentive to his position as candidate of a group to which he must answer (his extended family). All he has to do is channel enough advantages to his own group to ensure his position as chief, and, at the same time, he will be able to make a career in Parliament.

The verdict on these changes varies depending on the point of view and social position. What is of interest here is to understand that this evolution toward a model which is "half" true to the principles of Western democracy (the 1990 change was that everybody can vote, but only the chiefs can be elected) stems from Western influence on the text of the Samoan Constitution, an influence that itself stems from an initial Western misunderstanding, which took local valorization of hierarchy for a valorization of stratification.

The Chiefs, a System of Belonging:
The Samoan Universality of Hierarchy

Behind this misunderstanding lies the incapacity to understand that a system of statuary positions can also be a system of belonging for everyone and not a system of privileges creating an inequality among the classes.

Let us follow the Samoan discourse on this matter (my discussions with various Samoans in the early 1980s).

When a Samoan talks about his society in English, he does not differentiate between "culture" and "society," and, as is the habit in Anglo-American speech, he will even speak more often of "culture." But if he is asked, again in English, to characterize his "culture" in Samoan, once it is clear that the subject is the *faaSamoa* (as opposed to the *faaTonga*, for instance, or the *faaPapalagi*, the Tongan way of life and language or those of the Europeans), once it is clear that it is not a question of the history of his "country," *atunuu*, he will say that "the essence or the nature of Samoan culture is . . .": and what follows is usually a list of taboos and duties surrounding the *matai* system and religion. This will be introduced by the phrase: "*o le aganuu faaSamoa* . . ." The term *aganuu*, the dictionary translation of "custom," seems to be only another vocabulary item of the discourse on culture. But, like the concept "country" (*atunuu*), the word "custom" (*aganuu*) refers to the unit of social organization, the *nuu*, meaning both the groups that make up the village (each of which meets in a circle) and the whole village as these groups taken together. Furthermore, the first root (*aga*) means "the essence or the nature" of something, in the sense of "the true place (of this thing) in the overall order of the world," its meaning at all levels, and so on. In short, custom, that order of things which is the *faaSamoa* (the term is not obligatory because we are no longer speaking with reference to the neighbor or the outsider, we are speaking of the essence of the *faaSamoa*, we are speaking from the inside) is "the essence of the phenomenon represented by the *nuu*, *aganuu*. But the *nuu* is the realization, in the organization of the society, of the order established by the *matai* system.[13] Here I will stress two points: first of all, the organization of the *nuu* is the *matai* system, it is a *system* based on belonging and does not represent a system of stratification in the village society; secondly, no Samoan is left out of this system of belonging.

The *faamatai* ("the system of *matai* [names]") is, for everyone, the social system of belonging. Every person, in every social situation (therefore subjected to at least one prohibition and one obligation, and usually to several) acts (in accordance or in conscious and deliberate contradiction) with reference to a "place" (*tulaga, nofo*) that he sees himself as occupying with respect to the others present in this situation. We observe that the representation of this place always refers to the place occupied by the *matai* name with which this person is linked, with respect to the other village *matai* names within the "circle" of these names, the "*nuu* of the *matai*." The *faamatai* is therefore not "the group of chiefly families," it is not only the *matai*, the individual "chiefs": it is the fact that everything entailed in being part of society is *faa-matai,* "guided by the *matai* phenomenon:"[14] the representation of the sacred order of the ancestors' names throughout the country—a fluctuating representation at this level, but very clear at the level of each district and each village taken in isolation.

Everyone thus has in mind the circle of the *matai* of his village, and determines his own position with respect to his peers as though the interaction were homologous to that of the *matai* names from which everyone descends.

The *"matai* name" is the name of a memorable ancestor who has founded a family in the sense of having left the memory of a specific genealogy and a history of great and small events, often connected with wars, a memory that is passed on. In Samoa, every person belongs to a "family" (*aiga*) and often to several; and each *aiga* is something like a cult group, defined around the preservation of one or several ancestral names. There is therefore no such thing as a person who is not linked to at least one *matai* name. And when we see that reference to the place occupied by this name guides all personal interaction, it becomes clear that we are dealing with the most inclusive system of belonging.

The name of an ancestor becomes a *matai* name (*suafa o matai*), a title—as the literature has grown accustomed to calling it—if this name has authority over a land: a land that has been connected with the name since time immemorial, or that was given to this ancestor by another *matai* who had authority over this land, often in token of a service rendered in time of war. Today a *matai* can still create a *matai* name and give this new name a land over which his own name has authority. In this ideology, where continuity between the gods, the ancestors, and men is uninterrupted, men have always behaved toward each other as (they imagine) the gods behave toward them. The great *matai* names come down from the gods (they originate in the cosmogony); others can be traced back to another *matai* name (which originally created them).[15]

The name has a founding house (*maota*), and this house becomes the home of the *matai* and those he wants to gather around himself once he has been invested by the extended family. The name must always be carried by someone in order to stay "alive." The person invested with the name is therefore called the *"matai* of the family" (*o le matai o le aiga*). After a number of generations, the extended family (*aiga*) thus created is defined as follows: a member is considered to be any person, even one living at the other end of the archipelago (people are scattered far and wide by marriage), who can (and wishes to) state any genealogical link (paternal, maternal, or by adoption) with any of the *matai* who has succeeded to this name (and whose connection is known and accepted by the other members: as can be seen when this person comes to contribute to ceremonial gift giving ceremonies, and his/her contribution is accepted). He thereby becomes "an heir to the name" (*suli*); he can take his place in the "extended family circle" (*aiga potopoto*), which meets whenever there is a decision to be made concerning the whole family—and he can be a candidate to this name when the incumbent *matai* ceases to exercise his charge, and a successor must be chosen.

This set of names connected with a founding land might merely constitute a group of families living side by side, an inert list of family names and lands. To this, however, must immediately be added the village dimension, at least in the sense of *nuu*. Samoa is a network of villages ("country": *atunuu*), and its custom is "the essence of the *nuu*" (*aganuu*). This dimension is present from the outset because a land is always a "village land." It is located in the territory of the village, which means that certain decisions can have a considerable impact on the way this land is used. Even if the land holds a founding house—and in this event nothing and no one can annul it; it is an ancestral site, and it is believed that the ancestor is buried there—the village can expel the people who occupy it. The village cannot change the name that has title to the land, but it has every right over the individuals who live on a land belonging to the circle of village lands. These rights used to include the power to put someone to death or to banish them. Today they still include banishment, a sentence that can be pronounced against an individual, against a *matai*, or against several individuals, even a whole extended family, living on this family's village land. One can see the limits arising from this system. Not only is there no such thing as private ownership of the land, but the village can sever the tie that links individuals to their ancestral right to use a land, with the typically Samoan distinction between, on the one hand, the principle of ancestrality, which is off limits—this land remains X's land, and if those living there are banished, other members of the family, living in another village, can move onto it—and, on the other hand, the individual. This person is entirely subject to the consensual decisions of the group to which they belong: namely, first of all the extended family circle, which can expel one of its members, and then the village circle, which has authority over the families and the persons that comprise them.

How can a village decision be imposed on a family? Because every family is part of a circle of which it is only one component: the circle of the village families. Every family is a group that reproduces itself around the preservation of a name that must "live" and therefore must be carried on. This name is connected with a land; both are basic components of the social circle formed by the village. The village *nuu* is nothing other than a circle of *aiga*, a circle of chief *matai* names (which range from ten to more than fifty) together with their associated lands. To say that the village can dictate the way a family uses its land simply means that a family always lives with other families, in a circle, and that, in the event of serious misconduct, the whole circle can decide to expel this family, which is only one component of the circle, just as the extended family "meeting in a circle " (*aiga potopoto*) can decide to banish one of its members—in the same way as it must decide which of the individuals in this circle will be the family's next *matai*.

Every Samoan thus belongs to a sacred circle at every level. Outside the circle, he ceases to exist. The individual does not exist if he has no "family circle" (the literal translation of *aiga potopoto*) to belong to. The family (his place of origin) does not exist if it is not inscribed at the territorial level in a village circle (*nuu, nuu o matai*). If this kind of belonging is not in place, the individual cannot sit down in a house because every house materializes a circle of belonging; in this event, he is without a house, which is inconceivable in the Samoan culture; one must be able to sit down, and know what post to lean against when his family meets, the two being synonymous: when a person "belongs," he knows at what "place" in the circle he belongs. The same is true at the village level: the *matai* of a family could not sit down with other *matai*; he would not know what post to sit against when the circle of the *matai* (*nuu o matai*) met to decide village affairs.

Outside the immediate family circle, one is also a member of larger configurations. On a more conceptual level, there is what we can term "the circle of villages" that makes up the district or the one that makes up the whole archipelago. A family name is always part of a system of names, which is, in its broad rules, in the way it defines for all Samoans the quality of being a Samoan person, the *faamatai*. But the system can best be seen at work in the village community; Samoa is thus primarily a set of several hundreds of circles of names. In each village, the circle of these names is called the *nuu o matai*, the *nuu* of the *matai*. It is materialized by the regular meetings of the village *matai* (*fono o matai*, or simply *fono*). They meet in one of the village founding houses; in some cases it is always the same house, that of the name of the village's greatest and most ancient *matai*, and in some cases they meet in a different house each time, to honor several *matai* names. Physically all of these houses are comprised of a circle of posts supporting a huge, more or less conical roof. The *matai* sit cross-legged on the floor (a stone pavement covered with a layer of coral and then a layer of mats) with their back against a post. No post is the same as any other, and the seating order around the circle of posts is an instantaneous representation of the hierarchy of names. This hierarchy is both historical and legendary, and is inscribed in a series of statements, which relate the origin of the village and the hierarchy of its *matai* names.

Even today these phrases are used in greeting whenever one *matai* meets another. *Matai* greet each other through the intermediary of their ancestors, as it were, as though each was actually the founding ancestor of the *matai* name he bears, and had just relived a condensed version of this ancestor's history.[16] But that is what each *matai* is: not only does he bear the ancestor's name, he "is" this ancestor, from the day he is invested with the name until the day he dies or the family decides to take it away from him.[17] This is visible, for example, in the way children, even very little ones, address their father. Up to the very day before his selection, they called him "Pita" (from Peter) or "Siva" (from a compound name beginning with the word for "dance," *siva*) and so forth, using "his birth name" (the equivalent of our first name). They would use this name in all situations where a European child would say "Daddy": in Samoa, kin terms of address do not exist; only proper names are used. In short, the day before, they called him "Pita." The morning of the bestowal ceremony, of course, the children had known for quite some time that their father was going to receive the title *"Fonomalii"* (for example) and become the *matai* of the family. That very evening, without a hint of hesitation in their voice, they are calling their father by his new name: *"Fono!"* (the *matai* name was *Fonomalii*, but all names, ordinary ones or *matai* names, are shortened in address; the first part is kept or, more rarely, the last).

Beyond the village, there is no social identity that operates on a continuous basis.[18] The hierarchy of *matai* names, however, is used countrywide in the following manner. First of all, as we have seen, when *matai* from different villages meet, they exchange greetings using formulas that sum up the genealogical history of their villages (these are condensations, but it can still take several minutes to utter them because they are made up of several statements which describe the principal names of the sacred circle and their history). However each one recites the history of the other: "Welcome to you who . . . (come from village X)," "Thanks to you who . . . (come from village Y)." In other words, a good *matai* knows the basic history of the names of between a hundred and three hundred villages and, even if two *matai* are meeting for the first time, once they have exchanged names, each usually knows what village the other comes from and the rank his name holds within his village. The exchange of the formulas that summarize the village's history merely confirms this knowledge and creates a more intimate relationship, after which conversation can commence.

To sum up: a *matai* is at home anywhere in Samoa. In a less ceremonial manner and with reduced verbal exchange, the same holds for anyone, once they have told each other what village and family (and therefore what *matai* name) they come from. The fact that a *matai* is at home in any village, in short, that the hierarchy of the *matai* system is universal for a Samoan, is further shown by the following rule: when a family holds a bestowal ceremony for a *matai*, any *matai* passing through can also join in the ceremony and the accompanying exchanges. Once he has entered the house, he will expect to receive little or much, in accordance with the greatness of his name.

The *faamatai* is thus at the same time a hierarchy that can be observed daily in the village and an ideology of belonging to a system that for everyone defines "Samoa." To be "Samoan" is always to be able, through the agency of the *matai* name one carries or to which one is linked, to establish a status orientation ("respect"—*faaaloalo*) in relation to anybody one encounters anywhere in the country.

Let us now go back to the beginning and finish this point. Each person has a place in relation with that of the *matai* name to which he or she is linked. A village *nuu* is first of all, as we have seen, the circle of *matai*—which is the circle of *matai* names, the circle of the deceased ancestors, the latter personified by the *matai* (in the sense, this time, of the person bearing the name). This is the village council, which decides everything, by consensus. But the *nuu* is also the *nuu* of the "daughters of *matai*," that is to say, all of the women related by blood to the *matai* names of the village. They have their own meetings, their own ceremonies, and their internal hierarchy is modeled on that of the *matai* names. The same holds to a certain extent for the third *nuu*, that of the "sons of *matai*," which is comprised of the men in the village who are not *matai* at the time in question. Last of all, it is true, but with even greater nuances, of the "wives of *matai*," whose group is structured by the hierarchy of their husband's *matai* names.[19] It should be added that a woman's membership in the *matai* system is always governed more by her own blood ties than by marriage. These wives, who do not really belong to their husband's *nuu*, are, in their home village, full members of the *nuu* of the "daughters of *matai*" of their respective villages, and they reactualize this membership if they divorce or are widowed, and even each time they return to their village alone, which they do frequently.

Because of this, every man and woman, *matai* or not, carries around a mental image of the hierarchy of *matai* names which constitutes his or her ideological reference in relations with others. That is the *matai* system, a hierarchical system of belonging; it is at the heart of the *faaSamoa*, which identifies the Samoan culture area, and it organizes the Samoan identity into a series of connected and concentric circles: those of the families and those of the village, and less frequently, those of the districts and those of each island; finally, and on a more imaginary plane, those of each of the two Samoas, and even of the entire Samoan culture area, a circle which would be materialized if all the *matai* of the two Samoas, western and eastern, were to assemble and meet together.

Dumont's Distinction

Polynesia thus offers many examples that invite an extension of the notion of "inequality."[20] Our reflection is facilitated, however, because a predecessor once found himself in the same situation, that of discovering himself to be out of sync, as it were, and forced to apply a notion to his observation different from his customary way of thinking. Louis Dumont had this experience in his work in India. I have already mentioned the case of India, which at the same time resembles that of Polynesia, but reversing the directionality of the taboo. Dumont studied India in the 1950s; one of the concepts at his disposal at that time was the idea of "social stratification," which he had inherited from his studies as well as from his English readings. After his research, here is what he wrote, in an article published in a professional journal in 1960 and later included in *Homo Hierarchius*, devoted to the systematic aspects of the Indian caste system (Dumont 1966: Appendix A):

> [Concerning India] it is necessary to distinguish two very different aspects: on the one hand the status ladder (usually called "religious" status), which I call hierarchy, and which has nothing to do with the fact of power, on the other side we find the distribution of economic and political power (Dumont 1966: 317–18).

He added that hierarchy "culminates in the Brahman or priest"; and it is the Brahman who "consecrates the king's power," whereas the king "relies on force" (*artha*). The priest is therefore "absolutely" supreme, and answers to the king only on a lower level (Dumont 1966: 317–18).

From 1960 until today, few have listened to this author's proposal to distinguish two kinds of inequality. We will look at two reasons for this.

Reason 1: The Vocabulary of Political Anthropology

The term "hierarchy" belongs primarily to the field of political anthropology. The concept is understood *a priori* as indicating a phenomenon of power, eventually generalized or sacred power. One has only to reread a few passages from the works of Georges Balandier or from American anthropologists, even schools that purport to be explicitly based on Dumont's writings.

Political power organizes the legitimate domination and subordination and thus creates its proper hierarchy . . . there is no power without hierarchies. . . . The power, the influence, the prestige result from conditions, which are better known today. For instance the relation to the ancestors, the ownership of land, . . . the manipulation of symbols and rites . . . The so-called "natural" inequalities, founded on differences of sex and age and "processed" by the cultural environment . . . manifest themselves in a hierarchy of individual positions (Balandier 1974: 270).

Sometimes the author uses the terms "hierarchy," "stratification," and "inequality" (status inequality and inequality of power, here interchangeably); sometimes he seems to find "elementary forms of social stratification" in the "hierarchies" (of kin relations, sex, age), here citing Bastide as well as Murdock, who wanted—quite rightly, I think—*the term "stratification"* to be reserved exclusively for situations dealing with "*essentially distinct and unequal groups*," as in the case of slavery (original emphasis). Balandier cites together the cases of "truly political" stratifications as well as "societies based on rank, orders, and castes," including the case of Samoa, then mentions Sahlins's book (1958), with its revealing title *Social Stratification in Polynesia*. Nevertheless he once more concludes that it is preferable to use the term "stratification" when describing dominant inequalities other than those that create hierarchies within the kin group, and so on, and when "the divisions that are established between hierarchical groups are delineated on the scale of the society as a whole or on that of the national political unit."[21] In short, stratification includes the various hierarchies and is grounded in them. Consequently, both these notions designate the same logic, namely, the logic of the *difference of access* to social positions, even when one might claim that these are of symbolic value only:

> to list all those who have a privileged access to elements organized by any social system—men, objects, "codes," and symbols. This leads one to mention: those who possess power; those who possess rare property, those who possess social signs and symbols of the most valued kind, authorities, and prestige. . . . In short all those who possess some *power* and who contribute to the inauguration and the maintenance of subordination, and who benefit in various ways from inequality (Balandier 1974: 270, original emphasis).

One finds this same absence of distinction between hierarchy and stratification in the articles in general or specialized dictionaries, in English and American anthropology textbooks, and so on. Yet, to me it seems useful to distinguish clearly between the inequality of *access to things* (keeping Balandier's notion of "access") and the hierarchy within a *totality*. Nor is it enough to say that the object of the differentiation is sacred, and therefore the gradation becomes a hierarchy, a "sacred order." Indeed, if the gradation is made in terms of *access* to the control of "sacred powers," the result can also be stratification.

The Case of Samoa and the Example of Gender

It is also interesting to see what Sherry Ortner and Harriet Whitehead have to say. They edited a well known book on gender studies, in which Ortner devoted a great deal of attention to the example of Polynesia, dwelling at particular length on the case of Samoa.

> For Polynesia the "prestige system" is a system of hereditary ranking. . . . Polynesia thus belongs to that large class of societies labeled "hierarchical" in Louis Dumont's classic formulation. . . . Most recently Irving Goldman has (independently) discussed Polynesia in much the same terms in which Dumont discusses India (Ortner, 1981: 359–60).

The author immediately goes on to sum up what she considers to be Dumont's defining characteristics of "hierarchical" societies. The first is "what Dumont calls 'encompassing' status of prestige criteria vis-à-vis other principles of social organization." This means, Ortner continues, that people are ranked according to criteria "of social or religious value that theoretically transcend immediate political and economic 'realities.'" The second characteristic is "holism." The author understands that this term implies that, contrary to a view in which "strata" are set out and then connected together, the differences are the "functionally specialized precipitates of a prior whole." However, for Ortner, this would simply mean, "in terms of social practice," a system of reciprocal as well as mutual obligations: inferiors have obligations toward superiors, but the latter also have obligations toward inferiors, because of "*noblesse oblige*" (in French in the text). In short, the holistic hierarchy would just be a reciprocity operating within nonpolitical-economic contexts (Ortner, 1981: 359–360).

Elsewhere Ortner and Whithead explain that it was these "prestige structures" that anthropologists neglected, with the notable exception of L. Dumont, I. Goldman, and M. Bloch (1981: 14). Individual status results from the assessment made by all the other individuals. Thus, according to Giddens (1971) and repeated by the authors, "stratification of status is not, to Weber, only a 'complication' of class hierarchy."[22]

"Class" distinctions could be defined "with regard to production," while the "sources of status or prestige" would be: "command of material resources (including human labor power), political might, personal skill" in relation with a legitimizing system of beliefs and symbols. The content of the defining list is of little importance, however. We see that, for the authors, the difference between order of the social classes (which Dumont calls "stratification") and status order (which Dumont calls "hierarchy") comes down to content: the relationship to production and everything else. They thus totally ignore the difference between the two logics, insisted upon by Weber and later by Dumont. Let us qualify this in different words as a logic of access *versus* a logic of belonging.

This turns out to have far reaching consequences. In the study mentioned above, Ortner concludes that the system of the cultural representation of the man/woman relationship in Samoa is one of these "prestige structures." Thus one might believe it suffices to prove that, in Samoa and elsewhere in Polynesia, the difference is one of kin status used in power strategies (men give a high status to women-as-sisters, which enables them to use their sisters in strategic clan alliances by means of matrimonial alliances). We thus completely miss the crucial fact that, for some of these man/woman relations, the logic is one of status: it is of the whole/part kind when it pertains to the sister/brother relationship, while it becomes what one could call a "class" distinction—as well as one of power—when it pertains to men and women not related to one another.

In every situation where men and women are considered, from the Samoan point of view, as "males and females," each of the sexes carries its own definition (in the discourse of the other sex and in the general discourse of the two sexes), which allows one to measure inequality. Thus we find ourselves in a situation where fact precedes value. Without going into detail, let us say that, with a few exceptions, we once again find a certain discourse that Westerners also are familiar with in their own ideology: the "stronger sex" versus the "weaker sex." The forms taken by flirting and hidden premarital sexuality, and even parts of the wedding ceremony, express a clear male domination. In these cases, the Samoan discourse refers to "living beings": it lumps together humans and animals, and divides the world of the living into two sexes. The characteristics ascribed to either sex emerge from their respective "natures" (as ideologically constructed).

All one has to do, however, is to shift to the world of consanguine kin relations and, outside kin relations, to the formal relations between fellow villagers, to discover that the world of humans is completely disjoined from the animal world—which is quite logical—and that it no longer partakes of this inequality measured *a posteriori* and explained in the terms of "strong/weak." In this world, one finds: (1) the "chiefs," who, in a certain manner, might be described as situated beyond the gender distinction; (2) their "daughters" (all the girls and women living in the village and who are considered as the "heiresses" of the landowning families in the village;

(3) the "brothers of" these women (all of the boys and men who are not chiefs). The women we consider as the "women" of this place have a sort of *a priori* definition connected with their position as heiresses, with regard to the chief system. Even today it is said that these women are "the relation." They are not at all defined only as the "sisters of" certain men. The village men who are not chiefs are defined with respect to the women (terminology and attitudes): "brother of" (while, in the sociocentric vocabulary, the Samoan translation of " sister of" does not exist). In short, the former are the whole of the relationship, the latter, a part encompassed in it.

If one asks a Samoan to answer, in this context, comparative questions pertaining to the idea of one sex dominating the other, the unanimous answer is that the question does not mean anything. That should not keep the anthropologist from studying the manner in which a certain kind of male domination plays or does not play a role. Nevertheless he should bear in mind the fact that, at this moment, this question is his own, for from the standpoint of his interlocutors, these are not two categories of the same kind whose inequality of access to such and such a power could be compared.

A short example of all this is the brother's attitude toward his unmarried sister. A priori, he is the "part"; he sees the world through his sister (she is "in the pupil of his eye"); he is her servant (doing numerous household chores, including cooking and serving meals). This applies to brothers and sisters of the same generation regardless of who is the elder or the younger, and holds for as long as the sister preserves the reputation befitting an unmarried woman. There must never be the rumor or hint of a sexual relationship with a man. Should this happen, the brother suddenly becomes someone who can strike his sister, verbally and even physically. He can do this, however, only if he is older than she. If not, he must quickly denounce her to an older brother. The explanation given for this is that the sister is behaving like a "woman," (in the sense of "female"), and that the brother, then representing the "stronger" sex, must remind her of her obligations. The brother and the sister are suddenly transported to the level of relations between "male" and "female." On this level, "force or power" becomes the law. But for this power relation to be possible, one sibling must be older than the other. This is not at all surprising. The older/younger relationship is a measure of inequality of age, overlaid *a posteriori* on two "sames."[23]

Second Reason: the Novelty of a Discourse on "Values"

Another reason explains the reticence to enter into the logic of hierarchy: One rejects the pertinence of an anthropology of values. Dumont addressed this case in particular. This point of view was presented as a formulation of the comparison of "values," which might suggest an incidental remark reserved for the case of India. On the ideological level, the modern day Western world valorizes equality, Dumont wrote; yet, in point of fact, it is inequality that dominates. How can one analyze inequality—or what seems like it—when one encounters it in other societies? The usual choice of the political anthropologist is to turn to the idea, which in the Western world is the opposite of equality, namely, stratification, that economic or politico-economic inequality which can, in fact, lie behind the value of equality. But in proceeding in this way, one prevents oneself from understanding what otherwise could constitute a "valorized" form of inequality. Dumont had the conviction that he should look at societies that clearly valorized inequality if he wanted to formulate an anthropological concept contrary to equality. For him, India was a choice example. At the end of his analysis, valorized inequality (from now on called "status hierarchy") appears as something different from stratification in both its form and its content: it is "structural" rather than substantial, "religious" rather than political or economic, Dumont writes.[24]

This line of reasoning shocked many; it also engendered erroneous interpretations of the typology of societies. The "valorization" of inequality cannot help but shock. It was said that Dumont had limited himself to "paraphrasing" the "ideology" of certain traditional societies (Lantz 1986; the term is extended to the sense of superstructure, false consciousness, alienation of the dominated, and so on). It was also said that he let himself be taken advantage of, and had locked himself into a simplistic dichotomy, for he seems to have forgotten that inequality also exists in India, and, above all, that inequality exists in the Western world (Béteille 1986). The critics forget the fundamental difference that Dumont wanted to make between "valorized" social facts (he also said "ideological"), which are a representation shared by *the whole society*, and the opposite, which appear de facto to the observer, and which he recognizes as being at work. When Dumont later wrote that the development of Western ideology (the valorization of equality) seemed to him "exceptional" and "aberrant" with regard to various societies both present and past (Dumont was thinking of the "historical" character of the emergence of universalistic modern individualism),[25] the threshold of tolerance in the anthropological imagination seemed to have been crossed: nonegalitarian societies, he seemed to be saying, are the normal and natural form of social structure!

The distinctive opposition, however, "as analytical as one could wish for," according to Dumont, between *stratification* and *hierarchy*, has nothing to do with comparison, even if it is the result, in Dumont's thinking, of a comparison between India and the Western world. One simply notes that stratification does not account for certain social phenomena. One can now understand that the inadequacy of the concept of stratification as a universal sociological concept appears there where the hierarchical phenomenon analyzed is *global* (a fact of "consciousness," as Dumont says, "valorized" and "ideological," shared by everybody). Indeed stratification was understood by us as being the *opposite of one of our values*, and not only as the distinctive opposite of another analytical concept in an already scientific and specialized discourse. It is thus "encompassed" (*"englobé"*) and therefore cannot represent a value, which is, by definition, something that "encompasses," an organization-representation of a global system of social belonging. We therefore need something else to account for an encompassing inequality.

The notion of "valorization" can lead to some confusion: Dumont has sometimes been mistaken for an advocate of social inequality. Let us instead say that status hierarchy is an inequality that functions at the *level of the whole*, and as such is a system of distinctions that is immediately a *rule* (locally regarded as universal) *of belonging to the same group*. I hope that the few insights given above into the Samoa *"matai* system" have illustrated that point.

Indeed, the example of Polynesia is eloquent. Let us take a formal meeting in Samoa, for instance one of the kind in which the family chiefs deliberate at the village level to come to a collective decision. They meet in a circle according to a highly specialized code; everyone is different by their position in the circle (with respect to a system of axes orienting the house with regard to the center of the village), while all are alike because they belong to this unique "sacred circle." Disagreements may be expressed, but only "within the circle," and the outcome must be a "consensus" (even though, in the process leading to this consensus, some voices had more impact than others during the discussion). To close the reunion and seal the consensus, a ceremonial drink is shared. The decision can then be announced to the village. Sometimes, however, it happens that one of the members cannot hide his anger at having had his proposal vetoed by a majority that emerges in the course of the discussion. If he makes the error of abandoning the "polite" vocabulary and resorts to insults, if he makes the error of leaving his seated position and stands up, he offers the possibility of a space for violent confrontation, where "force" replaces "rank." Then the young men who have been waiting around the ceremonial house and who belong to the families of the other chiefs present at the meeting, lay hold of the person who has left the "circle" to resort to violent means (they remove him from the ceremonial house *manu militari*), and they respond with violence by beating him, even though they are not chiefs. In these cases they act as the "group of the village force" (formal appellation of a group of nonchiefs), obeying in fact an order given by the other chiefs present; and this space of "force" has now left the world of "respect" owed to rank: here a nonchief can strike a chief.

Formal Differences

This position, at the level of the whole—the "valorization" of hierarchy—endows status hierarchy with specific formal properties. Dumont hardly developed this aspect. In the vocabulary of the time (1966) he had only the contrast between structure and substance at his disposal (chapter 2). The indications we gave at the beginning of this discussion show how the analysis should be continued in order to go beyond an opposition defined only by the labels "religion" (status) and "power."

First the question of reference: With hierarchy, the reference of difference can no longer stand outside the field of relations, thus it cannot be substantialist; one can no longer think in the habitual manner, which leads one first to determine the nature of the connected elements and then to measure the relation between them so as to determine whether there is equality or inequality: A and B have x and y and are therefore rich/poor or the converse. Dumont rightly criticized the tendency to separate in this way fact from value in sociological analyses (1983: 202, 210–217). Alternatively, in the case of the distinction "divine/human," in the sense given above, we find a model for a certain number of systems of social differentiation. In India, the Brahman priest versus the other castes; in Samoa, the chief (the bearer of a title—an ancestral name—once he has gone through a ritual appointment) versus the taulelea (people who have only their birth name, i.e., all nonchief males).

Second characteristic: the status hierarchy consists of a gradation of prohibitions, while stratification is a gradation of having. More sacredness means—and is marked by—more prohibitions, which characterize the position in question. We have talked about this.

The third characteristic is also already discussed: in the having mode, there is a symmetry between the ascending and the descending orders, in short an absence of direction in the difference. Alternatively, in the gradation of the prohibitions, the differences are directional. We have already mentioned the case of India. In Samoa unidirectional opposition between statuses is everywhere. Upward, one offers food, and cooked food only; in Polynesia cooking operates a true ritual passage that gives entry to a circle of greater sacredness (this is the elementary sacrificial operation). Downward, one offers bark cloth and mats (and bank notes), which are soul containers, vectors of mana, in the Polynesian sense (Tcherkézoff 2002, 2003b, 2004:

chapter 10). Another example cited is the "chiefs' language": hierarchical direction can be introduced even in the everyday vocabulary. This and the other previous examples lead us to think that the addition of "hierarchy" to "stratification" may bring a better anthropological understanding in a large number of situations. At least if one agrees to say that progress in anthropological understanding is enhancing the possibility of intercultural dialogue (Tcherkézoff 2003a: Introduction and Conclusion). For instance: how do Samoans understand our will to study their "social relations of equality/inequality"? In the process of that dialogue, the question brought in by the visitor comes back to him with a new distinction. Retranslated in "anthropological discourse," the question addressed back by the Samoans to the visitor is: "Do you mean holistic hierarchies or stratified inequalities, for we have both?"

Notes

1. This text is partly an extension and partly a translation of an article written in French. That article is published in *Terrains Ethnographiques et Hierarchies Sociales*, ed. Olivier Leservoisier. Paris: Karthala, 2005. The French has been translated into English by Britt Veland and revised by Nora Scott.
2. See Tcherkézoff 2004, chapter 11.
3. A detailed description of this affair can be found in Tcherkézoff (2003a: 459–473).
4. See Tcherkézoff 2001a; 2001b; 2001c; 2003a: 473–494.
5. As understood by French holistic anthropology: that is, the Durkheim of *The Elementary Forms of Religious Life*, first published in French in 1912, Mauss and later Dumont.
6. Sahlins says only "burned."
7. In Polynesian logic, it is not the chief who is contaminated by this gaze; it is the transgressor who is "burned." However, since this symbolic cremation is completed by a real sacrifice, we have no experience of what would happen to a chief who was looked on by a lowly man who was not subsequently punished. Taboo does not obey a logic of experience, but rather a logic of "prohibition."
8. On "the chiefs' language," see Tcherkézoff 2003a: chapter 5; on the misunderstandings concerning an "aristocratic" regime, see ibid.: chapter 6. These two chapters contain all the necessary references, not mentioned here for lack of space, including an ethnographical summary of facts and a bibliography of old and more recent publications.
9. Let us add that, in the system of "sacred powers," the same individual, the "chief" or "sacred king," is placed at the top of the ladder of prohibitions as at the summit of the ladder of power. But the conditions of exercise and the symbolization of the two are clearly distinguished.
10. The Samoans call this vocabulary the "words of respect" (*upu faaalaoalo*) and those who speak English use the "polite language." Typically, the European expression used

locally is "Chiefs' language," thus immediately interpreting a hierarchy as stratification, something which is a complete fallacy.

11. On the generalization of the notion of the "family chief" in Samoa, see Tcherkézoff (2000).

12. Samoans also say outright that the characteristic feature of their custom is the *faamatai*, the "*matai* system." But this response is more typical of intellectuals, who spontaneously make a comparison with foreign social systems "without *matai*." I am interested here in the fact that, even from a purely insider viewpoint, the order of things is *aganuu*. Any time someone wants to justify an obligation or a prohibition to a younger person, not to an outsider, they invoke the "*aganuu* imperative."

13. For Samoans who put the word in writing, it is an institution and, as in English, they sometimes capitalize it *(Faamatai)*. But the term designates first of all the set of social principles that stem from the system of belonging constituted by the transmission and reproduction of the *matai* names. For Samoans, it is the functional equivalent of our reference to "democracy" or "equality." Everything connected with social relations flows from, or at least, people say, *should* flow from the *faamatai*, from the "spirit of *mataism*" (to use a local English neologism). Furthermore, in the current political debate, *faamatai* can also mean a budding political party or all the individual *matai* taken together. Recently, in reaction to certain tendencies of the present government (this note was written in 1994), several *matai* created an association to preserve and promote the values underlying the system of belonging constituted by the transmission of the *matai* names. They called it "*Faaiganuu Faamatai*" or simply "*Faamatai*"; its leitmotiv is the defense of the consensus made possible by the traditional practice of the sacred circle, in contrast to the decisions obtained by majority of votes expressed (Hon. Le Tagaloa Leota P., personal communication). See below the section on consensus; see also the magazine *Poliata Samoa* (no. 1, December 1994), published in Apia, which includes pictures of the Hawaiian trip organized by the association: the outcome was the proposal to create an Alliance of Pacific Cultures. It should be noted in passing that the word *Faiganuu*, like *nuu*, is a root "association, organized group" *(fai:* to do, make; *-ga*, noun suffix); the Samoan village, in the sense of *nuu*, is a "social organization" first, and only afterwards a geographical site.

14. It may be that, in pre-Mission times, there was a distance between *matai* names regarded as *paia*, "sacred-divine" (which had the right to this title, according to certain informants) and others not qualified as such (is it because they were sufficiently recent for the memory of their creation by another *matai* to have been preserved?) (see Tcherkézoff 2000). Today, and since the mid nineteenth century, it seems, the term *paia* is applied only to religion (and to the country, since "Samoa is founded upon God"): "Samoa" is *paia*, God's "name" is *paia* (O le Suafa Paia), and the Bible is the "sacred-divine book," O le Tusi Paia (but the church building is *falesa*: "house" = *fale*, "sacred, forbidden" + *sa*; the term *sa* was and is still used for all prohibitions having to do with the family, the village, the State, or religion).

15. Marshall Sahlins has already reported this use of the "heroic I" in Oceania and elsewhere, where the teller relives in a historical present the story of the hero (his ancestor) so vividly that not only is the action narrated in the present, but the subject of the action becomes no longer "he" but "I" (see Sahlins 1985: 47).

16. Throughout this section, I intentionally stress the *faamatai* as a system of ancestor worship and the *aiga* as a cult group articulated around a genealogy, in order

to correct the image usually conveyed by the literature of an aristocratic society with a system of chiefly families. But notions that, expressed in this way, look like "religious" concepts can very well be part of the social morphology and even provide the fundamental scaffolding for the whole social organization (we once would have said that they "function as an 'infrastructure'"; see Godelier 1979)— the Indian caste system is there as proof (see Dumont 1966; Tcherkézoff 1994b, part two).

17. A little nuancing is in order here. A number of great *matai* names are linked with a territory in several villages (as a result of past wars, marriage strategies) and are the source of numerous other *matai* names whose founding house stands in these villages. Succession to these great names requires that the representatives of all these villages meet together. Furthermore, since the beginning of the twentieth century, there is, over and above the village, the *malo*, the government; but in theory this *malo* is not above the *faamatai*. Until now it has not had authority over the *faamatai* when it comes to titles, but this may come about if a separate political class grows up. Meanwhile, the contradiction already exists in the area of criminal law.

18. Here a number of explanations would be needed. First of all, some people say that "the two village *nuu*" are the *matai*, and the daughters (and sisters, and aunts, and so on), *nuu o matai ma nuu o tamaitai*. The third group is also constituent of the *nuu*, but it is rarely called "the *nuu* of the boys/young men)": it is called "the strength of the village," in the service of the two other *nuu*, their *matai*, and their sisters and paternal aunts. The fourth group is a complicated affair. First, this group is a constituent part of the village inasmuch as these women carry on collective activities, but for some, this does not make it a *nuu* because wives are not members of the village (in the sense of members of the "circle" of *matai* names), since they originate from other villages (a rule of village exogamy largely prevails in Samoa). Second, the discussion concerns only the wives of *matai*; for the rest, the wives of non-*matai*, do not form an official group but are integrated into their husband's household (if the couple lives with his parents, which is far from always being the case when the husband is, precisely, not a *matai*), where they do many of the chores (the same may be symmetrically true if the couple goes to live with the wife's family, the non-*matai* husband may be given the heaviest household chores to do).

19. In the following pages, when the reference of the quotation refers to the French original edition, it means that the quotation presented here is a literal translation of the French original, done by the translators of this whole paper and revised by Serge Tcherkézoff.

20. See Balandier 1969: 93–103.

21. Note that, as for the last expression, we find a usage comparable to that of Balandier.

22. On this vast question of relations between the sexes in Samoa, see Tcherkézoff (2003a: 277–495). One could also show, by studying various Polynesian kin terminologies, how the terms used to differentiate age create a system different from the terms that distinguish sisters and brothers. The former cannot create a socio-centric vocabulary; they remain egocentric, while the latter have two forms: some permitting the masculine Ego to speak about a certain sister, others permitting the same Ego to speak about his sisters, or even about the sisters of the chiefs who have succeeded one another over the many generations of the extended family.

23. See Tcherkézoff 1993; 1994a; 1994b; 1995.

24. See Tcherkézoff 1994c.

References

Balandier, Georges. 1969. *Anthropologie Politique*. Paris: Presses Universitaires de France. [*Political Anthropology*, trans. A. M. Sheridan Smith. 1970. London: Allen Lane.]

———. 1974. *Anthropo-logiques*. Paris: Presses Universitaires de France.

Beteille, André. 1986. "Individualism and Equality." *Current Anthropology* 27 (2): 121–128.

Dumont, Louis. 1966. *Homo Hierarchicus: Le Système des Castes et ses Implications*. Paris: Gallimard. [*Homo Hierarchicus; An Essay on the Caste System*, trans. Mark Sainsbury. 1970. Chicago: The University of Chicago Press.]

———. 1983. *Essais sur l'Individualisme: Une Perspective Anthropologique sur l'Idéologie Moderne*. Paris: Le Seuil. [*Essays on Individualism: Modern Ideology in Anthropological Perspective*. 1986. Chicago: The University of Chicago Press.]

Giddens, Anthony. 1971. *Capitalism and Modern Social Theory: An Analysis of the Writings of Marx, Durkheim and Max Weber*. Cambridge: Cambridge University Press.

Godelier, Maurice. 1979. "Epistemological Comments on the Problems of Comparing Modes of Production and Societies." In *Towards a Marxist Anthropology: Problems and Perspectives*, ed. S. Diamond. The Hague: Mouton Publishers.

Lantz, P. 1986. "Holisme ou Individualisme: Un Faux Dilemme." *M.A.U.S.S.* 20: 71–87.

Mead, Margaret. 1926. *Coming of Age in Samoa*. New York: William Morrow & Company.

Ortner, Sherry. 1981. "Gender and Sexuality in Hierarchical Societies: The Case of Polynesia and Some Comparative Implications." In *Sexual Meanings: The Cultural Construction of Gender and Sexuality*, ed. S. Ortner and H. Whitehead. New York: Cambridge University Press.

Ortner, Sherry B. and Harriet Whitehead. 1981. "Introduction: Accounting for Sexual Meaning." In *Sexual Meanings: The Cultural Construction of Gender and Sexuality*, ed. S. Ortner and H. Whitehead. New York: Cambridge University Press.

Shore, Bradd. 1982. *Salailua: A Samoan Mystery*. New York: Columbia University Press.

Sahlins, Marshall. 1958. *Social Stratification in Polynesia*. Seattle: University of Washington Press.

———. 1985. *Islands of History*. Chicago: The University of Chicago Press.

Tcherkézoff, Serge. 1987. *Dual Classification Reconsidered*. Cambridge: Cambridge University Press.

———. 1989. "Rituel et Royauté Sacrée: La Double Figure du Père." In *Le Père: Métaphore Paternelle et Fonctions du Père*, ed. A. Muxel and J. P. Rennes. Paris: Denoël.

———. 1993. "La Relation Roi/Prêtre en Inde Selon Louis Dumont et le Modèle de l'Inversion Hiérarchique." *Gradhiva* 14: 65–85.

———. 1994a. "L'Inclusion du Contraire (L. Dumont), la Hiérarchie Enchevêtrée (J. P. Dupuy) et le Rapport Sacré/Pouvoir. Relectures et Révision des Modèles à Propos de l'Inde." 1st Part: "Un modèle Asymétrique"; 2nd Part: "Statut et Pouvoir en Inde: la Logique Concrète de l'Inclusion du Contraire." *Culture* 14 (2): 113–134; 15 (1): 33–48.

———. 1994b. "Hierarchical Reversal, Ten Years On (Africa, India, Polynesia)." 1st Part: "The Hierarchical Structure"; 2nd Part: "Rodney Needham's Counterpoints." *Journal of Anthropological Society of Oxford* 25 (2): 133–167; 25 (3): 229–253.

———. 1994c. "L' Individualisme' chez Louis Dumont et l'Anthropologie des Idéologies Globales: Genèse du Point de Vue Comparatif." 1st part: "L'Individualisme"; 2nd part: "La Comparaison." *Anthropologie et Sociétés* 17 (3): 141–158; 18 (1): 203–222.

———. 1995. "La Totalité Durkheimienne (E. Durkheim et R. Hertz): Un Modèle Holiste du Rapport Sacré/Profane." *Regards Actuels sur Durkheim et sur Mauss* 91 (1): 53–69.

———. 2000. "Are the Samoan Chiefs Matai 'Out of Time'? Tradition and Democracy: Contemporary Ambiguities and Historical Transformations of the Concept of Chief." In *Governance in Samoa*, ed. E. Huffer and A. So'o. Canberra/Suva: Australian National University (National Center for Development Studies, Asia-Pacific Series)/ University of the South Pacific (Institute of Pacific Studies).

———. 2001a. *Le Mythe Occidental de la Sexualité Polynésienne: Margaret Mead, Derek Freeman et "Samoa."* Paris: Presses Universitaires de France.

———. 2001b. "Is Anthropology About Individual Agency or Culture? Or Why 'Old Derek' is doubly wrong." *Journal of the Polynesian Society* 110 (1): 59–78.

———. 2001c. "Samoa Again: on 'Durkheimian Bees,' Freemanian Passions and Fa'amu's 'Confession.'" *Journal of the Polynesian Society* 110 (4): 431–36.

———. 2002. "Subjects and Objects in Samoa: Ceremonial Mats Have a 'Soul'. In *People and Things: Social Mediations in Oceania*, ed. B. Juillerat and M. Jeudy-Ballini. Durham: Carolina Academic Press.

———. 2003a. *FaaSamoa, une Identité Polynésienne (Economie, Politique, Sexualité): L'Anthropologie Comme Dialogue Culturel.* Paris: L'Harmattan.

———. 2003b. "On Cloth, Gifts and Nudity: Regarding some European Misunderstandings during Early Encounters in Polynesia." In *Clothing the Pacific*, ed. C. Colchester. Oxford: Berg.

———. 2004. *"First Contacts" in Polynesia: the Samoan case (1722–1848). Western misunderstandings about sexuality and divinity.* Canberra/ Christchurch: Journal of Pacific History Monographs/ Macmillan Brown Center for Pacific Studies.

———. 2005. "Culture, Nation, Society. Secondary Change and Fundamental Transformations in Western Samoa: Towards a Model for the Study of Cultural Dynamics." In *The Changing Pacific: Identities and Transformations*, ed. S. Tcherkézoff and F. Douaire-Marsaudon. Canberra, ANU-RSPAS, Pandanus Press.

Tuitolova'a, Agafili La'au. 1984. "Letter to the Editor. Reply to Bradd Shore." *Oceania* 55 (2): 146–147.

Valeri, Valerio. 1972. "Le Fonctionnement du Système des Rangs à Hawaii." *L'Homme* 12: 29–66.

———. 1976. "Le Cuit et le Brulé: Tapu et Mana." Ph.D. diss., École des Hautes Études en Sciences Sociales, Paris.

———. 1985. *Kingship and Sacrifice: Ritual and Society in ancient Hawaii.* Chicago: University of Chicago Press.

Chapter 11

Hierarchy and Power

A Comparative Attempt under Asymmetrical Lines

André Iteanu

Most dominant contemporary social science currents define the concept of hierarchy as a chain of command.[1] This is to say that, in their view, hierarchy is always and everywhere the outcome of underlying power relations, in the sense of inter-individual constraining relations, whose prototype is political power.[2] Therefore, for them, hierarchy and power are always strictly mingled to the point that hierarchy is deprived of any other meaning except as the sign of underlying power relations. This conception of hierarchy as totally submitted to power is congenital to a formulation of society as constituted by a sum of individuals who exert their natural free will and agency. Today it is largely spread out, not only in social sciences, but also throughout all dominant Western (Euro-American) ideologies. In short, that hierarchy and power are consubstantially linked is, in the West, largely a shared assertion and a value that informs a wide range of judgments, actions, and ideas, including the way in which most social sciences specialists conceive of society.

In contrast to these mainstream theories, I will argue that Louis Dumont's comparative anthropology allows us to envisage that certain societies, and particularly India, conceive of hierarchic relations, not as redundant with political power, but as opposed and superior to it.[3] Louis Dumont calls holistic all such social formations in which hierarchic relations, separated from power, are ideologically dominant. Therefore, for him, contrary to the aforementioned social science theories, the collusion between power and hierarchy is not integral to human nature, but the outcome of a specific social configuration. In comparative terms, two contrasted situations must be distinguished. First, in certain societies hierarchy and power are separated, and the former is dominant. Each society pertaining to this group recognizes a particular and unique set of values

---

Notes to this section begin on page 347.

according to which it orders the statuses it confers. From a comparative point of view, this set of values gives each such society its specificity. Second, in contrast, in the societies where hierarchy is indistinguishable from power, statuses are conceived as independent from values, and therefore no values are recognized. This exclusive orientation to power is so influential that the numbers of these societies apply it not only to the description of their own societies, but to all other societies as well. It thus tends to conceal their orientation to values and, as we shall see, poses to anthropology a complex analytical problem.

In the present chapter, I attempt to explore the distinction between hierarchy and power that Dumont has widely documented. As is well known, this author's positions have been heavily criticized by an unusually high number of anthropologists and particularly of Indianists.[4] For lack of space, I do not discuss here their views on hierarchy and what opposes them to Dumont. Of these debates, I only retain, what appears to be a widespread agreement; a vast majority of Indianists—even among those who criticize Dumont—share with him the view that caste hierarchy occupies or occupied an important place in India, at least at a moment of its history, and that Brahmans, or priests, are or were then considered as superior to the kings. When referring to Indian hierarchy, I attempt to remain within the bounds of this shared knowledge, while for the rest of this chapter I am mainly concerned with methodological questions.

As mentioned earlier, I start from a simple contrast. The form of hierarchy which Dumont asserts he has found in India differs primarily from its Western counterpart in that it forms a relatively autonomous realm, partially separated, among other things, from political power (see Dumont 1975, 1977, 1980, 1986). In contradiction to what most social science theories hold as true, this separation thus suggests that the lack of distinction between hierarchy and power is not a universal feature, but a specific ideological construct, operating particularly strongly in the West.

This simple assertion raises a major question that lies at the heart of the very activity of anthropological comparisons. If power and hierarchy differ so vastly in India and in the West, if only because, in the one case they are mingled and in the other separated, how can they still be compared?

To answer this question, Dumont adopts an encompassing view. He argues that hierarchy and power, like so many other social dimensions, are so different here and there that they cannot be compared without considering their position within the global system. While hierarchy in the West is a weak notion largely eclipsed by power, in India, it is constantly manifested all through the continent in the powerful caste ideology. Their magnitudes are therefore radically diverse. Thus comparison must be sought elsewhere, between elements that have a similar weight. In this view, Indian hierarchy and Western power equally represent a value dominantly shared in the societies to which they belong. Hierarchy in India is therefore not to be compared to hierarchy in the West, but to power.

This comparative displacement is considerable and carries many consequences and discomforts. To reduce the leap, it would be tempting to understand Western and Indian ideologies as two opposed cases whose inversion could be formulated as: while power is dominant over hierarchy in the West, in India hierarchy is dominant over power. However, this is to disregard that the adopting of power or hierarchy as a dominant value does not constitute two equivalent but inverse choices. When hierarchy is encompassing, it recognizes lesser values, including political power, by attributing to them a lower rank. When power is dominating, as in the West (Euro-America), it endlessly attempts to reduce all other values to itself, including hierarchy; otherwise, it excludes them. The opposition between Indian and Western ideologies is thus not an inversion but a radical structural contrast between two configurations based on different forms of relations, and even on dissimilar conceptions of society. The most crucial of these differences is that, in Dumont's India, society appears as an ordered diversity, while in the West it appears as a homogeneous field of potentially comparable elements (individuals).

In conclusion, I argue that the consideration of the distinction between hierarchy and power is a powerful comparative tool that preserves social differences, contrary to the universal use of the notion of power that assimilates all societies. In my view, Dumont's hierarchy is, thus, not only a characteristic of such or such society, but also an essential epistemological orientation that helps overcome the absolute reification resulting from the dominating extension of the notions of power.

Several excellent works have already presented and discussed Dumont's notion of hierarchy (Houseman 1984; Descombes 1996; Vibert 2004). In relation to these works, my specific contribution is to insist on the consequences of the distinction between hierarchy and power. I choose this angle because, in my opinion, it allows a generalizing of Dumont's findings to societies where obvious hierarchies, like that of castes, do not exist. It explains why I have been able, with other colleagues, to use some of Dumont's findings in the study of Melanesian societies, despite the fact that they have a reputation for their sense of equality and their absence of centralized power.

Hierarchy Here and There

Dumont developed his own sense of hierarchy through the study of India, a civilization reputed, long before him, for its highly ranked castes system. All through India, notwithstanding local differences, anthropologists have repeatedly reported endogamous and professionally specialized social units that they called castes. A crucial characteristic of these units is that they are ranked with each other according to their relative position with regards to a value that the Indians subsume under the notion of "purity." Among other things, commensality prohibitions, which forbid members of a purer caste to accept food (especially cooked) from less pure ones, demonstrated this order of purity.

Without going into details, it is important to remember some of the case's characteristics that led Dumont to depart from the habitual definition of hierarchy and to affirm that caste ranking was different from a chain of command.

First, the kings' castes, endowed with the political power, are not the highest ranking castes in the hierarchy; rather the eminent position is reserved for the castes of priests, the Brahmans.

Second, while, castes are generally ranked according to their relative purity, and not according to political power, there are times, when the kings' power comes to the foreground (like during wars). The kings then become superior, not to the Brahmans, but in the sense that they can act as their own priest to perform purification and other rites (Dumont 1980).

Third, this implies that, although the kings are hierarchically subordinated to Brahmans, or rather, because of this subordination, political power is not excluded from Indian society, but accorded a legitimate, if subordinated, status. This recognition is particularly clear in the fact that, when circumstances require it, the Kings endowed with political power can momentarily set aside the normal prominence of hierarchy and act as if they are superior. As mentioned earlier, in these exceptional cases, kings do not become superior to the Brahmans in status, but they can momentarily act as their own Brahmans to give way to political power.

Last, Indians do not perceive the caste system as an aggregating of identical elements (castes), which differ only in rank, but as a system of successive encompassment. This can be seen by the fact that caste members, irrespective of their status, do not position their own caste as one among others, but systematically divide the whole caste system into two groups relative to them, the superior and the inferior, the purer and the impure. Given this holistic view, one's own caste does not belong steadily to one of the halves, but varies with the point of view: looking to higher ranks, one identifies one's own caste with the lower castes; to lower ranks, with the higher castes (Dumont 1966: 80). In both cases, one's own caste position is only considered as meaningful in relation to the caste system as a whole.

In sum, Brahmans are not accorded the highest caste rank because they are richer or politically more powerful than the members of lower castes, but because they are purer. Purity is therefore superior to political power exerted by the kings, to whom it offers, nonetheless, a legitimate subordinated position. Caste hierarchy is thus neither a chain of command, nor *society against the state*, in Clastres's sense of the term (1987), which excludes political power, but a totality ordered by a common value—purity—distinct from political power, to which it offers a subordinate position.

That here, a value like purity can encompass lower values, likes power, without confronting them may seem quite surprising. This is so because, as Dumont noted: "While the West, under the logic of contradiction, approves or excludes, traditional India under the logic of encompassing attributes a rank" (1971: 76). This implies that values, like power, which are encompassed by hierarchy, are not confronted but offered actual autonomy within their own subordinated realm.

In contrast, dominant Western (Euro-American) ideologies stipulate that hierarchy is fused with power. Therefore, what is commonly called hierarchy—inequality of wealth, of races, of sexes, and so forth—is systematically assimilated to political power. This in turn implies that all interindividual relations are dominantly conceived as power relations. While in India, hierarchy depends on the value of purity, in the West it is predicated on power.

These two sorts of "hierarchy" not only constitute distinct ways to order individuals, but promote two radically diverse worldviews. While Western inequality, mingled with power, has to do with, among other things, force, "created" inequalities, with resistance, justice, statistical measurements, and with the eventuality for an individual to escape it, Indian hierarchy has to do with ontology of the person, with duration, and reproduction in time, with interiorization and acceptance of the status order, and with devotion. This difference of nature is so far reaching that even the Indian elite, raised on Western ideologies, today put considerable effort into erasing the former form of hierarchy, materialized in the caste system, and to replacing it by another social order based on power; which will, no doubt, include many political and economical inequalities. Clearly, their goal is not to reach "equality," but to replace hierarchy by power.

While we started with a Western definition of hierarchy as a chain of command, Dumont's analysis of the caste system has put us in the position to understand that the Western conception of inequality, intimately associated with, and grounded on, power, is radically different from the Indian conception of hierarchy as separated from political power. Simultaneously, this comparative view suggests that Indian political power—that of the kings, encompassed within hierarchy—is different from Western power, which is a dominant value and the exclusive yardstick to evaluate relations, both in social life and in dominant social science theories.

An Asymmetric Form of Comparison

Sociological theories that consider power as the universal characteristic of relations, oppose inequality constituted on power to equality where power is thought to be minimal. They therefore erect inequality and power as the core of all known social configurations. For example, several authors argue that inequality between men and women constitutes the base of Papua-New-Guinean societies (see for example Godelier 1986). The drawback of these studies is that to characterize inequality, they are brought to extract from their contexts all the elements they examine. For example, that women in the West have lower salaries than men and the ritual contrast between men and women in Papua-New-Guinean initiations are both similarly classified as inequalities. Extracted from any context, the notion of inequality is thereby reified. Leach convincingly compared such a form of analysis to a "butterfly collection" (1968).

To avoid such reification, Dumont proposed to restrict comparison to elements of analogous value magnitude, thus taking into account "people's conceptions." This is why, he argues, anthropology can neither directly compare Western to Indian notions of power, nor Western to Indian notions of hierarchy. Rather, hierarchy orders the Indian caste system, just as political power orders, in the West (Euro-American), relations between persons, who then see themselves as individuals. Therefore, Indian hierarchy, he claims, must be compared to Western power. This shift is crucial since it allows for formulating the contrast between two radically diverse forms of relations.

As stated earlier, hierarchy is characterized by the perception that a higher value encompasses a lower one. It is therefore inseparable from the recognition of different values within the same social system. On the contrary, Western ideologies that formulate all relations as power relations have no space for secondary values. When, for some reason, one of the latter manifests itself, power invariably attempts to assimilate or eliminate it.

One example will illustrate this situation. As everywhere else in the West, current French political ideology claims to be favorable to social and religious diversity. This is why, for example, Islam is recognized as an interlocutor by the French government and given funding.[5] This status is more or less respected for as long as Islam's claims remain in the political sphere. However, when its practice requires establishing a value hierarchy beyond the political domain, it is considered as incompatible with French political ideology and prohibited. This happened recently, when after a heated national debate, French Muslim girls were legally forbidden to wear headscarves in school. This measure was taken in the name of equality between men and women, that is, against gender hierarchy. In spite of the French commitment to respect Islam, political power was here unable to attribute a status of any sort to the gender hierarchy that some Islam currents practice.[6] Its only reaction was to suppress it by legal means, although one can reasonably doubt that this will contribute to rendering Muslim girls more equal to the others, or give them more chances of success in school. When confronted with such phenomena that assert a value different from power, Western ideology, even with the best intentions, finds no other choice but to suppress it by force.

In brief, in societies characterized by power, power exerts constraint over contradictory lower values to transform or to eliminate them. Relations of encompassment, when they exist (as historical remains, or as in the example given, in association with migrations), are therefore partially transformed into power relations.

As we have seen, this confrontation is absent form hierarchic configurations where higher values always attribute a status to lower values. In the Indian example, hierarchy cannot be said to be stronger than power, because it does not interfere in its domain. Describing this relation in terms of power domination would therefore be misleading. Instead, Dumont chose to use the metaphor of encompassment. In his view, the contrast between encompassment and domination reflects that the relations which power has to other elements are different from that which hierarchy has to them. This is true both in the Indian case, where the Brahmans are *superior* to all others in terms of purity, while the kings *dominate* in terms of power; but also, as we have seen, in a comparison which shows that Indian hierarchy *attributes a status* to other values, while Western power attempts to *suppress* them.

A consequence of the radical contrast between these two forms of relations is worth mentioning because it runs against a commonly admitted conception. Societies where relations of encompassment are dominant, like India, are characterized by a profusion of diversities because everything is attributed a status, and nothing is eliminated. In contrast, societies dominated by relations of power are characterized by a higher degree of homogeneity, because power recurrently attempts to eliminate all values that contradict it. Thus, hierarchy does not necessarily reduce all individuals to being the same, as power does not necessarily promote individual diversity.

The Terms of a Nondefinition

Dumont used the notions of hierarchy and of encompassment, as opposed to power and to domination, to refer his readers to the contrast between forms of relations, prominent in two dissimilar groups of societies. These notions do not exist as such in the Indian world, nor, probably, in any other society. He did not use them in their common Western sense either, but on the contrary, expected their atypical connotation to alert the reader to the contrast between his or her habitual notions and those prevalent in India. At best, these notions became part of anthropology's technical vocabulary. I have called such terms "displaced." In relation, but foreign, to both parties of the comparison, they allow anthropological comparison to escape some of the limitations associated with its Western origin.

The Notion of Hierarchy

As mentioned earlier, hierarchy—unlike evolution, Lévi-Strauss's binary opposition, or Durkheim's distinction between sacred and profane or social and individual—does not claim to be central in all societies. It is a limited way to construct an asymmetrical translation between two societies. As a displaced notion, its interest does not reside in the acuteness of its definition, in our usual sense of the term, but in its capacity to encompass different secondary notions—like value, encompassment, and so forth—that evoke, without totally capturing, the contrast between one society and another. Each of these encompassed notions presents a partial view of hierarchy as well as of the societies studied.

In practice, in order to capture a displaced term like hierarchy, the reader must not simply string up in a linear way all the notions used in its definition, but successively adopt the various complementary points of view that partake in its definition. While each point of view may be incomplete in itself, their combination constitutes an acceptable description. Unlike in a sum, such a totalizing definition is compatible with eventual contradictions between the diverse points of view that construct it.

Since the diverse points of view that partake in the definition of hierarchy have been described by Dumont himself, I will only evoke those which are crucial for my concern. I draw these elements from the small glossary, which Dumont offered in his *Essays on Individualism*:

> HIERARCHY: To be distinguished from power, or command: order resulting from the consideration of value. The elementary hierarchical relation (or hierarchical opposition) is between a whole (or a set) and element of that whole

(or set)—or else that between two parts with reference to the whole. It can be analyzed into two contradictory aspects belonging to different levels: it is a distinction within an identity, an *encompassing of the contrary*. Hierarchy is thus bi-dimensional (1986: 279, original emphasis).

Three main aspects of hierarchy—value, totality, and encompassment—are here emphasized. They are at once separate from each other and partially overlapping. Their definition employs in turn displaced terms that are not used in their usual Western sense.

Value

In Dumont's idea, value was probably the most general way (even if still insufficient) to describe the configuration which he calls hierarchy: "VALUE: Under this term, often in the plural, the anthropological literature refers to some extent to what we prefer to call hierarchy. Value is segregated in modern individualistic ideology; in contrast it is an integral part of representations in holistic ideologies" (1986: 280).

Value is used here in an unusual sense in which normative judgments are not separated from social life. Rather, value and ideas are given simultaneously. It implies that, in any given social situation, ideas cannot be enunciated or actions be undertaken, without referring them to a context of ideas and practices, a value. Or to put it differently, ideas and practices cannot be seized in themselves, but only in relation to a set of ideas and actions to which they belong. In this sense, each idea and each practice is immediately given with its relation to something else. This relation assigns it, or "is," its value. Therefore, value is not here a norm or an idea as such, but a relation, which is inseparable from the content of an idea or a practice: in its absence, the content does not "mean" at all. That the meaning of any idea or any practice is dependent on its relation to a context implies that this context has a superior value or, better, that the relation between the idea or the practice and the context is a hierarchical relation. Further, each such context, in turn, depends for its own meaning on its relation to some larger contexts. This cascade of embeddedness is in principle endless, but bound in practice at its superior end by a "paramount value." This hierarchic configuration has two implications. First, that any value is both consubstantial and external to the contexts that use it as a point of reference. Second, that an element is never identical to the value it refers to. Therefore, ideas or practices always partially escape the relations which link them to the superior value, something that Dumont described as a partial contradiction.

From a given social system point of view, the values and the hierarchic relations they elicit are consubstantial to meaning. However, from a comparative perspective, they are arbitrary in the sense that they are not universal, but the specific signature of a particular society. Under this light, one could consider, for example, any causal system—scientific or not, efficient or not—with its infinite potential for regression, as a value system bound by its socially accepted end points, its values.

Such a consecutive encompassment may seem exceedingly rigid and distant from any known form of social life. However, this is never the case because hierarchy does not abolish lower rank values, but only links them to higher rank values. Thus, each encompassed value has room for an amount of "logical contradiction." In India, for example, although the kings' political power is defined with reference to the higher rank value of purity, it is not threatened by the relative impurity of its holders. The very same characteristic accounts as well for individual diversity. While the highest castes worship the white gods, the lower rank castes worship the black god as their highest god (Dumont 1975: 92–111). This difference of reference reflects the fact that in hierarchic ideologies, values do not apply equally to all individuals, but relatively to personal status. The value "choices" of individuals reflect their value ranking.

Relation Between Totality and Parts

Hierarchy is a relation between a part and a totality. However, here again, the notions both of totality and of part do not posses their usual meaning. In the usual Western sense, a totality is an entity which leaves nothing outside of itself. This is not the case in hierarchic ideologies, where each element is in relation to a larger context, and each totality needs another totality to encompass it. Totalities are, therefore, not closed, but open. It follows that a totality is only such for its parts, and a part is only such for its totality, or for an individual that belongs to one or the other. This, however, does not betray a relativistic view, but that the stress is put on relations instead of on their poles. Or to put it differently, that parts depend on a context, which encompasses them. It implies also that, seen from the status of a part, a totality is transcendent, in the sense that it has both a status within the relation and a part that escapes it. In that sense, a totality is always both within and outside the relation of encompassment. This is what Dumont called the two-dimensionality of hierarchic relations.

Encompassment and Partial Contradiction

Encompassment implies that the relation between a part and a whole is not external to each of them, but a relation of "shared substances," or better, a relation in which the relation itself determines the substance, or the "identity" of the related elements, to use Dumont's term. However, since this relation deals simultaneously both with status and with identity, it appears to possess two partially contradictory meanings. From a first point of view, the part and the whole are one and the same thing; from a second one, they are opposed or rather contradictory. When we attribute to these two dimensions a similar reference (relation to the same value), they seem to stand in logical contradiction. However, this is not so for an insider who refers each of the two propositions to a different value context. The contradiction is, therefore, only "local" (if one does not consider the context), or apparent. From within a hierarchical ideology, the simultaneous presence of two seemingly contradictory propositions only reasserts the difference of status of the two distinct value contexts, on which they are predicated. In contrast, in power-dominated ideologies, contradiction evokes a clash between power and some secondary value that it plans to suppress.

Hierarchy and Power

Dumont's reappraisal of the notion of hierarchy is grounded on his experience in India where he was confronted with a form of hierarchy which does not conform to the usual Western (Euro-American) sense of "a chain of command." Therefore, while retaining the term "hierarchy," he redefined the notion to fit the Indian case. As is only normal, in the process the notion has become an anthropological concept. Although such a comparative redefinition of a term constitutes a most regular practice in social sciences, here it gave rise to an unusually high number of violent reactions. This is probably why, in an article published in 1971, Dumont thought it useful to clarify his position:

> Next, the idea of hierarchy, as the relation between the encompassing and the encompassed, gives difficulty to many and even seems to outrage some. Why, in the first place—some would say—introduce such a confusing language? [. . .] Others will state that they can think of "encompassing" about values or ideas, not about people or categories of persons. For example, they might admit that the ends of marriage encompass each other: religious duty encompasses progeny, which encompasses pleasure, or similarly the ends of life, *dharma*, *artha*, and *kàma*: that makes sense, but it does not say that the Brahmans encompass the

Kshatriyas, etc. It would do so only in the case of units of successive orders, as in an army [. . .] or in a multi-layered classification (vertebrates-mammals-lions, says Leach), or in the successive levels of segmentation of the Nuer system of descent groups, i.e., in general in cases when there is a hierarchy of levels where each level includes the inferior ones. *As for me, I am not saying that there is nothing hierarchical here, but what I want to draw attention to is a slightly different case which I take to be that of stronger or more perfect hierarchy* (1971: 68–69, added emphasis).

In this passage, Dumont's main concern is to comment on the radical contrast between himself and his opponents. According to him, his critics accept that abstract ideas or values can encompass each other, but they refuse the idea of encompassment when people or groups are involved. However, he does not explain this contrast. In my view, their position, as in that of more recent critics (see note 4), is understandable in terms of the relative value that they accord to power. Its underlying logic is that relations between concrete people or groups always constitute chains of command ordered by power; but abstract notions do not, and can therefore be accounted for in terms of encompassment. For example, Dumont's critics accept that encompassment is at work in Nuer's social morphology, because segmentation only outlines an abstract dynamic structure and not empirical kin groups. Similarly, they accept encompassment in natural taxonomies that do not deal with human beings and in the relations that link army units of different levels, but not in those that link higher rank officers to lower rank soldiers, which they consider as forming a chain of command. Conversely, the same critics deny encompassment in all cases where empirical people or groups are involved (i.e., Brahmans [priests] and Kshatriyas [kings]), because they reckon that relations between them must universally be described as chains of command.

My argument is, therefore, that in the view of Dumont's critics, ideology is the domain of encompassment, politics that of relations between people. It helps to understand, why, when Dumont applies encompassment to relations between Brahmans and kings, his critics consider that he unduly conceals the power struggles that invariably govern all social relations. In sum, in my view, the opposition between Dumont and his critics does not principally revolve around the definition of the term "hierarchy," but around a deeper methodological and epistemological contrast: while Dumont stresses the diversity of social relations that can be found in different societies, his opponents emphasize the universality of power relations.

As Taylor puts it:

After Foucault we are likely to see power's hands everywhere, omnipresent and in a certain sense omniscient, for just like Adam Smith's Invisible Hand, it appears to "know" just how to shape social relations without each social actor's specific awareness of what is going on, and to ineluctably sort people into two categories: the empowered and the disempowered (2004: 180).

As it proposes that all relations are not based on domination, I read Dumont's redefinition of hierarchy as a deconstruction of the reductive pretension of the notion of power to account for all relations. This is true in "remote" places like India, but according to Dumont appears to be equally so in ideologies where power is dominant, like in the West (Euro-America). As he puts it, hierarchy is indeed "stronger or more perfect" in India where it is separated from political power, but it is not absent altogether from other societies. There, it just assumes lesser forms, mingled with power and partially silenced by it.

A typical example of such a case is the dominant Western conception of gender relations. A powerful ideological trend pleads today for the reduction of gender difference, which it conceives as resulting from a relation of power. However, concomitantly, another ideological discourse, often sustained by the same people, pleads for the preservation of some form of "gender difference." "Although, these discourses do not exclusively conceive of relations between sexes as power relations, they avoid grounding gender difference on the values attached to the "old gender hierarchy," but no new "values" are explicitly formulated to support it either. Therefore, they remain purely rhetorical. In this example, as in many others, power relations are put into the foreground, while hierarchy and its reference to a value are silenced and reduced to a minimal expression. Although unexpressed, hierarchy is not totally absent but appears as less perfect and mingled with power. An anthropological view of these societies, which would content itself with a description in terms of power, only offers a thoroughly impoverished description.

In brief, Dumont's Indian hierarchy teaches us two lessons. First, it shows that the high status accorded to power in the West is not a universal social feature, but an ideological choice among other choices, a value. Second, that the ideologies which value hierarchy are not in a symmetrical position to those which value power: in the former hierarchy affords a status distinct from political power and from other values, while in the latter, power attempts permanently to suppress hierarchy and all values other than itself. This asymmetry elicits a contrast between two radically different ways to conceive social relations. Looking back on most critics of Dumont's notion of hierarchy, it is my contention now that what elucidates their exaggerated aggressiveness is not their disagreement with hierarchy itself, but through it, consciously or not, their deep opposition to the distinction between hierarchy and power. Just as four centuries ago, among the Tupinamba, Jean de Léry (1578) was confronted with an unpleasant dilemma when he was given a man's foot to eat, the Indian castes as seen by Dumont, confront "us," not as anthropologists, but as defenders of equality, and therefore ultimately of power, with the disturbing quandary that hierarchy may be the value preference, as against power, of certain social configurations. This is why many critics of the notion of hierarchy attempt to restore the plenitude of the notion of power, which, according to them, Dumont has devalued.

Hierarchy as a Comparative Notion

In contrast to Dumont, anthropological comparison does not start from universals, but from an examination of the major distinctions between the anthropologist's society and that which he examines. Apprehending a different society, therefore, simultaneously implies reappraising one's own society and deconstructing its categories. This is not to say that comparison offers a view of the anthropologist's society as refined as that afforded by its actual study. It only displaces the anthropologist's standpoint, so that he may gradually view his own society from the point of view of the main values of the society he studies. There is therefore an inherent hierarchy in the knowledge gained. Because of this dissymmetry, looking from one's own society to the society one studies is not simply the reverse of looking from the other way around. This is why repeated comings and goings between two societies are not repetitious, but possess the potential to improve the gained understanding.

Furthermore, to pursue this goal, a specific vocabulary is created whose notions are recurrently redefined. This gradual transformation of meaning is by definition endless, but not hopeless. Comparative understanding appears progressively while one is repeatedly coming and going between two societies, just as the recurring modification of the terms of a language gradually refines the meanings offered. This however does not imply that comparison is reducible to translation or that society is reducible to language or to ideology, as practices are in need of understanding, just as text is in need of translation (Dumont 1966: 56). Discovering universals is but the hypothetical and ideal conclusion of this lengthy process.

Because Dumont's comparison is not universal but a face-to-face confrontation of two societies, it is always located and partial. Its angle depends on the societies considered. A French view of a Melanesian society will differ from an Indian one, just as French society will be enlightened differently by the study of India and by that of Melanesia. Each comparison is, therefore, not objective but subjective in a particular sense—in that the subject is not an individual but a social subject confronted by a different social configuration. It is partial, because other views are possible that can illuminate elements that remained invisible for another study.

Thus, the form of understanding that one can expect to reach by such a comparison is not total, but forever imperfect, or to say it differently, partial. This imperfection, however, can be gradually reduced by repeatedly coming and going between the two poles of comparison. Such a form of knowledge, which is by definition circumscribed by imperfection, is not a Dumontian invention, but echoes established philosophical positions, like that of Leibniz. Because of this limitation, the discriminating question which such an anthropology poses is not that of the adequacy between the comparative view and "reality," taken as an objective social state, but that of the "translation depth," which this view achieves. How much understanding of the other society have we gained through comparison? And how does this acquired knowledge facilitate the understanding of other societies and even of human social nature?

Some of Dumont's critics have judged this form of comparison as derogatory because it does not account for the entire "identity" of the society studied. But is there another alternative to avoid the straightjacket of essentialism? For my part, imperfection is preferable to ignorance. After all, are we not currently reading translated texts—like the Bible, the *Odyssey*, Dante's *Inferno*, and so many others—with the justified certitude that we grasp a substantive share of their content, even if part of what is said will be escaping us forever?

Conclusion on the Notion of Totality

While reading the present chapter, many must think that I either ignore the current literature or pretend to ignore it, because I present a position which has been supposedly taken to pieces long ago and that all this is a tremendous waste of time: I do not believe so.

First, in my view, most critics averse to Dumont's position are not directed to it, or at least not directed to it in the way I understand it. For example, many think they criticize Dumont by attacking a notion of totality that leaves nothing outside itself. I agree with them, for this is precisely not Dumont's notion of a totality. As I have shown, totality in his sense of the term is necessarily open and in relation with a superior value that encompasses it.

Second, such a totality is not historically unchangeable; rather, on the contrary, it is the locus of permanent transformations. Dumont always chose to study societies, which were involved in a deep process of change. In India, he derived (rightly or not) his notion of the caste system from the comparison of two separated historical contexts—the older Varna theory and the caste situation he could witness in the field (1980)—of which, he argues, one probably transformed into the other. In the West, he studied the crucial modifications that occurred when economy as an ideological field started gaining independence from the realm of political power (1977). In Germany, he analyzed the transformations of German ideology under the pressure exerted by French Revolutionary individualist ideas (1994). Finally, in his *Essays on Individualism* (1986), he gave a sweeping vision of different crucial transformative stages in Western history. This suggests, I think, that it may even be impossible to propose an accurate hierarchical view of a society, which would not be caught in a moment of a crucial ideological transformation.

Third, other authors reproach the hierarchical view to transform individuals into puppets, deprived of agency and constrained in normative social structure. I think I have shown here that this is not the case. Dumont's comparison, which opposes hierarchy to political power, attempts only to account for a limited part of the lives and ideas of Indian individuals. Apart from hierarchy, these also recognize political power and many other values that must be studied in their own right. Because of the inherent limitations of Dumont's located point of view, so far these values elude comparison between India and the West. Unlike other approaches—for example, biogenetics or transactionalism—which pretend to explain all individual actions, thereby binding them in a total causal logic, hierarchical vision pays humans a specific respect in accounting only for a limited part of their social existence. This modesty in the face of the richness of social life is to be found again in the fact that Dumont's hierarchical view sees contradiction as an integral part of society. Although, for Dumont, the caste system is central in India, he made of the renouncer, the one who negates it by quitting the social system, a central inventive force in Indian history (1980: 267–287).

Dumont explored the notion of hierarchy hoping to promote a form of comparative anthropology, which preserves social differences. He always insisted that his project was not a theory but "research in the making." with concepts that should be permanently reworked to match newly collected materials and freshly developed ideas. In the present article, from his work, I retained the powerful guideline that power cannot accurately represent relations in all societies. Through this, I suggest that those of us who are confronted in their work with this experience can gain inspiration from Dumont's complex vision to elicit the nature of the relation, which they are given to witness.

Notes

1. Most of the ideas included in this paper have been developed through the years in intense discussions with the late Daniel de Coppet. I thank Jean-Claude Galey for the Indian expertise, Stephen C. Headley for editorial advice, and Cecile Barraud and the seminar GTASC of the EHESS for valuable comments.
2. See for example Bourdieu 1984 for whom relations in a particular "field" are defined indistinctively by power and by hierarchic relations, or to put it differently, hierarchy, wherever it is found, is the sign of power relations.
3. That is, that it is not a dimension of "human nature."
4. To name only a few: N. Dirks, R. Inden, J. Assayag, R. Lardinois, M. Marriot, G. Berreman, R de Liège, D. Kingsley, A. Appadurai, C. Fuller, F.G. Bailey.
5. This is most exceptional in a country characterized by a radical division between religion and the state.
6. This is however the crucial challenge set by the Western attempts to recognize differences. Can, for example, the domination of women by men, which, needless to say, is a recurrent cultural feature in many societies, be recognised as legitimate in the name of the equal recognition of all traditions? In France, at least, this is, for the time being, impossible and I doubt it is feasible anywhere else in Europe.

References

Bastin, Rohan. 2004. "Death of the Indian Social." *Social Analysis* 48 (3): 205–213.

Bourdieu, Pierre. 1984. *Distinction: A Social Critique of the Judgment of Taste*, trans. Richard Nice. Cambridge: Harvard University Press.

Clastres, Pierre. 1987. *Society Against the State: Essays in Political Anthropology*. New York: Zone Books.

Descombes, Vincent. 1996. *Les Institutions du Sens*. Paris: Les Editions de Minuit.

Dumont, Louis. 1966. *Homo Hierarchicus*. Paris: Gallimard.

———. 1971. "On Putative Hierarchy and some Allergies to it," *Contributions to Indian Sociology*, 5: 61–84.

———. 1975. *La Civilization Indienne et nous*. Paris: Armand Colin.

———. 1977. *From Mandeville to Marx: The Genesis and Triumph of Economic Ideology*. Chicago: University of Chicago Press.

———. 1986. *Essays on Individualism: Modern Ideology in Anthropological Perspective*. Chicago and London: The University of Chicago Press.

———. 1994. *German Ideology: From France to Germany and back*. Chicago: The University of Chicago Press.

Godelier, Maurice. 1986. *The Making of Great Men: Male Domination and Power among the New Guinea Baruya*. Cambridge: Cambridge University Press.

Houseman, Michael. 1984. "La Relation Hiérarchique: Idéologie Particulière ou Modèle General." In *Différences, Valeurs, Hiérarchie*, ed. Jean-Claude Galey. Paris: Edition de l'École des Hautes Études en Sciences Sociales.

Inden, Ronald. 1990. *Imagining India*. Cambridge, MA. and Oxford U.K.: Blackwell.

Iteanu, André. 1990. "The Concept of the Person and the Ritual System: An Orokaiva View," *Man* (N.S.) 25: 399–418.

———. 1995. "Rituals and ancestors." In *Society and Cosmos in Oceania*, ed. Daniel de Coppet and André Iteanu. Oxford: Berg.

Leach, Edmund R. 1968. *Rethinking Anthropology*. London: Athlone Press.

Léry de, Jean. 1578 [1980]. *Histoire d'un voyage fait en la terre du Brézil*. Paris: Plasma.

Parry, Jonathan. 1998. "Mauss, Dumont, and the Distinction between Status and Power." In *Marcel Mauss: A Centenary Tribute*, ed. W. James and N. J. Allen. Oxford: Berghahn Books.

Taylor, Christopher C. 2004. "More Power to You, or Should It Be Less?" *Social Analysis* 48 (3) 179–185.

Vibert, Stéphane. 2004. *Louis Dumont: Holisme et Modernité*. Paris: Editions Michalon.

On Dumont's Relentless Comparativism

Frederick H. Damon

"La notion de valeur fonctionne dans ces sociétés; . . ."
Marcel Mauss
Essai sur le don

L ouis Dumont's place in the history of anthropology is secure. The question this volume addresses is his legacy. Will he have bequeathed to the next generations the most productive synthesis about the social systems of South Asia and, based on that analysis, a developing view of the West since the beginning of Christianity? Combined together, and in the context of the largely Anglo-French ethnographic tradition, is this our discipline's most ambitious comparative project, at once regional and historical? Is his work an analysis of places, and times, which establishes a model for the analysis of other crystallizations of sociality? The editors and authors of this collection offer partial answers to these questions by trying to operationalize what they understand as Dumont's relentless comparativism. The volume takes up the challenge Dumont gave us by engaging three projects. First, it defends or perfects his core ideas for, we must insist, future elaboration. Second, it extends the scope of his regional analysis. Finally, it enlarges some of his ideas for transformations many of us face, developments which were not the problem of Dumont's time. His epoch faced the question of what were the different social systems occupying the world. While we continue to debate the answers to that question, his work may also pose the question of what they are becoming.

Dumont was an intense reader of his predecessors' work, both in the anthropology of India for the first phase of his research, and of the Western tradition that occupied much of the last half of his professional life.

Notes to this section begin on page 359.

To follow in his footsteps is to employ the same critical and probing spirit he used with his predecessors. In the closing essays of this volume two of Dumont's students, Tcherkézoff and Iteanu, defend their master's system. It is appropriate that this is done for a different place, Samoa on the one hand, and in terms that attempt to reach beyond India and the West on the other. This is necessary if we seek to test the pertinence of his insights beyond the axis of his central concerns. To just repeat his synthesis is to miss the point of his own endeavors. Between his India and his model of the West, there was and remains the complicated, vast, and interconnected region of Eurasia. Dumont's work must speak to that area, otherwise it must be judged radically incomplete. Beyond the subcontinent were social systems constructed by hierarchical ideas and practices that clearly resonate with those Dumont identified for India. And of course, to travel in today's world is to experience the often problematic fitting of ideas from the West, especially those Dumont identified as paramount, to different places and customary practices, an appropriation or insinuation that is rarely inconsequential. His *oeuvre* adapts to these challenges or else it is a moment in the history of anthropology.

In this concluding statement I draw out a number of themes and problems that, building on the work of this volume, hopefully extend its endeavor. While the editors' Introduction provides its own rationale for the significance of Dumont's work, I focus on issues addressed in the subsequent chapters. On the one hand I urge a regional twist to the collective essays presented here. On the other, I want to take up the question of "paramount" values that Robbins extracts using Dumont's analysis from both the hierarchy of India and the egalitarian ideal in the West. Between these two thrusts there exists an ambiguity over the word "value" that runs through the social sciences, and of course this volume. This ambiguity resides in the difference between the term's connotation as it derives from political economy on the one hand and the sense it received from the revolution in linguistics that de Saussure effected. Dumont's point of view, as is clear from Iteanu's closing chapter, follows from the sheer analysis of form the structuralist revolution inspired. (It also follows from Talcott Parsons, which is not quite the same thing.) I would suggest that the last thirty years, which has witnessed a renewed concern with political economy's "value," but built on structuralist insights, allows us to clarify the ambiguity in the current usage. That is a task, however, lying just beyond what I can suggest here although it informs some of the questions I hope a Dumontian orientation can pose for a future.

Let us be clear, first of all, about the scope of these essays and the people who have penned them. While generated by distaste for aspects of our present situation, our contributors are anthropologists of a rather traditional sort. Products of the ethnographic tradition which engaged Dumont, they have spent or are spending large portions of their lives in other social systems first, if now not exclusively, defined by principles articulated by terms other than those of the current dominant social order. Their contributions fit between or bound the places of Dumont's interests. Three locations are, arguably, adjacent to the West and South Asia: Fosshagen's synthesis of Ottoman sacralized power, Sneath's critique of the writings about the social systems of Inner Asia, and Hoskins's chapter on Vietnamese Caodaism. Both the accounts of Inner Asia and twentieth-century Vietnamese practices touch on an important lacuna in the Dumontian framework: the absence of an analysis of the East Asian hierarchies. Hoskins's elegant contribution, seemingly undertheorized, makes a crucial argument against some of Dumont's critics. The charge had been leveled that Dumont's model of Indian hierarchy was derived from a vision of India created by its colonial context. Hoskins dispenses with the implicit question of authenticity which that charge raises by showing that the logic of Dumont's argument is pertinent for a Caodaism which explicitly rises in an identifiable historical context.

In any case, for good methodological reasons in Dumont's time it was necessary to restrict the field of one's inquiry. However, interaction across this region long before the Western epoch is now a well established fact. This was a highly developed, integrated world predicated on radical cultural discontinuities. So a relative differentiation and interpenetration of people and ideas throughout this region must be taken, now, as the ethnographic context for our further interpretation. In his closing essay Iteanu warns against the butterfly collecting that sometimes perturbs our discipline; that tendency can not be allowed to occlude insights we need to generate with Dumont's analytics. Iteanu defends and elaborates on the Dumontian attempt to integrate a model of hierarchy articulated by the contradictory relation of pure/impure. He does this by reproducing the India/West axis of Dumont's original comparison. Without questioning the utility of this contrast it is imperative that we expand it to encompass the other systems or partial systems overtly defined by hierarchizing modalities. It was not just India that incorporated diversity by attributing rank.

With the possible exception of Robbins's chapter, which derives its problem from the present, the remaining chapters in this book deal with social systems, or relatively isolatable segments of social systems, that were generated by the flows out of the Asian centrifuges. One way of organizing a consideration of these essays would put them in a sequential order from west to east, an order that bears a rough relation to their temporal and spatial distance from the Asian hierarchies. The Ngadha marriage payment system Smedal analyzes from Central Flores is the furthest to the west. Certainly it is his analytical dexterity that allows him to infer the logic of Dumont's understanding of the Indian caste system inside the meanings and uses of buffalo, a human generated form from which life flows. Yet again, maybe he is revealing logical transformations that were most certainly part of the social systems generated across this region. Next to the east is Eriksen's discussion of the social system on Ambrym, in contemporary Vanuatu and thus part of the dividing line between Melanesia and Polynesia. Her problem is similar to Robbins's, and deals with Western religious transformations of the recent past, and I shall return to their central issue. But it also remains significant, perhaps, that while clearly intrigued by the possibilities Dumont's comparative project elicits, drawing from Strathern she feels she has to add a different axis to the contrast in order to make it productive. There is of course a vast region and considerable time between Smedal's Flores and Eriksen's Vanuatan Ambrym Island. But readers of this volume should be reminded of the Introduction's invocation of Wagner's work which is effectively located in New Ireland of Papua New Guinea. Such a location mediates Flores and Ambrym, and Wagner draws usefully on Dumont's, and Marriott's, discussions of Indian hierarchy. As is the case with Smedal's analysis, one might suggest here that the analysis derives first and foremost from the author's creativity, which is not to be doubted. But I would also like to suggest that it is a progressive transformation of interrelated cultural systems that allows models constructed for India to become suggestive for Melanesia. Iteanu asserts that Indian diversity, which can not be overestimated, follows from the encompassing hierarchy of Dumont's model. We know that that quality of diversity extends beyond India and that it does not derive from the isolation of peopled spaces. It derives, rather, from a property of these social systems, arguably a quality sharing something with what Dumont struggled to generate for India. Clearly, however, some attention needs to be given to the mechanisms that generate this diversity. If it is accurate, what role does Dumont's model have in India's history of continuous differentiation? And what role would the analogous structure have in, say, Melanesia? These are questions for a future.

In any case, next in this progression would come Tcherkézoff's discussion of Samoa, and off of that Hoëm's of Tokelau, a recent offshoot of western Polynesia dynamics. Both these essays creatively illustrate how a sacred rank order, whose legitimacy they gather by inspiration from Dumont's India, underlies these respective places. These are not caste principles in operation though they are clearly ranking orders generating considerable variation through time and across space. Tcherkézoff's presents the Samoan system as a circle of ranked names in a system of belonging. With little modification, it should be noted, Tcherkézoff's model could be appropriated for a description of how the Kula Ring is conceived and enacted. Although in the Kula the place of the gods is taken by the exchange of human constructs obtained from the sea, both forms serve to illuminate, to make visible by means of sacrificial destruction, relations, attributed rank orders, among various social units, including named persons. Arguably the orderly ranking that kula shells create helps generate the considerable diversity experienced in the system. Thus a set of differences from one order facilitates the elaboration of others not tightly constrained by the first order of differentiation (see Damon 1980, 2002).

Completing this sequence would be Valeri's contribution on marriage and rank in Hawaii. This piece is culled from work only completed for this publication after Valeri's death. One of the tragedies of our present is that he is not here speaking directly to the issues this volume engages. Valeri generated his Hawaiian material in close association with Sahlins while his initial intellectual commitments derived from Lévi-Strauss. Some of the essays in this set, as I have defined it, are fine illustrations of what one can do with Dumont's ideas when employed with respect to social systems sharing family resemblances with India. Valeri's analysis runs on a different track. It is about how hierarchies are generated. In his Hawaii marriage practices—or, perhaps better put, the denial of a marriage practice/exchange, and other exclusions such as human sacrifice—create the value that inscribes hierarchy in the Hawaiian system. As is well known the creativity of Sahlins's recent contributions to Polynesian studies began with a rejection of our crusty old models of descent and alliance while incorporating ideas about hierarchy from Dumont, Hocart and others. No one should question what has been gained from this. Yet readers must be clear about what Valeri's essay attempts: to show that the manipulation of marriage practices, a play of keeping and giving, generates specific ranked values and the order of ranking itself. The question of generation is important partly because of the new reading of India introduced since Dumont advanced his model. By this I mean Parry and Raheja's ethnographic studies showing that in India impure forces, *dan*, flow up the hierarchy (Parry 1980, Raheja 1988). At face value these new facts would seem to contradict the poles of Dumont's model. However, it is likely they do not because we do not yet understand how *punya*, merit, is generated and sent down for the flow of *dan*, which it is. Yet these relations underline the fact that if Dumont's original structuralist insight helped reveal a critical dimension of the subcontinent, it has not yet helped us see how that system was produced and reproduced. Valeri's essay moves toward that kind of understanding for Hawaii. If his essay is in part a good illustration of what we learn by the partial appropriation of models from India for looking at the Hawaiian Polynesian case, then it also suggests the favor be returned.

The dynamics Valeri attempts to elucidate may be at the limits of a system of relationships, and in two ways. One, of course, has to do with the transformation of the Hawaiian system by the coming of the European order. This arrival gives Valeri, in fact, not just the data he has to work with but a perspective on how Hawaiian forms led to some of its subsequent transformations. His essay contains an argument that by dispensing with their traditional forms of hierarchy in the early decades of the nineteenth century some Hawaiians facilitated the very preservation of that order, if in a substantialized form. The other limit is the aforementioned flow of sociality out of the Asian world, that is, the last four to six thousand years of history that generated these revolving experiments in human order. Hawaii was literally an ending chapter. And his attempt to show limiting forms of reciprocity, partly by taking people out of circulation, generates reflections on the respective chapters by Sneath and Fosshagen. Given the axis of Dumont's work, these chapters are perhaps the most exciting essays in this volume because they are emphatic testimonies to what we have to do with the legacy Dumont bequeathed to us.

One may only hope that these contributions are just the beginnings of Sneath and Fosshagen's work. For individually and together they open new vistas on the places beyond India, stretching to the north and east in the case of Sneath, far to the west in Fosshagen's treatment of Ottoman forms. Although these essays draw on the same literature dealing with the category of "tribes" of Central and Inner Asia—Sneath destroying those models, Fosshagen building on them—both erase regional stereotypes, that these were simple if vigorous segmentary societies. They are ranked feudal systems by Sneath's account; equally ranked and feudal but products of the accumulative dynamics of Lévi-Strauss' model of generalized exchange in Fosshagen's synthesis. It would be nice if these scholars could incorporate into their models the subsidiary exchanges Lévi-Strauss built into his form; such an effort might give us a new handle on the vast regional networks that for millennia were part and parcel of this continental flow of relations. That said, both authors present us models of hierarchical systems of considerable complexity. At the very least this makes Dumont's questions about the nature of other social systems' hierarchies pertinent. Collectively this work provides, moreover, continuity with the hierarchies work such as Parry's North India (1979) data demonstrated and of course proffers an explanation of a baffling aspect of Chinese history: How can the "tribesmen" of Inner Asia gain access to the tops of the Chinese systems? One answer is that our understanding of "tribes" is deficient. Our models for this entire region need a vast overhaul. And these essays may be a good point of departure.

Appreciative of Dumont's models for both India and the West (and Sahlins' work in Polynesia), Fosshagen generates a model for the Ottoman sultan that does not so much split the differences between these two as take an entirely different track: a social order facilitated by something tantamount to a complete withdrawal from society:

> The point I wish to make is that the sultans never became, nor could become, divine kings of the "primitive" Polynesian type or the Egyptian type. In the Turkic tribal structures there was no room for a sacred sovereign within the cosmology. Nor did the structure of Sunni Islam install the sultan with priestly authority or divinity. The route to sovereignty implied a withdrawal from society and social bonds. In a sort of reversal of the mythological structure of sovereignty described by Dumézil (1985) from ancient Indo-European cultures and by Sahlins (1985) for Polynesia, where the stranger king eventually is domesticated by the native people, the Ottoman sultan became a sovereign by gradually estranging himself from the social bonds he was entangled in (p. 200)

Is this the political equivalent of patri-parallel cousin marriage, a kind of continual closing in on itself? This would put us in an analytical orbit first tested by Julian Pitt-Rivers in *The Fate of Shechem*, a collection that tries to locate the values of this region in a denial of customary forms of reciprocity apparently found everywhere else (Pitt-Rivers 1977). But here, in Pitt-Rivers' reading, honor, and "precedence" define the social order (See Fosshagen, p 201 *ff.* though there is no reference to Pitt-Rivers' work). So far as I know Pitt-Rivers did not intend his model to be a refraction off of Dumont's, or of India. But it is interesting that James Fox uses the same word—*precedence*—which *is* intended to replace a Dumontian notion of hierarchy in his, i.e. Fox's, model for Austronesian societies (Fox 1994). In Fox's accounts Austronesian societies create social order at least partly by being *conceived* to follow from taking a position in a scheme of positions. The synthesis covers some of the same kinds of social facts as Pitt-Rivers.' Eriksen and Hoëm invoke Fox's work in their chapters, and Tcherkézoff could have just as easily. While there has been an attempt to look at these models as in competition with one another, I would like to suggest that in fact they are not, that they are covering slightly different dimensions of societies arrayed with respect to one another across this arc of human geography. As Pitt-Rivers' analysis, which in a sense Fosshagen has reproduced, pertains to those places to the west of India, Fox's captures a dimension of those societies laying to the south. This region arguably presents us with a unique combinatory, and one facet of its analysis must acknowledge that possibility.

These orders of facts are among those that lead to a desire to have the kind of analysis Valeri effected combined with Fosshagen's, and constructed in the context of the dialogue with Dumont. For the inversions of the Islamic structures led to some of the most extensive and richest concentrations of value the world had known. In his essay on Flores Smedal pulls the Parry and Bloch distinction between short and long exchange cycles into his analysis. It might be interesting to employ these with Sneath and Fosshagen's material. If the centers that get created in the swirls off this region's history look both magnificent and thin—"almost perfectly external to the social order," in one of Fosshagen's phrasings—they are part of long distance relationships of exchange, and of necessity of production, that endure through the temporary concentrations of power. (These two social facts are relationships, of course, that still baffle Western observers and intruders in the region.) And of course, the social wealth of this region significantly dominated the world until the West eclipsed it. And Dumont's West, of course, was in immediate play with the extended Islamic world, and a more distant relation with the East, as it was being formed. In this time zone Calvin represents a movement that succeeded in making everyone a stranger to each other, mutually independent. This then is the conceptual founding of what comes to be the center of Western forms of production and exchange. Is this Western creation in opposition to the regimes of the East? Whatever the case, these attractors function by negations, perhaps all the while intensifying the emerging individual's relationships to its gods.

One might be able to suggest that the historical trajectory just alluded to would also be appropriate to Robbins's essay, the discussion of which will close my commentary. The Urapmin of western Papua New Guinea are a small group of interior people partially organized by one of the more unique regional systems in Melanesia. Rather than integrated through chain-like exchange systems, participants in this system were ranked in relation to a center at Telefomin. That center recently collapsed, and the somewhat unique response of the Urapmin was to go there to retrieve an evangelical version of Christianity from which they more or less converted themselves. Robbins's elegant review of this material attempts to show how Dumont's work can provide a framework for analyzing radical change. The argument is that a Dumontian notion of value, one that entails a super and subordinate relationship that structures other elements in a system of relations, allows us to see transformations where otherwise we have seen hybridity or synchronism. Eriksens' chapter on the Ambrym follows Robbins because she approaches a similar situation. Arguably a difference that appears between her data and Robbins's is that the version of Christianity to which people were first exposed in her region follows more from nineteenth-century transformations than the late twentieth-century evangelical forms that have been percolating through Melanesia over the last forty or so years, and from which the Urapmin drew. In Eriksen's case the creation of a kind of abstract community vis-à-vis Christianity seems central; in Robbins's the focus is more on the individual's religious experience. Western revivalist histories thus are a condition for some of the overt differences we experience in the present. But rather than historical trajectories as central, I wish to focus on Robbins's phrasing of the "paramount" values idea. His essay to some extent provides an illustration of the logic Iteanu puts forth, and it is from this work that, I think, a future needs to be generated.

The idea that Robbins extracts from the two sides of Dumont's work is that social systems are going to be organized by one or more central ideas, values, and it is these forms that structure relations among other elements in the system of ideas and actions. The point then is that a social system is not created by a unitary value, but that one, or a few, values structure relations among others. Significant social change then is not just the advent of new items in the set but a changed relation among existing ideas which may or may not derive from some new intrusion or element. In his own case, then, drawing on a long line of Melanesian studies, Robbins argues that a kind of relationalism, an analogue of the Indian caste hierarchy, organized Urapmin society but that function is being taken over by a version of Western individualism articulated by the social system's conversion to Christianity. In this process much of Urapmin culture, suggests Robbins, has remained. However, the relations among many of these items have changed, and these will, in the context of other developments, lead to further transformation. The continuity in contexts like this is then often, in Robbins's understanding, illusionary.

This is an idea that needs serious development. Dumont, in fact, extracts a recognition of this kind of analysis from Marx that has, unfortunately, been too little recognized. I shall quote at some length:

> What I want to praise here is the recognition that the unity of a social system corresponds to the predominance in it of cert institutions which it is the duty of the sociologist to determine, not only as present by the side of others, but as giving its character to the social whole. In Marx's own words:
>
> > Under all forms of society there is a certain production which by itself and by its conditions determines the rank and influence of all the rest. It is the general light in which all the other colours are dipped and which modifies

them in their particularity. It is a special ether which determines the specific weight of everything that appears in it. (P. 27; cf. trans., pp. 40–41).[1]

The aesthetic feeling is not so frequent in Marx. It marks here an intense
perception of the specificity of each type of society and of its unity. We may
call it a holistic and hierarchical perception (Dumont 1977: 162).

We might take from this passage the realization that possibilities for this
kind of analysis have been available to us for some time. Robbins is
undoubtedly correct to suggest that thinking in these terms might give
us a new handle on figuring out exactly what is social change. Yet these
ideas also throw into relief important questions about the nature of certain structures. It is of interest that this idea shares a family resemblance
with, for example, the concept "keystone species" in ecology. This idea
highlights the way certain organisms so arrange an environment that
they organize possibilities for other life forms. The others take their
place in relationship to the "keystone." In the history of technology in
the West it is not difficult to suggest that transportation systems, at least
over the last two hundred years, have played this role. The transformation and elaboration of these communication systems thus regularly
define and redefine a myriad of other relations and possibilities. Here
then is an idea about structure that might generate some useful comparative work not just in anthropology, sociology, and history, but in other
disciplines that also struggle with ways for analyzing wholes and their
relations. Dumont opens a possibility that extends beyond his concerns
with India and the West.

Yet there is additional work to do here. More than one of the authors
in this collection, and Iteanu emphatically in his closing, point out
that in Dumont's model there is a contradictory relationship between
the encompassing and encompassed element in the definition of hierarchy. But it is not clear, to me at least, what the significance of this
contradiction really is—a suggestive classificatory tool most certainly.
However, if the idea is just that difference implies a contradiction then
it is uninteresting. It goes nowhere. But that is not the empirical situation we have with any of the societies brought under the filters of
this discipline. If organized by distinguishable key value systems that
structured other relations, what are the natures of these forms that
generated the regional relations and temporal transformations that, in
the last analysis, must be our object of inquiry? It may be argued that
Dumont's work transformed our understanding of two major parts of
the world and left us with an inquiry worth extending. This volume
illustrates the pertinence of the argument to other areas as it asks us to
continue the endeavor. That must be done.

Notes

1. The passage from Marx is from the McClellan extracts from the *Grundrisse*. In the 1973 Nicolas translation of this passage, found on pages 106–7, the wording is somewhat different but to the same effect, with subsequent illustrations of what Marx means by arguing that every analysis must begin with respect to the dominant principle in the society being considered.

References

Damon, Frederick H. 1980. "The Kula and Generalised Exchange: Considering some Unconsidered Aspects of *The Elementary Structures of Kinship*." *Man* (n.s.) 15 (2): 267–93.

———. 2002. "Kula Valuables, the Problem of Value and the Production of Names." *L'Homme* April–June 162: 107–136.

Dumont, Louis. 1977. *From Mandeville to Marx. The Genesis and Triumph of Economic Ideology*. Chicago: The University of Chicago Press.

Fox, James. 1994. "Reflections on 'Hierarchy' and 'Precedence.'" In *Transformations of Hierarchy: Structure, History and Horizon in the Austronesian World*, Special issue of *History and Anthropology*, ed. M. Jolly and M. S. Mosko, 87–108.

Parry, Jonathan. 1979. *Caste and Kinship in Kangra*. London: Routledge & Kegan Paul.

———. 1980. "Ghosts, Greed and Sin: The Occupational Identity of the Benares Funeral Priests." *Man* (n.s.) 15 (1): 88–111.

Pitt-Rivers, Julian. 1977. *The Fate of Shechem, or the Politics of Sex: Essays in the Anthropology of the Mediterranean*. Cambridge: Cambridge University Press.

Raheja, Gloria G. 1988. *The Poison in the Gift*. Chicago: The University of Chicago Press.

NOTES ON CONTRIBUTORS

Frederick H. Damon is Professor of Anthropology at the University of Virginia. He has long-term research experience in the northeast corner of the Kula Ring in Papua New Guinea, now augmented by forays into East Asia. He writes about exchange, production, technology and ethnobotany, and the deep history of the Indo-Pacific and the modern world as analyzed by a social anthropologist.

Annelin Eriksen is a post-doctoral fellow at the Department of Social Anthropology, University of Bergen. She has conducted extensive fieldwork in Vanuatu in Melanesia, and is currently investigating charismatic Christian movements in Vanuatu. She has recently published a monograph entitled *Gender, Christianity and Change in Vanuatu: An analysis of social movements in North Ambrym* (2008).

Kjetil Fosshagen is a post-doctoral fellow at the Department of Social Anthropology, University of Bergen. He has conducted long-term fieldwork in Northern Cyprus, first in 1994–95. He is currently preparing research on Islamic sacrifice and secularization in Turkey. Research interests: anthropology of the state, political anthropology, ritual, and historical processes.

Ingjerd Hoëm is Associate Professor of Social Anthropology, University of Oslo. She has held the position of Head of Research at the Institute for Pacific Cultural History and Archaeology at the Kon-Tiki Museum, of which she is now a member of the Board of Directors. She is currently heading the interdisciplinary research project "Identity Matters: Movement and Place." Her research interests include Tokelau, the Polynesian Pacific, issues related to the relationship between cultural and personal identities, and the study of communication and political processes. Among her latest publications is *Theatre and Political Process. Staging Identities in Tokelau and New Zealand* (2004).

Janet Hoskins is Professor of Anthropology at the University of Southern California, Los Angeles. She is the author of *The Play of Time: Kodi*

Perspectives on Calendars, History and Exchange (1994), winner of the 1996 Benda Prize for Southeast Asian Studies, *Biographical Objects: How Things Tell the Story of People's Lives* (1998), and is the contributing editor of *Headhunting and the Social Imagination in Southeast Asia* (1996), *Anthropology as a Search for the Subject: The Space Between One Self and Another* (1999), and *Fragments from Forests and Libraries* (2000). She spent two decades doing ethnographic research in Eastern Indonesia, and is now studying Caodaism from a transnational perspective in Vietnam and California.

André Iteanu is Directeur de Recherche at the Centre National de la Recherche Scientifique (Paris) and Directeur d'études at the École Pratique des Hautes Études (Paris). He has conducted extensive fieldwork in Papua New Guinea and among youth in Parisian suburbs. His publications include *La ronde des échanges (1983)*, *Of Relations and the Dead (with C. Barraud, D. de Coppet and R. Jamous, 1994)*, *Parle et je t'écouterai* (with E. Schwimmer, 1996). He has authored a documentary film *Letter to the Dead* (with E. Kapon, 2002). His current research focuses on the interaction between Western and Oceanic religious conceptions.

Knut M. Rio is Associate Professor of Social Anthropology at the University of Bergen. He has worked with Melanesian ethnography since 1995, with fieldwork in Vanuatu. His work on social ontology, production, and ceremonial sacrifice has resulted in the monograph *The Power of Perspective: Social Ontology and Agency on Ambrym Island, Vanuatu* (2007).

Joel Robbins is Professor and Chair of the Department of Anthropology at the University of California, San Diego. His work has focused on issues of religion and cultural change in the Pacific, and on the comparative study of global Pentecostalism. He has also had a long-standing interest in developing Dumont's theoretical contributions, as reflected for example in his book *Becoming Sinners: Christianity and Moral Torment in a Papua New Guinea Society* (2004). He is also co-editor of the journal *Anthropological Theory*.

Olaf H. Smedal is Associate Professor of Social Anthropology at the University of Bergen. He has conducted long-term fieldwork in Indonesia since the beginning of the 1980s: first among the Lom on Bangka (an island off Sumatra), later among the Ngadha in Flores in eastern Indonesia. He is an Associate Editor of the journal *Social Analysis*. His research interests include social organization and kinship, economic anthropology, symbolization, ritual, comparative epistemology, history of anthropology, and theory of science.

David Sneath is the Director of the Mongolia and Inner Asia Studies Unit at Cambridge University, lecturer in Social Anthropology, and a Fellow of Corpus Christi College. He is a co-editor of the journal *Inner Asia*. His most recent book is *The Headless State: Aristocratic Orders, Kinship Society, and Representations of Nomadic Inner Asia* (2007).

Serge Tcherkézoff is Professor of Anthropology (directeur d'études) at the Institute of Advanced Studies in Social Sciences (EHESS) of Paris-Marseille. He has founded, with Pierre Lemonnier, the CREDO (Centre of Research and Documentation for Oceania), organized by CNRS, EHESS, and University of Provence. After working in the 1970s on African ethnography, he has been engaged in fieldwork in Polynesia since the early 1980s. Besides his publications since the early 1980s on the theory of anthropology and holism, and in the 1980–1990s on the transformations of the Samoan society, his more recent books bring together the results of his field studies and an ethnohistorical critique of European narratives about early encounters in Polynesia. He is currently working on two new books: the study of Maussian holistic models of the gift applied to the Samoan case, and a critical reading of Dumont's models.

Valerio Valeri was Professor of Anthropology at the University of Chicago from 1976–1998. He is the author of *Kingship and Sacrifice: Ritual and Society in Ancient Hawaii* (1985), and *The Forest of Taboos: Morality, Hunting and Identity among the Huaulu of the Moluccas* (2000). He has also published essays from his fieldwork in Indonesia in *Fragments from Forests and Libraries* (2001), and another collection of more theoretical essays in Italian, *Uno Spazio fra Sé e Sé; L'antropologia come Ricerca del Soggetto* (1999). He did archival and historical research in Hawaii, and in 1971 began twenty years of fieldwork among the Huaulu people of the Moluccas. The essay in this volume was prepared for publication from an original work written in French before his death in April 1998.

INDEX